Best wishes to you. Hope you enjoy these memories.

Helen E. Nebeker

Bittersweet:

A Candid Love Story

Helen Elizabeth Nebeker

Acacia Publishing, Inc.
1366 E. Thomas Rd., Suite 305
Phoenix, Arizona 85014
www.acaciapublishing.com

Library of Congress Cataloging-in-Publication Data

Nebeker, Helen.
Bittersweet : a candid love story / Helen Elizabeth Nebeker.
p. cm.
ISBN 0-9762224-8-5 (alk. paper)
1. Nebeker, Helen. 2. Nebeker, Aquila Chauncey, 1919-2001. 3. Spouses--United States--Biography. I. Title.
CT275.N414A3 2006
940.54'21092273--dc22

2005037368

Cover design by The Cricket Contrast
Printed and bound in Canada

DEDICATED
WITH DEEPEST LOVE
TO THE MEMORY OF MY HUSBAND
Aquila Chauncey Nebeker, Jr.

You were, indeed, a valiant man; and your wife honors you.

And

IN HEARTFELT ADMIRATION AND GRATITUDE

To all the men who serve on the battle front.
And to their women, who stand unswervingly beside them,
in the home.

Table of Contents

Book One:
The Book of Love

Part I: Our Romance

Part II: The Testing Begins

Part III: "Now is the Winter of Our Discontent"

Part IV: If Winter Comes

Part V: Great Changes

Part VI: The Sands of Time

Book Two:
The Book of Life

Part I: Living the Dream

Part II: The Testing Begins Again

Part III: These Were the "Days of Our Lives"

Book One

The Book of Love

Love Letters from Two Hearts:
June 1944 – December 1945
From the European Theatre - WWII

Part I

Our Romance

1
The Letter

23 May 2005

My dearest, darling, only husband, Neb,

This is the last love letter I shall ever write you. These will be the final words of love, completing what you long ago called "Helen's Book," a sequence of more than 400 letters written almost nightly, over 15 months of separation, while you were fighting and waiting – and, at the end, playing softball – all over England and France and Germany. As I repeat, today, the words of greeting above, which I used in various forms in all of those letters, I want you to know – even though you have been gone three and a half years and after what would have been our sixty-first year of marriage – that the love, the longing, the feelings of trust and hope expressed in them are as strong and true and new today as they were when written so many years ago.

These thoughts which I write are not just "words" lightly written. They are etched in my very being as I have perused during the last ten days every single letter – some 800 in number – that you and I have written during those dreadful months of separation and fear and continuing hope and faithfulness. Those letters began the morning after you left me that last Sunday morning on October 7, 1944 to return to Camp Atterbury. We kissed and cried together, knowing your deployment was at hand. We had expected it – but not so soon. And never did we dream, that morning, that we would not again kiss for nearly sixteen months. And never did we envision the hours that we would both spend in writing those 400 letters. They would be written in the snow, under bombing attacks in the Battle of the Bulge, in the cities of England and France and Germany, in the prison camps guarding the German surrenderers, in the ball fields of French and

German camps. And mine would be written in the beginning in Indianapolis where I lived and end in Mesa, Arizona, where I had gone to live with your mother and father. These letters would end only in December 1945, when you began your five week journey home – you having been shipwrecked in the Azores Islands.

Re-reading the letters of our youth and our so-short-time-together-marriage has been emotionally, even physically, wrenching – at times almost unbearably so. And I have wondered why, after so many years of simply storing them in a box, I have been moved to resurrect the past. But as I have pondered and persisted in the reading, I have come to realize that in those letters, you and I had been eternally bound – for better or for worse – in ways that we would seldom again achieve. In those letters our spirits were united; your tenderness and concern and love for me were expressed freely and fully, without inhibition. We were each others strength and hope; you were my teacher, my guide, my confidant. I was your lover, your nurturer, your courage, your faith in the future. There was absolutely nothing – even displeasure with one another – that we could not share without openness and without fear. Only the physical aspect of our love was missing in those letters – even as we both greatly desired it. And wrote of it unabashedly.

And as I began to clearly recognize this testimony of our, at least, spiritual uniting, it came to me suddenly, as through revelation, that here, at last, was the genesis for writing my life story. MY life story – but really OUR life story. For my life really began only in the birth of my love for you.

So, in this last love letter in "Helen's Book," I am going to share with you my heart, my soul, my growth, my deep and sincere joy, my sorrows – and at the end, perhaps, all my regrets and fears as I face the last years of my life without you. This will be an open and frank letter. I will cut no corners, display no coyness. If others should read this, they must accept what they will find – and, I hope, think no less of me. And, my love, this letter may be as long as the book I had published so many years ago – which, of course, you never read. But, if what is written on earth is truly recorded in heaven, then you have an eternity in which to read it. (At least I hope you are in heaven.)

2
Confessions

First of all, I want to tell you that never – in our meeting, our courtship, our marriage, my subsequent 400 letters – did I lie to you. Except in two details – one a foolish joke that Betty and I had concocted before we met you that night and one that I had not remembered until you mentioned it in a February letter. We told you, in our first conversation, that we were from Texas (we never thought we would see you again nor wanted to, for that matter). Neither of us was a Texan. Why we did that silly thing, I can't remember, but I wanted to confess this sin on earth – before I see you in Heaven – since you will know all things then, anyhow.

The second deception was really a happenstance, not a lie. But in a failure to be completely honest with you would lie future problems for both of us. To clarify, when we met, I was ostensibly a young woman of 20 (you were then 24). I had a reasonably good job (can you imagine $100 a month?) at Billings General Hospital at Fort Harrison. I had a nice apartment – as you came to know – which I had just begun to share with a new roommate, Betty Daugherty. I looked a somewhat "young" 20.

The fact was, however, that in January 1942 – when I was 15, working a 40 hour week in an all-night drugstore, for $12 a week – I had altered my 1927 year of birth certificate to read 1924. The birth certificates were hand written, in ink, and it was not a difficult document to change. I had done this two years before meeting you so that I could get my first real job, in a defense plant office, and thus earn sufficient money to support myself. In that office, I met Betty, who subsequently became my roommate when my original roommate, Louise Poole, a very nice and staid woman of 24, left me to join the WAVES. At that time, I was a "paper" 19 years of age. The truth was, simply, that I became – at the stroke of a pen – three years older, seemingly for life. Now how – and why – could I have told you the truth about this? I never expected to see you after that evening. And anyway, I didn't really think about age, as such. So much for confessions.

3

How On Earth Does a Nice Girl Like You...?

Looking retrospectively at the really unintentional deception about age, just imagine all the questions which could have arisen, right on the spot, had I told you all of the above details. First of all, "What on EARTH was a 15 year old girl doing being out on her own? Earning her own living? Having her own apartment? Meeting a strange man in a cocktail lounge – even though it was a very sophisticated place? Where to begin? (As a good Mormon boy, you wouldn't have gotten past the first question – although I didn't know that at the time.) Well, I'd have to begin with facts of my life that I never really told you about – or even wanted to, I guess. And in that failure to reveal – as I have thought about it – lay another implicit lie that would have to be dealt with when you later met my mother and "dad" (or Darrell). I think, many years later, that I hinted at this. But you patently didn't want to deal with it. (Now in this last letter, you can skip over reading this, but it might explain many things to you.)

The fact is I had left what I called home at 15 for two specific reasons. My home life had become truly intolerable – not teen-age disapproval of parents but truly horrible. In November of 1941, just before Pearl Harbor, Mother had given birth to her third daughter, Susie, at the age of thirty four. This was her second child by Darrell – and of course by my real father, she had borne me and my younger-by-20-months sister, Jean. You came to know Mother and Darrell well – and liked them. But had I revealed to you all of my experiences before leaving home, we might not have been able to maintain the friendship that we did in the years to come.

At any rate, Mother was deeply resentful of her pregnancy. She had been forced to quit work before the birth; Darrell was always a poor provider so we had moved into a really terrible house; and the fact is that Mother did not want this new child; she had wanted none of her children and particularly me. As she said to me so often, "If it hadn't been for you, my life would have been different." Frankly, husband mine, I have always wondered if she and my dad hadn't had to get married. The gall was that even though I was going to high school full time and was working five days a week from 5:00 p.m. 'til 1:00 in the morning – riding the last bus home and doing my homework only God knows when – and paying Mother one-third of my meager $12 week, she seemed to feel that I was responsible for everything in the home, that my entire obligation was to her, the kids and the house work. Finally, in one of her frequent rages towards me, she told me that if I didn't "like the way things were going," I could get out. So at the end of my Junior year, with only 3 credits left 'til graduation, I packed my meager possessions and left. The rest you have come to know.

But I have never really told you that for three full years I had had to fight off Darrell's attempted molestation. (He was eight years younger than Mother.) And I couldn't tell her. I couldn't hurt her that way. And besides that, I knew Mother – extremely jealous – would never believe me. In some way, she would put the blame on me. Being absolutely honest, I wouldn't have known how to tell her. Such things were never spoken of in my house – or in my generation, perhaps. Even sex, itself, was a forbidden topic in "nice" homes. And certainly in ours. But in my vulnerability, I do know that God was in some way surely looking out for me and giving me the strength and the way to escape – to you, eventually.

Before that, in my new sphere of life, I began to make up for lost time. Working among military personnel – and particularly at the Army hospital – I had the opportunity for many dates with the men, as well as with other young men I had known from high school. At home, Mother had allowed me almost no freedom – and when I was permitted to date, she either treated my friends abominably or humiliated me in front of them by telling personal things about me. She was also a terrible flirt and inevitably stole the scene with her conversation. Several times when I had a date, she would have found some fancied thing I had done, and to punish me, would meet my dates at the door, telling them I could not go out that evening. I gradually stopped dating or else I met the boy someplace downtown without asking permission. But after I left for my new life, I was fortunate – and choosy – and all the friends I had turned out to be exceptionally nice fellows. They usually developed a more or less protective attitude with me and in spite of living on my own, in a much-prized apartment, I had no difficulty in maintaining my standards of morality. I am not sure that Darrell and Mother ever believed this, although I had never touched liquor – my father was a great lesson to me – I never smoked, and I was rather naturally religious, in contrast to my parents who had no religion whatever.

Now that I've answered the first three "What on earth" questions, I must move on to the perhaps most important, "meeting a strange man in a cocktail lounge," when I have just said I didn't drink. Well, after leaving home, I had learned to nurse a drink or two when others drank – and when it comes down to that, how do *you* justify your being in that cocktail lounge? The answer is, of course, that we were *fated* to meet that night! But beyond that certainty of fate, there is another story, the story of Betty's recent break-up with her current boyfriend, a lieutenant in the Air Force. (Betty never dated anyone of lower rank than Lieutenant, she had informed me.)

Thus it was, that because of a friend's heart break and her ardent plea for company, that on a cold, rainy, April night, so typical of Spring weather in Indiana, I found myself – for the first time ever – with another young woman, seated in the very select lounge of the downtown Claypool Hotel, nursing a Tom Collins, I think. (I remember this clearly, Neb, because it was the 28th, two days before a much-needed pay day.) Suddenly the serenity of the lounge was broken by a rowdy bunch of noncoms (corporals and sergeants), demanding immediate service. It was obvious that they had just been paid and had money to burn. As they crowded around the long bar, I noticed one particularly handsome corporal – blonde, six feet tall – standing out from the others. I still remember my exact thought, even the words, as I saw him: "Now there's a man I could go for!" (My love, how was I to even suspect that that cursory thought would be prophetic? And I have never told anyone – not even our daughter – the accurate account of our meeting which followed.)

Suffice it to say that, soldiers being soldiers, Betty and I were soon spotted – and quickly surrounded by six or seven of you and your eager young friends; we soon learned that only four days before you had arrived at Camp Atterbury from maneuvers in Tennessee and that you all were attached to Battery C of the 592nd Field Artillery Battalion of the 106th Infantry Division. You were all so young, so full of energy and fun and life. How could any of us have believed that night that in exactly eight months many of you would be lying dead in a field of snow or running for your lives from the dreadful German counter-attack (which would come to be called the "Battle of the Bulge") in the Belgium and French Ardennes countryside? But enough of that for now. On to our meeting.

Betty, of course, was disdainful and somewhat dismissive, but I enjoyed all of you – Heinze and Del and Kirk and some of them who never came back. After awhile, having consumed several beers, you all decided you wanted to go to the famous Indiana Roof – to pick up girls, I'm sure – but you asked me, specifically, to go with you. Even in what was really to become "our first date," I can see now that you were possessive – that you desired no intrusion by others. How strange that after this long time I should remember that. "The Roof," as we called it, was a magnificent space with huge revolving balls of light. And always the most famous of name bands were on the marquee; after all, Indianapolis was a swinging military city with the army and the navy and the air force bringing in huge revenue. I had never been there before and I think that either Harry James or Tommy Dorsey were the headliners. Anyhow, the sparkling revolving globes turned the crowded, smoky dance floor into a kind of fantasy. And how we danced, and how we talked. And I seem to remember that our first dance was to "Long Ago and Far Away," a most tender love song but very difficult to dance to. You stepped all over my feet because you really were much better at the jive than in a waltz. Now why doesn't that surprise me?

To be honest (as I have promised to be), I really don't remember much about the rest of that evening, because of the noise and the music and the press of people as the crowd increased. But I do remember two things clearly – do you? After that first dance – or perhaps during it – you fervently declared to me, "Little girl" (that's what you called me) "I have been a happy bachelor for twenty-five years and I have absolutely *no* intention of getting married before I'm out of the army. And, especially, not before I go overseas." (As though I had some intention of roping and tying you!) And I just as vehemently declared, "I have no intention of getting married – ever! I like my freedom. Why would I want to get married?" Oh how the gods of fate must laugh at the puny, pointless plans of mortals. Seriously, I believe that our Creator must have smiled above as he directed two of His beloved children into the path that we were to follow. We parted that night, having made a tentative date, provided that you got a pass and I was free. You would call. And so it began.

4

The Courtship

So the week came and went; you didn't call; I wasn't surprised. Either you didn't get a pass or you weren't interested. So what? I never lacked for a Saturday night or Sunday date if I wanted one. In fact, I sometimes had to see the same movie twice in a week because of the overlapping date partners I had. But the following week when you called, I had a little surprise for you. On the Saturday you hadn't called, in the company of my date for the night, I had seen you – with your buddies – accompanying a young lady whose slip hung beneath her dress. Such lack of taste! I razzed you about that – and you never forgot the episode, did you? You mention the "slip" in several letters through the months. But because I hadn't been offended by your failure to call – in fact, I think you were more concerned by the fact that I had been out with someone else rather than waiting at home for the phone – I accepted your request for a date the following Friday.

That evening was to be my introduction to your famous Dog House. That establishment was to become the hang-out for the whole Battery C of the 592nd Field Artillery Gang. It was a small bar owned by a woman whose husband – or lover or something – was in your outfit, I think. I never was quite clear about that, even though Dottie and I became friends and I visited with her in her home, which she shared with a daughter, several times until I left for Arizona. The daughter had a baby and I came to envy her so much as I visited and saw the love involved in the little one's care. But I wrote you all about that. The important thing was that the Dog House was like a family. It was a fun place! If Indianapolis had had an English pub, the Dog

House would have been it. I don't remember where it was, except that it was purely a local hide out, really, but you and I were to spend many happy hours there before you shipped out. You and the boys drinking your beer – and me being initiated into the fine art of beer tasting. (Come to think of it, this may have been one of your sixteen steps which will arise later.) I didn't drink much – you were always stealing my glass – but to be honest, I liked the taste and I was never affected by alcohol. I must have inherited my father Tom's "hollow leg."

All in all, I don't believe you and I could have found a better place to get acquainted – surrounded by friends, laughing and sharing and finding relief from the tensions of war and the pressures of living – than at what we came to call "Dot's Place." And I still remember it with joy and without any guilt whatsoever. Anyone who might read this with disapproval must simply consider that in these war years, in a crowded military city – where the men were in their twenties or younger for the most part – recreation involved drinking. It was cheap; it was convivial; it was something to do at a time when movies and dances meant standing in endless admittance lines of service men and their dates. And the USO was the last resort of the hopeless. That's how many service men felt, I was told. And especially you, honey, the "old man" of the group. I, myself, took the habit as a fact of life. My father drank, my German and Irish grandparents drank – good Catholics that they were. In fact, Grandpa Helfrich grew his own grapes for wine and made beer in his bath tub. My mother's father, Daddy Gwin, drank only in the cellar with his sons-in-law at Christmas, 'til Mamma Gwin – an Episcopal in name only – would discover them and read the riot act.

Even as I am writing this, dear love, I am increasingly aware, after reading our letters, of how my acceptance of your drinking in those days and my conversion to Mormonism before you returned had serious implications in our life through the years. But the past is the past. And while I may have regretted the changes entailed, what could I do about it? The conflict to come was inevitable. "Beer with the boys" would become through the years our "snake in the garden."

But back to the date Friday night. It must have been successful, because we made another date for Saturday. Betty was out and I think we just stayed in my apartment and lazed around and talked. This was your first visit to 2102 N. Meridian Street and you were pleased with the small but nice living room, bedroom, dining room, kitchen and bath.(Neither of us ever thought that before too long, this would be the last home you would know for eighteen long and miserable months.) But I do remember that you were much impressed with the order, the neatness – which has always been a hallmark of my living quarters. And in our talking that night, it was in this homey place that you first introduced your soon to become famous Sixteen Steps of what you considered womanly perfection. These were the steps, you informed me, that any woman worthy of being *your* mate would have to climb. Such arrogance, I remember thinking. But before this disclosure came from you, you had made your discovery of my "Rogues Gallery," as you came to call it through the weeks of dating and courtship that were to come. In fact, that night – it was now late May – I believe the courtship had already begun, unknown to either of us.

Those Sixteen Steps I never did pass, you told me in a later letter of reminiscence, because by the 9th step, you "knew it didn't matter." You were already in love with me – with my "sweetness," with my "smile," with my "gentle way of teasing," with my "beautiful eyes," and, of course, with my "beautiful body." Of course we both know that these were – and are – the words of all young lovers. But how wonderful to read them so many years later and to know that at one time in your life, I was totally beloved and necessary to you. And I think through most of our life, despite all other conflicts, you still thought me beautiful. How would you see me now, I wonder? And, my dear, I simply have to tell you – in true humility and disbelief – that just last Sunday, a man much younger than you would be now called me "beautiful," and when I demurred, he said, "No, you really are." How I would like to know that you would find me beautiful still. And how I treasure those rare times in the last months of your life when you would say, "You're beautiful!" But to get back to the point of the Steps, I do know that I passed, not necessarily in this order: (1) being a good housekeeper; (2) knowing what it meant to be poor; (3) liking beer; (4) being able to look out for myself; (5) especially being a good cook!

Oh, how you loved my dinner the following Sunday. So much so, that when I invited you for dinner the next weekend, you brought with you three unexpected guests. I had to send all of you to the meat shop (imagine having separate meat shops and not just grocery stores) for extra pork chops and you used up all of my ration points for the next six months. However, in return I acquired three devoted followers, who obviously hoped for future – and individual – invitations. Do you remember that day? Oh, I remember that day mounting another Step on your stairway, so you told me later, because I wouldn't let you help with the dishes. (Your punishment was to be in the future when, in camp awaiting transportation to Europe, you and your mates drew constant KP duty. I hope you thought of that.)

But back to your discovery of the "Rogues Gallery." It was obvious amazement, shock, dislike, and a sudden awareness, I think, at the sight of the 8x10 photos of all my current boyfriends. (At least, all those that were still in attendance.) I could almost read your mind then: Hey, "little gal" had a real following! Your friends adoring me was one thing but here competition had reared its ugly head! (You told me this later when the "courtship" was over.) These photos were displayed in frames in a glassed china closet in my very small dining room. There were Jack (navy & a two year suitor and one whom I knew loved me dearly), Charles (air-force and not really in the running, but a nice occasional date), Dick (navy – a real scoundrel but charming and handsome), Al (navy, handsome, older and wonderfully attentive), Willie (navy), and D.V. (my very first boyfriend when I was "young" and now in the army, ardently requesting me to come down to visit him.) After this long time, honey, I can't remember the rest. But I can look them up, because you told me to keep their pictures so that when you came home you could look at them and gloat because you had won me from them – even though you weren't as handsome. That's what you told me in your letter and I have all the letters to prove these things.

Anyhow, the shock must have been real because, as we were going back to the apartment that Saturday evening, you had told me arrogantly that I was the kind of girl friend you wanted – one who didn't have a lot of boy friends and stayed home quite a bit so you didn't have to worry about whether I'd be there whenever you felt like coming to town. So how I silently laughed as you examined the handsome rogues in my gallery. I was to remind you of that in a letter written April 19th of the next year.

The "Steps" and the "Gallery" were to become important, as our casual dating turned into courtship. The next date was at the USO and then we went on to swimming, more dancing, just talking. I remember my "affection" for you growing as the "Ten Easy Lessons" course you gave me "taught" me how to kiss the way you liked it (maybe that was one of the Steps), and we "necked" – very innocently you may remember. In fact, you wrote me in a letter ten months later that you were glad we had restrained ourselves: "How glad I am that during our courtship we controlled our emotions. Although there were times when I almost lost my head, even if you had complete control – or did you?" That's still my secret.

But gradually, we began to care less and less for the company of others and you never knew that I broke more than one date during that time when you were able to get an unexpected pass into town. And more than once, worn out, you fell asleep on the couch – or on the floor if I fell asleep before you did – and slept until it was time to catch the last bus at 3:00 a.m. back to the base. And in our long Sunday discussions, you learned quite early that I was afraid of marriage and never wanted to have children. And I learned from you that children were wonderful and nothing to fear but to joy in. And you made me believe, despite the fears from my early memories, that love could be permanent, even forever, for eternity. And you didn't teach me all this from teaching the Gospel – it came from within *you*. And I confided in you the pain I felt so often. I had had a ruptured appendix only a year before and suffered intense, recurring pain, the reason unknown. And you understood and worried about what you called "our pet pain" and tried to help me "take care of myself." You were so tender with me! And we were both so worn out – you from the constant training and catching buses in from Atterbury; and I from my ten hour days at Billings Hospital, some 25 miles away. But we didn't even realize it. We had fallen in Love!

On the 20th of June, you wrote that you couldn't get leave that week and I should take the bus down to Atterbury; the boys were waiting to make my visit pleasant. Neither of us thought of the long bus trip, the long work week ahead of us. I went gladly; you were waiting at the depot. And then, by 17th of July – as I read from your letters – you were going to see the Captain about getting leave for our honeymoon; he had already okayed our marriage. But that is getting ahead of our story.

No Wonder I Fell In Love With This Handsome Man!

Helen at 17

5
The Proposal

I can't remember exactly the first time you proposed to me. It had to be between the middle of June and the 1st of July. By my estimation, we had had some 10 or 12 dates, amounting to maybe 150 hours together. Not really much time. But in those days and half the nights, we lived intensely. However, I don't think I had really considered the idea that we might marry. (Remember our first declarations at the Roof?) In fact, occasionally, when you were on the training maneuvers, I had had other dates and was still writing a few letters. But 61 years later, the circumstances are etched in my mind. We had been to a movie and then met Del and Kirk at the Dog House. When we left there, you wanted to go back home – as you now called the apartment – to sleep a little before catching the bus. You really seemed quite tipsy, so we went home and you slept an hour. Then, when you were kissing me good-bye, you suddenly said, "Little cupcake, how about marrying me?" Well, I was surprised and I certainly wasn't going to take advantage of a silly, tipsy fool, so I told you to go back to camp and "sleep it off!" Those were my exact words. You remember the occasion in a 16 February '45 letter: "I shall never forget the night I first put out a 'feeler' under the guise of being tight. Ha! You thought I was too tight and would forget the next day – then I waited and watched you wondering if I would really ask you again." Again, my sweet, your supreme egotism. The fact is, I was really hoping you wouldn't. Too many problems, too many reservations, too little time. We'd have to talk.

And so we did. For you didn't forget. About a week later, completely serious and sober, alone with me in *our* apartment (for so it had come to be without us even noticing), you asked me solemnly, "Helen, little gal, will you marry me?" And then the questions of my heart and soul poured out.

6
The Valley of Decision

My greatest reservation about our marriage was largely rooted in the confession I have made to you about my age in Chapter I. I didn't have the courage to tell – or the desire – to tell you that you had fallen in love with a seventeen year old girl. You would have been horrified, I still think. And even had you decided not to marry me because of that, you would have liked yourself much less for having, in your terms, "been made a fool of." I cared for you too much to have so damaged your ego. But I knew I was seventeen and I suspected that perhaps I wasn't yet fully sexually mature and I was fearful of just not being ready for that aspect of marriage. But I explained these complicated worries to you (at least they were complicated to me) as simply fear that I might disappoint you sexually because I wasn't ready. That would be a catastrophe for both of us. My second concern was "our pet pain." It was so severe, so often now, and I didn't know what that might portend. And last, there was the matter of time. You knew you were going overseas sometime soon, but exactly when and where were the great unknowns. Should we just get engaged and wait for marriage or. . . ? The worries tumbled out.

And then, I remember with every memory of those moments – as I read our letters – how tender you were, how reassuring: there were no problems we couldn't work through, together. If I weren't quite ready sexually, we'd "work on it;" if the pain was bad, we'd see a doctor about getting it fixed; as to the time problem, I could choose whether an engagement or a marriage was the best choice. You made it sound so easy that I almost said "yes" right then. But wisdom prevailed and I asked for a week to think it over. The next day, we went to Broadripple Park to swim. And that day, as you lay on the sand so tanned and masculine and dear, and as I rubbed your back with suntan lotion, I thought how unthinkable it would be to part from you. I made my decision, then. For better or for worse. But I didn't tell you. When you next came, hoping for your answer, the "Rogues Gallery" was gone. You told me much later, in one of your sweet letters, that were to become my life and breath in the months to come, that you prowled, unbeknownst to me, the whole apartment to be sure that not one picture remained. And then you knew the answer was going to be "YES." And we would be married before you left. The die was cast.

7

On the Merry-Go-Round

The rat race was on! Saturday, August 5, 1944 was to be the great day – the only possibility in the Unit's busy deportation plans. It was now the middle of July. Your letter from camp, July 19, says you are out on bivouac and won't be back until the 27th or 28th – we'll get blood tests then; maybe you'll get a ten day furlough (have to see the Captain); all the boys want to come to the wedding – including the Captain. July 20: you think you'll get in Sunday. July 25: sorry, couldn't get back from the muddy training field. And so it goes. Always the damned army changes your plans. Ceaseless uncertainty and activity. Phone call: "Honey, can you find the Church, call the Bishop, see if we can have the service on Saturday night – 8:00, can't get in sooner, just getting off bivouac. It's going to be a hell-uv-a rush anyhow. And I want us to be married in the Mormon Church." Those, my sweet, were your reports from your camp-home-front.

And on my home-front, I'm in unremitting activity and stress: still have ten-hour-work day at Billings; have to beg for a few days off. Then there's the Church – whatever that is! I search all the directories. No Mormon Church. Where the h. . . is the Mormon Church? No one I know has ever heard of the Mormon Church. And (further confession to add to my list) I haven't told you, I won't tell you I've taken a temporary job as hostess, four hours a night on the week nights when you don't come in, at a classy downtown hotel restaurant. Because I simply must have a pretty dress for my wedding! (Still have to find time to shop for it.)

Honey, you never did realize in all those months what a struggle I always had financially just to eat (which I sometimes didn't) and to pay the rent and utilities and bus fare, etc. I wouldn't have told you, whatever the cost. But undeniably, my escape to freedom and independence had been costly and physically wearing. Incidentally, to this very day I can't find when we managed to get our marriage license. Are you sure we are legally married? Fortunately, somewhere in this chaos, you phoned me and I learned just barely in the nick of time that the Mormon Church was really the Church of Jesus Christ of Latter Day Saints. And the date and time were set. And by this time, I was facing physical and emotional exhaustion. And with a honeymoon (oh barbaric custom) yet in view.

But now I have to get back to the evening you brought me my rings somewhere in the midst of this upheaval. You had asked me earlier whether, because you had been robbed in the barracks of $100, I would agree – only temporarily – to use Betty Wichtman's first wedding ring, just for the ceremony itself. Then, as soon as you got paid and could borrow some money from your folks, we could go pick out whatever I would like. It must be hard for people today to understand that we couldn't just go out and charge something. Charging for things was unheard of – at least for poor people. And the first highly restricted credit cards became available only in the '50s. Recalling the event of the rings, you write me in a letter six months later:

> **16 Feb 45:** Then the story about my borrowing a ring from Del and Betty to use on that day – with you agreeing while all the time disappointment shone in your eyes! Oh what a cad I was, stopping you in front of windows to get your likes and dislikes in rings! What a night that was when I placed the rings on the ironing board and the joy when you opened the box to see what was in it!

And that is exactly what I was doing when you came in that night – ironing. I had gone to hang some clothes in the closet and returned to find the box on the board – and you sitting there immersed in the newspaper. I was truly astonished – and more pleased than you would believe. Those rings became a symbol to me of your love and commitment – but you may remember (if not, I may just tell you later in this letter) what happened to them. Continuing, you write:

> Then you came over to sit on the arm of my chair and with your arms around me told me how much you loved me and how proud you were to show them to your friends. My darling, for years to come, regardless of hardship, regardless of what the future holds, I have those sweet memories to guide my footsteps – to give me a lift when things are tough – to give me hope when darkness settles over the present. Those memories are mine – mine and yours – to share together during the despondent days when things aren't right. They are my hope for future times when you and I shall be together.

I read such words now, written in the aftermath of the most bitter of battles in the Battle of the Bulge, and I know – as I knew it then and know it after all the vicissitudes of our life together – that our love was meant to be. Oh, my love, how I love you as I write these words. And how I hope that you are loving me! (But I doubt that many of our future friends would ever believe that hundreds of such letters came from you to give me courage. You were not, then, "a man of few words and little emotion." What happened to you, my love?)

8
Another Confession—Will They Never Cease?

But it is time for me, in the context of this happy night when you gave me my ring, to remember what occurred in the midst of the happiness you felt. You write in the same 16th February '45 letter: "How perturbed I was when that guy called and you wouldn't tell him over the phone but you'd tell him in a letter" [about our marriage, that is]. You remained "perturbed" for some time. But I was never able to share with you the great sadness that was to come to me through that call. It was from one of my Rogues Gallery suitors – Jack Roberts, the young man who had known me since I lived at home, had known me when I was an honest fifteen- year- old and who, I knew, had loved me sincerely and deeply. I had written him as soon as I had known that you and I would marry. But when he phoned, he had just returned to port on survivor's leave, had called me from the first phone box, and had not received my letter, since he had been six months at sea.

How could I tell him on the phone news that would, I knew, sadden him? And how could I explain to him – in front of you? You would be either hurt or deeply angry, since I had told you nothing concerning any of my male friends. It was not your business, until I told you I would marry you. And after that, it didn't matter. I had cleared the decks, so to speak.

I wrote him, again, that night after you left, as gently as I could, the news of our marriage. Two days later (and I remember just as I am writing this that it was the day you and I had gone to get our license – August 2nd – and you had to return immediately to camp) as I was getting off the bus and crossing the street to the apartment, Jack was there. He had borrowed a car just as fast as he could after he phoned and driven all the way from Great Lakes to urge me to reconsider. He had already bought rings as soon as he arrived in port – and finally, at his base, he had found the letter I had written him earlier. I didn't want to invite him up to the apartment – he had been there before, the summer when I was recovering from my surgery. So we went to a drive-in and talked for a long time. He tried so earnestly to convince me that you were too old for me, that he had loved me and wanted to marry me when we had been together the June before. But I was still recovering from the appendix rupture and he didn't want to risk harming me, so he decided to wait for his next leave. Now he had driven down, hoping to take me to his home as his wife.

I must tell you in this confession that I had not heard from Jack in three months, did not know, really, that he had contemplated marriage to me, so had no idea of his plans. Now he was urging me to go with him to his home in Dayton, right then, and we would be married. And I could write you from there! He wanted to care for me for the rest of my life – had always wanted to, ever since we met. As we talked together through several hours, I knew once again *our* ordained fate. Somehow I knew, intuitively, that I would be more cherished with Jack than I would later be by you. And I remember that there was almost a brief moment or two when I considered going with this dear man I knew so well. But I also knew I couldn't leave you. Had you delayed, however, by one month asking me to marry you, I would probably have been Mrs. Jack Roberts. And perhaps never even heard of the Gospel! Jack later wrote to tell me he had thrown the rings in Lake Michigan and would never marry. And he wrote me once (where he got the address I do not know) after Quill was born in September of '46. I wrote him of your return and Quill's birth and I never heard from him again. But I have always had in my heart the feeling that this was the most unkind thing I had ever done in my life and there was no way to atone.

I never told you of this through all the years – would it have helped? Why do I tell you now? And why does my heart still lie heavy over this matter?

9

Apparently Not!

And even as I have just written those questions above, I suddenly, as in a blaze of light, know the answers to these questions. And after all the years between us, I am going to share with you my relationship with Jack – hoping you will understand how it concerns both you and me.

I first met Jack in those awful days after the birth of Susie – I wrote you about that in my second chapter – in that still-haunting- to- me house on Roach Street (appropriately named), in the area of Indianapolis called Riverside, where the Navy's Signal Corps training facilities were located. I rode the bus everyday, going to my night-time job in the all-night drugstore downtown, where I worked as a fountain clerk. All Riverside buses were always loaded with sailors of one rank or another, continually coming and going on passes or "leaves" or "details" into the city center. It seems to me, upon reflection, that those buses served the same purposes as Stake MIA activities do among Mormons – aid young men and women in seeking to find one another. Anyhow, I was on the bus at 4:00, five afternoons a week, after school, going to work and every night I came home on the last bus. It was in this way that Jack (and Jimmy and a couple of others who never made the Rogues Gallery) met me.

After a few times of riding to town, he asked me for a date. He was one of those that Mother "turned away at the door" when he came to pick me up – but he persevered. And he saw the ugliness of that house on Roach Street, with diapers hanging around the coal stove in the living room, the poor furniture, Susie crying. And Mother. He was there once when she threw one of her screaming fits at me and he endured her flirting and felt, immediately, I think, the sadness of my circumstances. (It was here that my mother took after my sister with a knife – and Jean wrote me just the other day that she truly believes I saved her life that day. At least that is how she remembers it.) But you never saw this house because by the time we met, the family had uprooted and moved to the much better Colorado Street address – Mother had returned to providing for the family.

Anyhow, Jack, knowing how young I was, barely 15 (he was 20, himself) became my faithful friend and squire. We went for long walks together in the park, in the bitter winter following the bombing of Pearl Harbor. He met me on weekends, making sure that I ate well, because he chose the places carefully. He became in my mind, I think, the loving big brother, the true friend that I had never had in my life. It was like the devotion our son and daughter had for each other beginning in their college years, as I'm sure you would remember. Then, in early 1942, before I left home, he was assigned sea duty. He wrote quite often, until in June of that year, after I had moved into my apartment, he returned from sea duty with a 30 day leave. At that time, I was just recovering from the appendix operation and because I had been so seriously ill, the insurance company had granted me six weeks disability leave with full pay! Waiting for the insurance to kick in at my new defense plant job, which my forged birth certificate had enabled me to get, was the reason for my delay in getting the appendix taken care of before it ruptured. (How complicated my life always seems to be.)

Well, six weeks freedom! Something I had not known since I was ten. No housework, no babies to tend, no school assignments, no working. And, most necessary of all, money to live on. And one morning when I was lying on the couch resting, with the apartment door open into the hall, Jack was standing in the door. He had come to ask me to drive with him to Dayton to meet his parents, and after visiting a couple of days and meeting some of his friends, he and his parents and I would drive to the Great Lakes Naval Training Center, to reunion with his brother.

I went with him. Even now, I don't believe I consciously thought of what the implications might be for Jack. Oh, we had fun; we kissed and played around, I guess – but always chaperoned. When he wanted to buy me a gift, I said "no." He bought me a watch, anyhow, presenting it to me on a beautifully starred night. I suppose I knew then that he was in love with me. But I was barely sixteen. Marriage was a long time in the future. So I really didn't have to think of any consequences: the leave was up, he drove me home, he had said nothing that would bind me. Oh, the cruelty of teen-aged girls. When he sent me a beautiful robe a little later, I sent it back; our necking hadn't been that serious. And then he was gone. We wrote, but the letters from him suddenly stopped. I had turned seventeen. And then, Neb, you and I met – and now in writing these truths, I am answering my own questions. If I had told you all this the night you gave me the rings, would it have changed the future for Jack? I didn't love him in the way a wife should love her husband. For you? For me? We did love each other as man and wife should (or at least we thought we did) and our fifteen months of faithful letters show that, though through the years we both may have wondered. But the heaviness of my heart lies in knowing that, however inexcusable because of my youth and naiveté, I did lead Jack on. And as a consequence, I had been fated to face the dilemma of impossible choice. And as punishment, I cannot atone. Will you ever understand this? And can you forgive, if sometimes in the dark silences that were to come between the two of us, I thought about "what might have been?"

10

Great Day in the Morning—Or Rather Evening!

Saturday, August 5, 1944, is here at last! The bride's maid of honor has arrived from Detroit. The taxi has been ordered for seven sharp. The Bishop has arranged for some music. The bride's bag is packed – the couple will stay at the Claypool Hotel – an added expense but who wants a roommate around on a honeymoon? (again that word.) Everyone is getting concerned. But the bride is in command of "everything" – she is beautiful, she hopes, in her lovely new blue dress. Bought as you never knew, until this letter, at the expense of those five weeks of one hundred hours of standing on her feet in the restaurant at night. But will the bridegroom (you) have remembered to bring his bride a corsage? The minutes tick on; evening is coming. Del's wife is tense (could they be at the Dog House?) Where is the bride-groom – and his best man with the ring? And then, there's a rush through the door and the bride is enveloped in strong arms, a freshly-shaven and handsome and spick and span uniformed man is holding her in his arms and she knows that all is well.

After that, the night is a blur. I know we had a long ride to the Church, and that the chapel was bright and that the buddies from the unit are there. Few other than that have been invited – Mother and Darrell. Maybe twenty-five in all. And then I spy my poor father, Tom, and I am glad he is here. And then we're standing before the Bishop – as I now know to call him. And there, before all assembled, we solemnly pledge our love and faith to one another. And then you kiss me strongly but sweetly, and I have never forgotten that moment. I recall this night very clearly in the letter I write you on our 5th month anniversary, when I assumed you were in an embarkation port, "I remember how proud I was of my guy, so calm and collected when we were before the minister. And me so nervous I could have died. Of course, all day long [I learned from Del later] the situation had been reversed. One of the things that will always be a wonderful memory – just as you say the first time I kissed you will be one of yours – is that first kiss as man and wife. I can feel it yet, warm and tender and reassuring. I had no fears after that. I think I knew right then that being married to you would be all that I would ever ask. To have you and to keep you."

And now, my darling, sixty-some years later, through all the adversity that was to come our way, I would still write these words, concluding with these that I wrote you then: "We were married for now and eternity and until you change your mind that's the way it is with me." Little did I know, then, what would have to be done before the "eternity" part was valid. I pray daily that it is.

But from that point on, all is a blur. I remember only that suddenly my beautiful corsage is being crushed (in all your stressful days, you had remembered!) and I'm being kissed by the whole army it seems and then we're off to the "reception" someplace. I know the boys are toasting us – and you are happily responding – and then we leave. I seem to remember a lot of boisterous good-byes and you're getting some rather off-color (I would call them ribald, now) jokes from your buddies. And then we're in the hotel lobby – what time was it – as Husband and Wife! And life will never be the same, again. For either of us. Come what may.

11
The Honeymoon
Or
How Did I Ever Get Into All This?
Or
We Begin to "Work On It!"

Thinking back, if I had it to do all over again, I would never have consented to going to a hotel for the wedding night; we'd have thrown Betty out for the weekend. After all, the apartment was mine. (But perhaps the decision was mine; I just don't remember.) Yet I don't think you minded at all, being in that luxurious hotel, instead of our old familiar place. You were such a show-off anyhow and you were in your element on our special night. But my twelve hour day of keeping everything under control, and the waiting, and finally, the panic as we got to the church and then, the overwhelming exhilaration as we said our vows – plus the confusion and partying – had left me exhausted, even drained. And you, dear heart, had been out on a week of field maneuvers and were certainly dead on your feet. And you had undergone the stress of the marriage ceremony, too. Yet you continued without any sign of failing energy to really party and joke and to return "toasts" without number. And above all, to crow. And you were strutting and crowing as we went to register. Unmistakably newlyweds anyhow, I could have faded into the woodwork at your brashness and obvious pride. I knew what everyone was thinking. And I was thinking it, too. And wondering how I would act and what you would do. And frankly, I was afraid.

But you must have known that. When we finally got to our room, on the fifteenth floor (how slow that ride seemed) you were so sweet. And in a few minutes, for the first time, I was undressing before a man, slowly, hesitantly (remember, I've already told you sex was never mentioned in my home – although you and I had, of course, talked about it before I decided to marry you.) And then, you were holding me in your arms and telling me not to worry about it, we'd wait until tomorrow after we had rested. And then you were kissing me, and then – well, we didn't wait. The "lessons" were to begin that night. And you certainly were a wonderful instructor. And I gave to you, without hesitation, the only real gift that a woman can give to the man she intends to love forever! I don't know whether you gave me the same gift – but I didn't care then. And I don't care now. I only know that you were the choice of my heart and I was content in your arms, as I went to sleep.

I slept well, and when I awoke you were still sleeping – sprawled across the bed, as would be your habit through many years – so I quietly went to bathe and make myself entrancing to you, overwhelmed by the questions crowding my mind. How would you see me this morning? Had I failed you, as I had been afraid I would? Truly, I just didn't know. In our generation, as I'm sure you will remember, "passion" wasn't explored visually (heavens! married couples were still sleeping in discrete twin beds in the movies and Clark Gable wouldn't even say "damn" until years later.) Passion, in the movies was the tide-breaking-over-the-shore or the crash of music in the night air as the sun sank over the horizon. I honestly hadn't seen or heard anything like that. (Perhaps this will help explain the remark I was to make a little later in the morning which hurt you, I know, because you refer to it more than once in an off-hand way through the letters.) But I certainly knew I wasn't the same "little girl" that I had been the night before.

Pondering, but composed in mind, freshened for the new day before us, I returned to find you seemingly still asleep. So, although I really wanted to shower you with kisses, I just sat down at the little desk and wrote you the very first love letter you would ever receive from me. I have never been able to find a trace of it; I don't even know if I finished it. But I do know that it began, "My wonderful new husband" – And then you were awake and calling me. And then. . . the "lessons" began anew.

12
A New Day

Surprisingly for me, these first hours in our room – remember now, that it's August in Indiana and I'm not sure refrigeration was even known then and this will give you some idea of the difficulty of the remaining day – were the easiest part of what I still call the "barbaric custom" of the honeymoon. My ideal of a honeymoon would be a time of peace, of getting to know one another in quietness and freedom from stress. But that was not to be for me. (When would I ever really know a time of peace and freedom from stress?) Following the "lessons," we went to meet Betty and Del down the street for a noontime breakfast. (Perhaps the crowded day's agendum was the reason for us to have spent the night in the center of downtown Indianapolis, where we would have greater access to transportation.) Anyhow, as we went to meet them, you seemed a little subdued, for you, and suddenly you asked me what I had thought of "making wiz ze love" – as you were to call it through our many letters. Note, dear husband, even your more mature inability to say, "What did you think of the sex?" How could I have failed to know – as I do now – that you were really asking me how you had performed – what with all the tiredness and stress and beers? It never occurred to me that your worries would have been the same as mine. I have truly come to realize, dear one, that you emotionally frail males are the vulnerable ones. At any rate, in my usually honest – some would say blunt, I'm sure – way, I said, "I think it's kind of dumb." (I think I was surprised by the question.) But you would never let me forget those careless words. So I know you were hurt by them. But immediately after, as we continued walking down the street and I naively complained of my "horrible backache," right there in the street, you were laughing at me and hugging me tightly. I came to know why. Once more, in your laughter, I was being tutored concerning "lovemaking."

And the tutoring continued as we met Betty and Del. In the Ladies Room, Betty, long time married, sought to counsel me on birth control. (Did I really seem so innocent to everyone?) But I cut her off, able to tell her, proudly, that you and I had already considered this. And we had definitely decided that we wanted Junior (as you always referred to him) just as soon as possible. You can see in this how convincing you had already been in changing my old ideas. But we will have much more to say on this in our letters. However, in making that decision, I knew, even then, that not only in me would you draw patience and courage and maybe even life itself, but that the hope of the son or daughter we had already discussed would be a source of joy to you, if it should happen. I think all men in war time take comfort in the thought that their seed lives on. But more of this in many letters later. We would soon learn again that truly "man proposes; God disposes."

After brunch, we were off on the dizzying whirl that would be ours – or mine – for the next ten days. Knowing you would soon be at war, you were determined to squeeze the most out of every day. So we're off to the Broadripple Pool, where we would spend a marvelous day in the August heat. Of course my naturally curly hair would be a mess – at least to me (you said you loved it) as we caught the bus and hurried back to town to pick up our bag and get Del and Betty to their train to Detroit before we caught ours at 6:00 for Chicago. We had our tickets but the train was crowded as were all trains from Indianapolis in those days. As I remember, it was about a three hour trip and my "pet pain" was on a rampage, as I had feared it would be. And you may remember that this was my second great worry, before I agreed to marry. But I tried not to let you know and we arrived at the wonderful Stevens Hotel, right on Lake Michigan lakefront.

It must have been about 10:00 in the evening and then my misery really began. You were at your exuberant best. When were you ever not in those days? And surrounded by married couples – the hotel at that time was reserved only for service men and their wives – with all the best services of the hotel at minimal expense – we discovered that we needed to show them our marriage certificate, since I had no identification as Mrs. A. C. Nebeker. I was so humiliated. Did I really look like "one of those girls" for whom Chicago was now so famous? Did they think we were shacking up, as it was called in those days? I really don't remember how, after much confusion, we were finally allowed to check in, but I think it was because a Colonel had intervened and convinced them that since you were at Camp Atterbury and deployment was imminent, I probably was a new bride – as you had noisily and vehemently been trying to tell them. So finally, we're in the elevator and you're telling everyone we were just married last night (was it only that short a time ago?) And I am near collapsing. But I try not to let you see – and the evening is still young, you say – so after a brief freshening up, we are down in the cocktail room with every long – married couple in the room (on their second honeymoon) sending drinks over to the table. And the orchestra is playing wonderful music and we dance and I'm so tired. But finally, about 4:00 a.m., it's back to the room and sleep. But not before we had successfully, as you so generously told me, "worked on it," again.

And so it went for seven more days. You never wore out – nor let me. We swam in Lake Michigan and ate and danced and I still remember how you loved the Mexican band in one little bistro. And always you drank much more than you should. But I didn't fuss because I knew this was your last fling. And I ordered a Tom Collins, which I could hold all night without drinking. And we ran all over Chicago in the subway. And I was so afraid because often you fell asleep and I had no idea where I should wake you to get off for the hotel.

But always you had time and energy for "making wiz ze love." For, as you had promised in our "engagement days," we would deal with my most worrying problems, "together." If I were not quite ready sexually, "we would work on it." And so we did, time after time, together.

And then the ten days of honeymoon were over. During these days and nights, I had loved you, as I wrote you later, "completely, honestly, and with no reservations – though there were a couple of nights when you got so drunk, I could have killed you." But this was war-time and death might really happen someday very soon. This dread hung over me ceaselessly – as I am sure it did you. For you were trained in the big assault guns, which surely meant onslaught at the German front. But at last the days of fun were over and I was exhausted and I slept with my head in your lap the long trip home. I had not once mentioned my now excruciating pain.

Swimming during the honeymoon

We arrived home, very late and unexpectedly – to find Betty and Bill together in our bed. You had been right – and I wrong – about Betty; you had called her the She-Wolf of the Bronze Room only shortly after you had met her. Obviously, serious changes were in the offing.

We had our complete ten days leave from Sunday the 6th 'til Tuesday the 14th, when you report. And then you are out on a five day field exercise. You write me on 15 Aug 44: "I'm in love with you, so much in love I can't even think about anything else." The letters stop, because you come home every evening that you can get a pass – maybe weekends. Maybe ten nights in all. We play at marriage as we can – maybe ten more days in all. The fact of war-time marriage has begun.

Part II

The Testing Begins

1
Can Love Really Conquer All?

And now, in these few remaining precious days, we try to feel some normalcy. With Betty gone for the space of a few days (maybe she can't face us or maybe she's off with Bill?) we can be alone together, reading the Sunday newspaper, me cooking breakfast while you're groaning over your hangover. At night, we do the old familiar things, a movie, the Dog House, a walk over the bridge. But in the air, for us, there is a melancholy, an urgency that is palpable. Orders to go are expected without warning. When they come, you will go – on the instant. No phone call, no goodbyes, no 'nothin'. One evening, in the midst of the tension, expecting you momentarily (I've been waiting all day for you to walk through the door) you do not come. Nine o'clock, then ten, then eleven; I have cried all evening, knowing I may not see you again. Exhausted, I fall asleep on the sofa. A fumbling at the door, the turn of the key, and there you are! My heart actually leaps up with joy. You stand there reeling. "Honey, I'm so drunk – got caught up with the boys. Can I come in?" You remember that evening well in your letters. But in your memory of it, you never mention that you spent one of our last precious nights together, sleeping on the sofa. And to this day that is one of the real hurts of my life – that in these last hours before our parting, beers with the boys would take precedence over your waiting wife. And so it would often be in years to come. My heart still aches when I remember that. And though I have long since forgiven, I cannot forget.

But in this cherished time together, we have talked over many things, as we will continue to do in our letters. Neither you nor I have the feeling that I should remain at Billings. The pressure is too great for me. (I really believe you fear the handsome service men.) I go to Billings to sign the resignation papers. I interview for, and get, another job. To start the first week of October, downtown and without the stress of travel. What are we to do about my living arrangements? The revelation of Betty's activities has stunned me – if not you, because of your "experience." Furthermore, as you will write not much later, you fear what her influence will be on me. It seems that if we thought we had problems before marriage, the ones that we were facing now were more pressing. And this time, we both understood that we would not be working them out "together." And most worrisome of all, I had now been forced to share with you the dreadful pain that was consuming me. You were insisting that I go to the army hospital for a checkup. But I simply hadn't had time. I promise to go as soon as I can get an appointment with an OB/Gyn doctor at the hospital; that pleases you, and me, thinkng it may be Junior on the way. But I am fearful that all our "working on it" may be causing some more serious problem. And I do not tell you; you have enough to face.

As I am writing this, it occurs to me, after reading for the second time all these letters – and as I am growing in wisdom – that one of us is always trying in some way or another to shield or care for the other. The reality is that neither of us could do that, really. I know that there are many things you protected me from when you were in that winter of destruction; and then all the days that were to follow in the mopping up, and the many horrors that you must have seen in those months into the summer of the next year. I watch, now, every movie of the Ardennes battles; I see the sad, emaciated faces of the people, the crumbled cities. And the dead bodies. And I know, that after the 106th was overrun, you were in some of those areas, mopping up, guarding prisoners. I never knew if you saw the "concentration camps." It is possible. And now I realize that you had truly been down into the Valley of Death. How you men were able to do that, I will never comprehend. But you must remember that here at home, we didn't see the pictures until much later. (And suddenly, it occurs to me, that you were never able to realize my fears when I went down into the same Valley, at the birth of our children.) Be that as it may, you simply would not speak of the war experience when you came home. If I asked questions, you turned them aside. But I do remember that some time later, before Quill was born, I got so worried about you that I made you go to a psychiatrist. You told me long afterward, but not in specifics, that you had "walked around your job" – you were working on the old Balsz School pouring cement – contemplating suicide and that suicidal compulsion continued until you were about 30. And shortly before your death, our son took you to see "Saving Private Ryan" and he said you sat stony-faced and silent, as though you were in shock, throughout the picture. But anyhow, I know the Doctor gave you sodium pentothal, to help you release whatever was killing you inside. I never knew – or even knew if you remembered – what ensued there in that office. But I do know, that at least for some short time thereafter, you seemed a "released" man.

Oh my dear husband, if you could have put your head on my shoulder then, in those awful days, and cried with me, would it have helped? You never did that. Not even when our son died and I so desperately wanted you to comfort me. And be comforted. And when I tried to tell you of my fears, you would not hear. I have often wondered when we ceased to share and grieve together? And do you cry now?

And you never knew that I bore the guilt for your despair for many years – perhaps even now I still feel that pain – thinking that perhaps it was because you were disappointed in me that the depression occurred. I rejoice that this generation will know about Post Traumatic Stress Syndrome.

Then that last wonderful week of companionship and love and fear. And, finally, loss. (We would write longingly of those days in many letters.) On Sunday, October 8, 1944, at exactly 3:00 in the morning, we kiss goodbye. We will not kiss again until January 8, 1946, exactly fifteen months later, when we will meet in Los Angeles for our long ached for "second honeymoon."

2
And Now My Life Is Gone

After you left me that night and I did not hear from you by phone, I knew that your outfit had finally received its call. The days drag by. Nine days have passed. The whole city of Indianapolis knows that its lovingly adopted Unit has gone, though neither paper nor radio carries the news. The Blackout is complete. Men, equipment, trains have stolen out like thieves in the night. On the fourth day, I receive a card from the army, an APO number to which I can address mail. In my first letter, now very fragile with age, I write:

October 11, 1944

> Dearest–
> Since you left, this has been the loneliest place you can imagine. I thought I had rather prepared myself for your going but I had no idea it would be this rough. Monday and Tuesday, I spent most of the time crying but today I can begin to see a little light and realize that won't bring you back and only makes me sick. You know, you've positively ruined my sleep! Every night since Sunday, exactly at three o'clock, I wake up. And if you're not there to kiss me goodbye, I can't go back to sleep. [Now follows some practical stuff] . . . I hope you're missing me as much as I'm missing you, darling, but you are not to worry about me. I'm behaving myself and taking care of myself just as I promised I would. I'm going to the doctor this week and hope and pray that it's really "Junior." I never believed I'd ever want a baby like I want one now. Funny, isn't it? . . I'm sending "your key" back to you. It can kind of stand for the key to any door of mine – especially my heart! You've got a right to it . . . 'til you're bringing it back to me. Your very loving wife

Of such stuff, of course, are love letters made. But as I am writing these words, I am wondering how many weeping young wives – 61 years later – will be sending their new mates off today or tomorrow, to suffer in the coming months in a war which is strangely like yours was going to be. And will they write four hundred letters? Or will they merely e-mail back and forth, thus losing treasured records of their past? And what will be their stories, when they finally meet at last?

I write you again on the 12th, but on the 13th, I sadly write:

> *October 13, 1944:* I've got some bad news, darlin' and I've never been so disappointed in my life. 'Fraid we'll have to wait a little while for an addition to the family. Guess we didn't get on the ball quite soon enough. But late or not, I'm glad I finally got over a few crazy ideas, aren't you? But disappointed as I am, maybe it's just as well – maybe later on you'll be able to be with me – it'd be kind of rough, without you here. [And again, in writing now, I am struck by how the Lord was protecting me, knowing what would come and how I would need you when our son was born.]

I continue on in the letter:

> Outside of vetoing Junior, the doctor wasn't explicit about anything. He just said he'd see how I get along the next week or so. I'm feeling pretty good though honey, so don't worry. I'll keep you posted on all developments . . . I'm always thinking of you. I didn't realize how much one person can mean to a person's life until you left. I only hope that you feel the same and don't gradually forget me as time goes on. I never will you.

And again, in all the care of my heart – and my honesty which I protested to you as I began this letter (and in which I have had to make so many "confessions") – I have not told you the full truth. But I will tell you a little more of it in my letter of the 14th:

> *October 14, 1944:* Honey, I don't want to worry you but Betty said I should tell you, so here goes. I may be going to the hospital. Chances are I won't have to because I'm getting lots of

> rest and taking my medicine like a good little gal. But if I shouldn't quite make the grade where do I apply. . . .

And then I go on to tell you other news: Barbara's husband, Jack, is back and she's going to have a baby; I've sent you a package; tell the boys "hello." "Sweet dreams and they'd better be about me!"

Again, I see that my instinct is to protect you. In the midst of cheeriness, I have not told you that my state is not good – I have adhesions, the doctor has said, but there may be more serious complications. Only surgery will tell. And I've had surgery less than a year and a half ago! How can I manage? I'll postpone deciding. . . I may feel better. And in the despondency of not hearing from you and my limited health, I pour my feelings out in my next letter:

> I'm so afraid that you'll begin to forget about me. Remember how you told me once that you were scared stiff about what you would do if I hadn't said yes when you asked me to marry you? Well, I'm scared when I think of what I'd do if you should decide you didn't love me and didn't want to come back to me.

How strange that, even then, I knew your antipathy toward illness. Though I was told by one of your closest men friends, when I faced serious illness, in later years, that you were so afraid of losing me in death that you couldn't cope with it. I wanted to believe him, but only if I see you again, "beyond the veil," and I am in your arms once more, will my heart truly know peace.

I did go to the hospital. But not till you were gone. And you never knew. The specialists that were called in advised me that while surgery might be able to help the adhesions, there was no guarantee of success; they might simply return as a result of the second surgery. Furthermore, because of the seriousness of the ruptured appendix and the emergency of the former operation, my ovaries had been damaged, and a portion of one had been removed. Additionally, I had polycystic ovaries, which might bring further problems. In essence, they said I might never bear a child.

Not bear your son! How could I bear this sorrow? And how could I tell you? And because I did not confide in you, again I had made a decision that might alter our future life. But in the little package I had sent you (after the letter telling you I was not pregnant) I had sent "Junior!" (In our planning, we always called the coming children Junior and Terry Lee. Do you remember?) I hate to confess that after sixty years I am not quite sure what "Junior" really looked like. But I know he was somewhere between a stuffed animal and a hand puppet. I had sent this only as a soon-to-be-forgotten amusement for you. But Junior came to be your treasure – your panacea for the darkness of spirit that engulfed you so often in our months of separation. The place he came to occupy in your heart is indicated in the letter you wrote when you received him on the 16th of October. You write:

> **16 Oct 44:** What a swell boost of morale I received this morning. Two letters and "Neb Jr.". . . I got a great kick out of Neb Jr – all the boys say he looks just like me - even to the red nose - Already I have started to teach him a few manners - although I find him rather affectionate – he reaches up and kisses me now and then – Darn kid picks up things pretty fast. He has even learned to salute. . . The little fellow is going with me wherever I go for as long as he lasts –

And "Junior" did go with you through the next fifteen months, spying on you, storing up your derelictions to "report" to me when you got home, "protecting" my picture from the boys.
Constantly he was in your letters. On October 24th, you write of him, (and by this time, I know that he has become a surrogate for you):

> **24 Oct 44:** Jr. keeps telling me that he is so lonely for his mama – he cries sumpin' awful at night – But then all the Dog House bunch helps me quiet him down – even the boys miss you – They all ask "how's your wife and my girl friend? Especially Kirk – yep – they all say to extend their greetings of one type or another.

And it is clear that Junior and I have become the mascots of the 592nd battalion, going through all vicissitudes with you. . . until you lost him in the violent storm that almost sunk you in the Azores on your way back home in December '45. I never saw my "first-born" again. But how glad I am even now that that small gift brought you such happiness, through so many months to come.

But now back to my more or less truth about going to the hospital and my gloomy thoughts of how it would affect you. You receive that letter on the 20th of October and you advise me about the process for getting the surgery done in the Army hospital then, adding:

> If that is the only way that you can get rid of those adhesions in your side then I'm all for it – the sooner the better – I hate for those damn things to hurt you every day like they have been doing. Only this time don't be climbing any steps until you are really alright – I don't think I'd worry half as much about you if you could get over them that way. . . don't put it off. . . as they may cause something that will stay with you always – you don't want that and I don't either.

And then, assuaging all my fears of being rejected, you write these words:

> Never have I been so happy as when I married you – Never to this day have I regretted for one moment in hitching my lifetime, and I hope, my eternity to you. . . . Those short months we had together are the dearest months of my present life. . . Darling, I love you so and long to be with you. Your husband always, Neb

But before you write that letter on the 20th I have received your phone call! And I write you that very same Sunday the 17th:

> *October 17, 1944:* Right now I could climb a mountain, swim an ocean, kill an enormous monster or even drink seven Tom Collins –and all because of your telephone call. See what an effect you have on me – and via long distance too!!!. . . I'm sorry you couldn't tell me where you were nor if you were leaving – but doesn't it stand to reason if they pay you in the middle of the month you must be pulling out? Oh honey, I hope not . . . I'm glad you liked Jr – I thought you would even if Betty did think I was crazy. Anyone can send other things, but not everyone can send Jr. to their husbands. By the way, have you noticed how

> he hangs his head in shame when he stays out too late on Saturday night – just like his father! [business then]. . . .In case you are leaving, when you get to France among those beautiful mamsels, don't forget you've got a wife at home waiting to take her honeymoon all over again. And while she's usually pretty even tempered, if she gets stood up on that date, she's apt to blow her top!!! (So beware, frail man, beware.) Also, honey, while you're gone, don't go too heavy on the beer — 'Nite my darling and all the love you could possibly want or I could possibly give. "Me"

Honey, after all these years, don't you think I could write wonderful letters? And why didn't we write love letters after you got home and we had more perilous times? Don't you think it would have helped?

In the letter of the 17th, I do not tell you about my hospital plans, but I do tell you that Betty has had an operation, and is now home in bed. "Female trouble," she has said, but I am almost sure that she has had an abortion. I can't afford the apartment by myself and I don't want to stay with her as a roommate, so I must make other plans. Mother has had me over to dinner and has asked me if I would like to move back in for awhile. She has a room available now, since Jean has left them to go make her home with the Edmondsons. I think she probably needs money – and knows I wouldn't come, unless I paid her some rent. Your family would also like me to come visit them. But don't worry; I'll decide carefully and then let you know. I tell you not to worry about me – you know I've been out on my own for some time and am perfectly able to take care of myself. Which, of course, I was. And so I quietly make the plans for surgery; tell Betty she will have to have her Grandmother (who has been wanting to, anyway) move in with her – as soon as I recover from the surgery. And I have decided to move back to the family homestead.

Since I've confessed in the beginning of this letter to you and you now know "facts" which you didn't know before, I know that explanations will have to be forthcoming. But I'll save this particular "confession" for a later date, because, before I involve you in what may be a lengthy revelation, I want to dwell with you in some of the lovely "nothings" which you wrote so lovingly and faithfully through my long, aching months which were to come. Never did any woman love her man more ardently and wholly than I did you. And as I sustained you, so did your loving words sustain me. Never, through all the month of October, while you were still Stateside, did you cease to write words of love. But in some of the late letters, I sense your edginess. You were short-tempered, looking for trouble. I wait for the fuse to blow. You write, October 27th:

> **27 Oct 44:** Darling, it seems I am in a bad mood – I'm about to blow my top – guess I'll have to try it and see how much trouble I can get into. [The supply sergeant has given you trouble.] All in all, this has been one of those weeks when everyone seems to be on edge – one way or another. . . .Honey, I'm afraid I'm going to have to take your lovely picture down – too many guys are throwing you good night kisses to suit me – Simply makes me green-eyed. I wish we could spend this, our first Christmas together, but the army has strange ways of keeping people apart for such occasions – We'll have others, I know, so we ought to be able to spend this one apart. It'll be mighty tough but I'll be thinking of you, as I do all the time. I love you so and want to be with you so very badly.

After this letter, you do get into trouble and get six days camp restriction. How much I now remember in the re-reading of these letters: your edginess when worried, the necessity to blow off steam in a trying situation. Sometimes, I wish I could do that. But I'm not a steam blower at heart. But when I do get angry – you know the strength of my passion. And thinking about this now, how I wish in years to come that when this kind of mood was on you, you could have said, "Honey, I'm ready to blow. Better tighten the hatches." I think I could have understood. The next day's letter reads: "The boys finally quit throwing kisses to your picture when I threatened to put it away so I'm keeping your pictures in front of me. Oh the love I have for you."

On the 24th, you have been quite happy – your mother has written to you – she is 67 and has told you that with Dad not beside her, she cannot sleep very well, and that she has had forty years of love for the first Aquila Chauncey Nebeker (do you know I almost cancelled the wedding when you told me the first son had to be named Aquila Chauncey? What a name to burden a young child with!) "Do you think," you write, "you could stand the second for that long? By then, we ought to see the third, even perhaps the fourth? Eh?"

On October 27th, having received your 24th letter, I write you "sweet sincerities," which I would still mean today and with an even deeper understanding:

> *October 27, 1944:* I'll bet your mother is pretty lonesome there in Mesa with your dad gone. I can't imagine me ever being able to sleep as well with you gone. I used to love to sleep by myself – but after two months of sleeping with your arms around me, never again. [Of course, sweet guy, after so many years that snoring did get to me. You didn't snore for many years though.]. . . after forty years she still loves your dad, but I'll bet "the day after forever" my love for you will be at least as much as it is now. I say at least because its bound to be more after we've gone through sadness and trouble, as well as happiness and joy together. Forty years from now we should have a million memories – things we've shared and loved together. I hope by then we have at least one son and perhaps a daughter whom we can see living our happiness over again for us. It's so clear to me now what you were trying to tell me those nights about children bringing people close together. If a love is true and deep and right, there must be children for complete happiness. And the right kind of parents know how to teach their children so as to bring only happiness with their coming. I know, too, that I need never worry about losing your love while bearing your children. Two months ago I couldn't realize that – I do now. Your loving wife

And so the mail almost speeds back and forth. In your letter of reply you write, regarding Betty:

> Too bad she had that "operation" – if it was such. So many want kids and can't have them, then others get 'em, but get rid of them. I sorta hoped, you know, that we'd have one on the way – but I'm perfectly happy with "Neb, Jr." He was so blue this morning but now his ambition is coming back and he is feeling

> better – He said to me just the other day – "Wonder if mama misses me like we miss her? He has some cute sayings and surprises me with them now and then – I seen [sic] him writing down various things – but he wouldn't let me read them so I guess he is getting a few things to report to you. I hope they are all good."

Would anyone we have known in the coming years believe that you could write words such as these? But in this same letter, you mention again:

> Then the time I gave you the rings and that guy called you – you wouldn't tell him over the phone – and me sitting there listening while my special green dragon was eating some of Doctor Nebeker's Indian Root and growing bigger by the minute.

Looking back, I find it interesting to read in your last October letter: "Today I was rather surprised to get a letter from a girl I used to know – How she ever found out my new APO address I'll never know – She thought that you must feel that you must be the luckiest girl in the world to have roped and branded me. . . I hope she don't expect a letter in return cause she ain't going to get any." I wrote you back to do as you wished (I don't think that pleased you!) I just didn't inherit a jealousy gene. And I find myself disdainful of women who employ that gambit – even now, in my old age.

In your letter of reply to the above, you write:

> **8 Nov 44:** I can't quite understand why you say for me to do anything I want to do in the way of writing other gals. Why should I want to waste my time in that way when my entire thoughts are with you and for you? You know how I feel about this particular subject and how hurt I was until you promised not to write to your old boyfriends. [That, of course, was when I wrote Jack about our coming marriage rather than telling him over the phone, which I have explained to you in detail. I had already broken off all other correspondence.] If I feel that way for you then I can't feel any other way for me. Faith and I think you are a wanting to correspond to all those good looking guys

> you used to know and faith if you forget not to write to them I'll break your lovely neck.

For ten lovely days in November our letters are filled with communication, confidences. On 4 November headed "Doubly Blue," you actually indicate that you had felt that I was sad and didn't "feel so good." Those were the bad days of surgery and recovery – accounting for the two days I didn't write. But I'm a "master spy" and had covered my tracks well in my letters. In this letter, you write:

> **4 Nov 44:** Darling – how often at night I reach out for you – how this shoulder of mine misses your sweet head resting upon it. . . As I turn back to memories, all your dearness comes rushing to make me feel glad – make me feel sad. Will the time soon come when my dreams, my hopes, my ambition will be influenced by you personally? For this, I continually pray . . .

My dearest husband, what beautiful letters you wrote me; how they sustained me; how constant they were. And yet, a great sadness in my heart even today is that never, as long as I knew you, did you let others suspect this depth of feeling within you. And my great sorrow even to this very minute is that I never heard you – in a talk, in a meeting, in any public circumstance – ever acknowledge your love of me and my influence in your life. No other recognition I received in my life – and there were some of note – would ever have meant as much as that to me. And as I write these words, I cry. How precious it is that the Holy Spirit has turned me to re-reading your wonderful words of love. They have eased my grief.

In the future, despite our difficulties, your jealousy remained. I wasn't aware of it, really, until our daughter told me not too long ago, how you resented, in the last months of your life, my having lunch with George and Nick. Heavens! They were my long-time colleagues and friends of both of us. How could you have resented such innocent respites from my "nursing duties?" And all of us in our sixties plus! And why didn't you tell me that it upset you? I would have thought it stupid for you to feel such jealousy, but I wouldn't have gone. But perhaps I am the stupid one. Because, in the course of my educational and professional career that was to come in later years, I was always associated with male colleagues and it never entered my mind that you would feel threatened by that; I was never a woman who played upon men or was interested in them other than as friends. Surely you knew that? Surely you remembered that I had pledged myself to you? Oh, my dear, why didn't I know these things? Why didn't we talk about it later, as you feel free to do in this letter? Isn't it sad that only in trial and error – and finally, in age – that we grow in wisdom?

. . . And thus the month of October – and part of November – has passed. We have written almost daily since you left; you are in an embarkation camp somewhere in New York, I believe; we have been able to talk three times on the phone; and we know that the dark days of sailing on the wintry sea are upon us. But the news on the European warfront seems promising. And we still have time.

3

Sailing, Sailing, Over the Bounding Main

The dark, oppressive days of winter are now descending –literally, and in what will be a prophetic way. In our letters, we are both striving to be cheerful. I am withholding my illness from you and the gloom in your soul is almost completely camouflaged. Each letter you write is captioned specially:

1 Nov 44: A new month to miss and to love you;

2 Nov 44: Great love I have for you;

3 Nov 44: A Dreamy Day: there comes a time in every person's life when tears must fall – Tears of happiness – tears of loneliness – tears of sadness. But the tears that fall from my eyes are a combination of all. The feeling of happiness comes to me when I think ahead of the wonderful time we are going to have together – I'll bet you a yankee nickel that the next time I see you I'll cry a great deal more than I did after I left you. The tears will flow freely since gladness will fill my heart. That will be the DAY – the great day!!

4 Nov 44: Doubly Blue: The feeling of loneliness is bad today – since I called you on the phone, today has been a combination of sunshine and showers. I think I'll go down to the PX and have a good cry with the boys! [Darling, you always could find the solution!]

8 Nov 44: Your letter (Nov 1) was wonderful – those sweet, sweet memories. . . those wonderful kisses of yours – the lovely way you respond when I'm making love to you. How could I ever forget how really wonderful you are!

In the light of all these words of love sent back and forth, is it any wonder that I never once missed the "social whirl" that I had had before you and I met and married? I don't think I ever once looked back on my former days of fun, despite the great boredom that I often felt, and would feel often, in the long months to come. But as I write this, I realize that, in truth, I had given up, for you, my hard-won freedom.

On the 9th or 10th of November, you are not getting mail, but are hoping that more chapters for "Letters from Helen" will arrive soon. On the 11th, "Another Day," I find out that you are at sea and that you don't like it. You haven't been seasick and this is a wonderfully descriptive letter. You really could have been a writer. You write:

11 Nov 44: Another Day: I have spent a great deal of time on deck – I like to watch the waves rise and fall – even like to feel the ocean spray on my face. Looking out over the rail, I can see only endless stretches of blue water – broken here and there with whitecaps. While on deck, the wind seems to play tricks on the fellows; many times off goes a hat and flies back to the water – some sink and others float a long time. One helmet we watched ride the waves clear out of sight – it may be floating still – I have been lucky as the little puffs of wind seem to like me – at least I still have mine. Down here in our compartment it is usually so

> damn hot. Reminds me of your apartment last July – sweat runs down in streams and at night we sleep with no cover at all. The air is bad too what with all the guys sick and sweating but it is not so bad at that – at least it is fresh near the floor – I am beginning to think I made a mistake taking the top bunk. The only advantage is there is more room up here and more light. There is a light over my left shoulder that burns all the time.

And then you conclude with words that again tell me we were destined to be each other's love:

> My darling: this is the time that I have hated to think about ever since I met you. Last year I signed for overseas service but for some reason wasn't sent – maybe it was because I was to meet and marry you – but I'm on my way now. I hope more than anything that you will be happy and keep well while I am gone – I pray that the day will soon come when I can come back to you. Every day I want you to think how much I miss you and how much I want to come home to you. I'll carry my love for you anywhere I go and will wear it as a shield against whatever may come.
>
> Never forget, I'll love you always. Neb

4
Keep the Home Fires Burning

And darling, during these days in which you write, on the home front, sometimes the fire burns warm and sometimes cold – not for you but for life as a whole. I write you another letter telling you the doctor has told me surgery will not be a solution to the adhesions (he has told me that, so that's the truth); the better thing to do is just build me up so they can't affect me so terribly. I'm terribly anemic and I do have to take some horrible shots – so that part is also true. I ask you not to tell your mother about me being ill. No sense in her worrying about me as well as you. I tell you (keeping you interested, you understand):

> You're not the only one who's getting plenty of sleep. And it's such a waste of time when I can't curl up beside you. I wonder if when you first come back, I'll have gotten so bashful again that you have to leave the room while I get ready for bed? Or if I'll let you sleep on the floor like Jean Arthur did her husband in that picture "Impatient Years." Of course Junior's future doesn't look too bright if I do that so maybe I won't. . . Give Junior a kiss for me and then let him give you a kiss from me. My love

Following your letter about me not being pregnant, I write:

> I'm glad you weren't too let down about the real Junior. I'll confess I was terribly. But then, as you say, there'll be time after this mess is over. And then we can both watch him grow up together, together instead of via letters.

About the other Junior, I write:

> You don't think you're telling me anything new when you say Junior is pretty smart and learns fast, do you? Heavens, the main reason I sent him to you was so he could keep an eye on you and take care of you – incidentally, I'd better warn you he's going to give me an accurate account of everything you do while you're gone so, my favorite husband, watch your step! And when Jr. kisses you, those kisses are really from me. And if he cries in the night, sing him to sleep with my song, "A Sig Nu Honeymoon" and pretend I hear it too. Ever loving wife, "Me"

Our letters from October 15th until you are at sea swing from sadness to joy. You write that you haven't received mail and "the book" said that I should write every day. I reply:

> *October 15, 1944:* But sweetheart, are you really sure the "book" said that? It seems to me that book said quite an awful lot for being as little as you said it was. But if it did say that, it only proves that that book of ours is never wrong. I don't know of a

mistake it's made yet, so I shall continue to write every day because I know what your letters mean to my day and I'll be very conceited and take it for granted mine are as important to you. I still wish on a star every night – for you. That's the only thing in the world I really want – just you. And no matter how long we have to wait, I know my wish will come true – when it's time. However far you travel, I know that you'll travel those same miles back to me (or else I'll haunt you for life!)

Despairing of my boring letters, I write:

If I were a writer or a poet, I could put my thoughts down so you could almost feel the horrible loneliness within me and know as clearly as I do how very, very much I love you. Since I'm neither, I'll just have to trust that you can read between the lines – read in every line the words, "my heart is lonely without you." And if ever words were true, those words are. With all the love in me, Helen

Replying to what you call, "one of your gloomy letters," I write consolingly:

I know just how you felt because, as I recall, about that same night I wrote a letter to you on the very same order. It's one of those cases "make me feel glad just to be sad thinking of you." If we both didn't have moods like that once in awhile, I'm afraid there wouldn't be much feeling between us. Many nights when I'm tired and discouraged, I hit the depths of despair and then I need your shoulder to cry on - just as you needed mine the other evening. Darling, I also know how you feel when you think of anything happening between us. I've had those thoughts and felt the same way. Of course, I know as well as you do that probably nothing will ever happen that would part us. And yet they say the best way to really love someone is to realize that he or she may be lost. Thinking like that every thought, every action, every memory becomes just that much more precious and dear. Why honey, I've got so many things to remember that we shared, from the first time I leaned over and kissed you to the night we kissed each other goodbye, that no one could ever

> get through those memories. My days are just one long thought of you. . . sometimes things do look pretty gloomy – but that's not the future, that's the present. If we start out by having the hard things in the beginning, as we are now, then everything good that happens later will seem twice as wonderful.

Did I really have all that wisdom at only seventeen? But how prescient I was when I also wrote in that letter: "When the time comes when either of us is afraid to express himself to the other, that's when I'll be afraid we're drifting apart." My love, when did that start happening to us?

In the next letter from ship board you tell me that you and the boys have played "Barber Shop" and your new G.I. haircut is a mess. You've read another mystery book and admit that you cheated and read the last chapter first. (I will reply in my following letter that I always do that too!) You haven't been seasick at all – and all the men who have been are now recovering and have been "raising hell in general. . . all in all it has been interesting." On Sunday, the 12th, you had powdered eggs for breakfast and then:

> **12 Nov 44:** went up on deck to Protestant services. The first ship board church I have ever attended and although I don't agree with some of the things that were said, it was rather touching and made a great many of us feel somewhat better about the whole thing. Maybe it was because the sun was shining and it was somehow warm out there – It was a beautiful day to be out – anyway you looked at it – the only thing missing as far as I was concerned was you. How very much I would have liked to have you with me to enjoy this new experience. . . . As I look over this vast body of water my heart fills with love for you insomuch that if every drop of water was love I could drink it all and have plenty of room for I love you with every part of me and will for always.

My dear, through all our years of travel which were to come – together and apart – you never lost your love of new experiences, new places, the travel, itself. But my pleasure was less in the newness of things than in being near you and, freed from the press of the world, recapturing, often in "old familiar places," the joy that we could always find in each other.

> **13 Nov 44: A Day of Memories:** – big things – small things – beautiful things – All day it has been the same – and what a wonderful day it has been – I am most happy when my thoughts are entirely of you. . . The first time that you kissed me is one of my most pleasant memories – I hear such sweet music and the lights are low –and we are talking softly not caring if anyone is around – then you reach over and kiss me in such a swift sweet manner that has stamped it deeply in my memory – Do you still think that it was worth giving – seeing the result that it brought? . . .I am so glad that I searched for 25 years before I found you but I am happier that I didn't let you go. Darling, I'll never cease to be amazed at your beauty. How often have I thought of how pretty you looked every time I came to see you – And when I held you in my arms before the mirror, I couldn't help but tell you what a cute kid you are. To watch you coming down the stairs was really a treat. How angry you were with me when I coaxed you to go through the fun house at Riverside and then some guy got in my way when they shot the air to you. My but you did blush a pretty red. . . . And I'd let you rave on if I didn't leave a 30 cent tip – but now I know how very much time I wasted while drinking a beer or two with the boys. You see, my sweet, even the times I made you angry come back to make me feel sad! That I could do such things to hurt you!!! My My!. . .I love you so.

How strange that in one brief paragraph, read sixty years after the writing, I can see clearly the seeds of disharmony that will haunt us in days to come. A 30 cent tip (which I could easily and quietly circumvent myself) but which in reality revealed our differing attitudes toward money. And the "beer with the boys" which ultimately in the process of events will become to me a great betrayal and rejection of our love. Neither of us could "express himself to the other," and as I had predicted long before, we were "drifting apart."

But this wonderful, lonely letter, written on the high seas, ends in your great physical longing – which will always be part of you:

Sweetheart, how are you missing me now? Do you miss my loving? Is [sic] the twins missing me? Ah if I could be one hour with you, I could tell you of all the love I have only for you. I could really convince you just how very much I miss you. I love you so. Your husband, Neb

5
Land At Last

17 Nov 44 – Too Far Away!: My Darling Wife, At last we have reached land such as it is. I don't know where we are except that the ship is somewhere in England! Just looking over the supposed landscape I can tell that I am in a much different country than the good old U.S.A. . . . From my experiences on the boat I can and have said that I am happy that my feet are destined to be placed in mud not rolled around by the motion of the ocean waves. . . during the trip I never got the slightest sea-sick but many were that way the whole trip. . . I am so much in love with you and the feeling of loneliness deepens in each additional mile that separates us – I find it hard to think of any thing else but you . . . and how much I love you. . . Your faithful husband

18 Nov 44: As an Englishman, I say 'top o the morning to you, old chap, with a hip hip and all that merry old crap!" I see a few old merry Britishers standing here and there and, I say, I can hardly understand what they say. Peculiar old ducks if I say so myself.

We got on one of those funny trains that you often see in the movies pulled by two of the dinkiest engines that you can think of and sat in what would be English first class fare cars – I never saw such funny things in all my life – The whole railroad seemed so quaint and small – The box cars were interesting as they seemed to be a combination of several parts. The body itself was about 20 feet long and was what we would call a flat car – The box part was separate from the bottom part – A crane put the box on the flat car and there you had a box car or the crane would take the box off and you had a flat car – that flat car was used for every kind of a railroad car you could think of – gondolas, dump cars, tank cars etc.

Darling, if we lived in one of these English houses and went out on a Saturday night tear, we'd probably end up in the wrong house when we went home! All of them are the same, built in rows on both sides of the streets in one long brick building – It seems that the towns we passed through are all the same with these long buildings the only homes. Stores, homes, the same, What a place!

The farms were the only place where I saw any houses all by itself – and usually that was plenty big – with beautiful green pastures all over the countryside – Of course, on the farms there were the regular stock, such as cows, pigs, horses, etc. The fields were separated by hedges instead of the usual barbed wire fence – since it is rather cold here the hedges were in the winter state but I can imagine that in spring the country here is dotted with beautiful green hedges. I could tell that the people here are in a war as all of them had shabby clothes with the women wearing slacks or man's pants. Of course, I just saw them from the train window and couldn't say for sure if the clothes were new or not or whether they were in good shape or not but from talking with the train crew I could tell they felt the war was on – all in all they seemed to be glad the Yanks were here and they were happy in general.

Honey, we are in a camp or something not knowing anything about it but straw mattress and windy windows and as time goes on maybe I can describe camp after I know what's what – Right now I am loving you greatly and missing you – And now and forever – Your loving husband

19 Nov 44 Information Day! : . . . I want to tell you a few things that I have done since yesterday. . . We get to this camp to find that we are to stay in barracks of one sort or another and they later turned out to be of the "one sort or another" type but I am happy that we have a room with a small dinky stove at each end and double bunks the size of a regular bed, (that is – double bunks – the top bunk off the floor at about the same height of a regular bed) and this is where we live. The building is one of the

> few frame houses that I have seen. I have seen just our area – Of course I can't say where, how many, size, etc. of the camp anyway. . .

The rest of your letter I wish to recall in full. It shows so clearly how we were able to discuss and compare as the miles between us grew greater. But a little background first. You had been able to call me on November 5th, our three-month wedding anniversary, and following the call, I had immediately written you:

> *November 5, 1944:* The thought of your climbing on a boat and sailing away leaves me weak in the knees. . . When you left me for another state, it was bad enough, but when I think of you being in different countries, it's almost terrifying. Not because of the danger –that's not quite real enough yet to really worry me – but you'll be seeing new things, getting a different outlook on things, meeting strange and probably interesting people. Meanwhile, I'll be here, wondering day after day if you'll be disappointed in me after you get back, if you think and dream of me as I do you. If as time drags by you'll forget me. [And then I fill the letter with the "cheery "home front news.] You're the only thing that really counts in my life and I know it will always be that way – for now and forever.

Now back to your reply on 19 November:

> Honey, I received last night the letter you wrote the afternoon of the long phone call and I must admit that there was food for thought in every line you wrote – however my darling, I shall say that that call was the sweetest thing! That without a doubt was the very best thing that I brought with me from the States. Now about the things in your letter concerning my worldly travels and the changes they may have on me – I am not afraid that the changes will affect me in any manner – Mind you, I'm not saying I won't change in any degree but I am saying they will be of no importance as far as our lives are concerned – Remember, darling, I talked to you once about this same subject and I think we both agreed that a little adjustment on both of our parts will take care of that in short order. I feel safe

in saying that all major changes in my life have already been experienced unless the war really gets me down and even that possibility shouldn't bother me as most of my life, I have been exposed to danger in one form or another. Besides that, I have been on my own for the last ten years and realize that you have also which should be the major safeguard for any change. My dear, I don't think that you need worry about any change either in habits, personality, or thoughts regardless of time!

I know quite definitely that you are the only girl I truly love and I shall carry that with me for all time – there can be no other takes your place either now or any other time – that is how deeply I am in love with you. The re-adjustments necessary will come naturally in case there need be any, but now, I miss you so.

Oh my dearest, how very young and naive you were then for all your 25 years! I, in my tender seventeen-year-old forebodings, was much nearer the truth. But time alone would reveal the changes to come. For the time being, your letter above eased my heart, if not my mind.

Your letters from England continue through November:

20 Nov 44: You'd be rather surprised, darling, to see and hear some of these here blooming Englishmen. They call things by a lot different names than we do and it is pretty tough to figure out what they mean. The other afternoon I was talking with a chap about 14 years old. He was not much larger than Jerry [my eight year old brother] and he was smart as a whip. My nephew back home who is 14 is as tall as I and weighs close to 140 lbs. Just as a comparison between American and the English. Over here they seem to be small on the average but the cops are all great big guys 6 ft or over. You have heard of the English Bobbies of course, and they are as peculiar as they are told about. They wear long blue coats with a funny shaped helmet of blue steel that has a spike on top. They really have a snappy salute for all officers, and they are just civilian cops.

21 Nov 44: clear and cold, and dark, and rainy. The other night I went down to eat chow, when I got through it was dark so on the way back to the barracks I thought, as usual, I knew where I

> was going but it turned out that once more I was talking through my hat! I must have walked, bumped or otherwise stumbled around for a half an hour before I gave up and retraced my steps back to the mess hall. . . it was so dark at times that often times we bump into someone coming toward us. Here and there you can spot a light but it only throws you off. Every night we put up black out curtains so our light won't be seen from any where.
>
> We only get about one pass a week and that is from 6 P.M. to 11 P.M. All towns in England close at 10 and there is an 11 o'clock curfew – next is the fact that walking is the only way to get there and back. Might get there but getting back during this black out presents the problem of ending up somewhere the camp ain't! They say you can't get anything in town which is okay with me as I haven't any dough, anyway.

23 November is a newsy letter worthy of being preserved for our posterity – as are almost all of your letters, but sitting here at the computer hurts my back so that I'm including in total only the very best:

> **23 Nov 44:** Faith and may I wish you a very happy Turkey day dinner! I had a fairly good slab of good old white meat plus a little dark on the side. Naturally the side dishes were all the same as a regular Thanksgiving meal back home – dressing and all – It tasted mighty good since we have been eating h. . . of a lot of powdered stuff. . . Sorta to make an extra day I went to town to see what the town was like. After dinner Hennessy and I dashed in for a couple of hours – It is just a short ways so we walked to look over the country side and to get an idea of what to expect in town we stopped in places along the way. We went into a drug store and found that is just what it meant. Nothing but drugs for family use – the man laughed when we said that we wanted to see an English drug store. It was almost dark when we started out and by the time we got down toward the center, it was so dark we couldn't see. The only way we could tell a place was open was by a small lighted sign in the window, which was hard to see. We'd stick our head in the door to find out what kind of a joint it was. We saw theatres, grocery stores

– cafes and then we run [sic] into a "pub" – so we went in to taste some English beer. The beer tastes to me just like American vinegar and comes in half pint glasses. The glass you hang on to 'cause you won't get another one but you will refill it if you can stand more than one! I drank two before I gave it up as a bad job The pub is quite different from an American bar in that there are generally several rooms – a lounge, a smoke room, then the bar itself. No one makes any noise in there and all talk is quiet and low – Mostly old men to have their daily bitter as the beer is called – there is light, brown, mild and bitter as types of the stuff – By the time we got through with two beers it was time to go back to camp as we have to be in by 11 P.M. All in all it was interesting but not much fun – My darling – on this first Thanksgiving Day of our married life I think of you and send all the love my heart holds. . . Neb

The next day you woke up with:

24 Nov 44: one hell of a headache – I kinda think that it was the cider I put on top of the two bitters – cause everyone who had cider last night felt the same! The cider was good but I guess it don't mix with beer!!! Oh my ackin' head! [You idiot! Even I knew that cider is the "hardest" drink you can get in European countries!] . . . Darling, this is one of my bad days and for reasons that are unknown to me I can't for the life of me feel happy about anything. Regardless I have thoughts of pleasant memories concerning one sweet cookie in the States – namely you! Darling, in the long days ahead remember this. I love you and want so much to be with you. Always, Neb

Saturday & Sunday: blue days of reminiscing; it's cold and windy; squad's day for the PX, but the counter is bare.

25-26 Nov 44: Time to hit the sack – remember the organ player at the Moritz and his tune on our wedding nite!!!? Love

27 Nov 44: Mail from me in only 10 days! You're glad I'm enjoying my little brother [Jerry] and Susie, my now three-year-old sister.

29 Nov 44: "A Rainy Day": And you're 'bitchin': I'm afraid the fuse is burning! You write:

> As each day goes by I become more disgusted with England and English people! Gad, what a bunch of bums – The favorite saying seems to be 'Got any gum, chum?" or "Got a smoke, bloke?' Even the white haired old people say it! Kids by the droves hang around the gate and fences and you have to wade through them before we go ten yards. [You have no idea that these are probably children from the slums, resettled in this rural area because the British dock areas – and the poverty-ridden environs around them – are being blown up by buzz bombs!] Then if you walk down the street anywhere, the people you pass gives the same old stuff. The gang on the whole is ready to bust out of this country – the sooner the better.

Again, most of you won't even think that these poor people have been at war for five years! How can you imagine their deprivation of the small things you all take for granted? You continue your diatribe against the army itself – how you hate being in the Service!

> The good old boys with the paper heads try to keep us doing something all the time – Hell, you'd think that we were back in the states with all the spit and polish that goes on here – Formations, inspections and all that crap – even in the back areas all that goes on. When I do the stuff I'm supposed to do – I'll be damned if I'm going through this stuff again. I half expect this outfit to stop a fire mission on the front lines just to have a show down inspection! But there I go bitchin' again so I cease– right now my morale is plenty low and I mustn't put too much stuff like that in my letters. . . .Oh! To remember your sweet kisses on this night sends thrills and chills up and down my spine! How I miss you tonight, darling!!!

As I read your closing lines, I am smiling – just as I smiled sixty years ago, remembering your exuberance, your enthusiasm for me and for life. You could not know then, as I would soon know, that the darkest days of the darkest winter of the darkest war in the history of modern man were only days ahead.

> **30 Nov 44: "What! Another Turkey Day:**... and while in the States people had turkey – your poor old husband had C rations – meat and vegetable hash in the can – plus two peanut butter sandwiches... Damn, no letter again today – what a life – Let me tell you, my dear, it is plenty discouraging not to receive any word from the very one that holds all the space in my heart! Yes – not only in my heart but in my entire lonely racked body, even down to my little toes! Great Scott! Whatta feelin'!

The squad has hooked up a portable radio and you hear short-waved music from the States. You continue:

> They played "You only hurt the one you love," and the good old look of homesickness came over every one of us! I got all choked up inside when I heard "Till Then;" I shall never forget the first time we heard that! The quiet attitude and the peaceful feeling that was there in that cute little bar in Chicago! Darling, as oceans of water separate us now, I continually think of you in every way and every day. You must never doubt that I love you – love you in a way that is great – wonderful and filling . . .

When I read such lines of love, I am reminded again, that in the dark, dark hours of these months, I was "your strength and hope, your courage. Your faith in the Future." And this gives me hope for mine – in the Lord's own time. But as you end the last letter of November, your humor emerges to conquer all. (How did you lose that wonderful gift?)

> Hitler fired a V2 into the air; it fell to earth he knows not where; He loses more damn V2s that way! P. S. I haven't seen any of those things yet and hope I never do! Love, "Me"

6
Back Home In Indiana

As all your dear letters are winging to me, back home in Indiana your faithful Helen continues to write the monotonous events of her life – sticking as close to the truth as her desire to protect you will permit. By the first days of November, you will have learned that I have moved out of our wonderful apartment –and though your memories with me are there, you are pleased. You had never liked Betty and have confessed you fear her influence on me. Well, perhaps that's logical – or maybe illogical – given the fact that through her persuasion, you and I had met! However, my sweet, you never gave one little thought about the wrench that move caused me. After all, that small place had been my home for three years. It had been earned at much cost. And in it, I had felt free – and confident. Now, in November, I have returned to the old environment from which I had fled. Did you ever once think of the courage required? But, so as not to harrow up your mind at this late date in our relationship, let me simply say that I made the change for four reasons: (1) to please you; (2) to help my mother out – financially, I thought; (3) to save money so that I could go to Arizona to meet your family – as both you and they desired; (4) to save money for our future together.

Let me clarify my desire to aid my mother – or Margie, as you were to call her through the years. Despite my mother's exploitation of me, despite her sometimes vicious temper toward me (none of which you knew until this letter), I truly cared for her. I hesitate to say I "loved" her but I am able to say, I cared for her deeply. Always from the time I was about three, I remember wanting to "help" her. I remember once, when I was no more than three, she had bathed me and lifted me onto the toilet seat, where she dried me. Then she left the room and, hoping to please her, I powdered myself all over. Returning, she was – in my memory – furious with me. She had wanted to put lotion on me first. And it was always like that between us. Whatever I did was wrong. And she always made such jokes about me to people. Because I was so small, I had been nicknamed "Teeny" (how I hated that name!) and always there was "a joke on Teeny." And laughter. And yet I always felt such sorrow for her. Was it guilt – because I somehow believed that if she hadn't had me – as she so often said – that her life would have been different? I just don't know. And I just don't know if she loved me. Though I do remember in later years – before she truly broke my heart, as you will remember, Neb – she said to me, "You are the only thing that has given my existence meaning!" And I carry deep in my heart the memory of a Christmas when I was maybe five years old. I had wakened and stealing down the stairs in the darkness, I had seen my tiny mother – herself only maybe 24 in this dark year of the Depression – with tears streaming down her face, trying – as I sensed even then – to rejuvenate my tattered "dolly" into freshness for the Christmas dawn. I somehow always knew she did the best she could. I think my sister does not have such tenderness for her.

I have not told you these memories before, Neb, because there were not reasons to do so. I had not told you the specifics of my leaving my home, until my confessions in this letter. But now you are entitled to know. Had you known before, perhaps you would have regretted my decision to return there. And had you known about Darrell, I really don't know what your reaction would have been. Had you known while you were still here – and knowing your jealous protection of me with others – I think you might have killed him. But because I had told Mother nothing about his actions, and because of his fear that I might, and because I was now *your wife*, I knew I had nothing to fear from him. In fact, I could return triumphant. So that, my love, is how I managed to make my return.

But to continue with my November writings. I am back at 132 N. Colorado. I am writing your family in Arizona and have sent them your picture; I am planning Christmas presents from you to all of them – about 16 if my memory serves me. And most important to me, I am planning carefully for the days when you return. "I expect," I write you, "that by the first of January our little family can be banking $120 a month! That means that by our first anniversary, we'll have over a thousand dollars." I even lay out for you projections for that vast sum of money (how times have changed.) First:

> in case, as you said, you got the chance to buy into some kind of business, you'd have the money. . . .I don't want you to have to start in on a job you don't care for and be miserable doing it the rest of your life. If you want to finish college it's going to be possible. If you want to lead a life of leisure the money is for that too. That way, maybe you'll never get the feeling that marrying me kept you from doing things you wanted to.

Had you remembered these provident plans of mine, in the early days of your return many months later, you might have understood better my reactions to your improvidence then. But it will become very clear to me in times to come, that in truth, man's plans are nothing, in the face of providence. Yet tempting fate even further, I write:

> And the second use for part of that money will be for Junior. I told you I thought families should be financially ready for their children and since the Lord seemed to think so too this time, I'm not going to give him a reason for disappointing us again! Now don't you think you've got a very smart wife? And besides that, she's so very much in love with you.

On November 5th, our third month anniversary, we have talked on the phone and I have written you words cited earlier, but I also reveal, because of your question about me being happy, how deep my misery really is at home. I do this very rarely:

> *November 5, 1944:* I can't be really happy until I'm with you. But as far as being fairly satisfied, well I am. Of course I have my bad times and the tired-er I am, the more often they occur. I'm sorry if I let my letters show it. I didn't mean to. Some times are worse than others. I've been by myself so long it's hard to get used to Mother and Dad's quarrels and the kids fighting. That's only at times – just remember it's because I'm tired and so very lonesome for you that sometimes there's nothing to do but break down and cry a few tears – and that's not because I'm a baby either. . . . You're the only thing that really counts in my life and I know it will always be that way. So for now and forever, Your loving wife, "Me"

It is during the first days of this month, that I miss writing you a couple of days. I mustn't let you know how slow my recovery is – and I am working so hard at my job at the loan company. During the holiday months of November and December, we will work 12 or 15 hours daily – stopping only in early evening when the boss treats us to dinner out. Then there's the trip home late at night, and the cold is devastating this year. You write several times that you have a bad cough. And knowing how you smoked, I'm not surprised now. But whoever, in 1944, had heard of emphysema – and the cigarette companies were making certain that the troops were well supplied. I still remember the slogan: Lucky Strike Green Goes to War. The seeds of your death were already being sown on the battle front – but *you* should have known better, my love. And several times you write, "I'd better stop smoking," but you never do. And I have other small problems: you request stamps and stationery and a schick razor and a scarf and a sweater as the cold engulfs you. Such minor things. But every errand requires more energy – the post office, the stores, the street car ride. And supplies in everything are extremely limited. I do my best, but it seems I'm always apologizing to you for my delinquencies. The home front is no picnic either, in these last months of a devastating year – in Europe and Japan.

But in between all the little exchanges of nothingness, our passion for each other endures. I write on 8th November:

> *November 8, 1944:* Sweetheart, don't think you can scare me with all that talk about the loving I'm going to get when you get home. If I remember rightly, I'm not exactly the one who can't take it!! The only thing I can't take are too many Tom Collins – after too many of those, I can't quite take the stairs either. But for the time being I shall cast no aspersions on your ability or powers of endurance. We shall wait and we shall see!?!

I include these words above in this love letter from me, dear heart, only to remind you that you had taught me your lessons well; I had learned the art of loving and I joyed in it. And when you returned home so many months later, we would need only to rekindle the fire. And for a wonderful while, we did. . . When did we begin to fail? And what could we have done? But in the midst of words of passion, I will also write [and this will be the truth of what I truly desired through all the years, though fate and circumstances were to dictate otherwise:]

> I'm just living for the day when all I have to do is keep house, cook for you, and be happy with you. I only wish there were some way of knowing when that will be. I long for you so much constantly that sometimes it almost seems impossible to go on with this useless, humdrum existence without seeing you, having you close to me once again. . . Having had you – even for only two months – I never, ever, could be happy with anyone else.

To the day of my death, I believe these words will still be true. Though many times I came to hate you!

And thus my November days pass – in the minutiae of life and words of longing and love. I do not write you on the 2nd & 3rd because I am so ill. But I do not tell you. In fact, in my letter of the 12th, I write:

> *November 12, 1944:* Just in case you should still be a little worried about my health, I'd better tell you that I feel almost as good as I ever did. It's only once in a great while I have any pain at all - and I never have that positively dead-tired feeling, No more dizzy spells and no more fainting. So you can be completely at ease about me and not worry about anything except getting back home to me.

While this is not exactly the truth, it suffices. And lest you forget, sweet husband, even in the days of illness that were to be mine, I <u>never</u> wallowed in sickliness! I never sought for pampering. It simply was not – and is not – my way. You and I were alike in asking no quarter when the chips were down.

But though I have cheered you on the 12th, in my letter of the 11th, I think I must have known that you were gone, again. And I am overcome with memories.

> *November 11, 1944:* I guess about my bluest, lonesome-est times are Saturdays and Sundays. I'll never . . . get used to not seeing you walk in the door Saturday evening – or waking up on Sunday without your arm around me, being able to lean over and kiss you while you lie there playing possum. You didn't fool

> me – ever – you big faker. I always knew when you were asleep and when you weren't. Oh darlin', do you think it will be as long as a year before you're back?

How could we have dreamed that it would be fourteen months more before we met again?

And on the 12th I mourn:

> *November 12, 1944:* You know, darling, my love for you grows daily. . . and yet, when you stop and think about it, we'll be practically strangers when we meet again. We knew each other only four months before we were married and then lived only two months together as man and wife. Those six months were wonderful and the only bright spot about our being apart is the thought of getting reacquainted and living it all over again. While you're gone, I'm going to be hanging on to all those things we shared for such a short time, loving you continually and deeply. I don't intend letting anything happen to something so lovely and wonderful as our life together as so many couples do because of separation and lack of faith.

On the 13th, "Oh what a day!" I receive your two letters written on the "blue days" of the 3rd & 4th. These are the last letters I will receive for over three weeks but I have written to you faithfully every day. However, from the 18th through the 20th, my letters are missing from your packet. And from my packet, your letters are missing from the 15th & 16th & 17th. They must have gotten lost in the 50,000 bags of mail you told me were waiting to be distributed or to go out. So Thanksgiving passes and I write you after work the next day:

> *November 26, 1944:* I'm so tired I'm almost hysterical and the first time somebody even looks at me, I'm liable to break down and cry. I may be a tough cookie, but fifteen hours is too much even for me. Looks like it'll be going on [work] for quite some time too. Sometimes I wonder if it's worth it. . . You know how discouraged I can get when I'm tired.

But the long hours of work are paying off. (Just as did my long hours of work before our wedding pay for my lovely wedding dress.) On the 29th of November, I write you that I am planning to visit your parents, perhaps in March. Your family has written me loving letters extending an invitation for however long I wish – and I know that you are pleased. Had you known how very difficult it was getting for me with Margie and Darrell, you would have been even more eager for me to leave. But I am not yet quite ready, financially, to make definite plans for Arizona. Long hours of work are still ahead for me.

And on the 30th, I got a government card with your new address on it. And I received a package from you – sent by your mother on your specific order – for my Christmas. I write:

> *November 30, 1944:* I had the awfulest fight with myself to keep from opening it. It had a "Do Not Open Until Christmas" sign on the outside but for the moment I almost forgot how to read. Finally, I decided I'd much rather have it under the tree Christmas. . . More love from your adoring wife
>
> P. S. You have the cutest dimples!

Part III

"Now is the Winter of Our Discontent"

1
Waiting On the Home Front

And in such small details of daily life, winter will usher in the coldest December recorded in Western history. In retrospect, its darkness and cold and malignancy seemed to be reflecting the mortal conflict now raging in Europe. In the East, Russia and Germany are locked in final deadly battle – a battle, many think, between dark and even darker force. In France, the Allied Forces wait to launch the final push across the Rhine to the heart of Germany and to final victory after six long years of war. And in Indianapolis, the winter reigns, temperature dipping to -12 degrees. And the wind blows cruelly off the river. And there is a coal shortage. And I receive no letters. Eleven days have passed; each day I write to you my letters of nothingness and love, trying in every letter to remind you of me, of the days we had shared, of a life that will yet be ours. On December 1, 1944, I write this nonsense:

> *December 1, 1944:* Dearest Dope: Maybe you don't like my name for you, but like Monkey-face, it's one of my favorite terms of endearment. You are a monkey and you are a dope and that's partly why you're my favorite husband. I love you just as you are – except once in awhile when you get the urge to sing to me, "Is you is or is you ain't my baby?" across a very crowded trolley. But even that's okay, if I'm not too tired to take it the way I should. This evening has been very nice. I spent the evening listening to the radio while I sewed and gave myself a manicure and did a few other things I've been saving for an evening just like this. I had looked for some mail today, but no such luck... I'm almost beginning to wonder if you're just a figment of my imagination or something I dreamed one night...If you were just a dream, that dream would be enough for me now

and forever....My darling, I love you so much. I'd like to show you how much, but I can't. All I can do is promise you a faithful heart. God bless.

As I read such letters, today, I remember how difficult it was to write day after day, trying not to bore you, trying to reassure you that I was not out playing the field like some of your friends – and their wives – were doing. I'm going to copy almost the entire letter of my December 11th letter to you just so we can both remember how very precious we both held these letters we wrote back and forth.

December 11, 1944: Dearest – This has been one of the nicest days I can remember since you left. I got ten letters all at once, and I was so happy I cried. It more than made up for those days and days when I didn't get the first line. All but two of the letters were the ones you wrote while aboard ship and I don't think there will be many things in my life that I'll treasure more than those letters. [Actually, I can't think of any other possession I have kept for 61 years!] All your letters are very dear to me but especially the ones I got today. Now I know those long nights when I had to almost fight to keep from crying on my pillow because I hadn't heard from you, you were blue and longing every bit as much for me. And when you wrote about all the little things you remembered like our first kiss, and our first Sunday together, our silly fight over thirty measly cents and other things it would be so easy to forget, I knew that as long as you kept remembering those things and feeling about me as your letters tell me you do, why you could be gone years and I'd never have to worry about us. . . . Don't you feel sorry for people who court each other, get married, and live their whole lives together without a chance to express their love in a few letters? It seems to me that one of the best ways to save memories of being young and newly in love is through letters. Just like you press a flower between a book to remember a nice party or dance, you save your letters as evidence of a perfect beginning to a lovely life together. And maybe sometime when the going gets a little rough, there all in black and white you have almost a panorama of things once shared together. You never can tell, sometime those little pieces of paper may be all

> that's needed to straighten out a seemingly hopeless muddle. That's one reason I'm glad you write me such wonderful letters – As long as I have those letters, I have you.

And then I continue:

> I don't know how I got off on that tangent but you know me. I'm certainly no one-track mind "Cookie." If I've bored you, I'm sorry – but them's me thoughts and you can take 'em or leave 'em."

After another page and a half [remember, all this is written in pen – not on a typewriter] I end:

> I'll come to the point and say what is really the whole idea for this letter-namely, I love you – and that's a gross understatement because I love you, I adore you, I respect (big joke) you, I miss you and I long for you, I dream of you, I talk of you – heavens that's enough – at least it will give you a vague, rough idea. And so, my darling, lest I flatter your ego, I'll say no more. Give my love to Junior, my hello to the boys and kiss yourself for me (amazing feat – let me know if you do it!) Until tomorrow, I'll dream of you and be constantly –
>
> Loving you, "Me"

But before I receive this treasure trove of ten letters, I have been without mail for two weeks and I have written to you about teaching my brother to dance, about changing all the furniture in my room and ending up with it all back in the same place, about my plans for the trip to Arizona. On one particular evening, I write again about our wedding:

> I remember how I felt awfully scared but awfully sure of what I was doing. If I live a hundred different lives, I'll never forget how proud and happy I was when you said, "I do" in your firm, sure tone. And after I said the same thing and you kissed me – such a sweet kiss, I could have died completely happy right then. I've never been sorry – one single moment – that I'm your wife, even with the loneliness of your being gone. In fact, every day I'm

prouder and happier and more in love with you than ever. . .
Forever, "Me"

It would be weeks later, on the German front, hiding in a foxhole, that you will receive this letter and write to tell me how it eased your heart. And on December 6th, having received your letter of November 17th – nearly three weeks in coming – I thank you for the advice you have given me about changes in our lives to come:

> *December 6, 1944:* You always seem to know just what to do or say to make us both happy....I shall have no more doubts or misgivings but continue to believe firmly and deeply that we shall pick up exactly where we left off after making perhaps a few adjustments . . . . You know, you never let me down and it's so nice to know you will always be there with the right answer when what I call a brain gets a little off the beam. Don't ever let that part about you change.

Oh how I wish you had remembered my need for your strength and guidance. I never wanted to be the strength of our family. I would have loved to have been your cherished "Little Girl" forever. But aren't you glad I provided you with another – our Deborah Paige – who would be the darling of our hearts?

The next ten days are filled with the trivia of my life: I've taken Two-Gun-Pete, that's Jerry, to the movies; my jam-packed bus had been narrowly missed by an express train because the driver stalled the bus on the tracks; mother and Darrell are fighting, and the kids are raising a ruckus. But on the 13th, I respond to one of your earlier letters:

> *December 13, 1944:* In one of your latest letters you said perhaps the reason you hadn't gotten [your transfer] was that *you were to meet and marry me* and I think that's really the reason. I don't think I'm being sacrilegious if I think that Someone took the trouble to direct our fate so that we could meet. Suppose you had left the country and I had never gone to the Claypool that night. I wouldn't be sitting here writing and you – well you might have been someone else's husband,

> sweetheart or lover. (And I couldn't stand that!) Even if it is lonesome, I'd much rather be your wife, waiting and planning for your return, than lead any kind of life I can think of. Of course, I would never have known what I missed. . . But I would have grown old without really living. . . Do you remember how you used to tease me and say you thought married life agreed with me because you could see happiness in my eyes? Well, it was happiness you saw – happiness and pride and love. And you were – and are – responsible for every bit of it. Because my idea of living is loving and being loved by you. It's because of you and for you that I want a home and family. I honestly don't believe any other man would have been able to change my mind about children as you did, so that I would actually be proud to have a child. Don't fool yourself and say that's just a woman's natural instinct because it isn't – it's you. I wish I could feel I'd given one-half as much to your life as you've given to mine. . . I'll be loving you always.

And, dear heart, as I think back over our long life together, with all its difficulties and failures and heartaches – and its successes – I know these words are still as true as they were the day I wrote them. I pray our struggles and endurance are recorded in the Book of Life and that we are judged with love and mercy.

On the 16th, 17th, 18th, I am most uneasy about you and even as I write of the coldness and the beauties of the Christmas decorations, I can't hide my concern. But I continue to write of the little things, like my little brother and his sweetness:

> Like tonight, coming home from the show, he looked up into the sky – the stars sparkled like diamonds on a black velvet dress – and he said, "You know, Helen, I'll bet Neb's looking up in the sky right now too and throwing kisses to you." [Poor, sweet little brother of mine. How sad his life was to be – and Mother was so much responsible for it.] In this letter, I also send you the words to a new song, "All of a Sudden My Heart Sings." [That song reminds me of us every time I hear it, all these years later.] And I conclude with: "It's a beautiful song even if the words were stolen right out of my heart, and every time I hear it

the longing grows that much worse. But it's a wonderful ache so I never pass up a chance to listen to it.

Yours and yours only, Helen

And on the 18th, deep in worry about you, I write hopefully:

December 18, 1944: It seems like an eternity darling since I've felt your arms around me and when I stop to think it's only been a little over two months, I wonder how the time I still must wait will pass. But no matter how unsure of other things I may be, of this I'm certain – we do love each other and in God's own time we will be together. Until that time comes, I know he'll help me to be patient and I pray he will keep you safe and happy. Until you left, I didn't realize how much I did believe in God – now I do – and I'm pretty sure it's the same with you. It's a big comfort to know there is Someone to ask to watch over you. . .

And in the days that were to come, these words remain a testimony of my faith beyond death.

And thus the dreary December days pass. The temperature is now 10 below; the wind across the bus stop howls; the skies are black but filled with glorious stars. There is no mail from you. Christmas comes and goes and I write you all the details of our Christmas Eve and Christmas morning with all the excitement and wonderful gifts – from everyone, my family, your family. And especially you. You have had your mother send me a beautiful Indian turquoise ring and bracelet. And a robe to die for. Mother has given me beautiful pajamas and in your robe and the pajamas, Darrell has said I look like a soldier's furlough dream come true. (But for you on your furlough, I'm saving the sheer black gown just like the one Paulette Goddard wore in one of her movies.) I close my first Christmas letter to you:

On this night of all nights, a night of thankfulness, I find myself more than ever thankful that we belong to each other and that God willing, we always will.

On the 26th of December, it is now 8 degrees below zero and I have been fifteen days without mail, I write:

December 26, 1944: The war news is not so good here, but it isn't leaving a depressive feeling. It's more like people have squared their shoulders, pulled up their stockings and settled down for a little harder pull at whatever they've been doing. You've no idea how useless I feel – not even having a war job – especially when for all I know you could be right in the midst of it. I tried to donate some of my beautiful red blood, but one of those know – nothing people (doctors to you) decided I needed it all myself. Well, I can always say I tried, but that's not much satisfaction.

And so the old year creeps to its close, dull, sunless, and my heart reflects that gloom. I try so hard to be cheerful, but my body is sick and my spirits low. So low that I even let you know about the chaos at home.

Sometimes for two cents I'd go back and live with Betty. Mom's too tired to do what there is to do in a house this big after she gets home from work. And I'm tired too. But Daddy just can't understand why I can't come home and clean up the dishes and put the kids to bed and do everything else. I appreciate him wanting to take it off Mother's shoulders but I'm human too! I guess we'll just never get along-he resents me . . . [and, of course, you now know why – as I did all along.] I don't know why I wrote what I just did – guess I just needed to get it off my chest, so I had to cry on your shoulder. Forgive me?

On the 28th, I write you about an article I had stumbled upon about how G. I. Joe is going to feel when he finally gets home to all the things he's been dreaming about.

December 28, 1944: It seems nothing is going to suit you guys so me and all the other soldiers' wives are going out and dig our graves, and pull the dirt in after us! After all, if you ain't going to love us what else is there to do? All kidding aside, people who write stuff like that ought to be shot. It certainly doesn't give Mrs. G.I. Joe much to look forward to.

[Had we pondered advice like this – and taken it seriously – we might have been better prepared to cope with the realities that would inevitably arise, when the thousands of military men returned, to the less than perfect lives they had been dreaming of; no wonder there would be so many post-war divorces.]

On December 31, 1944, I write:

> *December 31, 1944:* Well here it comes – the New Year in, the Old Year Out! It's kind of silly to say Happy New Year, because with things as they are, no one's really happy. But with the thought that the next New Year will see us together, I'll say it anyhow. And since this is the best way I can think of to start 1945, I'll say I love you.

We would not welcome in together New Year 1946.

2
On To the Battle Front

And as the last month of 1944 has dragged by in cold and fear and hope for me in Indianapolis, you and the 592nd Field Artillery Battalion – along with the entire 106th Infantry – have been moved to somewhere on the North Eastern coast of Britain, awaiting embarkation to the continent for the final assaults on the Axis forces. It has been almost exactly six months since D-Day, the Allied Forces deadly landing on the beaches of Normandy. And the Americans and British and Free French would seem to have an assured victory on their hands, even though the fighting is still fierce. But as I read your letters, I can feel the sense of foreboding as you move further from home.

> **1 Dec 44:** The starting of the month is not very happy for me – I am halfway across the world....At last I have seen a little more of England; the part I've seen is scarcely populated and the fields are not so pretty – signs of the war are not seen or the people must of cleared it up before I got to this country...the funny

thing about what I know is that the bath is in one room, the latrine in another and the wash basin in another. Just imagine me taking a bath in one building, running over to another to – well, I'd better not say!" [In the midst of everything, you always seem to be able to draw on your humor.]

2 Dec 44: Three to go! [to our fourth month anniversary]: Here as we sit my thoughts go back to the wonderful days I have spent with you! It seems that all I do has a direct bearing on you or rather you have a direct bearing on what I do. Dam it is mighty hard at times to keep from going berserk but I just holler out a few words of songs I know and think of you and that is what keeps up my morale.

[A few days later, your friend and mine, Ohlsen, will write me a letter, reporting on your activities – you've been a "pretty good little boy," but you've received letters from your "girlfriend, Rita," but not much. None of you have had a chance to go out – you just play cards and "Neb has been doing quite a bit of writing, so if you don't receive mail, don't blame it on him, blame it on the mail service. Neb is sitting right across the table from me playing 500 and singing at the top of his lungs. I don't know why the guy seems so happy but he's always singing." And then Ohlsen adds a cherished postscript: "Don't worry about your husband. I'll take care of him." [Ohlsen was a happy guest at our wedding just four long months ago! Did he make it home?]

On the anniversary of our wedding you write:

5 Dec 44: Yes Sir, four wonderful months have I been the luckiest guy on earth! But what a four – two perfect months of complete happiness and two that are happy but lonely. . . . How grateful I am that the army gave me the opportunity to woo and to wed you! [and so you rant on – I love it –] I am going further away from you than I ever cared to be...So once again I am on a boat going still further away. . . . The boat is quite a bit different from the one we came to England on but it is swell to have a little room to move around in. The waves are short and the roll of the ship is a lot worse than before, consequently a lot more guys are sick – Me – I haven't felt nothing yet. But it is plenty hard for me to stand and walk – Hit this side then that side! Just like a drunk trying to walk straight. . . Darling, I haven't ...received any mail from you since Nov 28. . . . Darling, I love you a great deal more as each day goes by. Never have I missed you more. . .

By December 8, you are "somewhere in Belgium," having come up through France, Luxemburg and even a small tip of Holland. [You and I would make this trip together in the early Fall of 1987.] Even as you describe the journey, your humor pops out: "Faith and I think it mean of me to be traveling over the world and leaving you behind! Much better I be behind with you!"

I want to record for our posterity, your description of the front line in what will be called the Battle of the Ardennes. Even as I write this now, there are very few who can remember that deadly time for Americans – and particularly the Infantry unit to which you were attached. They don't study the War now – too busy studying African History or the Women's Movement or The History of BeBop or whatever is the "in" thing now. But our grown grandson is intrigued with learning about those days of darkness and death-and survival. So on December 8, 1944, you write me:

8 Dec 44: . . .I thought that the country was low and level but here I am sitting way up here and in snow. Trees are all over the place and it is cold as hell is hot – The wind blows pretty hard some of the time and it goes cutting through like a saw. If my feet didn't get so damn cold I could love this spot. . . but I shall never like cold! Nor wet and baby, I've seen both so far here. . . The road up was covered in places with evidence of fighting but for the most part the people (or the army?) have cleaned the place up good. Here and there we saw wrecked German trucks and guns but not many were to be seen. A lot of houses were burned or knocked down by bombs or what have you! It was surprising how little evidence of fighting was around but I guess the Germans were on the run too fast to put up much of a fight- Me and my "little book" [dictionary?] was talking with a Belgian corporal and he told me that when the Germans came up over a hill, he shot ten of 'em! He was pretty proud of that – but he was hiding in some bushes with other civilians so how could he say who got who? I got some French bread from one old guy by using the "book" and a drink of apple wine from another. All we saw were old men – and kids – thousands of kids – every house had a dozen or so – but then again we saw lots of men that should be in the army but they just waved and made motions for a cigarette. Funny, I couldn't understand a word any of them said! [ha-ha!]

Darling – how I wish that it was you to share my tent with me instead of the old guy – Man, I'd cuddle up to you so hard and so close that it could get way colder than it is now and still we'd be warm. . . . Honey, I'm all right and will continue to be so but I could sure use a pair of rubbers or overshoes – size 10 or 10 and a half, plus more heavy wool socks – See if you can't send a pair out, eh?. . . . I must get under the blankets before I freeze. Until tomorrow or –

I love you, Your husband Neb

[You will receive overshoes from the army sometime on the 18th, just in time for the great German onslaught and the bitter battles of bombardment and death – and the murder of captured American prisoners in the snows of Belgium. I will not receive your request for them until long after that!]

3
Building Your Nest

As I read your letters from the front in Belgium, I am amazed at how you and your friends manage to hold on to sanity in the midst of uncertainty and bitter cold and Mud! Mud! Mud! You are getting entrenched for battle and you are busy building your nests. On December 10th, you write a most interesting over-view of your "work."

10 Dec 44: For the last couple days we have been busy as little bees - and twice as muddy. We are fairly comfortable, considering all that is here and around. But still work is to be done and I mean work! Somewhere in Germany [obviously, you have moved position in the two days between letters] there is a dugout and in that dugout is your little husband. It isn't bad however since it does keep us out of the weather. We have a good stove and plenty of wood to burn plus the guts necessary to work when we are wet from head to foot. Ambitious me went and rounded up some sort of a bunk and put a straw mattress of the home made variety in it. Then with my blankets I have myself a fairly nice resting place! At least it is better than pitching a tent on the wet ground that seems to be all over in this part of Europe. Darling, . . . if you and I ever have to live in a dugout, I'll know how to build a very neat one as there are plenty of examples around here. The one we have sure needs a lot of improvements – one at least and that is a door. Tomorrow I plan on building a door that we can use to keep old man winter out. Then I must build some kind of a box to put my stuff in to keep it somewhat dry – besides making various improvements on the inside. Of the ones I have seen Del has the best one – the guy that made that must have been a worker – he even put in a fireplace. It is lined with a red cloth and is big enough for just one man – there was a lot of work put into the place – wood floor and all! That is the kind of place I'm going to make if we stay in one spot long enough. . .

So far, I haven't seen any action yet and if things don't perk up a little, maybe I won't. But after we get settled more securely here I should think we will be pumping a few shells over that way. I hope they don't start pumping them over this way! So far so good! I have come to the end of a letter to the only One I love, Your Dugout Husband

On the 12th you write me words of love but,

12 Dec 44: Maybe I would like to be with you this night because I am rather tired from building cat walks, doors and other things to make life here in our "home" a little more comfortable – Honey, soon I shall have me a good bed-springs and although the mattress may be of straw, the bed will be quite the thing. Early this morning I made a reconnaissance over a hill back of us and found in an empty dugout – three springs, a big tub, a chair, a wash basin and a curved knife. So now I shall sleep well – take a bath and a shave plus use the knife for carving what animals that we may find! Little by little our dugout home is becoming a bit more livable – all we need now is to make a light of some kind – put in floors and make shelves and storage places for equipment – then come hell and high water your better half and only boyfriend will be warm and comfortable and safe. Faith and I think that I shall have all the comforts of home with the exception of my ever-loving wife. Oh my darling, how I love you this night! How I miss you as days go by. What joy will be ours when once more we are together again. . . My love for you, Your Neb

13 Dec 44: It's a nice day for the 13th. . . it hasn't snowed, rained or otherwise been miserable outside. The only thing that has bothered me is the endless sea of mud. Mud in places that must be at least ankle deep – and the dam stuff is wet too. Darling, you must come over to my house some night for our house warming. I laid one section of our floor today plus a few improvements on the door I made yesterday. The hinges I put on weren't strong enough so I had to round up larger ones. Now the door is in good shape but I think I shall put a window in it. Tomorrow I shall try to make up my bunk with the springs – then after lay the other floor sections so that should take about all day. Of course, this must take time because we still have to work on and fire our gun – now and then.

In later years, in Phoenix, when you would scrounge around to find odd-ball things to fix up something – and I would get so upset because you could have bought something new more easily – I should have remembered these letters in which you take such obvious pleasure in what is, really, great creativity. And maybe remembering this scrounger-rat-pack mentality of yours, I might have been less angry when, after, your death, in the middle of August, I had to clean out our attic and discovered old tires, worn out tools, pieces of roofing, and anything else you could find through the years. I have always said that you are the kind of man I would want to be shipwrecked with on a desert island! For more reasons than scrounging, my love. It is also in this letter of the 13th that trouble with authority rears its head:

> My good Sergeant is getting excited and he wants things done – everything at once – When he gets excited he ain't worth a dam – he wants to do my job and everyone else's all at the same time. Consequently he messes my ammunition all up and I have to do the stuff all over again so I can keep it straight – so I better get over there so I can keep track of what I got now! Soon I hope to have mail from you. My love, Your Neb

The work continues on the gun emplacement and upon your house. You are worried about your gun emplacement:

> **14 Dec 44:** I believe that after arguing for three days I am finally going to win my point in digging this place a little deeper and arranging it better. . . today some planes were reported coming our way but they never showed up over us. Then a German was herding sheep near our position so we rounded him up. While he was here a couple guys went over and killed two lambs – so we will have some mutton now. I don't particularly like that as the poor guy was an old man – about 70 years old. So he is the enemy but that is no reason to take his poor lambs. We got more to eat than he and I rather feel sorry for him. He was scared to death. This really has been a day of good news. Today our mail caught up with us but there is so much that it'll be a couple of days before they get it all assorted. Oh happy day – letters from you at last!!

Two days pass and you have not written. On the 15th you write "It is a "cold day" – [and already I am waiting for the steam to blow. I have been sensing the undertones in your letters recently.]:

> **15 Dec 44:** Honey, there was so much mail they didn't get it all sorted today but tomorrow morning we will get it, I hope – I had a blow up with my Sergeant this morning about the improvements on our shack. He wants to spend more time on

> our gun and let the house go. The gun is in the best shape of any but we still live in a pigpen type of hut – so I blew my top and he blew his – I got plenty mad but finally we got it all sorted out and are happy again! While I was in the States I took a lot of stuff and never said a word but now that I'm over here in combat, I'm looking out for myself first then others come. If I can make my life here as comfortable and safe as possible – I won't take stuff from anyone. I may get busted but I don't give a dam – This is supposed to be an individual war as well as teamwork – I got the team work to my satisfaction and now individuality comes in. I say to hell with doing anything just to please some guy with more rank than I have. I'll do my job and to hell with the rest of the stuff—!
>
> Some days are happy when everything goes well but others are bad like today – I just cut my finger and got some good blood on the papers so I am sending just a little more than my love tonight – I bleed for you [a drop of blood on the letter] Nice thought on this day of all days – BLOOD, BLOOD! Gad, I faint at the thought – oh horrible thought!

And you close with:

> Darling, my love grows for you like the new planted hay, like the sunflower in the summer sun – like a flood I can say I love you.

And in all of this, I am reminded of your volatile temper, your rejection of authority, your often present, but suppressed fear. And above all, of your wonderful blarney!

4
Battle of the Bulge: Baptism By Fire

The following is an excerpt from a broadcast by Cedric Foster, News Analyst, *January 21, 1945*: It is a recap of the situation which will be the subject of your January and later letters.

Tonight for the first time, there may be told the story which . . . is one of the most glorious episodes in the history of American arms . . . the story of America's 106th Infantry Division.

. . . It fought gloriously and it fought heroically in the full flush of German power on the 16th of last December. Two of its regiments were all but eliminated from the war. Three hundred men out of those two regiments were all who survived. Most of the others are presumed to be prisoners of war. . . On the 11th of December the 106th Division was in a sector of the front designated as quiet. Five days later on the 16th these men of the Golden Lion Division were struck by an avalanche of German steel and fire. The attack got under way just before six o'clock in the morning. In the battle that followed, the division suffered eight thousand, six hundred sixty-three casualties. 416 were killed, 1246 were wounded, 7,000 were missing.

Censorship can now reveal that the 106th was spread in a manner described as "pitifully thin," along a front of twenty-seven miles. . . along a sector just north east of the frontier of Luxembourg, Belgium, and Germany, ...in the general sector of the Belgian town of Saint Vith . . . twelve miles southeast of Malmedy. . . A field artillery battalion, attached to the 106th, was the next target. In thirty-five minutes more than one hundred rounds of

German fire had landed squarely in the midst of this battalion. At six o'clock, the Germans opened up on Saint Vith itself. The barrage was over at two o'clock in the afternoon [when the pre-warned civilians came out of their hiding places.] . . . It was not until 21st of December that the 106th went out of the line to reorganize. . .and on the 24th were hurled into the line on the northern side of the German force.

Darling, *your* version of the above described overwhelming attack of the Germans begins in your December 16th letter, a first-hand survivor's on-the-spot report:

> **16 Dec 44:** My Darling Wife, Today we received more or less of our baptism by fire, so much of the day was spent loafing underground. It was something that I have been expecting but so far haven't experienced until today. As long as a man stays close to the ground he is safe enough and, honey, I was not only close to the ground but I was under it! I finally saw some of those well known buzz bombs that every one is talking about. They went over and I mean they went! Fast but not too fast so I call them cement mixers – that is what they sound like anyway! Now when I come home I can say I have been in combat!

[In fact, your outfit was awarded 5 battle stars, although somehow, you failed to receive the last one before you were discharged.] Interestingly enough, in the midst of all this, you and the men are exultant about having received mail! You write:

> It was better tonic for all of us to get mail from home than even what a case of whiskey would have been! I can see now why they say back in the States "Write to the Boys." That really means something to me now. It is so important to everyone because everyone was happy today! Even me!

And then you warm me with your love before ending: "Sweet, it is my turn on guard so I'll take my thoughts of you outside with me cause I love you." It will be five days later, when you will write again:

> **21 Dec 44: 4 Days to Shop:** Things have really been happening since I last wrote – in fact, I haven't had time to mail the last letter. The house warming I have been planning on is very definitely postponed. We moved from the place and are now in

another one. I had just made my bedsteads for the springs I had told you about. . .but then we up and moved. But now I have a roof over my head and straw to sleep in so I don't say I regret the move so much. . .The only thing that keeps me happy is that your letters are catching up to me ....Honey, I could write pages about what has happened since I left America but it wouldn't do any good. So I'll just say that now I have seen combat instead of just training films. I am okay and plan to stay that way – I write you as every opportunity arises – that should be every day – ! Should be but here lately I lose track of time – days and weeks – Right now I am about freezing to death – but I shall think of you and get warm cause I have your love to keep me warm.

25 Dec 44: Christmas Day!: Here it is the day that I so wanted to spend with you! But No! I have to be here somewhere in Belgium in an open field going about the business of doing my job in the war. [And then you send me wishes for the day.] I understand that we are to have fresh turkey and all the trimmings this afternoon for our Christmas dinner. [When you got home, that was one of the experiences you told me about – sitting on a block of ice, you thought, eating your Christmas dinner, only to discover it was the body of a frozen German soldier!] This morning I got all the pancakes I could possibly hold – 10 all together. The Captain is really taking good care of us, both in being warm and having enough to eat. There are times we can't have a hot meal because we are on the move – but on the whole I am not hungry. If we lose or wear out our gloves etc then it isn't long until we have another pair issued to us. The only thing that is hard for me is keeping clean. For the reason we haven't had much time and then water is hard to get and heat. I shaved yesterday for the first time in weeks and pulled a mustache off that was a good fifteen days old [you later told me that you hadn't changed underwear in that time because the dirt kept you warm.] Am I glad you didn't see me with that – I took one look in a mirror and almost passed out – gad, hair one-half inch long going every which way and was I a sight with about 3 days dirt mixed up with that blonde hair – actually I haven't had a whole bath for three weeks and neither has anyone else – Boy do I smell!

Darling, my experiences in combat this far has [sic] been quite peaceful but a couple of times things were hot around us. So far I haven't anything to worry about and many times I think that we are on some kind of maneuvers some place - only in a serious manner. I have a couple of aching hands from handling shells but that is all that I can complain about. Incidentally, my sweet, I am getting along fairly well with my French - The other day I bought a little stove for two packs of cigarettes and I talked French to the old boy – with the help of my little book. Some nights we are lucky enough to be placed by a house or a barn and can sleep inside at least. Our last position was like that and I slept in a hayloft. That was really a break. The next morning there was about five inches of snow all over the place, and cold, man it does get cold where we are, in fact I think that it is cold all over now everywhere. . . I hear the Germans are supposed to have captured some of our, my – our mail. I don't believe that but it could be possible you know. So don't worry if you don't hear from me for days at a stretch - I'll be all right but mail delay can't be helped now!

Even though it is Christmas, I have work to do so I must leave you now but I shall have you in my thoughts and my love will grow as it always has but until that day soon, I say again and again, I love you dearly. Neb (Baby, its COLD!)

On the 26th, you are overjoyed because you "have received two most wonderful letters from me," the 14th-15th Dec ones:

26 Dec 44: That's just ten days ago, my darling. Almost the same as talking to you from the next room compared to what I have been getting. Baby, I got a lot of mail coming some time and I might add I'm getting damned impatient waiting for it to be delivered...You said you told me of receiving 10 letters from me (which made me happy) but so far I haven't received that one letter nor have I received any of the air mail stamps you sent nor any packages. Honey, my hands are so cold I can hardly hold the pen – and it is 3 o'clock in the afternoon – besides sitting by my stove - It is a wonder my hands aren't frozen stiff the way the weather is going. . . One of these days it is going to be actually warm – then I'll take a bath! [Then a lot of chit - chat about home.]

The gang seems to be happy and a bit tired from doing partially nothing – I guess – but we all did enjoy the colonel's Christmas present to us – He gave each section a fifth of good American White Horse Scotch – I had 4 jiggers of it and every one was a toast to the sweetest, wonderfulest wife a man ever had – Boy – it was good on this cold night. Darling, I have to improve my sleeping (?) quarters, just in case I get a chance to sleep a little some time – It is then that I dream so much of you but all during the night and day, I continually think of you and how much I love you. Neb

This is the last letter of the year which you will write and one which I will receive only many days in the future. After much heartbreak.

Part IV

If Winter Comes

1
Back Home Again In Indiana

But back home in Indiana, far from the battle's fury, I have received no letters from you in a month. Where you are, I do not know. If you're in danger, I can only guess. So in the letters of the last days of the year, I have poured out my heart to you in memory and longing.

On the 30th of December, I have written:

> *December 30, 1944:*. . . do you realize I'll soon have a birthday? Bet you can't remember the date! And do you also realize that very soon you'll be entering your sixth month of lifelong bondage – that we'll actually have been married five whole months?. . . It doesn't seem that long because we've really had so little time together. But those two months were wonderful. We had a much better marriage situation than a lot of couples even if it was short. At least I got to be with you in a place almost our own. I got to cook for you once in awhile, we had company come see us, we had companionship and love and enough minor misunderstandings to know the fun it is to make up and to know how we'd have to adjust ourselves so we wouldn't be hurting each other all the time. In two months with you I learned more about some things than I ever learned before in my whole life – the happiness of having someone who really counts, someone you love and live for. I know how wonderful it is to have someone to depend and count on – to know you love me. I learned not to be so afraid of some things, like growing old, and dying, and having a family. I learned to love with all my heart and soul and body as I never dreamed

possible. In fact, you've made me so happy that it would take a life-time of unhappiness to counterbalance my happiness.

After reading what I just wrote, I wonder if I ought to send it or not – it's been so very long since I've heard from you that by this time you may have decided your bachelor days had it all over wedded bliss and forgotten about me. Some things I write may sound awfully mushy to you but I can't help it – it's just my longing for you that can't help creeping out on paper. It all comes from my heart – besides before we were married, you used to want me to write you mushy letters.

2
My Valley of Despair

The first bitterly cold days of January break and I write you of the freezing cold, the failure of the buses to run, the bitterness of the days' monotony. And then, somehow the rumor breaks through the foreign censorship and in major headlines, in Extra Editions, coming home from work, on the evening of the 3rd of January, 1945, I read:

106th's STORY IN FULL!
DISASTER of FIRE and STEEL CAME IN FOGGY DAWN

The shock of the few details that infiltrated from foreign sources can never express the agony that was borne by all the people of Indianapolis. This was THEIR unit; these were THEIR men. And you were MY husband. And it would be another three weeks before there would be other than sporadic and erroneous news from the front. And it would not be until late January and early February that full accounts would emerge and I would know that you had survived all odds. My shock and agony is there as I write to you that night:

January 3, 1945: My dearest husband – This has been a day of such misery as I have never known, but now that the first shock has cleared, I refuse to believe what I read in this evening's newspaper. I know, I absolutely am positive, that you must be alive. I'm enclosing the front page article that was the first thing I saw . . . I need never fear death again because for a few minutes I was dead, mentally and physically. My heart stopped beating and there was no breath in me. Then the tears came and I could breathe again. After I could control myself a little, I could force myself to see that there was a chance it was just German propaganda, that you hadn't even been with the Division, anything. I knew you had to be safe and I'm positive of it now. Until the government informs me otherwise, I won't believe anything else.

Why darling, if anything happened to you, you couldn't keep our second honeymoon date with me – and you're not the kind of guy who'd stand a girl up! Besides that, honey, we've got a lot of unfinished business – swimming on Sundays, dancing on summer nights to soft, sweet music, breakfast to eat together. You've got to see my pretty new hat and my robe – and most important of all, we've got to provide an heir to the Nebeker name – you can't leave me without that. Oh sweetheart you must come back to me - without you I don't want to live either. Life without you would be meaningless, unendurable. When this little gal loves, she loves completely and wholeheartedly - too much so, I guess. But I won't even let myself think of your not coming back. I know you love me most when I'm happy and smiling, so dear one, I'll keep happy and smiling. And writing you and loving you.

I pray always for your safekeeping and return. God willing, you'll return and until then I only ask for strength of heart. Sweetheart, you know that as long as life endures, as long as there's a hereafter, my heart is yours. Helen

Reading these words so long after the fact, you might believe that they are theatrical, excessive – or maybe when you got them at the front they seemed so. But I can tell you truly that in my re-reading of this letter, I still remember the desolation of my heart. Only once again would I feel such agony of spirit. And it would not be when our son died. . .

On the 4th of January – the next day – I will write you [and I will recall this letter in full for you because it summarizes not only my despair, courage, commitment, call it what you like, but the experiences of so many women left behind during those long years of war]:

> Today has naturally been full of pent up emotions and a sense of dread, wondering if there will be news of you or from you when the mailman comes. But I feel more alive today and have confidence in God and our future. I'm not a very brave person but I've decided that I'll try to take whatever comes as I know you'd want me to. I know that whatever you're going through, you're taking it bravely and with faith and hope. I'd be a very poor wife for you if I couldn't carry on as ably. I'm going to pretend that you're no further away than a camp somewhere in England – I'll keep writing you and making plans for a future that you will share with me. A home, a family and each other for always – no war, no fear – just the privilege of making you happy. If God gives us this chance, if He brings you home to me, a lifetime won't be long enough to show my love for you and my gratitude. I don't care what troubles we have to hurdle together – I can take anything as long as you're with me. I don't say I won't make plenty of mistakes, but no one will try harder to be a good wife and mother.
>
> Right now darling, I need a Neb Jr. desperately – I need a blonde baby with your laughing eyes and monkey face. I need your son's arms around me – your son to keep me smiling when I feel like crying, your son to believe with me that you will come back. Sweetheart, once you're home again, I won't take a chance on this again. The sooner I find out I'm to have a child, the happier I'll be. So don't stay away too long because I need your help for that. Never think for a moment that I'll lose hope, or forget you, or stop loving you. You have to fight, I have to wait, and between us we'll do a good job. God bless you, my dear and keep you safe. You're my life and you must come back.
> Helen

And on our 5th month wedding anniversary, I write:

> *January 5, 1945:*. . .If you don't come back, I don't want to live either. I'd rather take my chance on meeting you in the place

> you call Paradise. We were married for now and eternity and until you change your mind that's the way it is with me. I'm going to sleep now to dream of us together. Before I sleep, however, I'll add one more prayer to all the others I've already said. I really don't have to pray because every breath I draw is a prayer. My love is with you through everything and anything and I hope you know it – can feel it. God bless you my darling, and bring you home to those who love you. Your adoring wife.

News is now beginning to trickle in from the front. I write:

> Still no news from you – but I'm positive it will take more than a damned old German to handle you. There's one thing I can't understand though, darling, and that's why other girls have had letters from your outfit as late as December 10th [that is before the German "putsch"] while my last letter was dated November 26th [42 newsless days!] Their letters were written from France and it does seem as though I should have heard too. . . Isn't it strange how fate works – it took the war to bring us together and that same war is now separating us – "strange are the uses of adversity."

As I have contemplated the above letters – and many others which you and I will write, I am struck by so much truth contained in our words – and I ponder, remembering how we will be tested by God – call it "Fate," if you like – in the course of our lives together. I comprehend so much more clearly the relevance of all things under God's hand. I can see, Neb, how the very meeting of you prepared me for the Gospel; I simply would have no choice in the matter. I was, in essence, a Latter Day Saint almost from our first evening together. Because, at your core, you were one, too. I could not write you in words other than I did – they were the "essence" of me, as were your words to me. I wrote words that I meant from my soul's depths and yet I would have to learn – and repent – of my inability to accept what was necessary and God's will in this learning process we call life. And you will have much to recall and repent of too, as the process of life HAPPENS! But this is all in the future. We have far to go in our journey of life. [And you have already gone further than that.]

3
A Brave New Year

Thus January begins to turn into that "brave new year." Letters, though not current, start to arrive. And the plod of days goes on: "It's funny," I write:

> . . .the way life goes on in the same old routine day after day when someone you love is suffering so much danger and hardship. My heart never stops aching for you and yet I still eat and drink and sleep as though you'd be coming home this very night. It's terribly hard to see God's plan in days like these and yet I know there must be one. I used to think it was being born and living and giving happiness and love. Now I wonder. And yet in just the last few days I've learned how much faith you can put in an infinite Being – how a person can go ahead just because of the knowledge that there is someone who cares what happens. I never feel that I have a right to ask anything for myself. But I can't help thinking that you deserve his protection and guidance. You may be a "rowdy Mormon" as you call yourself, but just the same, you have faith. . . and that gives me extra courage. Maybe it sounds funny to hear me talk about needing extra courage when I'm safe. But believe me, darling, to keep faith and to not know what is happening is harder than any physical pain I'll ever have to bear [and I have learned the hard truth of that in the last sixty one years]. I've had a taste of actual pain but I'd rather be in pure agony than to have you go through so much.

[How many years did I feel that through your long illness? And how I feel it today as our beautiful daughter suffers so much intolerable pain.]

MAIL TODAY! *January 8, 1945* [it's over a month old, but it's mail. And your words of love cheer me as nothing else can.]

I begin my letter of the 11th by telling you I haven't written for two days:

> *January 11, 1945:*. . . hated it but the last two days I've been flat on my back, so sick I couldn't even sit. Today, however, feel almost half alive. I didn't care much whether I lived or died but I took some kind of sulpha tablets and today I'm better. . . Those two days I was in bed, you've no idea how your four latest letters helped me. I couldn't sit up to read them but I knew every word that was in them and they were always under my pillow. You're a wonderful letter writer. You make me laugh, you make me cry; you write so I can feel your love as warm as your arms around me. . . And with every one of your letters, my love for you grows. Your letters, your picture with the smile I remember so well, are my most precious possessions, besides my memories. Besides you're so-o-o good looking and so crazy and you've read so many books too! That I should be so lucky as to be your wife!

I tell you that NEWS FROM THE FRONT lauds the heroism of all the units of the 106th. And that it had been commended for gallantry in stemming the German breakthrough on the German front. It is now in Belgium and has been since Christmas.

A Chaplain from the unit says that "for ten days they [you] went through hell and gave them everything they had."

[During this time, I have been really very ill – and in retrospect, I think I may have had the beginnings of tuberculosis. I took this illness with me to Arizona and it was well into the summer when I truly recovered. Calcified scars have been discovered on my lungs indicating that possibility of an arrested TB. That Arizona sun had to be good for something. But when you consider the terrible winter we had had in Indiana, with practically no coal for heating, and the terrible work burden – plus home responsibilities which I had borne, along with my great emotional suffering, it's a mark of my "survivor" quality that I even made it. God still had plans for me.]

106th With 8,000 Casualties Is Credited With Stopping Germans In Bulge Drive

Some of the troops of the 106th Infantry Division are shown as they marched on North Pennsylvania street in Indianapolis last Fourth of July when they were reviewed by Lieut. Gen. Brehon Somervell, commanding general of the Army Service Forces, shortly before going overseas.

By JACK REED

INDIANAPOLIS STAR BUREAU,
1297 National Press Building.

Washington, Jan. 18.—From the shell-swept, icy mud of northern France, where it crouched beaten to its knees by the might of Rundstedt's mechanized charge, the battle-broken but unbeaten 106th United States Infantry Division has risen anew to spearhead the Yankee armies at Malmedy.

The division, which bore the brunt of German attacks in the battle of the bulge and lost more than 50 per cent of its strength in the white-hot charge of the German panzers at St. Vith, has been reorganized, and with France, taking almost one-fifth of the total casualties of the battle of the bulge.

Missing List Comprises Bulk of Casualties

Its losses were 416 dead, 1,246 wounded and 7,001 missing.

Its boys, many of Indiana, many from Illinois, others from Pennsylvania, New York, Michigan and South Carolina, were familiar figures in Indianapolis for seven months last year when the division was in training at Atterbury. It left behind it, when it embarked for France last October, friends, sweethearts and relatives in Indiana who have been torn with the agonies of grief and fear for three weeks. German propaganda broad-

A HAPPY DAY! December letters, 5th, 8th, 26th. I reply:

January 15, 1945: Dear One, tonight I shall sleep with a happy heart and all because of some words written on some paper. It's like a shot in the arm hearing from you. I hate to think of me in my nice warm bed while you sleep in a cold pup tent – if you get to sleep at all. I'd much rather think of us both in a nice warm bed. But perhaps it won't be too long now. Forever yours, "Me"

And on the 16th, I become 18! (21 to you.) I write:

> I miss you as much as ever, but that awful fear is gone and my heart, she is beating right up to par again. Your loving wife

And now, the days are really good. All the details of the 106th are made clear and all parts of the unit are praised as valiant, enduring – though green – troops, who have helped to stem the German forces. Now, we are told, the tide is turning. I write you of how I have tried vainly to find you boots or overshoes at the army stores but they have actually laughed in my face; everything is going to the German front. I do manage to find wool socks and a wool sweater but they will probably be too big. Evidently all the materials are going to long, skinny, warm blooded Arizonans. I have received the letters about your dugout and I am so proud of you: " . . . I'll remember what a handy man you are and when you get home and we have our own place, you can fix doors and wash windows and paper walls to your heart's content." [And in our years to come, those are things we really enjoyed doing together. Our home was our castle.] In one of your letters, you tell me that Neb Jr. the II sends his love and I reply:

> Do you actually mean to tell me you took him all the way to Belgium? If you didn't lose him in the break-through and can get him back here, we'll really have a family heirloom. You know, it's not every four-month old son who can take a trip like that with his dad. What I can't understand is why you left me – his only mother – to break my heart over both of you. It'll be a long time before you'll have another son to take trips with you!!!!

January 22nd Another Happy Day! Four letters from you (Dec 1, 12, 13, 14) before the great battle, telling me about your nest building and I comment on that. But I am very concerned about the racking cough that you have been complaining about through several letters. I comment: "Darling, take care of that awful cold of yours [you call it the Nebeker Cough] as well as you can under the circumstances – I'm worried about it. I know how that cough tears you apart and I don't want it to get too big a start on you."

And it is in this wonderful letter – undated exactly – that you write these words that I am treasuring now so long after your death:

> New or old the love I have for you is as lasting as the sun, as beautiful as the moon and as steady as day and night. New, I say, since each brightening day brings more and more to add to the great store I have - old, I say, since I feel that *through all the eternities before this life I have loved you* and *will always love you* but for now I miss you so, Your Neb.

How can I ever doubt that we were meant for each other? Or ever doubt again your love?

4
Cheer From the Battle Front

In your letter of the first day of 1945, you tell me that you've dashed down to the mess truck and:

> **1 Jan 45:** . . . wrapped my belt around some real good turkey! Just to show you what a good meal we can have on the front lines – I say can have since most of the time we have B ration and C ration, so we really consider A rations a number one treat. . . I haven't got any mail for the last couple of days – I figure that I should have 27 coming from you! At least that is what the pages of that famous book "Letters by Helen" say. . . . Honey, Jr. hasn't said a word to me for a few days – maybe his head is "busted in" cause I haven't seen him running around lately. I have heard he is hiding in my duffle bag and that was where he was the last I saw him – but I'm sure he is safe and that he wishes the same as I that he could be back with his mother. Naturally, where he goes so goes I – then that would be simply swell – eh? Thanks for the kisses; here's some for you; Give me what I misses, Before I turn blue! Neb

> **2 Jan 45:** I got a hold of a pretty small steel box today that will fit right in my duffle bag – and that's where I am going to put Junior and all the souvenirs I have. No matter how rough it is handled, the contents will be safe from any breakage. It is also waterproof so I can keep some socks and clothes dry or at least keep them from freezing due to the moisture and frost in the air. Many of the containers we receive our supplies in can be made into various articles of use that would even surprise a cabinet maker. For instance, powder boxes can be made into tables, chairs, and firewood. . . Then there are a dozen or so different things that can be made from other containers. So I guess little Jr. will have a safe bed. He's my boy and I can't be the only monkey face kid besides myself in the great family of ours. Can I?

[I still remember the first piece of furniture you made for me in late '46 – a bedside table to put baby equipment on so I could take care of "Nebbie" without having to get out of bed. It was a monstrosity!]

And then you ask me about finances and whether I need the little spending money you have kept for yourself. I can tell you honestly, in my return letter, that I'm doing okay. Sadly, though, I have to admit that the savings plan is not doing as well as I had hoped. Christmas has taken its toll in gifts for the family; I have had doctor bills for my illness; and I lost days from work so the paycheck is lower. [I will not tell you, however, that I have taken a part-time job in the evening. The Loan company business has fallen off since the holidays and I no longer have overtime pay.] However, I tell you, I still hope to be able to go to Arizona – at least for a visit with your family as soon as I can. You write me two letters on the 2nd, because you have received four letters and the wallet I sent before Christmas, with the pictures. But you have not received the air-mail stamps. [You idiot! I sent enough stamps to last 'til the end of the war! Did it never occur to you that they were being stolen? I actually thought if I read "stamps" again, I'd scream! And you keep demanding more snapshots! In those days, with only our box cameras with no flash bulbs, etc. and in the Indiana winter where you seldom see sunlight, how in heck did you think I was going to snap pictures? It is a good thing for you that I was as patient as I was, sending you and your friends "cartoons" and perfuming my letters so you and the boys could have a bit of the feminine!]

Your letters through the 4th and 6th of January – 27 closely written pages of news – demand careful attention. Not only because of the interest but because they give a good picture of the average Joe's life during the great push toward the Rhine that now begins. Time is running out if the Allies are to beat the Russians into the heart of Berlin. And for you and your men that has meant 24 hour days, little food (Send me some chow! you write in one letter.) So I shall try to choose the most significant sections to preserve for posterity. But I want to also preserve the sense of our ongoing conversation – the dialogue of our hearts, as it were.

> **3 Jan 45:** Now the bestest and sweetest thing I ever received in my life was the wallet with the pictures – your family, my family, and most especially you! Boy-oh baby, what a treat. . . keep them coming. I still have your larger pictures and they are safe with Junior! The letters themselves were plenty but the wallet made today perfect.

[Only from reading letters such as this – written day after day by a lonely G.I., can today's generation really know what home and letters mean to their servicemen. And the same is true for those who wait for letters at home. As I would not have sent you V-mail – as it was called – so, today I would not substitute E mail for letters that demand one's commitment in time and thought and language – and can be kept for the future.]

> **4 Jan 45:** Darling, Mother's letter today was full of how very much she wants you to come out to visit, if not stay with them. . . Now you know how very much I want you to go out, at least for a short stay, but that is all up to you. The girls, as well as mother's letters are practically full of when you are going out – they'd love to have you and I'm certain you'd be happy with them. Mother must be writing quite a bit about our church to you. She does have that constantly on her mind. In fact, the church is her life outside of her family.

[Dear Mother Nebeker. How I was to love her – and be the torment of her soul, I'm afraid.]

> If you don't mind the letters – good – but if you feel you'd rather not – let me know and I'll have her take it easy on that subject. On the other hand, if there is any thing that you'd like to know about our church, I'll try to explain it to you. Quite naturally, I have a strong faith in God and the church – I continually pray for your happiness and safety. I am extremely happy that you have a faith in God and his powers. He certainly has blessed me beyond my worth and the greatest blessing was that you and I met, courted and became man and wife in His sight. As I told you many times before that the differences of our religions makes not the slightest effect on my love for you. I do hope that sometime I can take you through the Temple grounds in Salt Lake City, during the springtime. . . the lawns, the flowers, the pictures of different things and the beautiful organ music that can be heard, during the noon hour. . .

[We would have that opportunity many years later, when Quill was living in Sandy, and I still have the beautiful quilt that you bought me that day as a remembrance. I hope that our children and grandchildren may read your words some day and despite some memories they may have to the contrary, realize what a deep spiritual nature you had. But the strange contradiction of how "your" religion would come between us – or maybe "my" religion cause a rift – is one of the great ironies of my life. And ultimately, only God can make it clear.]

In this same letter, explaining your failure to write the previous day, you pen:

> . . . although it was a very easy day, I'll just say I was a very tired, haggard old man. Much worse than any of those nights that you saw me hit the sack back home, so I just slept through much of the day and even when I woke up I was sick as a dog – what with my aching back, cold, and the damn cough. Maybe I was so tired because I had only two hours sleep in 48 hours. I don't mind staying awake all night but when daylight comes, some officer usually finds some silly thing for us to do. I wouldn't be surprised to see at least half of the outfit keel over one of these days. Here it is 12:45 A.M. and I am going to bed

again so blamed tired I don't seem to care if school keeps or not. Rest assured, my own very sweet wife, that regardless of how I feel about other things, the strong love I have for you grows each day. . . Your loving Neb

Now to write in the face of all that, dear heart, is truly love!!!!

On the 6th of January, (three days after I will receive the awful news of your unit's destruction), you receive the letter I wrote on Christmas day. How glad I am that I had taken careful pains to create a vivid Christmas memory for you, even though you could not be there. [It was a special Christmas, I remember, because Darrell had been working and he and Mother had splurged on everyone. I could not remember them ever having a Christmas day like that, but I did not make that observation to you.] I read in this letter:

6 Jan 45: It is almost time for me to go off shift and thus to bed for the short space of a few hours – those remaining until daylight – but I just wanted to say how very much your happiness means to me – you quite naturally know that your being happy makes me happy. . . I still want you to be happy above all else.

And because I do know that, I try to keep my troubles from you and to insulate you from my ever increasing despair. In the 7th January letter, you are, again, bemoaning the mail failure – no mail in five days! (I think this is about the time I had gone some 40 days of not hearing from you.) But you have your "building" project to keep you happy:

7 Jan 45: Honey, once more my dug out house is starting to take shape! Tomorrow ought to see it almost completed - at least good enough to pull shift in – as it is my shift tomorrow night! So far I haven't seen one in the battery that will compare with it.

[How much this reminds me of newly weds competing with each other in their new homes.]

> Double bunks and plenty of living quarters – so if we are here for a hell of a long time, we shall be comfortable at least – that is if it don't leak!! Speaking of leaks reminds me of all the mud at this time! . . . it has started to rain and seems like every night now it rains, rains, and pours more rain. Consequently, all the snow is about gone and now we have mud clear up to our a. . . ! My clothes that I washed during rest are now covered with mud – my shoes stiff with mud – in fact, I am just plain mud. And I guess, my darling, that I shall be mud if I don't tell you what is foremost on my mind – that is my great love for you – how much I miss you – how much I long for you – In fact – just YOU!

MY, MY! Nebeker, darling, Can you write love letters!!!!!!!!!!

> **11 Jan 45:** (You're still writing 1944!) **A Rest!!:** Here I sit once again with darkness all around but just a little more relaxed than for several days. Partially because I just messed around all day and then again because I took one of my famous helmet baths! Can't you just see me standing in a tent with my steel helmet on a wet board floor trying to get in a bath, shower, rinse or what ever you may call it. Anyway, here I am again clean, shaved and ready for any chow that may come my way! [You seem to live in a world of exclamations!] Davis . . . is cooking a few steaks out of a beef that we killed today – I don't think that it will be so bad even if we haven't any salt or pepper! A snack here and there between meals is just the thing, especially at 2 A.M. . . The good old man Ohlsen done brung me two letters from you today – the 20 & 27 Dec – and I must say that they were as different as an elephant and a mouse! One was gay and the other was sorta blue and sounded rather like I felt yesterday. I am glad, darling, that your moods show so in your letters – Naturally I want you to be happy but I know that you know I want you to be happy, but I know that you know I want you to blow your top now and then too! Just like me! Don't hurt none, babe, don't hurt none!

Now, my dear, I'm going to reply to this letter in ways I haven't done before. You had no idea, at all, of how very miserable my life was after I left my apartment. [And I want you to remember what I say here in days that will come in almost a year to the month and even the day.] I never for one instant regretted marrying you and being absolutely faithful to you during the four months that you had been gone – nor in the 12 more that were to come. BUT MY LIFE WAS MISERABLE! The letter I wrote you on the 20th – and the 25th and many other dates – was mere camouflage – words to keep you happy. But, in my letter on the 27th, I simply did not have the energy to sufficiently hide my despair. I was lonely; I was over-worked; I was living in someone else's home, a home I hated. And Darrell was getting nastier with every day. And I now had no friends to cheer me up (boyfriends, if you like!) And what could I do? I did not want to burden you; there was nothing you could do! But I was as much a victim of this war as were you. I, too, was hanging on to the precious belief that we would be reunited and that all would be beautiful. So, as you see, beloved husband, even at this late date, as you say, blowing one's top "don't hurt none, babe, don't hurt none!"

Your letter of January 9, 1945 informs me that you have taken your own advice and blown your top, again:

> **9 Jan 45:** So now, you have a buck private for a husband [why didn't you go to Officer's Training as the Army wanted you to?] After 19 months as a corporal, I finally decided that the two lone stripes should come off in one way or another. Yep – I was busted high as a kite! But they still want me to do the same job for private's pay! Kinda nice, don't you think? It seems that a colonel gave our 1st sergeant orders to move our prime mover off the road as soon as possible. Me and the rest of the boys were getting our equipment off and were fixing a place for the ammo when our most gracious, great 1st Sgt came busting down and blew off – when he wanted the Cat moved away so the boys would have to carry the ammo back, then I blew off! So he runs to the Captain and the Captain says I'm a private but please to do the same job! Quite naturally, I'll do any job to get back to you quicker – be it private or general – but I'd just love to see some of these nuts carry a 98 pound shell over rough ground covered with snow for God knows how far – then let them blow off about steering a Cat from a position before it was unloaded! Especially a guy like our 1st Sgt. All he does is sit around in a warm house and have his dinner brought to him on

a plate while the rest of the boys eat freezing their fingers and drinking cold coffee. Man! What an outfit – But I guess I have blown enough now so I just want you to write and tell me you get this letter as he stated he'd be holding my mail back and if he does that there'll be hell to pay – if I have to talk to a general! You know how hot I can get when I get sore and baby, I'm sore – Hell, I was wrong for popping off but my good 1st Sgt would have seen what we were doing and just asked us to hurry it up, instead of thinking he could hollar around and have us jumping like a bunch of slaves. Not a guy in the battery – and I know them all – gives a hoot in hell for him and one of these good days someone is going to knock his teeth down his throat. Oh that will be the Happy Day for us all!!! Then all we'll need is for the officers to let us run our guns as we, who have been doing the hard work, know how to run them under most conditions. That will be the day when this outfit begins to do its share of winning the war faster, without breaking down a man's vitality!

So, darling, that is enough of "Neb's Gripe Session" and now I'll turn to much pleasanter subjects – namely You! Without the constant, sweet thought of you, I believe that the physical hardship of working all day and most of the night would have gotten me as it has a great many of the boys. Some of them are just about fagged out and they were in good shape too!. . . Do you mind if I just tell you of a love so great that it fills the universe – of a longing so painful that only you are a cure for – I love you so. Always Neb

And that's a day on the front with a once-non-com officer. Are better days coming, for both of us?

My letters of 29th, 30th, 31st, received. You are now missing 23 letters that you figure I have written and you can't understand why I am not receiving mail – you have written every day that you possibly could. I have been foolish and mentioned that mother and Darrell had wanted me to go out with a young male friend of theirs on New Year's Eve. I completely forgot your jealousy. But you are indeed angry and let me know it. (Hey, I didn't go! I baby-sat until 5 A.M. when they both rolled in, fighting as usual!) Again, you blow off:

11 Jan 45: and if they want this son-in-law as a friend they had better lay off that stuff! [I am laughing, even as I read of your anger.] I have never worried about this phase of our married life since the "Letter Incident" [that was my writing Jack about our getting married – are you never going to forget that? Oh, you haven't read my explanation yet?] nor do I worry about it now but I am inclined to be a little sore for having any one, your folks, my folks, your friends or mine, suggesting such a thing either to you or to me! While I was in England that short time, a lot of guys suggested to me, "Let's pick up some of this English stuff" but I was plenty satisfied just sipping beer in a pub with the boys. [And at least you have "the boys!" and can go to a pub!]

In this letter you suggest that I might want to get another apartment and find someone to share it. My goodness, dear, didn't you have any idea of the impossibility of that – to have an apartment was a dream! You didn't realize how lucky you were to have found a girl with an APARTMENT. And I only had mine by a stroke of pure luck! You'll learn about that process when you get home, next year. [I have often wondered, if I had kept my little home and had not gone to Arizona, and you had returned to Indianapolis, how different our lives might have been. One choice does, indeed, determine destiny.]

5

Fun at the Front

But in this period, you also report on a stroke of good luck in your "household."

One of the boys found a horse, harness and buggy so now we just ride around in our 'One Horse Shay.' Even has a couple of bells and we jingle, jingle all the way. Oh what fun we have out here in the country what with all the stuff we find – living in our dugout and doing our job for the war effort at the same time."

And then further good news. You haven't been "busted," only fined two-thirds of a month's pay or about $38. My allowance will be cut this month!

16 Jan 45: A Good Day!: One of the boys found a pair of skis the other day but the way the hills are around here skiing ain't so hot. If we get another good snow over this crust then I'll try my luck at a bit of fun – I haven't had a pair on since 1940 and I may be slightly rusty – Bet you'd like to see me fall on my caboose – That's what we need – a little winter sport to take our minds off this tough war situation. . . the menu called for beans – these damn beans – which reminds me that I hope you never cook beans for me unless it is in chile con carne, but no other type. I hate 'em! Even when they were only half cooked as they were today.

19 Jan 45: Friday, I think: Hey, Honey, May I say that this is "Good Friday?" At least, darling, I can say that this Friday is good to me! Here I get a full night's sleep plus all day tomorrow off and beside all that I got your package – and letters of Jan 1st and 2nd. What else could be better than that? Say little chum, that wonderful scarf you sent is the cat's pajamas . . . the combs may come in handy in about six months when my G.I. haircut grows back in. Then the towels came just when all my others were dirty. . . The candy bars were enjoyed by all – especially Boho – the bum! (He says I quote) "The only trouble is it ain't enough!"

20 Jan 45: Nice day! Know what I did on my day off? I goes back several miles to a nice place to take a BATH! Yep, the first bath I've had since I landed on these fair shores. The place we went was a big building with a hundred rooms – all bathrooms – I can't say much about the system of heating the water though! First a rather motherly looking woman would come in to wash the tub – then she would turn cold water in and then she would turn a steam valve that heated the water and then, damned if she didn't bring in a thermometer to see if the water was hot enough. When she got through with all the rigmarole, she left and I jumped in – damn near froze my legs off – so I turned the little handle to heat the water more – then I sat down to enjoy a good bath!!! Hell, in about two minutes I was roasting my fanny and had to jump up to cool it off. It wasn't long until I was sitting warm as a king and feeling twice as good. Baby, it was wonderful! . . . So here I sit tonight by a warm stove, drinking a little wine and then, eating my heart out cause I didn't get any mail from you today!

Honey, I really enjoyed myself today – the first time since I came to combat that I had a chance to get away from all this stuff. – No buildings wrecked by shells – no dead Germans laying around and no ringing of guns in my ears. My darling, you can never know how very much your love means to me – the very fact that you love me as you do gives me a definite purpose in life – gives me something to live for and quite naturally gives me something that I miss in person – and miss dearly at that. I can only hope and pray that my love – as great as it is – is enough to repay you for your faithfulness, your sweetness – cause God knows, I love you so. Your Neb

On the 21st of January – as you have received my fifth month anniversary letter (Jan 5) – for the first time you seem to realize that the letters I had written after the announcement of disaster for the 106th in the newspapers in Indianapolis, were written in the agony of my heart! You write:

21 Jan 45: Honey, for some reason or other I rather felt that for a time you were worried about me! I am rather dense at times and I didn't seem to get the meaning of [some of your] lines. Darling, are you letting the fact that all the letters I wrote you in December are being delayed get you down? Or are the newspapers giving you a bunch of stuff that is not true? Surely by this time you will have received at least some, if not all of the Dec letters?

[You will not know that only as late as January 8th, will I have received mail after 42 days and these will be the letters you wrote while you were leaving England! I could never, ever tell you of my great grief during that time.] But as you end your letter, you seem somehow, to become aware. You conclude:

> Never in all the days I have been over here has the feeling to be there with you – to hold you tight in my arms and whisper of my great love for you – been so strong as it is tonight – Darling, never forget that I love you truly and shall for always.

Your letter 22nd is filled with interest and advice:

> **22 Jan 45:** INTERESTING LIFE THIS ARMY! Here I sit in a small room of a barn with rock walls two-feet thick and I have just re-arranged the 13 pages of "Letters from Helen" [which is it – "Helen's Letters" or "Helen's Book?"] by Mrs. A. C. Nebeker that I received today. Pretty soon I am going to have to start a second edition of that book – I have all your letters that you wrote from Oct 10 to Jan 1 (four are missing). I may send them home cause I sure want to keep them and if I do there is going to be one mad censor – somewhere along the line. . . .Darling, I am happy that you have decided to go out and meet my folks around the first of March. There is no reason I would want you to stay where you are – in fact I think you know that I am very anxious for you to meet my parents.

And then you write four pages about your religion. "Darling, I have never said much about my church – mainly because – although it means a hell of a lot to me – I didn't want it to become a question between us – I think the world of my church and I'll never join another but you have your own ideas and ideals – and as you well know, I have a very healthy respect for them – plus your rolling pin, too!" Then you tell me about the MIA activities, the socials and the classes and dances. "And there are a lot of girls your own age – with your own ideas – and I know you may get a kick out of that – plus learn how not to burn my Sunday breakfast! (Joke)". And then you say you can't understand my not getting mail:

> Must be a slip-up somewhere. I don't want you worrying that it is because I don't write – or want to write or because I don't love you or have changed my mind because I'll never regret or change my mind or fall out of love with you since I love you deeply. Neb

12 Jan 45: Still in Belgium: My Sweet Kid – After I have been writing to you daily for the time that I have been over here – and then reading that you are not getting them – I did a little scouting around to find out just where and why the mail is! About all I could find out was that for some poor reason or another our outgoing mail has been held up by higher echelons since the December breakthrough! But now that we are off the secret list – as if it was ever secret we were here – the only ones who didn't know were the ones in the States – the mail must be going back to the States by now! I hope! Funny, my darling, why the army says mail to the soldier is so important – then they forget the mail a soldier writes. Most of the boys have been writing regular as all get out and still every one of them has been getting word back from their folks that no mail came – All the guy's folks are worried to death over them and now the boys are anxious for the mail to start home! And not a one of them wants that any more than I do! Beside, our morale is low because our loved ones back home are worried over us! Our officers ought to raise hell about that for us but I guess that the same thing may happen again.

[It's interesting to read this in the context of the Iraq war today: soldiers needing supplies from home; non-coms and officers alike unable or unwilling to exercise wisdom, or help, or just plain go to bat for those who depend upon them; the media always ready to exploit any failure or success on the Front. Face it: when your armed forces are for the most part simply decent, sometimes hard-working but always essentially "civilian" young men, unskilled in the art of warfare, there will always be slip-ups. If it weren't for our "professional" officers and men, we would certainly be doomed, as a fighting nation. . . War is truly HELL!]

And so the last week of January passes for you on the field of battle. One day you seem to be in a degree of safety and comfort – and the next I can tell that you are in the thick of the fray.

24 Jan 45: A Red Letter Day: Really and truly this has been a Red Letter Day for me – and all on account of you. But first, before I started this letter, I just had to heat me a can of C Ration to eat with my PX supply. You know how happy and lazy I am when I have a full tummy, so I thought I should reach the peak of happiness when I wrote this letter as I want it to be a good one. Honey, I shouldn't say that I had to eat to reach the peak – rather I should have said to retain the peak! I reached the peak tonight when Ohlsen handed me two letters from you – the 7th & 8th. What a difference in those two – written about 24 hours apart but still a lot happened during those few hours to make you happy. The fact that you received some of my letters on the 8th makes me very happy as it shows that at last the mail is going back – that now you should have dispelled many of the fears and worries that have been creeping into your letters no matter how hard you tried to keep them out. Not that I don't want you to worry over me (that makes me realize just how very much you love me and miss me) but not in the sense that it gets you down. . . Now for the minor parts of this my Red Letter Day. First, the sun was actually warm and because of that I had the very needed opportunity to straighten out my G.I. clothing – Of course, I had to thaw the ice out of them – even Jr. too – but I got what I wanted out of my duffle bag and then comes part two – A real chance for an extra special helmet bath! A warm room and plenty of hot water. So with a clean body and clean clothes throughout I read your happy letters. Part three – A beaming fat Belgian woman has washed my field jacket and tomorrow is going to wash some more of my awfully dirty stuff! Yeah man, I bet you're green eyed now – she's only about 65 anyway. Last night after I wrote you, I dashed down the road to see a movie. Damned good but I about froze. It was held in an old school house that had been hit by shells and the ventilation was rather windy. Supposed to have another one next week. I hope. . . Now, darling, don't go worrying that pretty head of yours over me. I can't tell much difference between all this and Tennessee maneuvers – only once in awhile some shells land nearby, but I hear them coming and duck plenty fast. Soon this war will be over, I hope, and I can come back to you as I shall, God willing and I do continually pray that he is! . . . for now I'll bear the pain of missing you and revel in my love for you tonight, tomorrow night and for always. "Neb"

25 Jan 45: [How the mood and circumstances have changed]: Xmas a Month Ago: Here on this eve I am so very tired that I can hardly see or hear for that matter. It seems that my shift really had some mighty hard work last night and today – We started at 10 last night working chipping trees – digging and stuff so we could still send the Jerries a few rounds of American ideas and by the time we got through it was 3:30 this afternoon – When I came off shift tonight at six, I just sorta sat around with Kirk and the boys – The peace and quiet was wonderful and the room is nice and warm. . . . Honey, did I ever mention what a set up we have here? Two old guys live at this house all by themselves and we just sorta took over just for my section – We have a room all to ourselves with a table, stove etc. It is surely swell from the usual dugout or wind break tent that we usually have to put up. Then there is the woman next door that has done some washing for us – but soon I hope we are on our way again – That'll mean that much closer to the time when I can come home to the only one I care about. . . .Darling, in my tiredness I have a strong burning love for you – a love that grows and grows as each day goes by – and I know for my part that it'll continue to grow. For always, Neb

26 Jan – In Belgium Still – but in a new position: You are really just beginning to realize the shock of the newspapers that the people in Indianapolis have received about the 106th and you ask for the paper clippings – You conclude a short letter:

26 Jan 45: What if the snow is 15 inches deep – what if the wind is cold – what if I freeze – I know that across the blue wide ocean, I have a very sweet, faithful, beautiful love that is reaching far over the miles to keep me warm – to give me the very inspirations and ambitions that I need! I can't seem to be able to wait until that most glorious day shall come that love and the person capable of giving that love, is sitting on the arm of my chair. It will be then that I shall say "My darling, I love you so."

A Cold, Snowy WWII Winter

You are concerned about my health and want a complete report. You think perhaps I should quit work. [Do you really think I can live on $80 monthly? That is, when you haven't been fined for insubordination!] But then if I am leaving for Arizona, we'll think about that later – after I've had a rest. Nothing to worry about you – only frost-bitten toes. May get a chance to thaw them out – otherwise in perfect health – in fact, feeling like a spring chicken. May have a cold now and then but nothing to worry about. Oh how we lie to each other!

> **27 Jan 45:** Am trying to take care of this boy so that you'll have a ready-for-the-Chicago-trip husband as soon as I get there – and I want you to be ready for it also! Naturally I want to kiss you, you dope! Plenty and long! But here's a million to start with now – via long distance!"

28 Jan 45: Rest Day: In this letter for the first time you tell me some of the disasters that have befallen the men you have trained with for so long. The ban has been lifted because by now their folks at home will have been notified by the War Department. You tell me about Del, the best man at our wedding, who has been two-timing his wife, Betty, for some time now. He was a machine-gunner.

> . . . and his crew was located several yards behind our kitchen. On that day we got march order early in the morning – Everyone was supposed to have been told we were leaving, including his gun. When we were ready to pull out, he hadn't showed up so a man went to see what was holding them up. The guy never came back and he didn't answer calls – we were in a big hurry so we just couldn't wait for them any longer. The Germans that came through us seem to be all right since Halberg was captured but later escaped in some way. [This area was the one in which many prisoners captured by the Germans were piled into a truck, taken out and, as they were ordered to get out for a rest, were machined gun, leaving none alive.] I am pretty sure that is what happened to Del – as no shots were fired over that way. You tell Betty that, anyway. I don't think that it shall be too long now that I'll know for sure – I couldn't tell you until I knew she had the official word. Nor can I tell you of any other casualties until their folks have been notified.

[Del was killed at the front, as Betty was informed later. How close they must have been to you, dear love, and what a miracle that you were unharmed.]

My darling, as I read these words now – and knowing your deep friendship with Del and so many of the young men in your battery, with whom you had trained for so many months – I can only imagine your grief, and perhaps your feeling of guilt, at having survived so many of your mates in those dark days of December. I have a deep-seated feeling that you still felt the grief and the guilt, perhaps to the end of your life. And yet, you kept your letters cheerful and the details few, even after the ban was lifted, so as not to burden me. Perhaps these were the memories that were to besiege you through those early years home when you told me that you had contemplated suicide. (Memories you could not share with me.) Many young men, today, are feeling the same grief and guilt. I hope they are getting the help they need.

29 Jan 45: Belgium: My Darling, I am not quite happy over the fact I didn't get any sleep for the past 24 hours! Most of the time I get a chance for a couple of winks during my shift, but today I just sat and wrote each of my sisters and my Mother a long letter – mostly asking them to send me some food. . . your letters are reaching me in the amazing time of 10 days – I think that yours are my life blood – and the sweet perfume on them is my inspiration. Oh baby – how I love that smell!. . . I shall never get over my empty feelings nor my missing you during these times when my heart cries out, I love you so. Your Neb.

My love, when I read your continuing words of need and love, I know, again, that you truly needed me in the long days you were gone. Despite the things that were to come in other days less needful, I somehow know I was appointed by a power beyond my understanding to watch over you, even though it had to be from a vast distance. But prayers and faith know no miles!

31 Jan 45: Still Belgium [This is a long and informative last letter of the year and I will record a great part of your letter verbatim.]: At long last we are back for a rest or something! Just somewhere in Belgium as far as I am concerned, but a good distance from the fighting. I'd much rather have stayed up there to get in on the finish (I hope) of this thing called war. . . . Honey, even here we have it pretty good. There are six of us living right with an old couple – I call the old man "Pop" and I got him saying "okay" and "check". The good people are afraid of the buzz bombs so they sleep down in the cellar and we have their bedroom and their beds. Of course, we have our own blankets and stuff. The mattress is full of bunched up cotton and I think the floor is much better but nonetheless a bed feels good after a couple of months sleeping on the hard ground. [No wonder you would never take me camping when you got home! And now I understand why you always rented a camper when you took the scouts on camping trips. How they used to taunt you about that – you Eagle Scout!!]. . . It seems that there is not a thing that these people won't do – especially for Americans! We want hot water – they get it for us – and anything else that they can do for us they're right there with it. However, we do a lot of that stuff ourselves and do not let them do too much for us. We give them everything from candy to torn up clothes – yep – I have lots of fun with "Pop" – He is teaching me French with the help of my little book. Darling, whenever you listen to a good radio program, just say, "Neb will hear that soon," because they have a good radio and we get re-broadcasts from the states. I hope we can stay here for awhile anyway. . . I miss you terribly and so long to be with you.

And so ends for you, the first month of the brave new year of 1945.

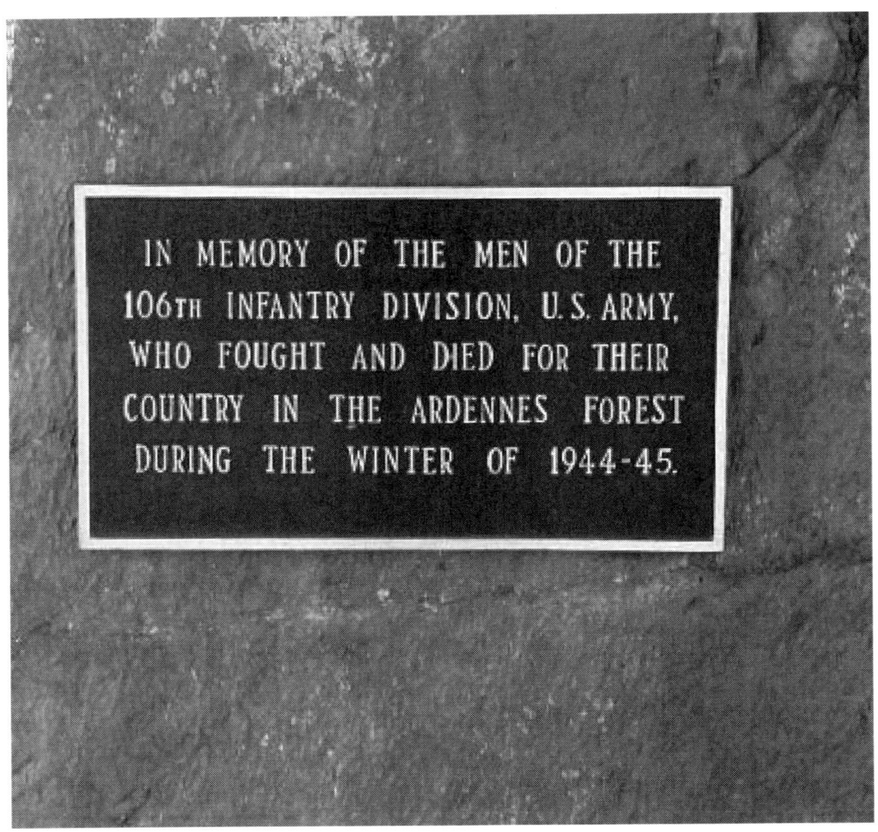

6
And Back at the Ranch

As I am reading and recording for posterity your January letters, I am also turning back to the ones I have been writing you in reply to your now-catching-up mail. In my letters, I write of anything and everything I can think of to amuse you and to keep your spirits up. And especially to remind you of "home" and of me! One of the things I mention frequently are the results of the weekly "Hit Parade" of songs. I don't believe that anyone not living through those years of war can imagine the influence and the great morale-building impact of that evening of popular musical choices for which we so eagerly glued ourselves to the radio each Saturday night. We, as a people, lived for that evening. And to deny that the songs selected each week created, to some extent at least, our vision of "reality" would be a mistake. In my January 20th letter I write:

> *January 20, 1945*: I'm listening to the Hit Parade right now, but since Frankie [Sinatra] isn't on it any longer, the program isn't as good. . . Lawrence Tibbett doesn't seem to have the feeling in his songs that Frankie did. Maybe it's because he doesn't have a crush on me! Anyhow you don't have to worry about Mr. Sinatra singing his love songs to me anymore! Now comes the three top tunes! #3 "Making Believe;" #2 "There Goes That Song Again." It's pretty new so maybe you haven't heard it but every time they play it I think of how I feel when they play "Til Then." And now the top tune of the week – "Don't Fence Me In!" – a song of a wandering foot-loose cowboy! And that completes my resume' of this week's top tunes.
>
> . . . I dreamed of you again last night. I must have a very vivid sub-conscious because my dreams are always so real. It's nice to have you with me, even if I have to wake up and find it only a dream. I wish we'd been married years so I could be

> living in our own home keeping things nice for your return. Even living in the apartment was more like our own home – at least you were there with me for awhile. But I'm not complaining – I'm perfectly happy. It's just one of my moods. [It is strange but I continue throughout my life to dream – and often those dreams have had incredibly accurate import!] . . . I'm glad I was born with a good imagination . . . because I can carry on conversations with you and sometimes almost really believe you're with me. You'll never be really far away from me – at least you'll always seem near. Guess it's because I love you so much that part of me is with you wherever you go. It's wonderful to love like that and I'll always be thankful I waited for you to come along even if I did have to beat you nearly to death to get you to say "yes" to my proposal! Thank heavens I met you during Leap Year!

And so it goes, day after day, letter after letter, of love and nothingness. On January 23rd, I will write again about Jr., in response to your letter about the metal box:

> *January 23, 1945:* I'm glad you have a sense of responsibility toward your son and that you're looking out for his safety. Be careful, though and don't let Junior suffocate in that metal box – I'd never forgive you if anything happened to him! [And I have just found the note I sent you when I shipped Jr. to you. It reads: "My favorite husband, This, darling, is "Neb, Jr." I'm afraid it's the best I can do in that way – at least for awhile. Hope you aren't too terribly disappointed and will treat your namesake like you should. He's a good boy and I couldn't resist sending him to you. Don't think I'm too silly. Neb, Jr. is smart too and you should be able to teach him lots of tricks. Your favorite wife (I hope), Me."]

It is in this letter that I also write you about the finances of our household and conclude with:

> Don't think for a minute, though, you sweet kid, you, that no matter how many raises I should get, you're going to stay home and have Junior while I support you. You talked me into the

> Junior idea and we're not going to trade places now!! So there!!!! Give my love to Junior and tell him I miss him. But it's nothing compared to the way I miss and yearn for you. I love you so much my darling and I'm praying only for your safe return. [And then I seal your letter with a kiss on paper in my new shade of lipstick!] New lipstick! – Do you like it? It tastes better than it looks! Sweet dreams!!! Me.

In my January 25th letter, I respond to the news that you have been "busted," writing:

> *January 25, 1945:* I couldn't figure out whether you were kidding me or not about being busted because you put Cpl on the return address. But even if you were I don't blame you for blowing up one bit. . . I can imagine that you really told the Sgt. where to head in but I don't doubt for a minute that you had reason to. You're not a person to gripe about hard work so he must have been awfully unreasonable. So darling, what do you care, Pvt Nebeker sounds just as good as Cpl Nebeker to me any day. I think I know how you felt though and I'm glad you told me about it. Sometimes I feel the same thing – everything seems to go wrong, nothing seems fair, and real happiness is just a word in fiction books. But don't let it get you down sweetheart; just remember that one of these days the top sergeant will no longer have any control of your actions. You'll be a civilian again and I and my rolling pin will be the sole master of your fate. Doesn't that sound lovely?

[As I read the last two lines that I've written, I think of how in days to come you were to transfer me into the role not of your sergeant restricting your freedom, but into that of your mother. Although your mother was a loving woman – and extremely good to me – you and she simply butted heads on every issue – and particularly anything pertaining to your personal freedom. I was to pay the penalty for that during many years and it was only after her death that you relinquished the concept of "being under her thumb," in your own words! But much more of that much later in this letter.] I also inform you in this letter that I have not received the foreign moneys that you say you've enclosed and that my letters I have just received look as though they have been opened. – although that may be by the censor. AND THAT I HAVE SENT YOU STAMPS AND SENT YOU STAMPS!!!!! "P.S. If you've been busted to buck private maybe next time you blow your top they'll bust you right out of the Army! Oh happy day!"

The last of my January letters are very long and detailed; I am planning on leaving home to visit your parents and I make my reasons very clear in one particular letter of the 26th:

> *January 26, 1945:* I'm not quite sure how you'll feel about me going so I'll tell you about the whole thing. In the first place I hesitate about going because Indpls is so near the center of everything – if you should get home unexpectedly, this would be a pretty easy place to reach, but on the other hand, no matter how short a time you might have, you'd still want to go home and I'd already be there. Then secondly, I was afraid I'd be inconveniencing your folks but your mother has assured me she really wants me to come. If I see that I am causing complications, I can always leave.
>
> Then there were and are some reasons why I want to go – strictly between you and me. Frankly, it's hell here at home – not because of me and the rest of the family but because of mother and daddy. I wouldn't be surprised if mother left dad tomorrow – in fact, if it weren't for Susie and Jerry I know she would. There's such tension between them constantly you can almost see it. Mother quit work about three weeks ago and since then – well I don't know what's happened. The poor little kids are always getting shouted at until I could just cry for them. . . .I'm not telling you this to worry you or make you think I'm unhappy – I just want to explain. Of course I could do like I did before [and these are exactly the kind of reasons that I had had to leave at 15], leave and get my own place but I'd be miserable by myself and if I shared a place with another girl, she'd probably be a second Betty and I know you wouldn't like that. So since you've always told me I was welcome at your folks, I think it's the best solution at least for awhile. Mother and Daddy can settle their troubles without giving me a nervous breakdown in the process. I've got a pretty good

> outlook on life and I refuse to have it spoiled. . . I feel sorry for both of them and yet there's no sense in all this trouble, so I can't be too sympathetic. Anyhow, honey, I hope what I'm doing is all right with you. If it isn't, write and give me the devil and next time I'll know. Even if there weren't these reasons, after being married half a year (in ten days) I really should get acquainted with my other family, don't you think?

I end with – "I love you so much and faith, you'd better have a bit o'love in your heart for me or else my heart, she will be broken. For always, Me."

Looking at this letter from a vantage point of years, it's difficult to imagine how a girl of barely eighteen could handle all of these problems – as well as all of the decisions of the past half year. Sometimes, upon reflection, I can't help thinking that either the Lord expected much too much of me or that he had great confidence in my powers of endurance. Either way, these were heavy problems! I could only do the best that I knew how.

In the January 27th letter, I send you "Your Hit Parade":

#9 "Don't you know I care" (well, don't you?)
#8 "Don't Ever Change" (not toward me anyhow!)
#7 "The Trolley Song" (and you don't necessarily have to sing it on a trolley if you know what I'm referring to!)
#6 "Sweet Dreams, Sweetheart" (my wish for you every night)
#5 "I'm Making Believe (it's better than nothing)
#4 "Accentuate the Positive" (Jive talk for being optimistic)
#3 "I Dream of You" (and I really do, too)
#2 "There Goes That Song Again" (good for recalling pleasant memories)
#1 "Don't Fence Me In" (that cowboy song again)
[How was I to know that cowboy song would become your favorite post-war theme?]

I end a long letter with: "As for me, my love grows with each day and nothing will ever change that. [It will!] You're as necessary to me as the sun to flowers, breath to life. [And you were!] I can't even remember how it was before I met you – I must have existed rather than lived [still true.] I know that more than anything else in life [and in eternity], I love you and want to be yours. For all eternity, Helen"

On the 28th, I write that I am giving notice at work and will be leaving for Arizona in two weeks or so. My Granddaddy Gwin is arranging the Southern Pacific train trip for me, and I will be going down through Louisiana and Texas, N. Mexico etc.

> *January 28, 1945:* It would be perfect if you were going with me. But one of these days we will be taking a trip together – the continuance of that wonderful honeymoon trip of ours. That's the trip I'm really looking forward to. When I can sit beside you and hold your hand while we both look at the sights together. Without you nothing is really much fun.

[And my darling, we did take those wonderful train trips together, forty-five years later from 1987 through 1993 – and one trip in 1975 – through all of Europe. Most of all, I remember our 43rd wedding anniversary in Vienna, Austria, where we waltzed together at the Schonberg Palace! And thinking of those days, after we had overcome so many seemingly insurmountable problems, I'll close with the same words I used in this letter of 1945: "There are so many words of love in my heart just clamoring to tell you how much I love you. But . . . I guess they will just have to stay in my heart until they can be told to your in person. With all my heart. . ."]

And so the month of January ends with me receiving your December 16th, 21st and Jan 15th & 16th letters: The lost money is in one of those letters and I've recorded previously your writings of the days of battle. . . I will write you back:

> I'll never, as long as I live, forget the horrible emptiness of those days when there was no news from you and every newspaper and radio commentator broadcasting the destruction of the 106th. I can just hear you calling me "worrywart," but there could be a time when you would fear for my life and then you'd know the feeling – that's the only way you could know!

[Did you, my love, ever feel that awful devastation when *my* life was on the line – or were you able to find solace with your buddies at the bar? Will I *ever* know? Never in *this* life, I'm sure.] And in this letter,

I'm worried about spending money for the trip. And I urge you to keep back some of my allotment money for yourself. I'm doing okay. But the last day of January 1945 sees me in a foul mood:

> It's a good thing you aren't here this evening cause if you were you'd probably divorce me or else turn me over your knee – and to be perfectly frank, I guess that's what I need. I'm in a very bad humor and there's no reason for it. Just tired, I guess, and that's no excuse – only an alibi. But regardless of my mood, my love for you never changes. That's really all that's wrong with me tonight – my love for you is unusually strong tonight and I guess I'm lonelier than usual. I never will get tired of waiting for you but I can get awfully bitter and disgusted with the necessity for waiting.

It will be almost exactly one year to this day that I will have need of being "turned over your knee" and in a metaphoric way, you will do just that! I will tell you the truth of this later, but will tell you that the *reason* will be the same!

7

"For Lo, the Winter Is Past"

February begins for me with the delivery of January mail – the 3rd and 4th combined and the January 17th full of your pleasure with the packages you have received. And your expression of your love for me. This is the letter in which you have been concerned about your mother worrying me about your church. I tell you plainly that "I have no intention of being forced to believe ideas that I really can't agree with, but just the same I'm open minded and if I can learn something better, why I'm willing. . . I wish I was there with you so I could rub your poor aching back for you. I bet I could really make it feel better. I think you've got the nicest back; in fact, one of the reasons I married you was that you had such a nice back – that and the fact that my heart, she would have no one else." [And that was simply the truth of it – and was til the end of your life.]

The first four letters of February are filled with daily news. There are rumors that the remnants of the 106th might be returned to Camp Atterbury and I'm getting cold feet about going to Arizona. My ticket is not finalized yet and I could cancel. Of course, I long to have you come home, any place, any time. I have received your letter about your day of rest and am glad your packages are beginning to catch up with you and believe that you still have five more coming. I'm sorry that maybe I've sent stuff to eat that you don't like but "I really didn't have time to learn all your likes and dislikes. I know you like steak and mashed potatoes and hate raisins and beans but there are a lot of things in between that I haven't the first idea about." And then I tell you about the weather and that Leona's husband is coming home and hasn't seen his six-month old baby yet. I close with:

> Dear one, I love you so very much that I can't tell you quite how much. Until I met you, I never dreamed I had so much lovin' in me. I think you've put a spell on me. But I love it. . . Take care of yourself and keep loving me as I will you.

My letter to you of February 5th is, of course, another anniversary letter. We have been married a full six months! Or, as I tell you, one-one hundredth of fifty years or 116 nights since I last saw you.

> *February 5, 1945:* . . . Sweetheart, thanks for the happiest six months of my life – even being apart, they've still been happy – guess it was just knowing I was Mrs. Aquila Chauncey Nebeker, Jr. – and to me that's the best name in the whole world.

[And I think, my dear, that I can truthfully say that I have never done anything to disgrace that name, in all the years we've been together.] Also, in this letter, I tell you that my train ticket has finally come – at the appalling cost of $91.80! [Can you imagine traveling by Pullman practically across the country for less than $100?] I will leave on February 22nd at 2:40 and arrive in Mesa on the 25th. . . The $91.80 doesn't include meals or my night's stop-over in New Orleans. I forget to tell you that the stop-over is so that I can meet and spend the evening in New Orleans with my cousin Pete's new fiancée. You are going to question me about that later! Your mother has written sending me some "family record" sheets to fill out and I am scared to death about them. "I only hope I can trace my family – and that there are no murderers or thieves in the family. . . I don't even know my own grandmother's maiden name!" And "I close my letter with so much love in my heart that it is aching from the weight of that love."

The war news for this week has been very good – though everyone knows that "each mile gained has meant hardship and bloodshed. The Russians keep pushing on and the Siegfried Line has been penetrated at some points, the radio reports. The war news from the Pacific is good, too – Manila retaken, American prisoners freed from concentration camps, air raids on big industrial centers." Men are returning home on furlough. Maybe you? I've been training a replacement for my job – and I'm very tired. And there are no letters now for three days! And I've had a very strange dream about you. You were home and "I stood on the top of a very high hill and shouted it so that everyone would know that you were back and then, just before I woke up, I lost my balance and fell down the hill. My dreams of you certainly take strange forms and shapes. I can still feel the bruises from that downhill trip." [Reading this so far in the distance, I am amazed at the symbolic significance of this dream. When you come home I will have been a member of the Church only three months. I really know nothing about the Gospel except that the Book of Mormon is true and that Joseph Smith was truly the Prophet of the Restoration. But I have no depth of testimony. And you will return home still the "rowdy Mormon" that you had proclaimed yourself to be when we first met. Certainly I will suffer the bruises from the fall in more than a symbolic way. And how often I will have such revelatory dreams in the future.]

But I end this letter, as I have so many before, with new words of love: "I still love you with all my heart. You're the stars in my sky, the water in my swimming pool. . . Honestly, I love you so much I can't imagine life without you." [Many years later, these words will also seem revelatory.]

My February 8th letter to you reports that there are definite reports from the media that the 106th is returning. Since I have no letters from you, I begin to ponder possibilities:

February 8, 1945: "I find myself thinking that . . . you're on a ship coming home so you can't write. . . .The papers report that the Russians are in the suburb of Berlin. . . so maybe you can take another boat ride home." And so it goes, day after dreary but busy days. And as always, I try to find some new way to say I love you:
" . . .you're as important to me as – my nylon hose, a bathing cap when I swim, lipstick and powder – in fact, dear, you are my heart. I love you above anyone, anything, and I've got a feeling I always will. Goodnight, sweetheart, God bless. "

On the 10th – still no mail and winter in full swing again with the mid-west alerted for terrible flooding – I write you that I will leave in eleven days and ask you about Jimmy and Louie and Smokey – you have only been able to tell me about Del. And again I write my words of love:

February 10, 1945: I'm a little on the lonely side tonight and I could sure use the sound of your voice or the touch of your hands. In fact, I just want you. . . .You'd think after all this time my love would have reached its full growth but it hasn't. It's like Jack's beanstalk, it just keeps growing and growing. Sometimes it almost scares me. I wonder if a person can love too deeply. I guess it doesn't matter as long as you're loving me too. And I won't even think of what would happen if you should ever stop. . . I love you more than Anthony did Cleopatra, more than Juliet did Romeo, more than Ella does Patches [who in heck were they?]. . . today, tomorrow and forever. "Me"

On Valentine's Day I received your January letters of 12th, 25th, 26th, 31st, and I now know you are back in Belgium. I'm interested in all the people you are meeting and happy when you are getting some rest. I let you know how unhappy I am about spending so much money, the train ticket and the state taxes I have had to pay; the cost of the injections I have been taking worries me, but since I'll be leaving that won't be a cost anymore. And, of course, I intend to find work as soon as I get to Mesa. But most of all I seem to be worrying about where I will be when you get home. I think the letters you are writing, together with all the news, has really made me feel you might be home soon. [But of course we know that it will be almost another full year before we are once again together.] On the 16th, the thermometer has zoomed to an incredible 67 degrees. How am I to know that is the coldest I will be for many months to come – I'm headed for the Arizona sun. On the 17th, I go to say good-bye to my poor dad, Tom. He was "really feeling bad today. He'd been held-up night before last. Two fellows hit him on the head and robbed him." Problems are continuing with mother and Darrell. In response to a concern of yours, I write:

> Darling, don't you ever worry about me even looking at another man. I trust you with all my heart and I'd sooner die than do anything that would hurt you or make you feel disappointed in me. I told you once that with your rings on my finger, I'd be the most faithful woman you could ever want – and I have been. I can make a lifetime career out of just loving you.

[I could not possibly know that before many years I would also have an almost equally important career in a field I had never dreamed of – it was just "fated." But, almost prophetically, in this same letter I mention, . . . "I should have gone to college or at least business college," little dreaming of what I would eventually do!]

On the 19th, I receive six letters and they tell me about "Mom" and "Pop" and all your adventures. And on the 20th, your sweet response to my letter of January 5th and my great grief over the disaster of the 106th and my fears for you. And all the rest of these last days before my departure are taken up visiting with family and friends. Everyone seems to know I will not soon be coming back to Indianapolis.

And now it is February 22, 1945 and the great day is here; a new day begins in the life of Mrs. A.C. Nebeker, Jr. I am on my way to a life as foreign to me as your life in the Army has been to you. A new life, a new family, a new faith, and a great hope and faith in the future with my "old" love, when he returns home.

Part V

Great Changes

1
The Adventure Begins

February 22, 1945: Train Day: "My Darling, Here I sit in a hard seat in Union Station waiting for my train which is an hour late. Fine start for my nice long trip, huh? A train station is a very interesting place to spend an extra hour or so in case you didn't know it. It's almost like seeing a dozen or so different movies all at the same time. Take this little sailor and his girl-friend over here. She's got an engagement ring and I just know from the way she's looking at it that it is a new possession. She's trying so hard not to cry and he keeps looking at her with such loving can't-bear-to-leave-you-look that my heart aches for both of them. Who knows how long it will be before they see each other again.

Then there's this little boy over here in his little sailor suit eating an apple that's almost as big as he is. Everyone is getting quite a kick out of him. Of course there are the usual soldiers and sailors doing their best to keep up civilian female morale by giving every pretty girl one of those wolfish whistles.

Here comes the signal that my train is finally coming in. So 'til I'm settled, adios senor.

<u>Later:</u> Well here I sit in my nice comfortable chair car watching the fields roll by and talking to you at the same time. There are ten of us in this car and just between you and me, they all look like bores. The women all look snooty and high toned and the men are fat, forty and nearly asleep! It's much nicer just sitting here thinking of you. . . I've got my chair facing the window and right in front of me a nice little table to set an ash tray and a drink on. How about it, could you go for a nice mixed drink – don't think they're serving beer.

<u>Still Later:</u> I got sleepy after that last line so I think I went to sleep. Anyhow, here I am watching for the Ohio River which

we're about to cross. Gee it's wide and the water is way up too. Sure hope this bridge holds until we're clear across. In just a few minutes we'll be in the Louisville station so Bye

Louisville, Ky: This station is pretty small to what I expected it to be but it has the usual hard uncomfortable seats for waiting – and I've got a two hour wait ahead of me. We got in the station about six-thirty and after checking my bags, I decided to get some food. I hadn't eaten since this morning and I was starved. Naturally the only place to eat was the station restaurant. Honey, if all Kentuckians eat this kind of food I had to eat this evening, I know why so many of them come to Indiana. The food was horrible. Sitting here by myself, you have no idea how lonely I am for you. Since you've been gone, I've learned that loneliness doesn't decrease with time, it only grows greater. Anymore it's just a constant ache and the only cure for it is you. I wish the War Department would hurry up and arrange that furlough!

More time has passed: . . .I am in my nice comfortable lower berth and the writing is rather up-hill & down-hill but I did want to tell you good night. Between this paragraph and the last one I wrote, I made a new acquaintance – a male too. But I don't really think you'd mind. He's just a kid – maybe a little over eighteen. I was sitting there in the station and a couple of times I noticed him smiling at me so naturally I smiled back. Pretty soon he walked over and asked me if he could sit down. Pretty soon we were talking and he told me about his mother and dad and showed me some pictures of his girl. Then we talked about our own states and really had a nice two hours. Then my train came in and I started to get a "red-cap" but nothing would do but he take my suitcases and carry them out for me. He put them on the train and then he held out his hand to shake my hand and said, "Gee, it's been nice knowing you" and left. That was one of the nicest compliments I've had in a long time. I didn't tell you this to make you think I talk to every stranger. But I thought he was such a nice kid – not fresh but just friendly and I thought you'd enjoy meeting him too. Now here I am, all tucked in my nice little room, all ready for some sleep. Good night, darling. Until tomorrow until I continue this travelogue, A heart full of love.

February 23, 1945: A New Day: Right now it's 11:30 and I've already put in a full day. I got up at seven so I could get out of the dressing room before the rush started. I didn't sleep too well last night because the jerking of the train brought my "pet pain" to the surface in a rather violent manner. But it's not so bad this morning and so far I've really enjoyed the day. I had a good breakfast even if I did live in fear of spilling coffee all over my lap. I spent a long time in the diner because the man above me was still sleeping and the porter couldn't make up the berths. We've been in Alabama ever since this morning and part of the time we seem to be way up in the hills. Mud, mules, misty fog, and red clay ground seem to be the general characteristics of this state. Most of the houses are rickety old shacks and it's almost impossible to think of people actually living in them. Most of the people are darkies – I don't think I've seen a dozen white people. These colored people aren't like those we see in Indpls – they all wear the proverbial turbans and gay colored, raggedy clothes that you read about in books. After seeing this state, all I can say is "Thank heavens I'm not a native of Alabama."

Time Passes: Well, darlin', here I am at last in New Orleans. I've seen rivers and lakes, mountains, valleys, green grass, lovely flowers, big navy ships anchored in the harbor and last but not least, one of the most beautiful sunsets that I've ever seen. Now I'm here in my hotel room on the third floor of the St. Charles and it reminds me so much of our Chicago honeymoon room – only the bed isn't as big. . . .It's so much like the Stephens, I almost expect to suddenly feel your arms around me. But since I can't have you, I at least have your picture with me and there you sit on the dresser winking at me – in an awfully fresh way.

Honey, Gloria, my cousin's fiancée will be up in a few minutes so I'll close until later when I'll tell you all about "My Night in New Orleans."

Oh my aching feet! It's your wandering wife again and have I wandered tonight! Relax and I'll tell you all about it. Gloria came after me with a girl friend and they really outdid themselves showing me a good time. I hope sometime I can return the favor. First of all they took me down to the old French Quarter to the Court of the Three Sisters and you should have seen what I had to eat. I can't even tell you what it was 'cause they ordered it for me. But the first course was shrimp with a creole sauce that was simply delicious. There was enough for a full course dinner but no here they came with a plate of the best looking fried oysters, some potato salad made with Roquefort cheese, french fried potatoes and some kind of nice light wine. I never enjoyed anything so much in my life. Then we walked miles and miles looking at the different shops, the famous spots until I was ready to drop. Then as the crowning act, I took a ferry boat across the Mississippi River. Oh, how I loved that. It was beautiful and the air was so warm and clean. But after that, I could stand no more so here, at three in the morning, I'm talking to you – but I always did like to talk after I got in bed.— It's awfully lonesome here in this room and I want you so badly. I'll bet I wouldn't be so cold if you were here. Until tomorrow, night, sweet dreams, I love you so. Me

February 24, 1945: We're now out of Louisiana and just leaving Houston and I aid in helping a bridal party – a young woman and her air cadet – find each other in the crowded station. "I'm tired out so: I'm going to bed, honey, so good night. I love you so much. Me"

February 25, 1945: I've had a good night sleep in my upper berth only we are up about 1800 feet and "I can hardly take it. I sure hope Mesa isn't that high. . . I think Texas is pretty – I'll take it to any state yet!! . . . Tomorrow, when I write I'll be in Mesa. I have been so lonely today that I would almost say I'm brooding. . . . What I'd like to know is why I love you so!. Maybe it's your red nose. Anyhow, until you lose whatever you have that keeps me under your spell, I'm yours forever."

February 26, 1945: "MESA, AT LAST!" . . . I got in this morning at 6:12 and your mother was there to meet me. Neb, honey, she's swell, every bit as nice as I knew all along she'd be. I sure am glad you made me her daughter. I'm absolutely thrilled with Mesa. The view of the mountains is enough to hold a person spellbound but when on top of that you have blue sky, green grass and trees, oranges, lemons and grapefruit growing on trees in your own front yard, no wonder I'm breathless.

After I got here I unpacked my clothes and your mother and I had breakfast and talked for awhile after which I pulled a fadeout and went to sleep. I am utterly and completely exhausted and on top of that I caught cold in my cold upper berth last night and I am about to cough my incision open. After a few hours rest, though, I think I'll feel better. After I woke up from my short nap, the mail man had left me three wonderful letters from you – not to mention the one waiting for me when I got here this morning. I gather you're again doing your bit on the front with no prospects of returning home for awhile. . . .I'm beginning to need you far worse than the army does – they've had you for four months, now I should have you for four.

After dinner, your mother and I went to the store and on the way, we went into the temple. I've never seen such lovely grounds in my life. I'm beginning to wonder why I waited so long to come out here. . . . My cold is getting worse by the second so I'm going to be dosed with some hot lemonade and go to bed. Much more coughing and I'll burst a blood vessel.

Tonight I want so much to have you here – it's been such a lovely day and to spend this night in your arms would make it complete. I never imagined that I would long for anyone's touch as I have for yours these past months. . . .I love you with all my heart. Your very tired wife. Helen P. S. I meant to make this letter much more interesting but I'm too tired. I'll do better tomorrow.

And so you see, my darling, that I tried to share with you my trip across the continent, just as you had so carefully shared your ocean crossing and other travels with me. How glad I am from this vantage point of time to remember all the wonderful trips and travel time that we had together. Every penny we spent has been worth it for the memories I carry in my heart these lonely last days of my life without you.

My next letters are concerned with meeting your family. On the 27th, I am at Stell's and tomorrow we will go up to Prescott to meet Anne's family and your dad. I have talked to them on the phone. But I am still very much under the weather and Ivy is trying to baby me by giving me medicine and trying to put me to bed. I've put her off by telling her I have to write you:

> We've been here in Phoenix [at Stell's] since noon. Stell has a lovely home and I think she's swell, but much different from what I had pictured. I'm really quite envious of her home. I want one more every day – with you there to keep me company. . . my chief ambition is to make a happy home for you. I don't know why, maybe it's because I don't feel so good, but I'm so lonesome for you I could cry like a baby. Aren't you ashamed of yourself driving a woman to tears?. . ..Be careful so you can hurry home to me. My heart forever. Helen

> *February 28, 1945:* I've met your dad and he's a grand guy. Something tells me he and I will get along. [And we always do. I loved him very much and there was a time or two when only he kept me from returning to more familiar places before you got home!] I love your whole family, honey, just as I knew I would and I think they like me too. Stell told me she wouldn't trade her new little sister for anything and IvyRae likes me too. She came and got in bed with me first thing this morning and we had a real nice chat for about forty minutes. Poor little thing. She wants a baby sister so badly. She also insists that I'm going to have a baby girl this summer. How would you like that??? She's brought the subject up more than once and I think she's going to be rather hard to dissuade.
>
> By the way, how's Junior? Give him a big kiss and hug for me and be sure to take good care of him. To Junior's daddy I send more love than any gal ever sent any guy. Love forever.

2
Back to Your Life on the Ardennes Front

1 Feb 45: In the first letter from you in this month, I learn that you are in a "new home" but I gather it is somewhere in the same area as when you were first attacked so furiously. It is on this date, that you get my letters of January 3rd & 4th and learn of my great despair at that time and my continuing fear for you. "Any way, honey, what do you mean that I'd make a target of myself for some Jerry. . . how can they catch the fastest runner in Arizona. Baby, you're stuck with me – I am ungetriddable, especially where you're concerned." You are teaching "Mom" to "jive" and have taken "Pop" to a movie and had enough French to make him understand the "drift" of 'A Guy Named Joe.' Good, simple people!" By the 5th of February, you have received all the mail for 1944 "except for four days that are "kaput" – but then I have already forgiven you for those – after all you couldn't help it! Eh?" [My dear, why the question mark?]

5 Feb 45: Another "anniversary" letter. And in this letter [having just recently read from other sources the horror of what the 592nd, Battery C, Field Artillery had survived in the late battle] I can understand the deeper emotion of your words:

> . . . For two months and 5 days I don't believe there ever was a happier man. . . the only thing that has kept me happy [during those dark days] is that you are waiting faithfully for my return! Naturally, Jr and his papa are anxiously awaiting for that time to come [when we are together] My darling, you shall know just how much my love for you has grown in the last few lonesome weeks. Baby, you can never guess just how really lonesome they are either. I keep constantly remembering how lovely you were on that blessed day – dressed in blue with my red flowers on your blouse. Then, too, I can remember how very nervous you were when we started for bed – Ha – You soon overcame

> that – didn't you! . . . So with all the longing I have in my heart, I wish you a very happy anniversary and I do hope that your happiness has been as complete as mine. The love I have for you constantly burns within my bosom and I am longing for the days when I shall never be missing you again, at least, not for so long. . . . I love you so. Your Neb

As I read words like this, written when death had really been imminent – and even these few days later remains a distinct possibility – I wonder how different it might have been had you returned to me much earlier than you were to do. Did those many months of what you considered "useless duty," after all the others had returned home, change you, harden you? Would you have been a different man emotionally, if these memories of battle had been fresh within you? We'll never know. Nor could we have changed any of it anyhow!

February 6th-8th are not happy days for you. You are back on the front line again, living in dugouts and doing a little work on the Jerries. Those 155 big guns somehow seemed to survive. But again, you are "fixing up your house" and "all is rain, mud-rain. I hope tomorrow it don't rain – It is turning too much like Tennessee!!!" But obviously, all is not well, otherwise, with the troops. It seems, reading between the lines, that different groups have merged because of the losses, and the different contingents are just not getting along. You write:

> Something is wrong in the section but damned if I know what it is. Anyway, honey, I am happy regardless of what goes on around here. And the only thing that keeps me happy is the fact that sometime soon I shall return to you and our life together. If you ever changed your mind and thought that some other guy could make you happier – I'm afraid that this old heart of mine would break. . . you are so sweet, so loving, so faithful. . .

[In many of your letters, I glean an undertone of "unfaithfulness" either on the part of the men's wives or the men themselves. And I know, of course, that Del has been writing to two girls – his Texan and the Redhead – and that you have discontinued your closeness with him since he announced his intention of divorcing Betty and marrying the red-head. Perhaps you are worried that something like this might happen to you. Perhaps that is part of your eagerness to have me in Arizona among family.]

I'm going to include almost the whole of your February 11th letter, simply to show how you make light – to me – of what you are actually experiencing in this bitter winter in the bleakness of the Belgium forests. I have just read portions of a book written by one of the survivors of your 592nd FA Battalion, and he speaks of the men riding the trucks with toes so frostbitten they may never heal. And the lack of food. And the ever falling snow or rain. Here are your words:

> **11 Feb 45:** My Darling Beauty, What a country! Here for a week it has been raining and spring was in the air. Today it settled down and started to snow – even turned cold enough to freeze slightly on the surface! That really makes it rugged.! Darling, from the letters I received from you yesterday – I take it that you have some funny ideas about how tough it is over here. Honey, I've never had an easier life in the army as I am having over here! If I get cold I dash into our shelter or dugout by the nice warm stove. I have either slept in straw or some kind of mattress every night – at least it is dry and my bedroll is dry enough to keep me warm in zero weather. And I'm safe enough although the incoming shells worry us now and then – so honey, don't worry your pretty, very pretty at that, head over me! At least, about being warm – when you read about guys freezing in the papers – that is the infantry, not the artillery!! Those poor boys are really the boys who need worrying about. . . Darling, yesterday I was back to our first position to find out about Del – I didn't find him but I found letters he received from the redhead plus her picture – and letters from his Texas Girl – the dugout showed no sign of any struggles or bloodshed – which convinces me that he is a prisoner. I wrote Betty – and the Texan – but damned if I'll write the red-head. He told me when he got back he was going to divorce Betty and marry the redhead – what a dope!
>
> On the way up we were going up a very ruined street in a town and at the end of the street a guy with a movie camera was taking a newsreel shot of us coming up the street. I was

standing up in the back of the truck about the middle up front – there was a guy on each side of me. So if you see a newsreel shot of St. Vith with a truck coming up the street and three GIs standing in the back, the middle one is me!! I love you so.

And so, my love, runs one unexpurgated, first hand view of the soldier in St. Vith, on February 10th, 1945! You see, again you are protecting me from worry insofar as you are able. And in your next letter, you tell me that our thoughts have been running together; that the jokes I had sent had been a laugh for you all, and that you always knew I was a "smart cookie" but you hadn't known I was also a mystic! On the 12th, you are finally having your long awaited "housewarming."

12 Feb 45: It's not the same house, but it's better and I am the guest of honor. I have the bottom bunk on the right side and that is the springs off a day-bed. It is nice and soft – I sleep like a baby on it. Lately, I sleep like a baby but for some reason, I get the blankets awfully dirty! Do you think it's because I go to sleep with muddy clothes on? Can I help it if they dry off and the dirt drops off? The housewarming is really a housewarming – we found a regular GI stove that the Jerries were so kind to leave us. . . it really throws off the heat too! It makes me feel sad because here I sit sweating from the heat and you sit half freezing back there! Maybe it would be nice for you to come over and warm your feet since you haven't my back to use as a foot warmer. I think that your feet will not be the only thing that would be warm if you were here. Oh yes, my sweet potato, I'd give you a loving that would melt your toes, crinkle your hair and leave you warm enough to cook an egg on your forehead. But truly dear, I continually long for the time when your presence will make music in my soul. . . when I can reach out for you and you will be there, when I can draw you close and whisper, "I love you, darling!"

[As you would say, dear, Faith and I think it's more than the heat of the stove you are feeling tonight! And I know that feeling well!]

13 Feb 45: Things are looking up for you. You are now getting supplies from the PX – stationery, toothpaste, shaving cream, a can of fruit juice, cigarettes and candy bars – But now you want a batch of homemade fudge. [You ain't gonna get it from me!] But you have discovered another dislike for me to remember – anchovies! Above all, I am to remember that you "like meat and mashed potatoes, potatoes and meat! Then on Sunday I like something just a little different – mashed potatoes and some kind of steak. . . .but I know I don't have to worry about your cooking.." And again you are into your building projects:

> "Today I made a boardwalk out of our dugout to the gun – besides a couple of steps leading out the door. Every day that we stay here I find some little thing to make or to do that will make it just a bit nicer for us to live. I have an idea for tomorrow already! Right after chow tonight and just before a disappointing mail came in, I heated a bucketful of water to wash and shave. Now I had a nice mirror I had previously found, but I didn't have a place to put my helmet to wash in. So in the morning I am going to build some kind of washstand!

But lest I get any idea about your handiness about the house, you conclude your letter:

> . . . before you get any idea about me doing (any chores), I'm warning you right now, darling, when I get home I'm not going to do a damn thing for a couple of weeks except make "plenty of ze love to you" – God knows I'm storing all I have just for you.

[And I think God knows that you never spoke truer words!!!!]

14 Feb 45: You receive my "sixth" month anniversary letter.

> A letter so full of love, sweetness and, oh so touching. I now fear that the one I wrote you will not even compare with it. And I tried so hard to convince you just how really grateful I am that for six months I have really been a happy man. Somehow I feel that I can never catch up with you in expressing myself in

> letters. Your way of doing it has really become a source of happiness to me.

[As your words have done the same for me in *every* letter you write, my love.]

> Today for once, has been a nice day. The sun has been out most the day and a lot of the mud seems to be drying up. In fact, the mud is now only ankle deep instead of clear up to my a. . . But here and there patches of snow still dot the countryside. All in all, it is pretty nice – even the landscape seems to know that spring is just around the corner and that soon there will be no more shells to injure its surfaces!

Your next passages are concerned with my trip to Arizona. You wonder:

> Why the h. . . are you going clear down to Louisiana when you could have gone straight across to Arizona? No wonder it is going to take you three whole days and nights – besides costing you extra dough. But then it will be a nice trip and you'll see part of the states I haven't – so you'll have that over my head!! [What is this, a competition?] Here I left Virginia and in 3 days I was home and it only cost me $61.85, which is the regular one way fare!

[I will tell you later of the extraordinary pains and pull my grandfather had to use to get me the ticket and the accommodations that he did. After all, I couldn't make that trip, alone, as ill as I had been, without a bed to sleep in and a comfortable chair car or roomette. Besides, I had never traveled and I wanted to see all that I could see, plus I wanted to meet Pete's [my cousin's] new fiancée. But I'll get back to this maybe later when I answer this letter. As to the Texas context, see Confessions!]

And then your letter ends with the husbandly advice I so cherished, always.

> Since you are there [in Arizona] first for a vacation and a visit, then for a stay – provided *you* want to, I want you to listen to this husband of yours when I say I want you to take it easy for a spell – I want you to go to Prescott and visit the girls – I want you to see as much of the state as possible – I want you – in other words, to rest up and relax. After all, the State of Arizona is noted for its health-giving properties. Take a good rest and don't worry about a thing – not even me. Cause when I get home, you're going to be a busy little gal, keeping up with me – returning all my stored up love – having little Junior and Terry Lee – cooking my dinners and sitting on the arm of my chair. And honey, that's going to keep you plenty busy!. . . You are the only thing that counts in this man's life! Be happy! Be cheerful! Keep smiling! Keep remembering – I love you dearly – Forever.

And Baby, that's some letter!

15 Feb 45: You're not too happy – the mixture of squads:

> Our section is full of new guys and for quite a time we've had a few troubles in the way of arrangements. Here I am a happy man but soon I'll be tearing my hair! By the way, honey, my hair has come back in a little thicker. . . I used to be a blond but with seven layers of dirt I can't tell just what color I am now. It may even be gray – what with all these inspections, etc.

On the 16th, you seem extremely sad – full of reminiscences which I have quoted in part earlier. You end with – and I sense real despair in this –

> **16 Feb 45:** As each day passes my gratitude to you increases, my gratitude because you are the one my love grows stronger for as every hour passes – you, my darling, are indeed my sunshine, my hope for happiness, my hope for life – You are the one – the only one – that I can say I love you so dearly. Thinking of you, Your Neb P.S. I miss you, too!

17 – 18 Feb 45: Again, you ask why I have gone Southern Pacific instead of the Santa Fe. Then you discuss books – you evidently are having time to read and tell me you have just finished reading Thunder Mountain "which is oozing with sex," and is a good story too – [I can't find the last page of this letter. Maybe it "burnt itself up" before I got it!!!??? I later find that it has been severely censored and cut to fragments.]

19 Feb 45: You have not received mail from me since my anniversary letter on the 14th and I can tell you need a letter badly.

> "Without a letter from you for a couple of days and with rain spattering down, a despondent feeling has crept over me. Maybe with the dawning of a new day and another Sunday, I shall receive a few sparks of good cheer from you." The 19th is shower day! "I took a regular shower and I mean with hot water too. . . and good old Palmolive soap. A room was rigged up and big vats of water supplied heat – after the water was pumped up from the muddy creek. Here I had just finished washing the second layer of dirt out of my hair and the soap was running down into my eyes – when the vat ran dry! What pain! What misery! Eyes burning and no water! I had to wait a full ten minutes for water to wash the soap out! You ought to see me hopping around – yelling for water! But I'm clean, at least, or rather I was awhile ago. . . Where, oh where, has the little mail gone!?"

[You chicken, you. I went 42 days without a single bit of news that you were even alive!!]

20 Feb 45: Happy Day! Not because you have received mail but because you are finally back with Emile Heintz's section. Your old sergeant and your old Dog House Gang – those that are still alive. So you're happy with your friends and you find another high-spirited horse, and you all proceed to have some fun in the sun. Life has picked up for you after so long a time and I am so comforted.

21 Feb 45: On the 21st you're either drunk or demented. You pen what I can only call "An Ode To Spring." Your spirit is soaring "the birds are singing their glad songs; the fields, once well-tended, are awakening to the energies of a new life." [I'm sorry, honey, but this is so unlike you I can only break up in laughter – not <u>at</u> you but <u>with</u>

you.] But this section I do not laugh at- – I sense your longing:

> When the spring season turns the wintery corner, a young man's fancy turns to love - Love of a home, of peace and happiness, of a wife who waits patiently for his return. There can be no better season for hope of a new and happier life than the season of spring. So that is how, on this wonderful spring day, I sit so forlornly with my thoughts full of a world that could be – a world full of peace and neighborly love, without the angry recoil of guns sending their messages of death through the pure clean air. It is for such a time I hope – I earnestly pray for. . . I dream of a house with lawns to be cut – with fences to be fixed – with you beside me while tiny arms creep about my neck. . . I dream of the complete happiness that only you can give me – all these things are to be mine when another spring commences in the not too distant future. How insignificant the short space of time this war is compared to an eternity of love and happiness a man can have with a wife like you – so faithful – so understanding and so beautiful! Is it any wonder that on this lovely spring day this young man's fancy turns to the deep love he holds for you – only you! Is it any wonder that he loves you so, Always Neb.

And I defy anyone who reads this to believe that this was a man without spirit and soul and love. Sweetheart, this was and is the man I hope to love through all eternity!

> **23 Feb 45:** For 11 days now I have had to more or less, go on loving you without the benefit of reading of your love of me. Of course, I have reread a few of your old ones – especially the one of Feb 5 – but now I hope to read some more soon that says "I love your so "Your Neb

24 Feb 45: Still no letters. You are wondering if I have changed my plans about going west. You are anticipating your mother's disappointment if I have. If I have, you are afraid I won't receive letters you have been addressing to Mesa. You write in a kind of desperation:

> Darling, oftentimes you remark about your letters not being this or not being that. During the last two weeks I have missed your letters almost as much as I miss you! Naturally, sweetheart, I know that you have written and that the delay is over here somewhere, but the long waiting has given me much the same feeling that you must have had last December. I don't really believe that you will ever quite understand that your written expressions, regardless, are as food to a starving man. They are all the personal contact I have with you, they are the only things that are precious and dear to me in this far away land! You must know, my love, that whether or no you are bawling me out for drinking too many beers with the boys, or telling me of a new dress, movie, or telling me of the great love you have for me – all these are the food I must have to keep me happy amid all the horrors of war! So you see just what a delay in mail has for me – and for my buddies! But I have hopes that very soon the situation will be as normal again. When that happens, I know I shall read of smiles, of loneliness, of love and of great happiness. For when you are happy, my own darling, I am also happy and nothing, no not even mail delays, can ever or will ever, make me lose faith for a future, hope for a quick reunion, or a love for you that truly fills every pore in my body – for I know that I love you deeply, Your husband, Neb

25 Feb 45: Still no mail, but you admit that it has only been two weeks and you have fun writing about the Pony Express delivery. You had wanted to grab a plane and meet the train when it got to Mesa – wondering if I would have fainted, kissed you, or beaten you with my famous rolling pin. You expect me to write everyday now that I am there and to tell you all about my trip – and all the troubles you expected me to have:

> I bet I'll get a kick out of hearing of the travel troubles you had on your way out! All people have travel troubles and are you to be different – Oh no! . . . you don't think you can get away from travel troubles, now do you?. . . and if you didn't write me while you were on the train, the last three days – I'll just mark it down in my little black book and a great day will come for the accounting of the books! Heh, Heh, I've already got one black

> mark but I ain't agoing to say what it is – I'll wait until some dark night then I'll spring like a cat and scare you wiz it!

[Of course I can honestly say that I scarcely had any difficulty at all with the traveling because Daddy Gwin had made such careful preparations for me and I seldom have difficulty with people in any situation. Furthermore, I have written you about the trip – and on every single day, too. And I suppose the "one black mark" is because I wouldn't "tell that guy on the phone" about our getting married!] It's a good thing that with all your threat, you end with:

> My every thought, my every prayer is for you, with you and about you! Is it any wonder, my darling, that I love you so – Your Neb (I think I could really "make wiz ze love to you this night! Yeah man!)

26 Feb 45: Four letters from me today, but they are quite old, the ones missing from your "Book" – the 13th, 14th, 16th & 17th. You tell me not to worry about sending the things you've asked for that I haven't already sent, instead you:

> need some kind of a light, even though I have a flashlight. I wrote Dad to send me a carbide light but if you can run across some other type run by flashlight batteries – then send it along. I mean a light that spreads the beams and doesn't make a spot of it – say something like a railroad lantern! As I do most of my reading and writing during the long night, I need some kind of light better than a flash light.

[My dear, do you realize that giving me a request like that is somewhat similar to me asking you to go pick out a brassiere for me? It's entirely out of my purview! Although, come to think of it, when you came home, you did stand in a long line at Korricks to buy me some very scarce nylon hose. But, of course, all the ladies made a fuss over you and let you go ahead, because you were still in uniform with all your battle stars! I never did try to find the lamp – the only thing I failed you in.]

So my darling, I have read those sweet words that mean so much to me and once again I am just a happy, carefree boy! Of course, you know what those sweet words are – I love you so,
Your Neb

28 Feb 45: And February ends with you happy because "Ohlsen, the sweet kid, has brought me a total of nine wonderful letters. Seven of them were yours from the 6th until the 12th and the other two ones that mother had written." You are happy because your mother is happy that I am coming. Naturally, you're afraid she'll spoil me and you say, "I want to do it when I get home." You have been concerned from my letters at my being so tired and you urge me "to take it easy and rest up. Then where-ever – when-ever – if-ever you go back to work – just don't work so hard cause I really do hate to have you tired -every night!" Then, of course, you are worried because I have mentioned some of the boys having come home on furlough: "I hope none of those furloughed boys were some of your old flames or I'd send my green daggers clear across the wide blue ocean to haunt you!" [Dear love, in our whole life together, there were times you might not want me (for one reason or another!) But you sure didn't want anyone else to have me, either!]

3

"Oh, Brave New World!"

Darling, as I have re-read our letters of the month of March and begin to write this section of my letter to you, I find that I am disturbed by an almost overwhelming melancholy, a grieving kind of sadness that I don't understand and which, to be honest, has left me weeping. Everyday in this month, I have written you long letters filled with so many first-time experiences. I marvel at the beauty of Arizona, from the Valley to the mountains of Prescott. I have met your wonderful family – and been literally swept up in welcoming arms of love. Something I have never experienced in the whole of my life. I have sisters now and brothers-in-law and nieces and nephews, who seem to truly adore me. I have already made friends with other young women who actually like me – something which previously, life hadn't provided – except for Dot and Leona at the Dog House after I met you. I have been to your church and been welcomed by young men and women alike. And I have even found a good job at the Arizona Department of Licenses, having been interviewed and hired by the Governor of the State, himself. What is it that is missing? What is it that I feel?

I begin to re-read your letters. I learn that you are now undergoing a full time training schedule, with classes to attend that you hate. But I also learn that it is "also the close of another period of complete happiness in my life. . . the greatest fact is that my love for you grows daily, deeper and more filling than yesterday." On the 4th, you have received seven letters from me and your "heart's singing with joy and happiness. . . darling, how you belong to me! But you don't belong to me half as much as I belong to you. Every hair, every cell, every bone and every beat of my heart is yours. . . " But then, in your next letter I read this strange passage:

> **5 Mar 45:** "You know, honey, combat does some mighty funny things to a person, but thank God that I am the same old husband you married just seven months ago. I've seen much and heard much more but I'm more deeply in love with you than ever – Should it be that we are apart in the next seven months or seven years – I know that I shall love you as deep and true and a great deal stronger than I do now!" [Why does this bother me, now?]

On the 8th of March you have obviously moved again – you say cryptically – and I now know that your letter of February 17th had been severely censored and half of it missing:

> **8 Mar 45:**. . .took a turn into Germany, then came back to live in houses for awhile. . . it looks as if I'm going to be rather busy the next few days. . . If one could only believe all the good things he hears over here, then life wouldn't be so bad! They tell us one thing and then a couple days pass when up pops all the bad things a man can take – One of these days we'll get some of the good parts. . .

On March 11th (You've missed a day and you will miss writing 7 days this month – this is unlike you even in the midst of battle. What is happening? What has happened?) You write:

> **11 Mar 45:** Being so far behind the lines now gives us nothing to do to speak of and I fail to see why that will help us to get home sooner. It's not that we've moved back any – it's because the lines have moved and we haven't followed them except for a couple of days, then we come back to a position that we have been in for quite a time. What I'd really like is to move forward as fast as we can go and in that way all the boys will be able to get back home all the faster. . . .
>
> Because it is Sunday, two kegs of beer came in . . . and I've had several good old brews. Funny how little things like candy or beer or movies can mean so much out here. Over here getting rations is like getting a pass to town. . . tomorrow we have another movie, which most of us will go to regardless of what the picture might be. . . .The last letter I got from you was the one you mailed in El Paso. . . [and you are anxiously awaiting further news.] Sweetheart, I must be content on this Sunday remembering another when you and I spent loafing on the floor reading the papers and otherwise being lazy. One of the most enjoyable days I ever spent in my life – It was on that day when the deep love I have for you started to blossom and to grow into the most important phase of my life. . . Always Neb

12 Mar 45: You have received the letter I mailed on the way to Houston, and are evidently surprised that I have not had the travel problems that you had predicted in your February 25th letter:

> I've always thought that I was a pretty good traveler but you got me beat seven ways to Sunday. What with all the help you had from nice young men getting your bags on the train – then even trying to be a Cupid's helper. My, My! What a gal I met up and married with. With so many service men on the trains today – I am glad you met a nice guy that just wanted to talk while you were waiting for your train. There are too many that will try to get a nice gal to talk with and then try to get her to "shack up"

> with them on the way. I must admit that I wondered if you'd meet up with that type, but I knew that it wouldn't do him any good. I guess I've seen too damn many guys, ordinarily good guys, that are on the make when they are away from camp. Or maybe it is the tall stories they all tell when they come back. Anyway, I wouldn't trust any guy with my private life – if a man can have one in this army?

And here, again, I'm left with a question – what has happened? But at any rate, I will reply to you in my letter of the 29th: "Incidentally, I'd almost forgotten your little expression "shack up," and by the way, you seem to know how soldiers act on trains pretty well! – the Voice of Experience?!?"

13 Mar 45: You have finally received the box I sent you with the stationery and the socks and candy and other things you have no use for now: You continue:

> . . . I may not get the chance, honey, to write you again for a couple of days – we have some traveling to do and you know I can't write while doing that. ..It looks as if I'll be out of this war for awhile. Just how long I can't say, but I'd much rather stay here than go beating around the countryside somewhere. . . I took a good shower yesterday and changed into clean clothes for the first time in weeks. It sure did increase my morale, just to be clean once more. Damn near froze last night though. It seems dirty clothes keep you a lot warmer than clean ones even if it isn't as healthy. And of course, we have had our stoves, a distinct advantage over a lot of other outfits.

You will not write me again for four days.

> **17 Mar 45: Back in France:** . . . Just what we're doing back in France I don't know nor how long we are going to stay. But it will give us a good rest. Our outfit is in a big building that used to be a sewing factory – We sleep on regular army cots and I might say that it is crowded as hell – There is no plumbing in here and we have a rather tough time washing, etc. – But there are a lot of bars in a block or two and Kirk and I drink a beer

now and then. For the next couple of days, I will be busy with this and that fixing up the joint and the equipment. Then a training schedule has been made out for us – hikes and drills – everything just like the States. It makes me wish I was back on the front lines – We had it a lot better up there. . . My darling, I love you so much and miss you so damn much that I think soon I shall go nuts with my longing for you. Love for you, Your Neb

Your letters of March 18th-22nd (you do not write on the 19th) are filled with response to my letters written early in March when I have arrived in Mesa and am discovering all the new things. One letter involves your answers to my concerns about religion making a difference in our relationship. You write: "Did I marry you because I loved you or was it for religion? It wouldn't make a damn bit of difference if you were a pagan. I love you. You are you!" Then you are concerned about your mother's influence: "There is a lot of difference in Mother's and my opinion of the Church. She is inclined to be narrow-minded about some phases of our faith, whereas I ignore many of the old fashioned ideas. Rather I mean the interpretation of the ideas is old fashioned – as is the usual viewpoint of people 20 and 60, anyway. – If you want to look into mine or any other [religion] your decision will be agreed upon by me."

In the letter of the 20th, you begin:

20 Mar 45: By golly, I must really like the beer of France or some wine perhaps – cause here it is a couple of days since I've written you. I really ought to bash myself in the head for slipping like that. Our training schedule is in effect now and after hours there are a lot of taverns across the street and around the corners. But right now I don't think you'll mind my catching up to my beer, eh? Just for a little while – okay?

The 21st is a brief message concerning censored mail your dad has received. The 22nd you have received three more of my letters about your family and my stay. And then you conclude:

22 Mar 45: Honey, I found I am 64th on the list for passes to Paris. . . Outside of movies every night and a couple of beers,

> there is nothing for us to do around here – I hear tell of a dance to be held soon but even that is a rumor. We are enjoying ourselves as much as we can, however – it is better than the mud of the front at that. Regardless of what day it is you can rest assured that I shall be missing you and loving you. . . .
> Your, Neb

On the 23rd, you have been on a ten mile training hike. . . . "When I got back dinner was ready so we ate then Kirk and I took off on a pass for the town. Naturally, the first headed for was a bar. Do you know we had to go to five before we got a beer. . . " And then you tell me "every afternoon we play ball –" and the letter continues for two pages about the ball game you have played that afternoon.

And it is as I end this letter that I know I need search no further for the reason of my "overwhelming melancholy," that "grieving kind of sadness" that I hadn't been able to understand as I began this section of March letters. For here, laid out in subtle details of your changing life is the genesis of what will be the ironies of our mutual "brave new worlds." Most overwhelming to me just now has been the shock of finding that an important element of our love has changed. *I will no longer be vital to your survival,* as I have been the last eight months! *I will no longer be the anchor of your life,* as I have striven to be through the long, dark days. No longer facing the horrors of the battle, free from the imminent threat of imprisonment or death, once more among your friends of the past, a newer, safer reality now begins to define your existence. Despite the ennui of daily routine, the boredom of the training exercises, the bleak, uncomfortable barracks environment, you have an expanding social world. You have movies every evening; you are able to frequent almost nightly the French cafes and bars. The USO is available – and there might even be dances. It is almost Camp Atterbury revisited. You write:

> We have found another Dog House. . . All the gang goes there just like they did the Dog House in Indpls. Get about 20 guys in there and then try to move – It is worse than a crowded bus – but at least the boys are together for a couple of beers – Couldn't find anything to drink so we went down to a USO show. . . There you have, my darling, the things that I am doing for amusements – the usual training, complete with parades is

> followed also – in fact it is beginning to be just like Atterbury except that I can't jump on a bus and come home to you!

But then you do conclude with words of love:

> And I want so very much to come home to you. Every hour, every minute that feeling increases. Right now is just a blank spot in my young life – I shall not live again until I reach out and find you in my arms. My darling, I love you so very much and miss you so terribly. But I know that you love me and that ours is a love for All eternity – Your Neb

As I review what I have just written, I am asking myself if I regretted these changes in your life – the freedom you would have after the ordeals of the past months? If I sensed the implications for our future in your need for freedom and excitement – and beer? I think not, because our letters were criss-crossing and thus did not have the immediate impact that I can absorb reading them now. Did I ever wonder if there would be another "Helen?" I really don't know – at this point, anyhow! But this one thing I did sense. In your mind, at least unconsciously, I was no longer your major concern, your first responsibility. I am "in my place," in the midst of "your family," where the "green-eyed monster" will no longer worry you!

Your last three letters of the month – again you will not write on the 30th – my letters are coming in quickly, assuring you "that I love you." You get another package – late and the sweater is too big. I tell you the MIA lesson has been on the Seventh Commandment and ask if you know what that is? You tell me that naturally you know what it is but think it a funny subject for MIA. [Did you never suspect how many service men were meeting together in that group?] In telling me of your love and my letters, you write: ". . . without your daily letters, it *would have been*" impossible for any happiness to come my way." [How strange to me now is that use of the subjunctive!] Tomorrow you go on pass to Paris, the City of Lights.

4
March "Reprised"

And now I find, in the light of the discoveries I have made as I re-read your March letters, that I have need to re-evaluate my own March letters – to search for currents, revelations I have not seen before. In several of your letters you have written that you "sense a note of happiness and fun" in me, that you "know that I am happy and having fun" and that everyone in your family is "crazy" about me and that Anne, Stell, your mother, all wish me to stay with them, and I am free to choose... But in your March 25th letter, you have written: "Darling, I wonder if you ever feel sorry that you left Indpls and went out there. Naturally, I know you wish I was there with you but under the circumstances, I wonder how you feel about it all."

I had to search through my April letters to find the answer I sent you: 8th April "I'll admit that once in awhile I get lonesome for that old town and places and things that I'm familiar with, customs I'm used to. I miss my folks, particularly Jerry. I get tired of these little modern houses and really long to see big houses like we have in Indiana. But I'm very glad I came here and I wouldn't be back home for anything. I'm glad your family isn't too disappointed in me and as long as they can put up with me, I know I'll be content to wait for you here." But even as I read these lines, I recognize the truth behind the optimistic words as you, my dear, apparently did not. That is, having uprooted myself from the only home that I had known – my sweet apartment – having left my parents' home which had never held anything but unhappiness for me, having cut myself off at your insistence from every friend that I had – I couldn't help that they were male – having no job to return to and a subsistence of $70 per month from you, *what on earth could I have done??? Without you, I was more alone in the world than I had ever been!* This is what cries out to me as I again peruse the letters from March. And what else cries out is that only in the one brief quote above from you on March 25th, do you perhaps sense that all might not be as blithe as it seems. Nor do you ever seem to realize that *my existence now* depends upon you! And upon your letters.

I read this in my March 2nd letter: "This has been another lovely day but I've been so lonely I could just have bawled a couple of times today." Maybe it was just a touch of nostalgia or something but so far as you're concerned it's been a bad day. Looking over your family picture books, I'm worrying about your past life and its good memories for you and I write: "I'm kind of wondering if after all these things, maybe your life with me may seem like an anticlimax – just a part of a settling down process that you may not like so well. I don't want it to be like that – I want to be remembered as part of your good-time days too. . . I couldn't bear to think of you wishing you'd kept your vow to be a bachelor" And then, I'm terribly concerned about the Church: "I don't know whether I could ever make such a radical change in [my beliefs.] . . . What I need right now is just a good firm hold on you so I can put my head on your shoulder and have a real good cry. I know I shouldn't worry you with letters like these but I just have to get some things off my chest once in awhile." And then I end with: "You must know my darling from this letter and the hundred and some others that I've written that I love you with all my heart and soul. If you don't know it, you never will. Each day you're gone seems longer and lonelier and my need for you gets greater. Please don't find another cookie over there but hurry home to be mine." And in another very wise letter – I think – I reveal:

> I can remember a time when I would have been afraid to express real and deep feelings. But with you it's so natural I never even think about it – my heart tells me I love you, so my pen sends the news on to you so that never for a minute need you doubt that you're everything in my life. When two people are really in love, the problem isn't, as so many people think, to keep each other guessing, but to keep each other believing – not through fancy words but from expressions straight from the heart.

And as I read these letters to you, written from my lonely heart, I see not only my love for you increasing, but sadly for me, your love, after the middle of March, changing in its emphasis.

It is in my letter to you of March 8th – when I have received thirteen wonderful letters from January 6th to February 24th, that for the first time I will write, in answer to your questions about my health- because I had missed writing you my daily letter:

> *March 8, 1945:* For two days I suffered like hell – the third day I was given some kind of sulpha drug and presto, I was well. . . About my "pet pain," I won't say my side doesn't hurt because it does, but not too much or too frequently. And it's been that way for a long time so it'll probably continue. My "pet pain" is just part of me anymore. But never fear, I'll keep myself so I'll be ready for anything when you get home. I wouldn't miss that second honeymoon. And as for Junior, I can handle him too when the time comes. But please, honey, don't plan on him exactly nine months to the day when you get home. I'd like a little time to be a wife instead of a mother. Just a little while to play and dance and have a good time with you before I start my role of nursemaid. . . I haven't changed my mind about the little monkey but it really won't make a lot of difference if he's a couple of months younger than he could be. As for the little gal, give her a couple of years after Junior!

[And, of course, always in the back of my mind was the thought that I might not conceive and this delay might soften the blow for you. But you would not know this until you read this last letter which I am now writing. "Oh, how the best laid plans of mice and men". . . and Helen. . .] I conclude:

> I wish I were there with you so I could give you a kiss and tell you how much I love you. But even if I were it'd be like explaining the distance to the sun, or the sands in the ocean. I'll only say I miss you so much, your kiss, your laugh, your arms around me, just every little thing about you. All my love, Helen.

And in the observations of the above may lie the answer to many of the problems or questions which were to come our way not many months later. And certainly, in them, you must hear the crying of my heart. And I am wondering now, how two young people could keep alive, after such a short marriage and so many months of separation, the fires of love!

5
April Letters

As though the tears of the March doldrums are being washed away by the warm airs of spring, so are my melancholy thoughts of the past month of letters eased and warmed by your April letters. To quote the poet, Spring is truly in the air for both of us.

After a few days in which you do not write, your letter of April 5 – our eighth month wedding anniversary – tells me again that all is right with the world, that you need me, and especially that you love me. You return from your visit to Paris, revivified and full of all the things that you have seen and done. Your description of your activities and sightseeing recalled for me the year that you and I first saw Paris, together – October 1987. I, like you, had been there once before. But together, you and I explored, in love and companionship, every detail that you relate in your letter:

> **5 Apr 45:** We left our billet area by truck and got in gay Paree 3:15 minutes later – as it was necessary to wait for our passes and rooms, we finally got settled. We were lucky enough to get a Red Cross Hotel right in the center of everything.

[I am reminded by this that the very same thing happened to us when you finally returned home and I met you In L.A. It took us over three hours to have the Red Cross find us rooms – after those long months of waiting – and another two hours to finally get registered. Those were among the longest hours of waiting I can ever remember! I wonder why!?]

> After eating a very good meal at the Club for 10 francs (20 cents) we took off for the clothing exchange and shower department on the outskirts of town where we all got a

> complete new outfit – plus a shower. After that we started for the cafes and high spots. There was one street called Pigalle – a street of bars, cafes and night clubs – the hottest spots in Paris. In every one of the places you could get any kind of a drink that France has. . . .the bars were beautiful with music and mirrors and beautiful women – everyone of them a prostitute – I got a kick out of watching one redhead – in 45 minutes she had 3 guys up and finished with 'em. I asked one guy how it was and he said "it" happened so fast he didn't think it was worth 300 francs (6 bucks). I am thankful honey, that my love for you is strong enough to chase such gals away. I haven't "cheated" on you and I don't believe that there is a woman made on earth that can make me forget what a great privilege it is to love you so.

Needless to say, my faith in you had always been strong, but these words did much to cure the ache that had oppressed me during the March letters. You continue for six pages, telling me of your visit to the Follies: "It was the best hottest show I ever seen [sic] with more beautiful gals- I saw one that reminded me of you so much I almost cried – I wish so much for you to be with me to have the fun I was having."

The next day you and your friends – I don't know these men – toured the city by bus, went to a dance at the club where you jitterbugged with a WAC, and went to the hospital to visit some of the boys who had been in your Unit. You do not tell me any details, and of course after your return home, you say nothing about that at all. I never do learn exactly who was killed or who wounded of all those boys I knew in Indianapolis. You simply cannot speak of it. You end this letter:

> I got blisters on my toes and now I am limping like a cripple! Finally I caught the trucks and am now back with the boys. Had a lot of fun and spent a lot of dough so now I can go on with my army 'stuff'. My darling, so rolls to a close 8 months of happy married life – what a swell person you are for keeping me extremely happy and grateful that I was the one you married. . . within my bosom swells a heart so full of love – so full of longing, and all for you. . . I love you so – Your husband, Neb.

I can easily see from the next letters you write that your pass to Paris has really revivified you. Now you write wonderfully descriptive passages of the countryside, references to the money situation in France, happiness that I am with your people and that they love me so much, as I seem to do them. In your letter of April 8, I know that you are again subtly telling me that you are in a different camp, that just outside your tent there is an old bomb crater with fresh running water in which you can swim.

> **8 Apr 45:** Tomorrow we put up our bigger tents and get set for more living here. We are to have regular cots, electric lights, radio speakers – plank floors and walks. After awhile, this place will really begin to look like a real camp. The grass made good sleeping last night but I was cold for the first time. Just as a sample of Army chow on a Sunday – I just finished a dinner of meatloaf, potatoes, fruit salad, tomatoes, bread, butter, and peanut butter. Darling we are going to town for showers – Always on a Sunday my missing you is greater than any other day but every day is a day I love you so Neb

> **9 Apr 45:** My dearest Darling, The first day of our new training schedule seems to indicate that from now on the training will be worse than ever before, even that of the States. I was on detail today but the boys said it was going to be tough. . . Reveille is before dawn (4 A.M.) and right after that is calisthenics. . . all in all it begins to look that we'll be garrison soldiers again. . . .We are supposed to move in to the big tents tonight. The POWs [prisoners of war] put 'em up today but not enough – so for the night we will sleep 10 men in a tent. They really hold 6 men as they will tomorrow. How would you like to share my bed roll with me now in my tent? Too public, eh?

And then your life sustaining words of love.

10 Apr 45: You are really down today. Is it because you are exceptionally tired from the training or is it the despondency that seems to hit us both, almost on the same dates. You begin:

What a hell of a day! I have missed you so terribly that several times I almost reached the breaking point. And then to make matters worse no mail again today! That makes five days in a row and I need them so very much now – my morale has hit an all time low. The mail train better find us again soon or I'll blow my top. . . . I find my love for you increasing so fast . . . what words can I use to explain the beauty of the love I have for you. . . .It will be almost a year since I first met you – a year full of the sweetest, dearest memories a man ever had. . . Memories of past summers and years have fallen along the wayside and only the beauty of the past year remains.

You know, darling, it seemed so natural for me to be there [in my apartment] after the first few times. I always marvel at the ease of our companionship. . . Because of that ease, I have wondered if you had thoughts of marrying me before that first night we talked of it? It seems that I know you must have but I'd really like to hear what you thought of it.?! Naturally, it had been in my thoughts for several weeks before I could loosen my tongue enough to form the words. But God, I didn't know I was going to love you so deeply that every part of my being would pain so because of this separation. Had I known, I would have run off with you sooner. . . My darling, I love you. Yours forever.

And so I know in May that my fears of March were vain. You loved me – and you needed me.

11 Apr 45: Today we spent mostly in bed since there was a 15 mile hike last night [you are now over half-way to being 26 years old! Isn't that quite strenuous for that age?]. . . .The only work we did today was an hour cleaning the gun. . . the army is a funny thing – up on the line where we fired the gun everyday, we cleaned it up every chance we got – sometimes not for a week. But now we have it in fairly good shape and still spend an hour a day on it – just to put in time. All in all, I've been in the army two years and now find myself in basic training again! What a hell of a life! I see that they are stringing wires for the lights in our tents. It won't be bad at all when that's finished and the radio speakers are put in. Right in back of the tent street is our ball field – in the corner of the field is a volley ball court. So there is my "home" – the only thing lacking is showers and "etc." – that still is in the primitive stage.

In this letter, you tell me for the first time that you need money. You haven't been paid; you're still paying off your "fine;" and you borrowed money from the Captain for Paris. You dope! I've wanted you to stop sending me your extra money. I will send you the money the day I receive this letter. You end with your truly horrible verse: "it would be swell/ For a kiss on your lips/ To dwell! I love you so."

12 Apr 45: It's hot; you're thinking of me in my white two-piece bathing suit; you have severe laryngitis and the Doc has told you not to talk for three days. You are going to a movie on the wet grass and the bugs are bothering you. And you remember the very first letter you wrote me back at Camp Atterbury, when you were asking me to come down to camp for the week-end. Of course I still have that tattered 61 year old letter, written as you were waiting for a movie to start out on the camp field: "They're setting up the movie stuff and the sun is going down so before long the great event will start. I wish you were here so you can shoo these gnats away – Then maybe I would hold your hand." I didn't know we would be married, then – but I kept the letter for some reason – and I wouldn't take any amount of money for it today! As we were both to say, so often, we were simply "fated!"

It is in this letter, also, that you tell me:

> ...the last two nights have been dream night and both times they have been of you. They are the first for a long time – maybe because for the last week my missing you has been the worst it has ever been! I can't remember many details except I was a civilian and I came home to you after working in a mine all day! One night we went to a movie and I sat looking at your beauty instead of watching the picture. The other night was a bedroom scene.

[And I think I will close the door and leave the reader here.]

Darling, I must tell you right here – that even now, these letters of yours are bringing joy to my heart and to my soul. They cancel out so many memories of the silences in your last days of suffering when there was no way I could give – or receive from you—the love that joined us, despite all the obstacles. Surely, the Holy Spirit has led me to this task which I have undertaken.

13 Apr 45: 5 Letters! – all the ones you have been missing:

> You'll never know how very much I enjoy your letters. The boys think I'm nuts at times when I laugh while reading 'em – like when you wrote of Dad helping you with the dishes. Or about your 'train experiences.' You see, honey, I don't just read your letters, I live it with you. . . It looks as if I'm about to have competition. I'd better say lots of sweet nothing to you or I'll lose you to one of my nephews. I knew that those kids would like you, but, damned if I thought I'd have to fight 'em off. By golly, darling, not only the nieces and nephews but the folks also seem to have fallen in love with you. Mother is so pleased with you, dear, and she said Pop was really having a time with you. . . It seems to me that you are good for the family and the family is good for you! . . . .Your leaving now would be the same to them as when I left – in fact, more so.

[How wonderful it is to read these comments from your family, because I had somehow often felt that your mother, especially, had been unhappy with your not marrying "a member of the Church." That was always her first question about anyone: Is he/she a member of the Church?] This letter of the 13th is six pages in small script and ends with:

> Speaking of love, sweetheart, did you know that there is a P.F.C. [oh, you've gotten one of your stripes back?] that is going crazy because he loves you so damned much? That there isn't an hour goes by he doesn't long for you? Did you know that this guy is Your husband?

14 Apr 45: Saturday, an Inspection followed by a Division Parade with a lot of standing; and then you pull guard duty, during which you write me. The troops have heard the news of President Roosevelt's death and

> are stunned by it – if only because we wonder if it is going to have any effect on our coming home. . . they said in tonight's paper that the war would be over in Germany in the next few days. . . .In my opinion, it will be a couple of months then a few fights here and there for a couple of years. It is those couple of years that I'll be sweating out and I hope my name won't be on that list. But at least I feel that I'll be coming back in one piece however long it will be. God has been kind to me with his protection, so far, and I am praying he will continue to be so.

And then you promise me to "take me out on the desert on a clear moon lit night – I'll bet you jump when you hear the coyotes howl – hope you jump right in my arms!" Sweet husband, you never did take me out on that desert night even though I asked you to. You obviously, by the time you got home, wanted *nothing to do with camping out,* ever again!

I almost forgot that it is in the letter of the 13th, that you also address my worries about things I have been reading in the church books – particularly about baptism by immersion by the proper authority and also the necessity for "eternal marriage." I really don't understand it and am deeply concerned about "holding you back" in some, to me, unfathomable way. Comfortingly, you try to assuage my fears:

> Hey now, what is all this bout you holding me back in some future time? Do you think I'm going to let you feel that way because of something you read in a book? When I fell in love with you, I wasn't going to let anything stop me from having you, because I do love you so. . . . Don't worry about it, little chum.

[How was I to know that I would be destined to worry about it for twenty-five years, until you finally decided to "tie the knot" leading, we hope, to our eternal union?]

April 15, 1945: You receive on this Sunday, my anniversary letter of April 5th and now have all my letters from October 10, 1944 to

April 5, 1945 – minus only the four when I have been ill. You have not done quite as well in your writing, [but I give you an A-plus and think you are qualified to teach a graduate class in "How to Write Love Letters."] My anniversary letter – as you call it – goes thusly:

> Well congratulate me, darling, I'm celebrating my eighth wedding anniversary! (Sounds important, doesn't it?) No one would ever guess it was only eight months instead of eight years, would they? You know, you really ought to get married yourself! There's no life like it. If I didn't have such a grand husband, I'd be delighted to marry you myself. But I'm not sure my husband would approve. Of course, he neglects me terribly – trots around all over the country and leaves me here at home – but just the same I loves him. However, I might play Cupid and help you find the right mate for you. I'd choose a fairly small girl – say 5'3 3/4" – that would make you look bigger and stronger by comparison. She should weigh about 115 and I think she should be on the blonde side – that way all your children would probably be tow heads like you were. Of course, she'd have to have freckles – otherwise your dad wouldn't approve. Not too serious, but she ought to have at least one brain in her head. Above all, she'll have to love you heart and soul – monkeyface and all. What about it – think she'll be hard to find??
>
> This has been such a lovely day that I wish I could write and tell you about every single second of it. I can't understand what makes everything so wonderful. Even at work I don't get tired or bored. I just rip through the day and the days are much too short. . . the days are so full and busy and everything is so lovely that it's like having a song in your heart. And I know every morning when I wake up and see the sun and smell the flowers, I know surely and strongly that someday soon you'll be right here seeing it all with me. . . . Need I say that I love you or do you know that I do and will, Forever, Helen

And suddenly I remember that this is the way it was here in Arizona, after I got through those blue, blue days of March and felt the coming of Spring. But always underneath the joy runs a current of sadness: "Hurry home so you can show me how pretty the desert is in moonlight. A little romance and moonlight is what I'm craving –

providing you're my partner." The fire of Spring is always there for the young – even when one is married! And, almost identical to the letter you have written to me on the 12th, I write:

> Tonight as every night for the last nine or ten months, I find myself so much in love with you that nothing else matters. On second thought, it's not been nine or ten months – it's been a full year that I've been completely, madly, head-over-heels in love with you. Someday when we haven't anything else to talk about, I'll tell you the exact day, month, and almost the hour that it happened. (Didn't think I had such a good memory, did you?)" And I still do.

My April 15th letter is shrouded in gloom. The national grief at the loss of F.D.R. is impossible to comprehend.

> *April 15, 1945:* I often wonder if you have days when it seems that things will never be right again? You never seem other than happy in your letters and sometimes I wonder if I'm abnormal – you know, a case of psychosis. I hope I get at least one letter from you tomorrow. It's been fifteen days since your last letter was written – and I want to hear about your pass to Paris. . . . I can sit here and think back to so many lovely Sundays we spent together and I want you here so badly. I don't think I'll ever take being with you on Sunday for granted because I'll always remember days like today when you weren't here.

And so, with our mutual longing and words of love, the first half of April, Eliot's "cruelest month of the year," is over and spring is waiting to be born.

6
"Spring is sprung/ the grass is riz. I wonder where/ the flowers is."

For you, the last days of the month have begun in the heat of the European sun, with the ever constant threat of rain and the constant whine of mosquitoes, the grueling grind of the new training system, constant guard detail, and the competition of the soft ball tournament. On the 20th of the month you are playing for the championship of the Unit's Battery teams. I assume you win, but do not know for sure because the next letter I receive is that of the 24th. Obviously, you have received unexpected orders and you are on the move again – being transported by train quite a distance into Germany. You write:

> **24 Apr 45:** For the first time in several days I have the chance to write to you. I am miles away from where I wrote you last and right now I am sitting in a boxcar somewhere in Germany. Sorta reminds me of the times I saw men on the bum – riding the rails here and there. I am just as dirty as they were too – but it won't be long before I can wash up again. Awhile back I was almost certain that we were on our way home, but orders change and who knows when that great day will come my way. . . Coming through France I saw some mighty pretty country and it was country I had never seen before. Join the army and see France is the by-word now. There is very little of the country that I haven't been in and I expect when they finally get through moving us around I'll have seen that part. . . The train ride up here was pretty interesting and somewhat cold! At night I crawl into my bedroll in the box car but during the day, I'd be out on a flat car looking at the scenery, sunning myself or reading the war news. We'd stop every so often for a couple of hours and have chow or stretch a bit – so all in all it was different than

riding the trucks as we have been doing up to now Although I am further away from you than I ever have been.

[You get around the censor so cleverly. Imagine only having one letter completely rejected by that officer, up to this time. You are a smart cookie! And I can assume that you are now occupying the towns that have been over-run. I also know that you have been guarding German prisoners in your previous camp.]

Guarding Prisoners of War - WWII

25 Apr 45: Sweetheart: Oh what a beautiful day to be in Arizona. I could really appreciate the warm sun or the green trees, if I were there with you. . . Oh yes, we could listen to the birds sing and watch the bugs buzzing around. . . however, here I am with a bunch of boys, waiting in a bunch of trees, across the Rhine somewhere in this damn country that started all this hell!! I wrote you a letter earlier today but the little man with the scissors said that I couldn't send it as it had some military information. In all the letters I have written that is the first I have ever had returned.

As we came through towns yesterday evening, the people, what few there are left, just stood and watched. Some tried to wave and be friendly but no soldier would wave back – so the people would just stand there and watch us roll by. From what I saw as we passed through towns, I should say that if there is another war after this one, it will be well over 25 or 30 years from now. It should take the Germans that long to rebuild. If I was on the Judgment seat, I'd say flatten all their towns, cities and villages so that they could expend all their energies into building something to live in instead of building things for destructive purposes. Take for example – a city about like Indpls and blow up all the buildings until just the walls are standing. Then chase all the people away and you have about what is happening to these "war starters" over here. Oh no, there is no love in my heart for any of these damn Germans – ought to shoot them all – then maybe Americans could live in peace for a long time!. . . .A Jugful of kisses to you from Me and Junior – You beautiful thing, you!!

26 Apr 45: Darling o' Mine,. . . .This tree I am leaning against is not quite big enough for both Kirk and me – He is reading a "murder mystery" while I write you and over against the next tree, Wendley is writing to his WAC. Heintz is over there playing ball with Hallberg – we are all just loafing around for today is "Sunday," at least we are considering it Sunday even though it is really Thursday. Now when Thursday does come around it will probably be Sunday. . . The Army does strange things to people!

There seems to be a law that it will cost a man $65 to get caught talking to any German. We can't give them anything or receive anything from them. Who would want to anyway is beyond me. There are plenty of civilians, mostly the very young or old but some young babes about 19 or so. There aren't any young men around to speak of – they're all in the army or dead, I guess. It was a lot different in France and Belgium – there we could talk, etc. as much as we please, but not here. I'd like to talk to them with the speaking end of a rifle – anyway I can't speak German! So my darling, as the spiders crawl over me day and night, my thoughts of you and our future home linger – But as Junior was saying the other night, "I want my Mama," and you are the only "Mama" I'll have from now on – I love you – Neb How's for a kiss/Me pretty Miss?

[My, you are a goon – and I prefer that to the great hatred you have just expressed for the conquered German!]

27 Apr 45: Another place! My Darling, Here on the wet grass in a different part of Germany, I sit. For the first time in a couple of months, it has rained hard upon your husband's pup tent. Not only that but the wind is blowing and I am cold. Seems that winter hasn't left yet – I shall probably only have time to write you short notes – there is so much to do. We have to fix up the place we are to live in – and take care of our other duties as well. Once we get set up though and get on some kind of schedule, then things ought to be nice for us. We are to live in buildings and I understand they are good ones – with big rooms, baths and electric lights. That will be quite a treat after living in tents and such for the last month – gotta close – guard duty – I'm longing for you.

28 Apr 45: Cold again: Instead of sitting on wet grass and writing you as I did yesterday, I am laying in my "sack" still freezing and trying to keep the pen from shaking. Took a little trip with Hallberg to another town today but the truck we were to come back in didn't show up so. . . we hitch hiked! Hitch hiking in Germany – yes sir quite the fun. It was plenty easy though – all we had to do was to stop a truck, get on and ride to where we are and there was nothing to it. Only instead of a truck we got a ride on an "Alligator" – that is a truck and a boat combination. It was hard to tell if we were riding a highway or a river – it was that rough!

29 Apr 45: Two letters today! . . . the Army has slipped us a low blow again! We work plenty hard cleaning out some German barracks for our living quarters and just as we get them in shape so we can move into them – up comes a Major and tells our Colonel that we can't have them – Instead a Negro outfit

moves in. . . .Those barracks were really the stuff! Great big rooms, double beds and individual closets with plenty of floor space for comfort. The only major repair needed was new window panes and there were thousands of those in the basement – Oh well, just another army trick! For the time being we are still in our pup tents in a wet grassy field and it looks like we'll be for some time yet. I don't mind that so much except that it rains a hell of a lot and is cold much of the time. Maybe they can find some other buildings for us later on!
Everyone has their ears glued to the radio and they make a dash for the newspapers. It looks like the end is pretty well in sight – there's not much left to overrun and . . . what is left of the Germans is fast being taken. I was guarding some PW the other day and even they wanted to know when it would be that they could go home. Just how soon, after this is over, I can come back to you is what is bothering me now. . . .I hope I can keep that first anniversary date with you!

30 Apr 45: Little Gal, . . . I see that I forgot to thank you for the brand new dollar bill – so now I thank you! It will be supplied with all the major items of the overseas experiences of one Aquila Chauncey Nebeker, Jr. That is really the only souvenir I desire of this stuff going on over here. Some day I shall forget I was even in the Army. Oh happy day, come speedy my way!

Now we are to build our own houses! Of course we are to sleep in our pup tents, but we have to build some kind of house to get out of the rain. With all the places around too. I sure wish somebody would get on the G I Ball and do something for the men once. I begin to wonder when all these breaks we read about will come our way. Ho Hum – I think I am finally getting fed up with this army life. I loves ya!

Neb with his mess kit -- somewhere in Europe

Darling, as I conclude this month of April letters, my heart simply aches for you and those of your friends who have lived through the Battle of the Bulge four long months ago and have known scarcely any degree of comfort since that time. Certainly, you have received none of the glory that the people back home know you are entitled to. And when I think of the long nine months you have yet to experience before you return home – not to even think of my months of waiting – I can understand the violence of your feelings about the Army and your service in it. I'm not sure I fully comprehended it until I began this project of mine. You were indeed, a valiant man. And your wife honors you!

7
But In Mesa

My letters to you the last half of the month are full of response to your letters – and news of my daily living. On the 17th, I have received the details of your Parisian adventure and I write:

> I'm glad that you didn't take advantage of some of the "fun" the other fellows had but you didn't have to tell me that you didn't. To even think of you "cheating on me," as you put it, would mean that I no longer love you as I do. When you love someone completely, you trust them completely! But I was interested to hear about the girls. Poor kids, maybe that's the only way they have to make a living. The way you talked about the beautiful women, they must be something. . . But I don't care how beautiful they are just as long as you don't begin to wish you had married a beautiful girl instead of me.
>
> I can't help being happy that you're somewhere in France rather than Germany, but that camp of yours sounds far too permanent to suit me. I've had such visions of your being home soon. Besides that, I can't help thinking that this stiff training program of yours means more and tougher action – maybe in the Pacific. That's one thing that really frightens me. . . .How are the blisters on your feet? That WAC must have been a pretty heavy dancer to do that to you. If they're no better, better tell the General you'd like a few days off to rest and recuperate. I'm

sure he'd be glad to accommodate. . . Before I bid you adieu, I must tell you that just anytime I'll share your bedroll. The other guys in the tent can just tend to their own business! P. S. We'll try that "triplet" suggestion of Rae's when you get home over my dead body. One cousin at a time is enough for her. And if there were three, little chum, it won't be I who will be carrying them on my back. If I carry them the first three- fourths of a year, from that time on you can do the carrying! So think twice, my friend, before adopting my young niece's suggestion!!!! I loves ya.

April 18, 1945: My first April in Arizona evokes this bit of poesy:

Just the 18th of April/And what do you know/It's so doggoned hot/I wish it would snow! These unsympathetic Arizonans are consoling me with "You ain't seen nothing yet!" Maybe I'll have to go back to Indiana just to get cool It was so warm today that I decided to change from my winter apparel of hose to my summer attire of bare-legs. Already my legs are as brown as they were last summer. The lady I work with told me she didn't approve of bare legs – it was indecent! But I stopped her sermon by telling her if she thought that was bad, she ought to see me in a bathing suit. She had no come-back so left me in peace. . . .Sweetheart, if I could tell you how much I love you, I would but since that is next to impossible, I'll just say goodnight, sweet dreams; I love you so.

April 19, 1945: In reply to your letter of the 11th, as to when I first fell in love with you, I reply after deep and honest consideration:

I suppose, from the first night I met you, I was unusually drawn to you – not that it was love at first sight – just that I knew I liked you. First of all because even though I hadn't had a very proper introduction, you didn't act as though you thought I was a common little pick-up. And even when I let you come up to the apartment, you behaved yourself pretty well. But I wasn't falling in love. [I have already given some of the details in an earlier section so won't repeat them.] Then on our first real date – if you recall the USO, I had a good time even though I felt rather

> uncomfortable trying to crash the gate. After that, it was just a growing affection for you. That ten easy lessons course you gave me helped a lot plus whole Sundays spent together. . . .But I was still fighting an internal battle because I was still determined to be an old maid. Even that night you first asked me, I didn't know. I thought maybe what we both felt was a passing fancy – besides, I thought you were drunk. . . .Anyhow, it simmered in my mind until I knew if it wasn't you, it would never be anyone. I still didn't like the thought of the physical part of it – I was afraid. But that day at the pool [I've already told you about that] I knew definitely, for sure, that I was in love with you. I wanted you so desperately I knew I couldn't stand it if you weren't my husband. Then you asked me again. . . That, in short, is my love story. . . . It doesn't tell of the happiness in my heart those few weeks before August 5th rolled around. . . It doesn't say much about how I worried for fear I wouldn't be right for you, be able to make you happy, especially the first few days after we were married. And I never can tell you how much I loved you for being so patient with me, trying to show me what you could and letting me get used to being married. [And didn't I learn well, my love, oh didn't I learn well?] Until tomorrow, I send my love to you and once more I remind you, I love you – forever – Helen

And so go my "sugar reports" as you call them throughout April. I tell you all the details of my life – going to the dentist; agreeing to be a volunteer at the "Hospitality House," a service club for the military in Mesa. I did hard labor there, too, the first afternoon cutting and squeezing *twelve gallons* of oranges, lemon, grapefruit. I washed dishes, swept floors, filed records and arranged flowers for the recreation room. "By that time, I was so tired I could have dropped and I was all prepared to take it easy. But the head lady caught me and asked if I could possibly come back at eight because they were short on hostesses. . . ." And then I write of the dancing etc, concluding:

> To be perfectly frank, I enjoyed myself thoroughly. . . As for dancing with the boys, that wasn't my idea at all, but even that was fun. The boys cut in so fast I didn't even have time to ask

their names so there was certainly nothing personal about it. Inside of me, I honestly believe they need me at the canteen and I know that whatever I did down there would be strictly on the up and up. But if you aren't happy about it – if you feel that you'd rather I didn't, I want you to tell me. I don't want to do anything to make you unhappy. And I couldn't do it without telling you. . . .but they've asked me to help Friday, Saturday and Sunday, and I'd like to. . . After dancing with all those kids tonight I wanted so much to have you there so you could hold me close and I could really dance and enjoy every single dance. When I'm having the nicest times, I'm the loneliest for you and as far as I'm concerned, God never made another man. I'm so terribly in love with you that there could never be anyone else.

April 22, 1945: It's Sunday and I write you:

"Mother is still at Sunday School – I just know your mother thinks I'm a heathen because I don't even go to Sunday School, let alone church. I know I should go but it gives me too much time just to sit. I'd much rather stay here at home and be doing something. I used to go to church all the time and I'm ashamed of myself. But if I don't enjoy it, why go? Mom never says anything – she certainly is lenient with me." Then I tell you about my afternoon at the Canteen – cutting and squeezing more fruit for punch – but I "drafted a partner and it didn't take long. After I finished all that, we played some music and you should have seen the kids around the piano singing barbershop harmony. I stayed until seven and then bade them all adieu. Mrs. Kinsey asked me to come back Thursday and bring a cake so looks like I bake Wednesday night."

I walk home alone, in my very first dust storm.

I was rather afraid because the wind was blowing hard and the sky looked so black and turbulent. But in a way it was beautiful. Walking that distance I thought of you and missed you every step of the way. It's that way all the time – the only thing I can think of is I want to be close to you, feel your arms and lips until I think I'll go crazy. If I'm not thinking about it, I'm dreaming about it. Another six months without you and I don't know what I'll do. I still think I had better come find you!" And then, curiously, I mention "those beautiful girls you saw in Paris didn't make you rather regret the fact that you had a wife at home, did it?"

I end by telling you that, of course, I have already consulted with your mother and she has given her opinion that there is nothing wrong in working at the Canteen. And I have reminded you that you have felt free to visit Paris and the hot spots and to dance with a WAC at the USO. [So I am not expecting your disapproval. But I will wait for your reply.] Perhaps fortunately, I get your lovely letter of the 13th!

April 24, 1945: I write you a long six page letter. My last week or so has been boring at the office because I don't have enough to do. I am really suffering from the 97 degree heat which leaves me completely exhausted. There is a chance I could lose my job because the State is cutting the Highway Department's budget by 50%, so by the 1st of July I'll probably be out of a job – new employees are always the first to go. I am concerned about your parents and my intrusion. In a way, I rebuke you:

> . . . I doubt if either of us will realize until our son brings home a wife, just how hard it must be for your folks to get used to a daughter who has been raised in an entirely different environment. I know that sometimes your mom must be aggravated with me and yet she is always so sweet to me. Please honey, don't send your folks any more instructions on how to treat me. In the first place, it will make them think that I have been complaining to you and in the second place, it hurts their feelings because they try so hard to make me feel at home and they think you feel that they won't. Besides that, there are times that I feel that I ought to be told what to do and I want their advice. Like when I decided about working at the service club, until I could get a letter from you expressing your feelings. . . But if you tell them not to boss me, they won't feel free to even offer advice. See what I mean? Anyhow, we seldom disagree on anything – 'cept I know Mom's disappointed because I'm not interested in Mormonism and I don't care to go

> to church or MIA and the rest of the stuff. I can't help it because I lack interest. Maybe when you're home it'll be different. She never says anything, though, and I don't worry about it anymore. So if I'm to feel free to discuss things with you as I always have, you'll have to promise not to let them creep into the letters you write her, because I love her and don't want to hurt her either directly or through you. You have a wonderful mother, I think, and I wouldn't trade her.

This is how I always felt about your dear mother – although, because of you, I would have to hurt her in the future. But as I read this letter from the vantage point of being a mother-in-law myself, I think – that for an eighteen year old wife – this letter is quite thoughtful, loving and mature, don't you? But I have to include my ending to this letter – not because it's good but because always I am trying to express my deep love in a different – if not better - way.

> Sweetheart, I thought you'd like to know
> That someone's thoughts go where you go
> That someone never can forget
> The hours we spent since we first met;
> That life is richer, sweeter far
> For such a sweetheart as you are.
> And now my constant prayer will be
> That God may keep you safe for me.

[Honey, I've had graduate students that couldn't surpass "them thoughts." And how many husbands have wives who write "poetry" to them?]

April 25, 1945: Just everyday doings – six pages again. My conclusion (always trying to keep you interested, of course):

> For the 193^{d} time I bid you good night via a letter. That's a lot of nights (plus the four I missed writing =197) to save up love so don't be a crazy kid and ask me if I "want to make with ze love tonight." I don't think you'd have to worry about me not being in the mood. Of course, it goes without saying that that applies only to you and to no one else. "Loving" by itself stands for

absolutely nothing in my life but "loving you" – oo-la-la! P. S. If you sign your letters 'Your husband, Me,' how am I s'posed to know which husband?!

April 23, 1945: My dearest sweetheart. . . Those dreams of yours about taking it easy and reading your paper while I "remodel our little love nest" makes a nice dream – but that's all it is! Don't you know, my darlin' that the only reason I'm getting all that experience [on a girl friend's house] is so I'll make a good supervisor for you while you do all the work. So "dream" while you may. The time is coming!

[This letter is received out of sequence, hence its order. But I didn't want to ignore the significance of your dreaming.]

April 26, 1945: It's been cooler but when it reaches 113:

I think I'll probably be dead. I took my cake down to the service club and the boys seemed to like it – at least there was none left. All of the fellows tonight were British boys – a nice bunch – polite and mannerly. They seem very bashful and quiet on the whole. One – just out of high school – spent quite a bit of time telling me how they played cricket and soccer, but in the end I decided I'd take football and baseball. The English are good dancers, too. They haven't the sense of rhythm that American boys have but they evidently spend hours learning exact steps and then working out variations. But most of them want to learn to jitterbug before they get home. As well as they dance though, there isn't anyone who can begin to measure up as well as you do. – I won't say it isn't fun to dance because dancing is always fun, but with these kids, it's strictly business – or whatever you want to call it. I like to know they're having a good time and at the same time I'm hoping that people over there are being nice to you.

I also hope that you aren't disappointed in me for wanting to do something like that. It's rather hard to put in a letter why. It's not that I wanted to meet fellows or anything like that – as I'm afraid you might think. It's just that all the girls at work do something – even if their husbands are here – and I felt so left

> out. And besides, it's been good for me. On the nights that I help, I know they're depending on me and if I'm in a not-too-happy mood, I know I have to get over it fast or else I'll spoil someone's good time. It's something to look forward to – just as you like to look forward to a beer with the boys. Don't get the idea it's just fun – I've worked darn hard there since I've been going. But it's different from a day's work at the office. It's something I'm doing for someone without pay and it leaves a nice feeling. If you are hurt or disappointed in me then I'm hurt and disappointed in myself too. For I have tried so hard to decide if I should do it and what you'd think of it. But I'll know for sure when I get your letter.

April 28, 1945: Upon rereading this letter of the 28th, I am mystified, because you cannot possibly have received my letters concerning working at the Service Club in time to write back to reprimand me. But I am apologizing to you for:

> being the most stupid, inconsiderate fool that was ever married to the sweetest husband in the world. And that's for even thinking of the stupid canteen work. . . .I never realized how you would really feel. . . I didn't stop to think that no matter how much you trusted me, you wouldn't like to think of me dancing with anyone while you weren't here. . . So sweetheart, if you will say you forgive me. . . never again will I think of anything crazy like that. It's strictly "all off."

I really can't remember why I decided to quit. Was it because I was thinking of how I felt when I knew you were off to Paris and seeing the beautiful women – or at the USO dancing with the WAC – or did some service man "get fresh dancing with me," as you suggest in your May 8th letter? The one "bawling you out" for giving advice to your parents. In that letter, you are obviously miffed that your intentions about that have been misinterpreted. Your words are, "I shall keep my nose out of things so far from me. For the worry I have caused both you and my parents, I humbly beg forgiveness – no use in saying I'm sorry but the true fact is I really am!!"

But I know you well enough to feel your anger. Then, to me, very broadmindedly – but scathingly – you write:

> Darling, had I known your opinion, I would have suggested the USO or the Service Club or whatever it is. . . the letter you wrote concerning starting there hasn't as yet been received but later ones have and I want you to know you have my full approval. It rather surprises me that you would think otherwise about it – Of course it does make me jealous as hell to know my wife is dancing with other Joes. But on the other hand, I know you'll have fun and get a kick in doing so.

[How broad-minded you are my love!] And then the venom fairly drips!

> Naturally, I know the hardships encountered in, shall I say the "ordeal" of being married with the husband overseas and by now you must know that it is plenty tough – being tough on you is nothing compared to how tough it is on me – what with everything so damn free over here. But you know what I mean and I'm afraid I'll mess it all up so I'll just leave it at that.

Yes, I *do* know what you mean. And I truly "thank God" that I had remembered your jealousy in time to mend my mistake and apologize before you have time to rebuke me in any way. But then, immediately after this reminder, you catch yourself and write sweetly:

> You have fun at the club, you hear, and remember that your better half is over here waiting for the day he'll be sailing back to you and there's no mistake about that.

And then you thank me for the pictures I've sent, concluding with:

> I know that back home there is a wife waiting for me with a love that is true and good – a love that is comparable with my own – one that is strong and beautiful – one that sings – I love you so. Where's the bathing beauty snapshot? I like 'em!!!!

The matter of the Service Club is finally concluded when you receive the letters I have written you on the 22nd-25th. Your final comments are:

> But whatever the reason you decided to cease the Canteen activities has, frankly, made me happy again. . . As long as you seemed to want to go, I was in agreement but I must admit I did feel slightly uncomfortable about it. There are plenty of nice guys that go to the clubs but there are the other type too, and those are the guys I wouldn't want to be dancing with my wife. When anything concerns service men, you'll always find the type of guy that is looking for a "shack up job" and they seem to think a married gal is the easiest. [Will there always be this double standard?]

But to end my month of April, Anne and Milton and Jerry and Gene have been down; Dad has gone and "I hated to see him go. You and he are so much alike and while he's here, it's like having your laugh, your smile and crazy way of playing jokes on people."

And as our ninth month of wedded bliss draws to its close: I'm lonely; I'm missing you. I'm wondering "where the flowers is." And if they will truly ever bloom, for me, for you, for us.

Part VI

The Sands of Time

1
Sweating Out the Peace

The month of May is to begin for you with the receipt of all my missing letters up to through the 19th. You are extremely happy – especially with the letter I have written about when I had fallen in love with you. You write:

> You'll never know how much I needed that, to build up my courage for the time remaining that I may have to spend over here. To know once more the love you have for me. . . .The first night I had any idea I was in love with you was one night last June when I was out in the field laying in a pup tent. That was the night I knew my 25 year search had come to an end – Course I had to bolster up my courage like all other young men [and then you write of "our little difficulty" my lack of sexual experience – sorry, men, but you can't have innocence and experience at the same time!]. That situation will always be an example for me in other troubles that come our way. A little talk now and then can always solve any major item, honey.

So May Day is happy for you and then on the 2nd it snows and turns cold again and you come back from a little trip yesterday, to find that your outfit has been moved into real houses. [I am now able to conjecture that these little trips you are continually making are probably the transporting of newly surrendering troops (some 290,000) throughout all of Germany to the vast "Caging" areas that are being constructed. The chaos occurring all along the Rhine was massive beyond comprehension, according to Dupuy.* And the 106th had been given this almost impossible task of transporting and guarding the prisoners, as well as building accommodations for them.]

*Dupuy, Colonel R. Ernest, *St. Vith: Lion In The Way.* Nashvile: The Battery Press, 1986.

May 2nd you write:

2 May 45: Each section has a house all to their self and the houses are all the same – Must have been a government project – it may have been like our defense Projects back home. The houses are the same in rooms but the one we are in hasn't any furniture – although we have a table and a few chairs. I was lucky enough to round up a regular bed with springs and everything – except a mattress – It reminds me of another time I slept on a bed without a mattress only that time I had a much better bed partner! We cleaned up the house somewhat and started to live in grand style. No one knows how long we will have to be here so we are going to make it the best we can. At least now we can sit down instead of squatting! If you get what I mean. That is something and no lie! [According to Dupuy's record, at this time there were absolutely no sanitation facilities except for "straddle-trench" latrines.] It seems that we will have to make a raid to get us some comfortable chairs and good tables. . . I hear tell of radios . . . one of these days. Then we'll really be enjoying our life here! Darling, the day the news comes out that Hitler is dead finds me very much in love with you and being away from you makes my heart strings strain for want of you. . . .Neb

3 May 45: Good News Day: The month seems to be the day we are waiting for so long – at least the way the news has been coming in the last few hours. Everywhere the Germans seem to know that there is no more use to fight any longer. Why, I'm willing to bet my last mark that this war will be over in another week. Then maybe we can start working on getting me home. . . Honey, we are getting settled fairly well in our house. It is better, at least, than sleeping in pup tents and freezing to an iceberg. We got a regular set-up for washing our clothes and I'm going to do a lot of cleaning up. I must have almost every piece of clothes I got dirty. We have a couple of stove irons and that will let us put a crease in pants that for months have hung like sacks. I expect for shoes to be shined before long – then we'll really be "Garrison soldiers."

5 May 45: You write: 9 Wonderful Months! And then you send our now usual anniversary thoughts to me, but in this one you add:

> Honey, it seems to me that Jr. should have been raising his head now but I'm glad "it" won't happen until I can be there and be a civilian once more. After all, an event such as that should really happen when I can see the little tyke the day he appears and not a couple of years after. But until that time I'll have to be well satisfied with my present Jr, until the day comes when I can do the job up right – with your help – of course, you sweet kid you!

[Isn't it interesting that you never once doubted that we would have a Junior – while my thoughts always pondered the possibility that we would have neither?] You continue:

> My darling, the goal I have in sight, and one I shall always keep in mind, is to make you happy and to keep you that way – If at the end of 50 years you can say, 'Darling, I'm happy, then I shall feel that these months of separation have been but moments of longing and waiting.

[If we had known the long road of struggle and sorrow and pain and disillusionment awaiting us, would we, could we, have endured those seemingly unending last eight months that lay ahead, before we held each other close again? Or was there, really, any other choice?]

The next week of letters is almost too difficult for me to read as I try to continue to write. They are so full of contradiction – the war is over in the minds of the gang. You and Kirk, and Emile and Pete and Hallberg are still together. You have better physical comfort, even a radio. You are even getting some rest between guard duty. All the boys are carrying my pictures around and you can't get them back. "Darling, they tell me the war is over but I've been hearing that for a week. They say this time is the straight stuff and if so that is great news, but I guess that won't affect me for awhile, at least, but I got hopes." You tell me to go back to Indpls if I want – it's natural to want to see the old home place. The 8th is, of course, your letter of rebuke, which I have already commented on in relation to the Service Club matter. But the letter of the 9th is full of expectation and joy at being safe, even as it is also reveals to me a sad awareness of the many problems that will be involved in your returning home. And there is an undercurrent of uneasiness, a tension. About where we will live and what we will do after the great reunion. This tension will be so obvious to me that I, myself, am full of tension and apprehension even as I am writing. Maybe it's because I already know, and suffer, the minutes and the hours and the days still to come. A time of separation that will be as long as the one we have already endured. Even at this time in my life, I cry out at the loss of time and youth and possibilities for these plodding days.

> **9 May 45:** My Darling . . . I long to take you in my arms on this day of happiness and tell you of a love never heard before. I say this day of happiness because, all over the world people know that it is one day after V E Day – the day you and I have waited for so long. It is on this day that we can feel rather assured that bullets and shrapnel won't be flying around in the air, as I have seen it so many times. . . It is on that day that the process of waiting really begins. Heretofore the day of reunion has been just a day of hope – but now it has become a reality – with, of course, the exact time, day and month a matter to wait for. . . I know that it shall be a great deal harder to wait until that happy day when you and I shall be together – at least for me – than it has ever been before. Now I have no purpose of being here to keep me occupied – all I know is the longing to be home with you – however that very happy occasion may be postponed for a time. The only hope that makes this existence possible for me is that someday I shall be enjoying the sights of Arizona with you.

And then you go into the decision as to where we are going to live, what you may choose to do for a career and conclude:

> In the meantime, many great days are centered on the love I have for you. You and God alone know I love you truly.

10 May 45: You are once again a Private – and this time you have no redeeming factors to call upon and very shortly you will hear from me about it. You and your Peck's Bad Boys have celebrated V E Day belatedly, and have flooded a wine cellar:

> I never saw so much wine in one place in all my life – there were stacks and stacks of great big kegs all over the joint. It seems the celebrating of V E Day was just a little too much for the lad – anyway the Captain said I was too "noisy" and now I am a private. I'm a happy man regardless. For a long time we haven't had a decent recreation program – so we find a wine cellar full of wine and make our own amusement, only this time it seems that my amusement is going to cost me a little dough. . . .When we were at Rennes we had a beautiful recreation program every night but here we don't do anything but our duties and that gets mighty tiresome. Of course that isn't an alibi for me getting so damn drunk. . .

Of course, this time, you are going to hear plenty from me – and you are not going to like it!

13 May 45: Mother's Day and I get greetings from you and Junior. You are trying to figure your "points" toward a discharge and know that you will fall short of the 85 necessary. "With all my figuring I can't get more than 47, but I have hopes of complete victory [Japan] before many months have passed and I'll be known as a civilian once more."

14 May 45: You are now free to tell me the areas in which you have been the last months:

> That time last February when we got that 5 days rest we were in a little village near Liege, called Villers Aux Tours. That's where I stayed with "Pop." Most of the time while we were in combat we were around St. Vith, Malmedy and Stavelot. That was all in the First Army's sector. We stayed in that part of the country until after the Ruhr River battle, then we went back to St. Quenton, France. That's the place where we lived in a factory and that's where I had the 3 day pass to Paris. When I got back from Paris, we moved to Rennes and started basic training all over again! From there we came up here.

And then, again, you share your details of your comfortable, easy times during the Ardennes battles:

> I wrote several times about how soft we had it. Actually, we were only shelled in two positions and then only a few came in. There we were with three squares a day, warm dugouts to sleep and work in – and we'd only fire about 20 rounds a day. Actually for us the war over here was a picnic but it wasn't for others. The shells that came our way didn't hit too close to where we were except a couple that hit in front of us. . . .

I guess I will never really know the extent of your danger.

16 May 45: You receive my first letters of May, tinged with:

> undertones of unhappiness – something that is bothering you – giving you unrest of mind. I sincerely hope that the three day despondent mood has passed and all is rosy again, but if it hasn't, you just unload your troubles on your better half and I shall lend you my shoulder to cry on! . . . It gives me pleasure to know that there is one who shares the simple pleasures that I do. It gives me courage to face whatever may lie ahead of me at this time. . . I'll always bear my love for you honorably and honestly. . . .

2

"Tomorrow, and Tomorrow, and Tomorrow Creeps in this Petty Pace"

Your sensitivity to the desolate undertones of my first letters in May, suggests that I have done an inadequate job of keeping up your morale. This beginning of another month does find me plunged in deepest gloom, though I have tried to hide it. Work has been extremely demanding and the State is bankrupt and I haven't been paid. But maybe, if I lose my job, I might go back to Indiana; I'm worried about being so long with your parents. My "pet pain" is emerging again. But the truth of all of this is that my heart and my body are pining away for you. I do not yet know how deeply my health is going to be affected in the next months. It is a fact of my whole life that my mind, body, and spirit are one – and when one is suffering, the others are affected. That is exactly what is happening to me as I write these words. As the anniversary mark of what would be our 61st year of marriage approaches – and I remember all these things – my heart, my mind, my body is aching for you. Age does not really change us, as the young so often think. "Personally, if you don't get home this summer, I know I shall die – which reminds me – I took out some insurance day before yesterday with you as beneficiary, so if you don't get home, I'll know you just wanted my insurance!!!!" But most of all, I believe, I am worried about the impact that time can always have on any relationship. We change, we forget, we give in to loneliness, we grow. Knowing this, I write longingly:

> . . . if I leave you alone too long, I'm afraid you'll begin to get bachelor fever again – you know, that "free, white, and twenty-five" stuff. . . .I hate it because I want so much to be near you but I never worry for fear anything will happen between us. I know there will be times we'll both get plenty lonesome and blue, but I know that I, for one, will never try to ease that loneliness by the companionship of anyone else. And I know that no matter what happens you'll always play fair and square with me. When I read so much about the incredible numbers of divorces and lives that are ripped up by separation, it makes a person stop and think. But if it is within my power, I mean to stay just as I was when you left so you won't be disappointed. . . The girls at work call me a freak because I don't run around with other guys but you can count on me continuing to be "a freak." Mainly because I happen to love you so much. What I want to know is, does ya love me? Do you want to kiss me? Are you lonesome for me? Well, why don't you say so? Why don't you Kiss me? Why don't you make love to me? Helen

And so my month goes. I try to fill up my life with busy-ness. I clean the house; I go to a movie; I'm meeting with a Church group of young marrieds – all of whose husbands are gone. All of them have children – or are pregnant. I go swimming. And I have just discovered that your mother thinks it's wrong to go to the movies or swimming on Sunday. But, I tell you, I don't really feel it is, so I will continue to do so – and your mother never says a word in rebuke. But despite all my efforts to stay happy and upbeat, I write you on our 9th month anniversary:

> *May 5, 1945:* I sure would like to go out on a fling, like I have once or twice before in my life – you know, a couple of Singapore Slings and a double Tom Collins, with maybe a couple dozen cherries thrown in! I'm so doggoned tired of being "good" I could scream. So darling, when you get home, you can just plan on taking me out for a good howl. You may have to drink lightly to see that I get back home okay but one night is mine!! Did you ever get so bored that you wanted to throw milk bottles or break dishes or just go quietly insane. Well that's me! But I guess I'll survive until you get home – just don't take too long. . . .I hope this ninth anniversary you're still pleased with your wife and love her as much as I do my husband.

In my letter of the 7th, I ask you if you remember when I sunburned my back so badly "I could hardly stand to wear a blouse and how embarrassed I was when you and Betty tried to convince me that it would be all right to go without one? And another time, in your screwy way, you picked me up right in the middle of the street where everyone could see and carried me down the street? I could have boxed your ears – but still I love the little bit of cave-man in you." [You would do the same thing when you finally came home, picking me up on the steep climb to the Long Beach Amusement Park and carrying me up to the top. I could still have boxed your ears!]

May 10th, I have learned that you are back in Germany and "I really hit the bottom" feeling that "you'll probably be kept there for some time to come. I guess I never admitted to myself how much I was planning on your coming home." On the 11th, I write, "I've been awfully blue today – every time I think that it will probably be at least another eight months before I see you, it makes me sick. Before your letters came saying you were in Germany, I kept pretty happy but...now I imagine it will be quite some time. I suppose by tomorrow, I'll feel better about the whole thing. I hope." But always I am happy that your living conditions have improved.

And so I write every night without fail – letters of four to six pages. And on May 14th, I write you my 212th letter since you embarked. And I have received letters from you through the 2nd of May. In reply to those first two letters of May from you, I comment:

> how nice and long – you certainly were in the mood to 'talk'. Why don't you do that all the time? But then, you're like that – sometimes you talk and talk and other times you just won't open your mouth. Like when I get all nice and comfortable in bed, with my head on your shoulder and want to talk, what do you do? You go to sleep!! It makes me very unhappy. Next time you try that, I'll bet I find some way to keep you awake!!!

[In all our years of marriage, dear husband, you never did get the point of what I have just written. And that is that for a woman, "after-talk" is the final part – and one of the best parts – of love-making! Even if you have to force yourself to keep awake, to your mate it says, "I love not only your body, but your thoughts and feelings." The only thing I can compare it to is how you used to have to have a cigarette after making love. If you had "hung in there" for only a few moments, you might have been surprised at the long- range results. I say this not only from personal experience but from my depth of literary research – as well as from discussions that I have heard from other women! Of course, now it's too late for you to profit from my advice!]

As I write you through the last of May, I make a desperate attempt to be cheerful, send homey news and try to keep track of what the future looks like for us. I go skating, I play volley ball, I've begun to make good friends with the service men's wives.

> *May 17, 1945:* I played volley ball and I made nine points in one game. But I played too hard cause my "pet pain" does really hurt. They are a very nice bunch of girls and since we were all wives of service men, we had lots in common. Just imagine though, I was the only one without at least one baby! And most of the girls were around my age, too. Two of the girls who came over were well on their first baby and you should have heard the others trying to scare 'em. Believe me honey, you haven't

heard anything until you've been in a bunch like that. It was a new experience for me and I really enjoyed it.

On May 19th, in response to your letter of the 9th we chat about Junior again and agree that it is best that you will be around before he arrives. I'm learning to drive – and I seem to be going back at least to Sunday School. I ask, for some telepathic reason, whether you've gotten your stripes back yet – you deserve them, I say. On the 21st we have heard that General Hodges' First Army is now on the way to Japan via the United States.

> *May 21, 2945:* Now I'm in a stew trying to figure if you'll be on your way home or if you'll stay in Germany. Oh, darling, I want so very, very much to see you but I don't want to have to tell you "goodbye" again, ever. And especially if you had to leave me for more fighting. But it's not in my power to decide the issue. . . I'll try to believe in my heart that it is for the best. But I'm not kidding, when I say that even the thought of maybe you'll be on your way home soon sends shivers up and down my back... anything that is connected with you is the main thing in my life.

May 22, 1945: I'm ecstatic – the first shipload of 1st Army soldiers will dock Thursday:

> All I can think of is that perhaps you'll be coming home too. And yet there's always the thought that perhaps you're part of the 15th Army now. . . I do wish I knew so I could settle down. This "up in the air" feeling is driving me crazy. [And then I wonder if you have plans if a furlough is in the near picture:] If you have any ideas, tell me about 'em. I have a general idea – I mean I want us to have more time like we did last summer. I want you to have a good visit with all your folks of course but I do want us to have some time just to ourselves – doing exactly as we please, even if we pitch a tent out in the middle of the desert. I just want to be with you all by myself. . . .With the stars and the moon making me feel oh so romantic, I find myself needing you and loving you in a way impossible to describe. So across miles of land I send My heart forever.

But I've had no recent letters!

Finally, your letters of the 8th and 9th arrive, in one of which I have detected the deep feelings about my "Service Club" project. But in my return letter, I respond in no way that reveals my sense of a kind of underlying threat – if that's the way to interpret it. After all, every one knows what a service man means when he says. "Everything so damn free!" So my letter to you practically drips syrup. No long distance fighting for this little cookie, smart gal that I am.

And, like you, I am concerned about the future: "I wish we still had our apartment somewhere so that we'd have a little to start with – something a little definite. Don't you think it would be nice to be coming back to a place like we had before you left? (minus Betty, of course.) But those things will solve themselves in time."

My letter of the 24th contains these words: "Sweetheart, are you a Private again – your return envelope was Pvt – if so, how come? I never did get the details of the last time." And again, the issue of the Service Club: "I'm glad I decided against the service club, but just the same, I'm glad you thought enough of me to say it was all right. But I didn't decide not to go because someone got "fresh" with me. . . It was just I got to thinking of how I'd feel in the same situation so that was all there was to it!" [Oh for the privileges of the spinster!]

May 26, 1945: The fur is going to fly today. I think I've had about all I'm going to stand from you, even though I begin sweetly with "Neb, dearest." And I thank you for the Mother's Day letter from you and Junior and the information about the number of your points and the places you had been previously. Then I let you have a piece of my mind, as the adage goes:

> To say that your letter of the 10th left me quite provoked is putting it very mildly and I'm not joking. I could understand and sympathize with you when you were busted last time – there seemed to be a pretty good reason for it and I took it as just one of those things that could happen to anyone. But when it happens for the second time – or is it the third – in a little more than three months and especially for the reason that you set forth, I'm really sadly disappointed in you. Your statement that you entered the army as a private and would end as a private, regardless of what happened in between times showed an awful

lack of thought on your part I think. I'd hate to think that I'd hold a job – and being in the army is a job – for over two years and at the end of that time had nothing to show for it except some not so good report on my "Service Record!" I know that promotions are sometimes next to impossible to get but I see absolutely no reasons for demotions. Don't think I don't realize that it's tough on you being over there with not much recreation but I really feel sorry for you if you can't find anything to interest yourself in except drinking the German's "red wine." You know that I've always thought that it was a man's privilege to drink if he wanted to – it was no business of mine. . . but I've a feeling you've been carrying it a little too far. I know a war can upset everyone, not only you doing the hard part of it but even me who you might say, does nothing. Still, how would you feel if just because there were no dances to go to, no you to be with, I decided I might as well drown my sorrows? You'd probably feel just as I do – disappointed, provoked, with a little doubt as to my ability to control myself. I must confess that only once before have I felt toward you as I do tonight – perhaps you remember that other night? I've had my say and I'll probably be the ex- Mrs. Nebeker after you get it. I'll probably wish tomorrow that I hadn't written this but since it is exactly how I feel, I'm going to mail this before I have a chance to change my mind.

Naturally this doesn't mean that I'm not as much in love with you as ever cause I am. But I do think you need to do a little thinking just for your own good. Don't be angry, darling – someday our roles will be reversed and you can call me down. As a matter of fact, if you'll recall, when my thinking hasn't been so clear, you've talked it over with me. I've had my say and nothing more will be said about it on my end of the line. I do hope though that something is *done* about it on your part. 'Nite, dear – If I'm in no better frame of mind tomorrow about the whole thing, I probably won't write. I don't like to write when I'm not in the mood!

And I do not write you again until the 29th. In this letter I apologize – not because I'm wrong in what I've said but because I had no right to "pop off" as I did.

> *May 29, 1945:* Doggone I've missed writing to you the last two nights but I just couldn't write until I got out of my horrible humor. Sunday night – the first night I didn't write – I went to bed at 9:30 and at 4:00 A. M. I was still wide awake, tossing from side to side. The trouble with me is my conscience is too good. . . . I miss you so much and love you.
>
> With all my heart.
>
> P. S. Do you still love me even if I do write hateful letters?

On the 30th, I can tell I'm working off supreme frustration. I don't have to work because it's a holiday, but I clean mom's house from 8:30 in the morning until 5:

> *May 30, 1945:* I took the stove apart and cleaned it from top to bottom – took me two hours – cleaned up the back porch and sorted and dusted all the canned food out there. Cleaned out all the drawers in the house. Then I killed about a million and a half spiders that I found. After that I did a good sized washing and by the time I'd straightened up the house, it was time to iron. I ironed for nearly three and a half hours and then thank the Lord I was through. Now here I sit on the front porch all cleaned up and looking and feeling like a human being. Incidentally, how'd you like to trade me jobs for a little while?

And then I give you the marvelous news that if you get home this summer while the temple is closed, we can have the apartment all to ourselves. . . "it'll be almost like having our own place. I'm hoping and praying that you'll be home sometime this summer." And 61 years after this letter is written, I'm still wondering why the Lord couldn't have indulged me in this one little prayer. Our life might have been so different.

May 31, 1945 finds me at the very lowest ebb of morale since I've been in Mesa. I've written you 227 letters; there is nothing new or happy to tell you. The promise of Spring is gone.

And there is no mail.

And for you, too, May is ending with one rumor after another – now to the Pacific with a furlough in the USA prior to going; now to being part of the Army of Occupation. "Of course," you say, "any change is going to take a lot of time – mostly waiting for transportation." On the 24th you put forth your plan for a furlough:

> **24 May 45:** Here is what I think will be a perfect furlough. When I get there we rent an apt. for a month and live there, just you and me. When the time comes I want so much to have you alone with me – no one else – in-laws, roommates, whoever. Honey, we'll sleep as late as we want – you can burn my toast every morning – we can go swimming every day if we want. In other words, darling, we'll live just like a couple of married people for a whole month – Baby, I can hardly wait to get there to you – now how's that for making up lost time. . . . Say, by the way, don't start reading a bunch of stuff about how to treat a returning soldier and try that stuff out on me – The paper is full of what a mistake that is – actual experience of men who are home. I am just the same monkey that left you and you never can tell when I'll stop on the street for you to scratch my back – or pick you up and carry you – or kiss you hard in front of everyone. . . Forever, Neb

And you will do all that too. But you will be changed!

On the 27th you have my letters from the 1st to the 20th. You are still guarding the "cages," "but a new outfit is coming in to relieve the Unit. Emile has been promoted to Staff Sgt, with the departure of Heintz, and Kirk has been promoted to Emile's rank – You are happy for them. And you are optimistic about making our August 5th anniversary! You reply to my plan for the furlough:

> I want to spend about one day visiting the folks and about 29 days making love to you! And I don't want to be interrupted in that love making by a lot of kinfolk running in and out. . . Now come – furlough of mine!

The last three days of May, for you, are a see-saw of rumors, news about Kirk's furlough to England, maybe three weeks. Hallberg has been poisoned or something – and has been taken to the hospital and your last thought for the month is:

> My darling, you know what I'd just love to do? Crawl into bed with you and make wiz ze love the whole night through. Does that tell you how a man who has been away from his wife 235 days feels? Oh yes – I could reach over and kiss the devil out of you. I'm just waiting to play with the twins again – I wonder if they get lonesome for their daddy?

[I started to "drop the curtain on these words," as I have done once before, but your daughter says "no! That's cheating." So I'll confess you were definitely a "breast" lover. How you loved your "twins." And they were "spectacular," as you used to say. But they became a great embarrassment to me – and I never told you this, dear – when I was baptized in the Mesa temple font, and clad in that too tight "jump suit" they provided, rose from the waters completely revealed in front of all those who had come to participate with me. My complete embarrassment is my major remembrance of that sacred ordinance. Remember, I was a nubile 18, and someone should have prepared me better. But I will admit here, my dearest husband, that after 235 days away from you, I was in complete agreement with your plans for the night because, as you said, "Naturally I want to do all that because I miss you so – and because I love forever."].

3

Fooled With Hope: Hope is a Waking Dream

"June comes busting in all over" and the first two weeks of your June letters are full of news about possible departures, then changes in departures, then unhappiness because you've received no letters for nine days. But amidst all of this there is still a lightness in your constant writings and you do not miss writing a single day until the 17th, when you will go on a short furlough to Namur, Belgium with Yost – a long-time buddy. Then you will return to Heilbronn, where I now know you are. You have not yet received my chastising letter of the 26th and I am holding my breath as to how you will receive it.

On our wedding anniversary I receive another of your wonderful letters of love. You still haven't received letters, but you think Ohlsen may be holding at least one for this day, because everybody in the outfit knows this is your special day. Closing your long letter, you write these words which will again bring comfort to me:

> **5 Jun 45:** For every hour, every minute of a full year now, I have loved you completely and insanely. Never has a doubt of that love entered my mind, never has an ounce of regret pressed my soul – The moments of our darkest hours over here my main worry was about you. . . Surely God has been good to me in giving you to be my wife . . . each passing moment brings me closer to the time when I can hold you securely-tightly in my arms and pour out my great love. . . a love that belongs to you in its entirety because it's you and only you that I love so truly, Your husband.

The next day, 6th, you receive the letter you are waiting for but it is my letter of the 29th, apologizing for the angry one I had written on the 26th. You are not exactly happy as to what it implies and write:

> **6 Jun 45:** I don't know whether to be mad, cry, or tear up that letter when it comes. However, I know this, I don't particularly like to have you miss writing me – even for a day-regardless if you are happy with me or if you are giving me hell about something – after all, honey, maybe I need a week of your hell raising letters – that really shows me how great your love is for me. (Your evident anger about a little thing like being busted made me laugh even though you may have thought it important.)

I have asked you if you have been sick and you reply:

> Naturally I've been sick! I'm sick of being over here – I'm sick about not getting your letters regularly but most of all I'm downright lovesick for you. I miss you so much it isn't funny – in fact it is depressing. . . I want so badly to be with you and to hold you in my arms – to kiss your beautiful face and to hear you whisper of your love for me (if you still have any) [my dear, how could you ever have doubted it?] I want to tell you how very important my being married to you has been – I want to tell you (and convince you) how terribly I love you – and baby, that time is coming soon. . . [And then you add a postscript:] Don't worry – honey – I need to have you give me the devil every day – it increases my love for you.

[You are indeed a strange man!!!!]

You celebrate D-Day (the 7th) with a swimming party at your new Red Cross recreation center and then go off to play another ball game. You have been pitching for several weeks now with much success but tonight in-field errors lose the game. At the end of the letter you write (about the previous day's letter): "I never realized that you were mad at me for getting tight and, as usual you are entirely right – I'm a cad – a low lifer and I'm sorry – but I do know this – I am not sorry that I love you more than anything on earth and will forever." And so another little rift has been mended with thoughtful words and love – on both our parts.

The soft ball games are becoming increasingly important to you. They are tough rivalry games between your unit and others around the area. The "boys" as you always call your outfit friends have won $50 on your pitching. You tell me you never bet on the games because you know you would be nervous and lose. But you sure wish you could bet – and pick up some money for our "honey-moon." After the game, you go to a movie and tomorrow you are going to a USO show – in the wonderful "swell new theatre" the PWs have built.

On the 8th of June, you are writing me at

> "6:15 A.M. – and proves that even in the very early hours I am thinking of you! I guess that there hasn't been an hour – or minute that at one time or another I haven't been writing you. During the fighting I'd write you even at 2 A.M. – or 3 A. M. or 5 P. M. And so on. . . .I am constantly thinking of you." [You are sending home your box of souvenirs. And you close with words that will send me into sheer delight.] "Darling, I am almost positive now we are back home bound! – back to the States . . . by July or the first of August. And it isn't very long before here I come. . . get ready for the loving of your life."

9th June – now the news is that it's probably the Pacific for your group, but with a stop in the States and furloughs. However, you have to train replacements for the 155 guns and then you start on your way – maybe a month or so yet. You still haven't received the "ominous" letter and seem a little worried:

> **9 Jun 45:** I have been curious to know just how bad you gave me hell! Maybe that curiosity will be killed in the heat of your words – but of course, you are right, regardless of what you said – If it will make you feel better, I haven't been tight since that day nor have I raised my voice above a whisper – which is somewhat unnatural for me!. . . You might not know that you have been selected as the "Pin-up Girl of C Battery. And I don't mean because of your swim suit pictures either. It is the "chin" photo [one I always hated] and the "Smiley" photo that done it.

[I had no idea that my pictures had been entered into a competition – although one time I did wonder why all your friends had been carrying my pictures around and you said you couldn't get them back.]

The 10th of June is a Sunday and you reminisce over past days, take a short swim and plan for the night's ball game. You went to the movies last night and saw "Music for Millions," one that I never heard of. But you say, "I cried like a baby for it showed me how you must have felt during December and January when you never received any mail from me." For you to cry like a baby is something in all our life together I never saw you do! I take that back; you cried *with your grandsons*, when you saw Quill's body, but you did not cry with me!

In the middle of writing the above, you receive mail – one which you "are afraid to open," but you "muster up your courage" and decide to comment on it *as you read it*. Your comments follow:

> **10 Jun 45:** I'm sorry you were disappointed in me. I must do better. You seemed not to know that when a man is discharged from the army, he is discharged as a private so that his rank may be filled in by another man – although his rank is held for him if he reenlists within 90 days. See what I meant by coming in as a private and going out as a private, regardless of what happens in between? Okay so far – Demotions happen plenty of times because there are too many of one rank in one outfit – there doesn't need to be a reason at all – i.e. since we have been here there have been 4 staffs, 2 buck Sgts and a number of corporals & PFCs busted for very little reason at all – just too many in the outfit – see what I mean? Score one for you – you are absolutely right about my drinking, however, I assure you it was not as much as you thought – but you are right – regardless of the amount. I hereby promise to cut it out or at least keep it down! I have always been sorry for "that other night" but that's all hashed over before.
>
> I agree with you wholeheartedly about your writing me exactly what you feel – be it happy or unhappy – I love you more this minute because you did write this straight from the shoulder. I am all to blame, honey, and – although the harm's done, I am sorry it hurt you so. Oh my darling, I hope that we will always "talk it over" together whenever any problem arises – you are so sweet and I'm such a louse – You have been right all the way through and I have been an ass – I'll try not to let it

happen again!!" [You see how easy it is to resolve questions when you are in long distance correspondence? And why didn't we continue to write letters after you came home?]

Darling, the ball game is about to start and I must go but I love you more than life itself and would never hurt you knowingly. You must know that I miss you so much it hurts—
Your husband Millions of kisses for you!

You win the ball game and the guys win another $50; the 12th you're supposed to play the 29th Field Hospital team but it's too muddy; you hitch a ride up to see Hallberg and he, like me, has had appendicitis and "some infection has set in and they were trying to draw it out – He'll probably end up with those blasted adhesions like you got but may be back in about five days." And it's turned cold again and you can't go swimming! On the 14th, you really need me to share your bed roll because you are

shivering under a raincoat and an overcoat. But the cold just kept on until I was nigh unto froze. They have the damnest weather over here – when the sun shines it is hot as hell but when it rains it is as cold as any day last Jan. So there I was just wishing I had your warm body to cuddle up to. Bet you a dollar that neither of us would have been cold had you shared my bed roll together!

And it is on this day that you will pitch your first game for the Battalion soft ball team, a game which may change your life. For better or worse I do not yet know. There is a game to be played on the 16th – on which your mates have bet another $150. Again you don't bet because "I'd probably throw the ball all over the lot trying to win – So I do the work and let the boys get the pay!"

On the 16th, you are definitely sure you will be on the way home and want to know just where Lesueur Street is in relation to places you might remember and are happy that there is a phone by which I can be reached. . . "The really tough part is not the 'ifs' of coming home but the 'whens'. It is fairly definite we are going back to the States but no one knows just when we are starting." And you conclude your letter of rumors with:

16 Jun 45: Honey, your letters are becoming important – not only to me but the boys in the battery. They ask me if I got a letter

> today and if I did then they dash out and bet more dough on the ball games – They seemed to think that since I was happy about getting one of your letters – then we'd be sure to win the game. They had close to $400 to bet on the game tonight but the other team backed out of the game. Your letters make me happy because they convey your love for me and every one makes me love you more dearly.

[I think you ought to get a percentage of all that money the boys are making on *my letters*!]

17 June 45: You write that you've just been informed that you and Yost are going to Namur, Belgium for a three-day pass.

> There is a rest camp there and it is our turn to go again. We went through there a couple times during the fighting and it is only a small village but there'll be the USO shows and the Red Cross clubs. It'll take a couple of days to get there and then three days there and two days coming back. So that's a week away from all this [blip] around the battery. When I get back, I hope there'll be something definite about leaving.

You will not write again until the 24th when you return to Heilbronn:

> **24 June 45:** tired, dirty and sun-burned to a crisp. The dirt and dust was flying thick in the back of the open truck, then the sun shone down on us all the two days we traveled. The only joy in coming back was reading the five letters that were waiting for me. The last one was written on June 8. . . there should have been more recent ones waiting but for some reason the mail was held up for several days. But the five that were here filled me with happiness! We went all over Belgium through Luxemburg down into France before we came back to Germany – From Brussels to Antwerp to Nancy-France. We covered all the high spots in between. We stayed overnight in Nancy in a swell place but the town was no good. They closed all the places at 8 o'clock so Yost, Slatten and I got plenty tired walking around the town. . . While I was gone the official word came as to when we are to leave here for the states! We are to stay here

until August and about the middle of that month are to be on our way back home. . . I would have liked to be with you on "our day" but we'll be together at least by Sept. – can you wait that long, darling?

[Have I a choice?]

As of the above letter of yours, you have received my letters of the first half of June, so I think I will turn to them briefly, just to remember what I have written, nothing of import I am sure.

4
Chit-Chat

I was absolutely right. My letters of June are almost nothing except "high" and "low." You are coming home soon – I can almost expect you any time; you are not coming home – it may be weeks. You have received my letters; you have not received my letters. I do write you about Conference Sunday: your mother left at 8:00 and did not return until 5:30 – how can anyone stay at Church that long? I have gotten very sun-burned walking downtown while wearing a sun back dress – I am brick red. I enclose a clipping and want to know "why you have to be one in that measly 10% of men that doesn't wear a wedding ring – maybe you're just ashamed of being married!?" On the 4th, "I'm walking on air, floating on clouds, I'm practically out of this world," because you have written that you are "probably preparing to return home." I assure you I won't "swallow any of that stuff about how to treat returning servicemen" because I "know that you're going to be you when you get home and the only thing I'm going to concentrate on is loving you. And if you have changed and don't stop me in the middle of the street to kiss me, you'll no longer be my favorite husband – I just want you back!!!!"

June 5, 1945: Ten months today: *You are coming home*! "All day I've been in the clouds so happy that nothing could worry me. I sure have taken a teasing today about my smile. My boss told me that it always made sunbeams but today it was the sun itself. He even suggested turning off the lights and saving electricity. But I just politely ignored the whole screwy bunch." My letter shows that clearly I am expecting you any day! And I inform you, firmly, that I do not "putter around the house!"

June 9, 1945: I have read your letter of the 29th which tells me that it may be sixty days before you have any idea of when you will be leaving. I try my best to put a happy face on it assuring you "September before you leave Europe, it's just three months longer I have to live without seeing you but it's also three months closer to the end of the war with Japan. . . In three months time you might even be a civilian, regardless of my not having triplets!" But I, for the first time, show concern about being pregnant:

> One thing, honey, I wish you wouldn't plan on starting the family when you do come home on that furlough. In the letter I got yesterday and several before that, you've mentioned that little item and the fact that you hoped I hadn't changed my mind about the A. C. Nebeker Jr. Family. Well, I haven't, not one iota. But since I've known you might be coming home soon, inside I've been trying to decide what we should do about that. And my commonsense says it would be better to wait until after the war when we're kind of settled and know what we're going to do. I couldn't stand raising our baby in someone else's house – either your folks or mine and if you had to leave me again, that's what I'd have to do. And without you, I'd be scared to death. Naturally, this kind of long distance talk isn't so good for discussing a subject as important as this but I just don't want you setting your heart on it. Of course, this "mother complex" I seem to have developed the last few months may get the best of that so-called common-sense of mine – but don't count on it too much.

I continue with four more pages of chit-chat, closing with "I love you truly, Me."

10th-12th: I write but I am severely sun-burned, to the point that I can scarcely wear clothes or sit down or stand up. I have been completely unaware of what an Arizona sun can do if you stay out in it all day. My letters are short during these three days. But I am so severely burnt that I have had to stay home from work – I can't even put on clothes!

The 13th finds me disconsolate: "If you left the 10th [which of course you did not], I suppose it will take a couple of months. If you don't get here soon, I'm going to be a complete nervous wreck. Right now I'd like to have about ten bottles of beer and drink every one of them myself." Had I known I would have to endure six months more of this kind of agony, I might have taken up drinking in earnest – had something else not happened.

On the 15th I indicate how deeply I am into a near break down:

> ". . . can't seem to settle down to anything anymore. Can't sleep, don't want to eat, don't want to work. . . I'm so bored with life in general I could scream. I think when I find out for sure when and if you'll be home, then I won't be at such a high point of tension. If I can last that long."

Then I tell you about the new girl at work, married to a sailor, who is two months pregnant.

> One of the girls had asked her – this is the game the girls play at work – if she loved her husband. In all earnestness she told us she didn't know – when she was with him she loved him, but after he left, she forgot about him. She tells us she seldom writes unless she wants something, while he writes twice a day. The other day she wrote him that when his letters came, unless there was money in them, she just put them up until she didn't have anything else to do. And she's mad because the husband is glad about the baby. Today she said, 'Oh, hell, what did I get out of being married 'cept this!!!' Talk about true love! And she's really a nice girl, too. In a way, she reminds me of Betty. . .

I end a very long letter:

> "Honey, how I'll ever survive the next few weeks [it will be *months*] I don't know. I wish I could go to bed tonight and not wake up until you were with me again. Oh, that happy day!"

The next five days my letters seem so boring to me, I can scarcely stand to read them but on the 21st I write, following your letter about me being pin-up girl:

June 21, 1945: it's probably because you either bribed all the fellows with candy bars or threatened to bash 'em in the nose if they disagreed, or maybe even invited them up for a post-war dinner. Anyhow, so long as I'm your pin-up girl, what more can I ask. I love you so much that all I ever really want is just for you to love me forever as I will you. I can't even dream of anything more wonderful than the time you're back home for keeps, when we have life together and I really become a "pin-up girl" trying to keep Junior's three-cornered trousers in place. A future like that is worth waiting for-worth being lonesome for all these months. I'm glad you got thirsty for a drink that night in April a year ago. Just imagine some other cookie being your wife!! or me being Mrs. Someone Else! I loves ya, honey.

As we complete the ninth month of our letter writing, we receive the letters almost within a week of each other. On June 25th, you have mine of the 12th and 16th and you write me what will turn out to be disaster for your homecoming plans. You could not have known it when you signed on, but it was to give us both great grief. You write:

25 Jun 45: Honey, today I got the first real break since I have been in the army! I was selected to play ball with the Division Artillery soft ball team. But the break that goes with it is what pleases me – namely that for the duration of our stay here in Europe I don't have to pull any details – no guard, no escort – just play ball. There are 20 of us from 4 battalions that get this break. We have plenty of good material and should win all our games. They are making us uniforms and getting a big bus for our road trips. We will travel about half the time playing other outfits on our way. Sometimes we will go for 500 or so miles to play a couple of games. Later on we may tour France and Belgium cause they want to do this thing big. For a week or two we will practice then be on our way. At least it will be a great deal more pleasant for me than pull guard every day! Darling, your statements in your June 12th letter concerning "making wiz ze love" made me happy – It shows that we have conquered that adjustment and that you don't think that it is "dumb."

[Oh, my dear, how unkind of you to remember so long that careless (because uninitiated yet) remark of mine. But 13 years later, you will make a statement to me that far exceeds the carelessness of this – and I do not think you *ever* apologized for it!] "But I still think I am man enough to last the night or at least a great part of the night. It has been a long time, hasn't it." And then you convey concern about the pain I still have:

> I can't help but feel that it contributed to our "pet pain" and we'll have to control or limit the quantity of said subject. . . Quite naturally I feel that the love makes our marriage a more complete union but even without it our marriage is a beautiful thing. . . .I am proud of the fact that we can discuss such matters easily and intelligently. It is just one more indication of when I am asked, "Do you love your wife?" I can answer strongly, "You're damned right I love her!!!" When you mentioned the experience of the new girl in your office, I thrilled to the fact that I know you know you love me and vise versa. A marriage is not a marriage if both parties have the least doubt, don't you think? As with me a person that really loves another should find that love growing stronger with every passing day.

The letters of the 26th-27th contain news of sore muscles from two full days of practicing and getting your muscles in shape; sympathy for my sunburn; assuring me that you have lost only 15 lbs and that you still weigh 180.4 lbs. [Now there I have it in your own words that you weighed over 180 lbs when we married. In later years you insisted that you had never weighed more than 170 lbs in your life. I thought you were one great specimen of manhood when we were married – and you remained so until you became ill in 1994.] And you assure me that you haven't lost your hair – it's just the G. I. hair cut. You now have my letters through the 16th with the snapshots that I have included.

In this letter of the 27th you reply to my letter about the future family:

> **27 Jun 45:** Darling don't worry too much about the "future family" cause maybe I'm not man enough although I certainly hope so – However, when I get home we'll take the necessary

steps to be sure that nothing happens while I am away – if I have to go to the Pacific – as much as I hate to admit that I am in agreement with you about being settled before we bless this world with an offspring. However, I am inclined to think if we actually want a Jr or Terry Lee we'd better take the advantages of any opportunity that comes our way, regardless of the economic situation. We tried for a couple of months and nothing came of it but a lot of fun, so maybe another month will pass with the same results – How about that – sweet?

[My only comment is that the gods must have been splitting their sides in laughter, again!!!!!]

On the 28th & 29th, you are playing your ball games – losing one (because you were not pitching at first and then it was too late to recoup) and winning the next. And then you're off on a tour and your letters of the month are finished and you will not receive the rest of mine until July, when you return to base camp.

And it is in this way that we strive to keep our love for one another safe in our hearts – and in our minds. I guess from this vantage point of time – exactly 60 years – we deserve a medal for constancy and determination in the face of many odds – if nothing else!

5
Love Is the Whole

As July begins the eleventh month of our marriage and the ninth month of separation, only the memories of the brief time of love we have shared – and our hope for future sharing – sustain us both. This month – with your duties involving your assignment to play ball – will bring me, waiting in my first summer experience of the blistering Arizona heat [remember there is *no refrigeration available, not even in stores or restaurants, only swamp coolers*] far fewer letters of consolation and hope. And mail time is now slowing down so days will pass without receiving mail. And the duty itself, although it relieves you of the hated guarding of the German prisoners in the "cages," will not be the pleasant experience you had envisioned. One letter is indicative of several:

> Our trip was longer than any of us thought it would be – partially because we got lost a dozen times as it was the first time we went up there. We left here right after our game Saturday (we won 4-3) and traveled up to 1 A.M. before we hit Limburg. We stayed in some outfit's headquarters – slept on the floor – for the rest of the night. Sunday morning, after taking a few wrong roads, we got to where we were to play. It was one of our Infantry outfits (the 106th) and they had been out there for a couple of months. Right up on top of high mountains where the wind and rain plays. The men were sleeping in pup tents and taking training the same as we done [sic] in the States – For dinner they fed us fried chicken and that really was good after eating the stuff we have been getting at the battery. We were afraid we would have to stay up there for the night so we got the game going as fast as we could – Then a strong wind came up just as we started the game – I was afraid we'd lose but the other team made several errors and we came out all right. In the last inning it started to pour down rain in buckets full but even that couldn't make us lose the game. Honey, I was never so glad to leave a place – it was right after the game too – we didn't lose any time either. That truck fairly flew out of that muddy windy mountain spot.
>
> There were 22 of us and only one truck – I rode in the trailer with the wind and the rain in my hair. When I got back today the old Nebeker Cough had caught up with me again and I got a cold – Nothing new has been added except a few more spots of love for you – Baby, I got plenty of that. . . Forever Neb

Thus go the road trips – varying only in time and place. The news of your homecoming consists of, time after time, "We may leave here sooner than we expected or stay here longer than I hope for. It is all a matter of finishing our job up and waiting for a boat." Your entertainment, when it comes, is a swim, a movie, or the USO show. You express extreme tiredness in nearly every letter and wish you had me there to wash your O.D.s and give them a good press. There are no PX supplies of stationery and all the boys are out so it's difficult to borrow. [I haven't sent you a supply because I thought you were coming home.] The weather is bad and the food gets worse every day. "All in all, the army ain't no place for this Joe!"

But on "our day-July 5th" – you write me words of love:

> **5 Jul 45:** I still wonder how a beautiful girl like you ever coupled up with a guy like me – but you're mine now and I do love you so very much. And the best part of it all is that I find my love being returned – that makes me fall in love with you every day just as I did the day I saw your beautiful face sitting by my side at the Roof from the first time to the last time we were there. I love you so damn much. Neb

You journey from Bad Ems to Frankfurt to Andernack back to Heilbronn and there is no mail, again. The next day there are two – and you're glad I'm learning to drive, but I'd better "get good enough to drive with one hand for you'll need your other one to 'protect' yourself – as you said one time before – Anyway you shouldn't have gone out with a guy that couldn't keep his hands to himself! [And if I hadn't, whose letter would you be reading now?] I did pretty well at that, when I was courting you – or did I?" [Yes, you did, because otherwise you'd have had a slapped face!] Important news is that only about 35 men of the original battalion group that you fought with are left – the rest are new guys so it seems to you that you are in a new outfit. And it's possible you may be soon.

But still, despite all the monotony and deprivations of your life you take the time to write me on the 12th:

> **12 Jul 45:** I got the sweetest, beautifulest wife a guy could ever have or want. When you speak of being so lonesome and lovesick – remember that you aren't the only one – after all, honey, I got that feeling the same as you and I got it bad. I get so restless just waiting to be on the move to you – if I was, I'd know that in a month or so I'd be able to see you or at least talk to you over the phone. The way it is now, it is just a big tease! In all my life I have never been quite so happy as I have since I met you – There is something about you that puts my heart to singing. Honey, I go now – I go trudging up to my lonely bed –

lonely cause you ain't in it, but I go with lovely thoughts of the gal. . . That's all the world to me. Yours for all Eternity

By the 15th, you have only missed writing me five days while you were traveling and you have just received my letters through the 5th. But for the rest of the month there will only be the letters of the 16th, 21st and 23rd. The 16th has unpleasant forecasts. You have been classed as a combat trooper and may be shipped to the China-Burma-Indonesian front. But maybe – or maybe not – a furlough first.

16 Jul 45: I'll be as mad as a wet hen if, after all my plans, they ship me without a furlough that I have wanted so much. I need to see you for I miss you something awful – I need your soft lips on mine and your arms around me once more. Oh my sweet, I love you so much. When I get home and get through kissing you, your lips will be quivering and so sore you won't be able to eat – cause I just love to kiss – even if you laughed at my 'ten easy lessons'!! Shame! Shame!

The letter of the 21st finds you in a box car:

21 Jul 45: at last I'm on the move! The last couple days has been a series of running around rounding up my stuff – packing it and trying to find out where the hell we are going! Two days ago orders came in transferring us old men out of the outfit. . . the only ones left are those with high points. Kirk, Pete, Nick, Hudson, Hallberg and all the rest are being split up at last. We all rode the trucks down to Karlsruh where we split up. The only man that you know that is with me is Hallberg. The orders are sending the men all over the ETO [Europe] and some unlucky ones are headed direct. I am one of the lucky ones!!!!! Right now we are sitting in the yards of Lyons, France, waiting for an engine to pull us on our way – It seems all we do is go a few miles then wait several hours for another engine. But it is here now.

22 Jul 45: We found yesterday we are headed for Camp Lucky Strike, near Le Harve. That means we are headed for home! I heard tell that we will all be home and on our furloughs by

August 10th. Of course, no one knows how long we will stay at that camp or how long the trip across will be but it will be a great deal sooner than staying with the division.

23 Jul 1945: Honey, after much delay we finally arrived, a couple of days ahead of schedule – that's the reason we had to wait so long in places. The French didn't have our train on schedule – but we are here now and being processed. (Later) The man said we my be here anywhere from 2 to 7 days and then we are CBI [China-Burma-India] bound via the States . . . Darling, get set for that furlough and prepare for a great loving cause Here I come – all the love in the world!!!

6

Promises! Promises!

And as you sweat out "all the butt-ends of your days and ways" – to quote T S. Eliot – back in Mesa, during this long month of July, I will write you 140 pages of everything I can think of to make your days easier, your tension less, and my longing for you ever on your mind. [This will be the equivalent of 14,000 words.] And I am not too sure that my physical discomfort is too much less than yours. Had we realized what was yet to come, I think we both would have just given up and gone off somewhere to die – I know I would have. And in fact, my body almost did. As I have said before, I am one of those unfortunate beings whose heart, mind and body are one – when part fails, the body fails. It has been that way for me ever since I can remember.

I will try to give only a brief recap of the major affairs that I report or discuss with you, never knowing whether you have received my letters or not. I've been to Prescott, attended the Rodeo, ridden in the Parade and, by sheer accident and stupidity, taken the wrong horse home from the Fairgrounds. I had wondered – as I rode him – why he had suddenly turned so uncontrollable. I managed to make it back to the barn – only to find I had ridden the sire – a bad stallion and the sire of my much gentler mount. Everyone was amazed that I had even made it without accident. And, of course, I would never live down the "theft" of a horse among my Prescott relatives. [That adventure consumed five pages.]

Naturally, I'm still on the "is he or is he not" coming home emotional see-saw. But on "our anniversary," I write sweet words of "the happiest moment in my life" and try to counsel with you about the possibility of getting an apartment to keep after you leave for the CBI. I write you of the extreme heat and 120 days so far without rain – and I hate the "swamp coolers. It's like living in a bath tub." I've been bitten by a spider; I'm sun-burned; and above all, I'm pining with love for you. I'm so lonely, I wish I had a roommate – even Betty!

In reply to your letter about our "future family" which is a reply to my letter about, as you put it, "said subject," [is that confusing enough] I write:

> Sweetheart, I'm not "worried" about our future family as you put it. In fact thinking about it is getting to be a source of real pleasure to me – a far cry from my feelings several months ago. As you put it, I'm beginning to wonder if we shouldn't take advantage of any opportunities that arise because it just might be that we'll have to work pretty hard at getting a family started. And since I've been feeling so well, I think maybe when you get home, I'll work on that little item – provided I can get everything arranged like I want it. Anyhow, I'll be thinking it over 'til you get home. I love you so much when you talk things like that over with me – it makes me much less lonely – more like you were here with me. I think that's a very nice part of marriage. [And one that you would cease to honor later on, as new love dimmed.]

On the 8th, I write you that I am attending Mesa Second Ward and like the Sunday School class because I can talk and express my opinions and find out things.

> *July 8, 1945:* When you get in a class of returned missionaries, it's really interesting. And they're all so nice to me, I don't feel strange, at all. One of the boys who did his work in Samoa told me after class that after some of the remarks and statements I

> had made, he was going home and re-read his Book of Mormon because he couldn't have a person who was a non-Mormon get ahead of him. I didn't tell him that your missionary book and your Book of Mormon with all its underlined passages was getting a good reading. But I'd not get nearly as much out of it without your notes in it – so thank you, sweetheart for making such good ones! You never can tell – I might be a Mormon yet. I'd hate to think of poor Junior being part Presbyterian and part Mormon. Of course I'll have to really feel it's right – no half-way beliefs – so I won't be hurried.

[So you see, my dear, you really are a part of my eventual conversion – from your thoughts while we dated until the last night we kissed goodbye.]

During this month I have three very vivid dreams about you. In one, "I go to a baseball game and there, out in the pitcher's box, you were. We must have seen each other at the same time because we both broke into a run at the same time. And after we'd "greeted" each other, I put my arms around your waist and remarked how thin you were and your exact words were 'Now let me alone, sweetheart, I like it that way.' And that was the end of my dream." [As I read this now, I see how predictive it really was of the extreme independence that you would require throughout your life. And for the most part, I reserved restriction against your freedom. I only wish your mother had been as wise as I.] "Shortly after, I dreamed that you called me from San Francisco and we talked for a long time. That was such a real dream that I actually woke up the next morning wondering if you had really called. Aren't you ashamed haunting me in my dreams like that?"

On the 8th, I write reluctantly, but with a clear purpose in mind:

> Tonight I don't feel so good. That darn pain in my side has been on a rampage again for a week now – off and on – *and without the aid of your love-making that you think affects it.* [Did you get my point, my dear?] It makes me so angry that just when I feel so good and almost certain it's gone for good, back it comes. If it keeps up, I'll have to be paying the doctor another visit.

July 8th I go to a ball game:

> "I hate to admit it, honey, but you couldn't even begin to compare with the pitchers on those teams in looks or build – don't worry, dear, it was two girls' teams."

The next night I'm swimming; then I stay overnight with a girl friend. Then the papers report that "the 106th is scheduled to leave for home by November 1st: next week it will be January and prob'ly the week after that it'll say 1950 or so. It sure is disheartening to say the least."

On the 10th, I have written you, to date, 267 letters. How can I find anything else to interest you? I know!

> "Do you know that I've got a love for you that surpasses any in the books? You're such a good looking kid with such a nice back to kiss – not to mention what nice lips you have-and in a pair of trunks you can't be beat – and besides that, how you can make with the love! Is it any wonder I love you completely, madly and forever and ever?"

On the 11th, I ask you some touchy questions about the church which I don't feel I can ask anyone else about. "Things I'm able to read and find out for myself, other people are only too willing to tell me about, but things I do need some explaining on, no one helps. And sometimes, they just don't know. I ask them a question and they say they don't know – that they haven't studied as they should. 'Course Mom or Melvin know but Melvin makes me kind of antagonistic and mom gets off into different channels. 'Course you're not to repeat this, you know!" It has been fourteen days since I've received a letter at this point in July. I threaten, "if any more weeks go by when you only write two days out of seven, then the same thing will happen on this end!" Unusually, for me, I also conclude with a real complaint:

> "I'm so miserable from the heat that I think I'd just as soon dig my grave and crawl in. Between the heat and my side it's a cruel world here lately. To my favorite husband always, all my love."

On July 14th I write that the last letter I have received was written the 27th of June – so maybe you're on your way home; I've cut my hair and I really like it – it's certainly much cooler for me in this awful heat; the Americans are making "quite a fuss" because the non-fraternization rules have been lifted in Germany and "all because of the meaning that fraternization has taken on. Silly, isn't it? If a fellow's that kind of a fellow, he'll take a girl be she American, French or German and no amount of rules will stop it." But the most important thing I write of is another dream I had…I could not have known – or even suspected at the time – the significance it had. If I had only understood, it might have changed things on January 16th, 1946. But only in my re-reading has the psychic or "spiritual" revelation emerged:

> *July 14, 1945:* You were home and we were really having a wonderful time. We were in Phoenix window shopping and in one window was the most beautiful black gown and negligee, also a slip and brassiere and I remember that I wanted them so badly. But instead of buying them, we stood there and laughed because I was pregnant and couldn't wear them. Now why do you suppose I dream wacky dreams like that? And they're all so real and plain. I even remember which store window they were in.

And then I wonder how long it will be before we can have Saturday nights like we used to – a dance or a show – and Saturday nights as a weekly occurrence again – only this time with no army to interfere.

> You know, my darling, that loving you is one half of the entire happiness in my life – the other half is being loved by you in return. And I'm living for the day when we'll have an honest to goodness family – together. And the only letters I'll write you will be notes I'll leave in your pockets so you won't forget me while you're away at work.

Sunday, 15th July is a really lonely day for me. I've been to Sunday School, and I'm hot and tired after walking home so I fall asleep for two hours. "I've had that continually sleepy, tired feeling for a week and I hope it's worn off by tomorrow. Mom has worried herself sick because she thinks I have been working too hard." [And the fact of the matter is that I have. Work plus the travel entailed plus the waiting and the loneliness is slowly but surely now, wearing me down.] I get out your letters and re-read them and loving memories are revived. I write, after that:

> *July 15, 1945:* Our letters back and forth are as good as a well-kept diary. In fact, they're probably more complete than most diaries. I hope that you still miss me and love me as much as you did when you left last October. I've gotten used to the idea of your being gone but I still love you and miss you more and more with each day. Anymore, my one and only thought is for when you're home. I want very much to have a home and be settled – to have you with me every day and to have a "tomorrow" to count on. I want to get Junior started so that we can be young with him and really be close to him. I want you to have a good job and me to stay home. I don't mean when I say settled that we're not to have fun like we used to because I think we'll always have fun. But fun is more fun when you've something of your own to anchor to. For no other man could I want things like that, but for us together. That's my dream." [And in spite of everything that would occur in my life, that was always my dream.] I end this nostalgic, perhaps childish letter with: "I just want us to be happy together. So many marriages last such a short time but I do pray ours will last at least an eternity. I love you my dear with all my heart. Helen"

July 16th is a happy day with two letters and a whole box of souvenirs you have sent – hand crocheted table cloth and embroidered dresser scarf, a German bayonet, a picture book of lovely scenes of Germany. And pictures of you! "I love you so much for thinking to send such lovely things." And so go my letters through the entire month. I tell you of friends I have made at the office and our outings to movies and to an occasional dinner out. On the 23rd, important news is that I'm sending you a real "pin-up" picture of me.

> *July 16, 1945:* I think it's the best picture I've ever taken. I'm taking no chances on your forgetting me or falling for some German gal cause it just happens I love you from your head to

> your toes and I insist that it remain mutual, even if I have to continue to have someone else pose for my pictures so you'll think you've got a good looking wife!

The next day I write that the picture is on its way – but I didn't get a folder for it because it would have been too heavy to air mail. . .

> The moon is out in full force, tonight. . . There are too many moons going to waste – it's downright extravagance. If you'd come home we could do something about it! I don't know whether I'm going to be able to last 'til November or not!
>
> *July 25, 1945:* The mail situation is disheartening and I've stopped looking for mail almost entirely. It's been fifteen days since your last letter was written and that one was nearly two weeks in coming. But pay no attention to me because to put in bluntly, I'm in a hell of a mood. I need some company or something. . . But forget it, chum, I'll get over it. . . Oh, honey, I give up – I just can't write anymore –
>
> *July 26, 1945:* I finally got mail from you again – and only twenty four days old. . . Incidentally, they want to use my "bathing beauty" picture in the Highway Magazine, perhaps in color, but I think I'd better not let them. I like being your pin-up girl but I don't know whether I'd like to be in a magazine or not. I had showed the picture to a good friend of mine there in the magazine and she insisted on showing it to the editor which accounts for the "bid." Then I tell you how homesick I am: "I can't think of anything much nicer than to be drinking coffee and eating do-nuts in the kitchen with mother and the little kids. That is, outside of having you home. Imagine me being homesick!?

The last days of the month find me truly ill:

> I'm just tired from the awful heat. I think it's the heat – but whatever it is I've been under the weather for at least three weeks and yesterday and today, I've really been sick. Everyone has made it a point to tell me how bad I look – and Mr. Hogan

> has just told me, if I like, I can take Thursday, Friday, and Saturday off and maybe a rest would help. He says he remembers his first summer in Arizona.

Then I tell you how pleased I was when your mother told me that you had sent money to buy me an anniversary present for our FIRST YEAR as man and wife. And I'm going to buy a lovely pin for my new suit I'm saving, for when you get home.

And I also tell you, that as your present – because I haven't wanted to send anything since you were in transit – that on August the 5th I will have deposited in the bank, $500.00! For your homecoming. [Now that does not seem like anything today, but consider that the whole time of our marriage, I had earned, and received from your allotment checks, less than $2500. And I had taken a trip across country and paid rent, travel, and living expenses in Mesa, out of that measly sum. Five hundred dollars was an incredible amount to have saved in less than twelve months! I end the month, reminding you that "I never forget how wonderful you are at 'making wiz ze love' and I don't think I ever will." [And I still don't!]

7
While Passion Sleeps

Our letters of August 1945 are among the most difficult for me to write about, in this long, long final letter which I am writing to you sixty years later in life. By number and by volume they would seem to indicate a great loss of interest on the part of both of us. But the fact is that they indicate a time of such hope, such joy, and such continuing disappointment that the pain is close to unbearable – at least for me. In the first fifteen days, you surpass me – for the first time in all the long months – in the number of letters you write. There are seven to my three. And the tension of those letters is gripping. By the 25th of July, you have arrived at Camp Lucky Strike, hoping that you will be on your way home. On August 1st you write:

> **1 Aug 45:** By now I thought for sure that I would be on my way home you. But evidently they have forgotten about us being here. [It is a fact that they, indeed, never knew you were there!] Of course, I have only been at this camp for 10 days, which isn't long in itself. However, it is a century compared to a like period three months ago. That is because this is the first lap of the journey home. . . I want to get moving-and fast-so I can be with you – and what do I get? Just to sit, lay or sleep on my bunk most of the day anxiously awaiting to hear my name on a shipping list at last. . . It is rumored that we will all be out of here by next Saturday. According to others in the same shape as myself, the average stay before shipment is two weeks – now that gives us four more days to sweat it out. . . as your letters are not coming here, but are being returned home, I hope, I have taken time to read your letters of May, June and what I have of July's – up to the 6th – and I have gotten quite a kick out of some of them – and a great lift to my morale. . .

The great lift to the morale of both of us is the letter we will each write on our anniversary, during these miserable, wearing days of August. Since these will be our last anniversary letters – and our first yearly marking of the great event – I will preserve them in part here.

> *August 5, 1945:* My dearest husband, It's really true-for exactly one year and half an hour, we've been man and wife – the happiest year in my life. I'm sorry that we couldn't be together but the wonderful V-mail that I got yesterday, with the news you were honestly on your way home, has taken any unhappiness from my heart. To know that before too many days pass, I'll be in your arms again is happiness indeed. . . .Next to seeing you, it was the most wonderful anniversary present I could have asked for. . . . I want to tell you especially tonight how very proud and happy I am to be your wife. The happiness you've given me is the kind that I can never repay. . . You're everything I could ever ask for or want. . . I love you above everything in this world. I thought a year ago, when for the first time I could say "my husband," I could love you no more but I do. Tonight I have more love in my heart than I ever thought possible and I know

> that every year it will be the same. . . .I'm counting the minutes until you're home.
>
> My heart, forever.

And on the same day, you send me this sweet remembrance:

> **5 Aug 45:** My Very Sweet Darlin', At eight o'clock this day when we celebrate our first wedding anniversary, I am one very blue and discouraged lad – Blue because I can't reach out to enfold you in my arms and tell you what is so important to me – namely that I love you truly and for the past year I have loved my dear wife most dearly. . . because for one year I have had the privilege of having the most wonderful girl for my wife. Darling, I am most grateful to you for the love, encouragement and yes, the bawling outs that you have given me during the past year. I have come to realize just how much my love for you means to me. There is nothing so important or necessary as the love alive and burning inside of me – a love that is for you and you only. I have come to realize that, although we have been apart for ten long, hard months, your love for me is bright and strong like the star I have wished on so frequently. . . .Darling, today I send to you my complete love – a love I have had for over a year – and I say I love you dearly and I miss you terribly.
>
> Forever, Your anxious husband

But, of course, on the 5th – that great day of the first year anniversary – you are still in camp, "discouraged because I still sit here at Camp Lucky Strike, France, instead of being home or on the high seas. . . already some of the boys that came with us are on the ocean – also tomorrow morning some more are supposed to take off – so it shouldn't be long before my turn comes." On the 28th: "I am plenty burned up with being here so long – If I have to stay another month or so, I hope they move me out of this camp – these canvas cots, the poorly cooked food are enough to send a guy to the hospital." And on the 30th, you are still bemoaning, "I never heard of such a stalemate as we are having."

And, back home I know even less. Only on the 5th of August do I get your V-mail, dated July 25th, informing me that you are at Lucky

Strike, that all your clothes have been turned in and all the other stuff and that all you do now is "wait around to grab the boat." Because of the seeming immediacy of your departure, I cease to write, knowing that you are probably homeward bound at best – and won't get my mail, if you are still waiting. And the mail situation, for both of us, will be as pressing as it was in the black days of the Bulge Battle. Other mail to service men is being processed, but for those in camps, great delays occur in both the sending and the receiving of mail. Which naturally causes a build-up of tension.

On August 15th, knowing that you may never get the letter, I have to write. The War is over; the Japanese have surrendered. Of this momentous occasion, there are really no appropriate words:

> *August 15, 1945:* When definite news came, no one knew whether to shout or cry or thank the Lord. It was a very inadequate feeling after four years of war. As for me, practically my first thought was, "We're practically "Mr. And Mrs." instead of "Pvt. & Mrs." Imagine me married to a civilian. It's a feeling I can't describe when I know that I don't have to think in terms of hours or days or weeks with you anymore. I can begin to think of years with you. Not just furloughs but lifetimes. It's almost unbelievable and a little frightening, too.
>
> I've been on needles and pins for days now waiting to hear from you and I'm not sure how much longer I can stand this tension. To quote a song, "Baby, won't you please come home?" Darling, I love you tonight more than last night or the night before or any time – more every day of my life. I love you and oh, how I want you. Hurry, little chum, I'm an awfully lonesome wife.

I will write you only one more August letter – after I receive, finally, yours from the 10th to the 15th. Some of the matters of these letters I have already referred to but there are other interesting happenings, such as a short respite you were given from the camp, when:

> They took us 20 miles to a town called Fechamps where I swam in the English Channel. I think if the water hadn't been so cold, I would have started swimming the Atlantic – just so I could be with you. The beach was one long stretch of rocks – all of them

were round and smooth. There were big ones, small ones, in-between-ones. Even in the water the bottom was the same. You can imagine me and my tender feet trying to walk on such as that. The water was cold, clear and clean – in fact, it was the cleanest ocean water I have ever swum in. There were a bunch of cliffs like the Cliffs of Dover and it was really a very pretty place.

On the 8th, you express your tension:

8 Aug 45: If my body finds itself still resting uncomfortably on this canvas cot on the first of September, I am afraid that I shall be at the end of my string. I am so impatient to start for home that I can hardly contain myself from dashing on one of the boats that are always in the harbor – That boat which will have my name on the passenger list, must be on the way somewhere, sometime. And to make matters worse, it is raining, cold as the North Pole – muddy as a wet race track and beside I got a summer cold that is about to drive me nuts by itself. But I think I can survive all the waiting, disappointments and the goodbyes if – in the end – I can spend my thirty days with you. [You are still expecting to be sent to the Pacific, even though peace may be in the offing.]

Darling, I may sound rather despondent – if I sound so it is because I really am – and the mail situation doesn't help any either. I haven't received any letters since I have been here and the other guys have gotten some at least.

The 10th finds you expecting news of Japan's surrender and you are sure you won't be shipped there, now. And your hope for a speedy discharge is greater. But your "heart has been singing for joy" since you got my letters at mail call.

10 Aug 45: And I have been really looking the spots off that "Beauty on a Rock" picture [a small photo of the larger one to come]. Of course, I never have told you how very beautiful you are, but now, to my own private pin up I just have to say you are the most beautifulest creature that has ever been made in the form of a woman And those cow girl shots are the stuff, too –

but I saw those green dragons until I recognized the guy with his arm around you was my nephew.

Your letter of the 11th carefully answers questions I have asked you about the church. You close with:

> **11 Aug 45:** I have rambled on-on a subject I know little about in all its entirety but there is one subject that I know in its entirety – and that is I love you so deeply and so dearly that in all my happiness I shall bear that love for you." And you add a postscript that pleases me greatly: "By the way, honey, I am desiring one of those little rings that I can wear on the third finger of my left hand – I don't know the size but you can go with me and pick it out – I think we can afford one now, don't you?

The August 13th letter, addressed to "My Beautiful Pin Up" [underlined three times] begins:

> **13 Aug 45:** Just now, at 4 o'clock, I got a large envelope containing the most beautiful picture I have ever seen in my life [my, my, how you do carry on, dear] – the enlarged shot of "The Beauty on the Rocks," a title that I have given my favorite photo of you. When you said it was good, you weren't kidding – it is good – in fact, it is excellent. That, my sweet, is the most precious hunk of woman that was ever made – and to think that beautiful gal belongs to me – I'll tell you I am so thrilled and so proud of my own favorite pin-up. . . I am certainly anxious to get home to you so I can show you just how very much I love you – how completely and madly I am in love with you.

[Enthusiasms like this make me wonder – I thought you fell in love with my spirit and mind, and now I discover it was really my body. And I enclose this bit of rhapsody on your part just so my grandson can know that his grandma "really was a hottie!"]

On the 17th, you are again bemoaning no mail! You are missing about twenty letters that you think I have written: "If there ever was a time when letters meant life or death it is now – there is nothing to do in this out-in-the-sticks camp but wait for the afternoon mail call. The last I have from you is the 'Beauty on the Rocks' which you mailed July 25th. Baby, I need a letter from you!!" And then you add this grim news: "I think we may be stuck over here for a couple more months" and then you write "prepare thyself just in case we have to wait *a few months longer.*" And then, Lord give me patience, in the same letter, two pages later, you write about being separated into Reception Centers – and your center will be Fort MacArthur, Calif. And that's where you'll get your furlough from.

> If I can, I'll call from New York or at least send you a telegram but I'll call for sure when I reach the reception center. After I leave here it will be a month at least before I can get clear out there – at least three weeks. By that time, I'll be so crazy you may have to put me out on East Van Buren Street – as the saying goes.

And I'll have to go with you! Is it any wonder that both of us are on the point of absolute collapse before the month is over? And the worst is yet to come!!!!

August 19, 1945: Sunday: This letter is truly revelatory of the depth of your despair and somehow I know that you are going to suffer physical consequences. When there is no way for you to release your tension, it must erupt in violence – or illness. [And you do not seem to have had the "beer" that is always so helpful for you in times of stress.]

> **19 Aug 45:** It would seem that my feelings would be somewhat relieved if I would go out and bang my head against a brick wall. For the last couple of weeks, tension has been mounting inside of me until I don't see how I can stay here much longer without the risk of going completely batty – here three weeks ago I was so sure I would be loafing around a Phoenix swimming pool with you on this particular Sunday. But no, the army has to snafu and keep us here in the rain and mud – just look at the weather for today - or even glancing out the flap of our tent – damn, all you can see is rain and about 4 inches of oozy mud. That alone is almost enough to drive a man to distraction – or at least to drink – which reminds me that for six weeks all I've had to drink except water and coffee was one can of American

beer – This has been the extreme of cold summers – Here it is August with weather comparable to November back home . . . It almost breaks my heart when the summer keeps passing by and I sit here and sweat – and I don't mean from the heat, either.

But then you try to be upbeat and just hang in there-which is all that either of us could do.

20 Aug 45: A Lucky Day! I happened to call out the mail today and in all the letters I found 15 from you – I don't believe I would have gotten them if I hadn't been calling them out. I bet they have been here for a week but no one ever called 'em out, so today I got sore and did the job myself – and I got 'em! It took me an hour and a half to read them all and it was the best time I've spent since I got the last ones – over two weeks ago.

And then you write me some very sweet words:

There were so many things that pleased me and I was very happy to learn that you really enjoy the friendship of those gals. Now you know somewhat of my feelings when I dash out for a few beers with the boys – One can have lots of fun, at times, thataway. [Except you were never left waiting at home, alone, nor was I drinking beer!] I don't believe that I have to tell you how very much I admire you for the way you have fitted into my family or for the "hardships" that you encountered in doing so. I realize that it hasn't been an easy thing for you to go out amongst strange relations-with strange living habits and my love for you has increased a million fold for the way that you have come through. Sweetheart, I have always known that you were much too good for me – If you receive a little happiness out of the small things I am able to give you-then I am so very pleased. I did so want to give you something nice for our wedding anniversary, but the fifteen bucks was all I had. I am glad that you wanted to get the lapel pin – for that is one of the things I suggested to mother to get you. . . It was a very small token of appreciation to show how thankful I am for the honor it is to have you for my wife – I am grateful for the full year of

> completely being happy and proud of your allowing me to be your husband. Someday I'll show you just what I mean.

[These words are very precious to me as I copy them, for not often, when you came home, did you verbalize such sentiments. And it makes me remember how, not too long hence, I would act, briefly, in a way not to make you proud of me. I have always regretted it – but I understand the "why" of those disappointing actions now. And I will explain them fully to you later in this letter.]

It is in this letter that you will also tell me about some of the tales that some of the "guys" have brought back concerning their sexual adventures in Paris. Your opinion is:

> The French are the dirtiest people I have ever heard about – they talk about that stuff like you and I would talk about going to a movie. Educational, you know – but I'll still take my "little book" – eh? Which, by the way, reminds me that I have gotten out of the habit of sleeping on my right side – it is the left one now. Lately I haven't slept so well because it is plenty cold here at nights and I only got extra blankets last night – I could go for plenty of your cuddling – now or any time.

Back in Mesa, I have received your letters from the 10th to the 15th, and in one of them is your new address so that your mail will be getting to you. I'm happy with your desire to have a wedding ring: "it's really a silly little thing, I guess but I really wanted you to want one. Of course, maybe you're just trying to please me and don't particularly care for one, but whichever it is, it really makes me happy." I'm pleased about your thinking about going back to college.

> The government gives $75 a month and if I worked, you should be able to graduate easily. I'll be the happiest, proudest wife in the world when I walk down the street with my civilian husband. I hope it's not too much longer before you're home because I've practically reached the breaking point. I think each day that passes now is more unbearable than the last because of the loneliness inside for you. Each day is at least 48 hours long and sometimes I think I'll never survive. The girls at work

say if you don't get home pretty soon, they're going to be nervous wrecks too just because it's contagious from me. So you see, honey, you've got more than one woman waiting for you to get home.

My next two letters have only one thought: "I'm really dying to have you home and the suspense and waiting gets on my nerves. *I want you home!!!!!"* But I have had a letter from one of my "Rogues Gallery" friends. He has just learned of our marriage – never having received my letter – and sends his congratulations." [His name was Al Bartzak and he was a really fine man.]

On the 31st, I receive the very sweet letter you have written me on the 20th [see above] – the day you had received 15 letters from me – I assure you that I'm not getting skinny; that I've decided not to let the magazine have the negative of my picture for publication [I want no green-eyed dragon when you come home.].

August 31, 1945: I don't think I'd like to find myself on a newsstand, especially in such brief apparel. For you, it's okay – but for other people, I don't think so! Listen, my sweet husband, when we were first married, I succumbed fairly gracefully to sleeping on the left hand side of the bed after having slept on the right all my life. But if you think – after finally getting used to the left – I'm going to make a change, again you're nuts! Either you start sleeping on your right again or one of us sleeps on the floor!!

My last letter ends assuring that I will start writing every night, now that I have your new address – and know that you are stuck in purgatory for only God knows how long! And *your* final letters of the month – faithful and true as you are in your writing – show that you are, indeed, in hell.

Today marks the 31st day that I have been in this mud hole. . . It rained plenty hard last night and just as I was coming back from the Red Cross too. Before I got back I was wet from my short blonde hair to my boot enclosed toes The first three tents across the street were flooded with about 3 inches of water on the floors. Our tent is on higher ground and we only got dripped on – got a big hole right in the top of it. After it quit raining we dashed outside and found the water rushing down a hole in the middle of the street. It wasn't there before the rain and it was deeper than the longest pole we could find. Maybe we are over an underground lake – could be we sink?

It was still raining this morning but our spirits rose when they brought us slips to fill out. They were slips telling just what reception center we want to go to. I filled mine out for Ft. MacArthur – it shouldn't be long now, honey, before I am home. . . .I'm sure it will be before my birthday [Oct 4] or at least by Christmas. So hold tight, darlin', and I'll be seeing you.

24 Aug 45: [You must be really ill, because you never complain:] For the last couple days I have really had the misery – we played a ball game in the rain the other day and I must have caught a cold in my back and legs. Or maybe it's just a bunch of sore muscles but I sure had the misery. So I lay on my canvas bunk for the last two days and now I'm fit as a fiddle. [The rest of the letter is just "maybes" of hope, expectation, and rumor.]

25 August 45: So today is just another day to sit and twiddle our thumbs or argue what is going to happen to us poor boys. We've discussed, argued and otherwise fought over the various subjects of being discharged, shipped to the Pacific, waiting until all the high point men are shipped home. And whether we'll ever smoke Lucky Strikes again after staying so long in this forsaken place. . . After [everything] I have reached the conclusion that all we know is that we are here.

And then you tell me of former buddies you have run into – and they have reports of other friends of ours. Only Hallberg is still with you – and isn't it strange that he was the one who escaped from the Germans in the Ardennes and is still with you. The sun shines for you on the 27th; you go to see a Negro USO show; you are absolutely unable to sleep all night. And you love me. On the 30th of August, you finally receive my letters of July 7 & 8 and they make you glad – especially about starting a family. And you only hope you're man enough. [You were, my love, you were. But how my heart is aching for you as I read these letters. I am glad we do not yet know what has still to come.]

8
"The Very Thought of You"

September begins with the fulfillment of what I had feared for you as I had read your August 24th letter: You are, indeed, ill:

> **24 Aug 45:** My Darlin,' Remember I told you once that the Army chow would finally get me down. It has – and I mean it has. Here I sit in the hospital – with Yellow Jaundice – of all things. No one seems to know much about it except it is caused by a deficiency of certain food. . . All they do is put you on a non-fat diet and give you lots of fruit to eat. Of course, I only came in here today and they say I'll be out in a week or 10 days – and all that time I have to go without any meat – and the way I love meat too. Last night we were laying around shooting the breeze about when we'd be apt to go home and all at once Halberg said, "Neb, you're turning yellow" and sure enough, when I looked in the mirror my eyeballs were yellow and my skin had a yellow-ish cast to it – I didn't feel sick or anything [those aches and pains you wrote of on the 24th, were all symptoms of jaundice, my love] so I went on sick call this morning and Doc sent me up here. It seems that improper food gets the kidneys down, then you turn yellow. But I feel fine and sleep like a log – especially in my bed of sheets and a pillow. . . So in a few days, I'll probably be back in my old tent waiting for the boat with the rest of the guys – then I'll probably turn yellow again just to get back to the sheets!
>
> It is a lot better here than where I was – the movies are better – the Red Cross is better equipped and there are more "reading materials." In fact, it is pretty good all the way around unless they start sticking needles in me – or something. And as long as I feel okay, I won't mind waiting here rather than down

in the mud hole. As far as my shipment is concerned, this won't affect it one way or another – I'll go as scheduled but it is the same old story – no news. (Pardon me here comes my vitamin pills) Right next to me are two big black Negroes and they sure razz me about being a "yellow boy." How you like a yellow man for a husband?. . . The only thing makes me mad is for some reason I gotta wear these ugly hospital "bed uniforms" and honey, they're pips. But yellow or white, I loves you with a love that is burning deep and every day I am hoping it will be the day I'm to start on the journey home to you.

September 3rd: Your days consist of lying in your bunk, reading, walking back and forth to the Red Cross and writing to me. You say that there are many others in the hospital with jaundice [so that seems communicable rather than just a matter of food deficiency. You have a full scale hepatitis epidemic going.] You write: ". . . some of the color has gone but there is still a lot left. I was yellow from head to toe yesterday but today only in spots on my legs and arms. The rest is still a yellow blotch." And there are movies:

3 Sep 45: Awhile ago I saw a movie that really made me homesick for you and the family. It showed what happened to a guy that had been away for twenty months and just got to his home town-Boy, I had a hard time keeping the tears from rolling, I wantta go home to you! Sweetheart, as I'll lay in my sheets, I'll wish like hell that soon I can reach over and kiss you-tell you how very much I've missed you and how very much I love you.
Your "Yellow-y" Neb

And on the 5th – our 13th month of married life - you write another dear epistle that I will always treasure:

Darling, if this stuff keeps up, it will be a year since I last saw you. And that's much too long to be away. Here it is exactly 13 months to the day when you and I stood together, and said "I do.". I still do, do you? In another month plus 5 days – it will be just one year since I left you that Monday morning. You were crying that morning and so did I – but now we need only to wait for time to pass, without the fears we had then. Those are passed and I hope for all time. If in this past year of separation I have helped make it possible for me to stay home with you from now on, then I won't mind so much the time that we have lost being together.

Of course, I would have liked to have been with you all that time and I like to believe I was, for my love for you is so great that it linked me to you in every thought and in every passing day. Many times I had only to close my eyes and there you were-sitting on the arm of my chair, scratching my back, kissing me tenderly, or walking across the floor in those cute white panties of yours. You never did know how I loved to watch you walk across the floor like that, did you? You have a lovely back and those panties fit you just right. It is going to be a great day when I can once again be with you. Just your smile is worth traveling 5,000 miles to see. . . and I pray that it is soon for I am almost beside myself in wanting to hold you tight - to feel your head on my shoulder when we are asleep at night – and to feel your soft beautiful fingers running up and down my back. Oh you are so sweet!

And darling, I love you so much that it is impossible for me to describe it in mere words – I'll wait for awhile till I get home and prove to you that it is a love that will last. Forever, Your Husband Neb

As I have included here – as well as in other places – intimate details of our physical love for each other, perhaps, dear husband, you feel it an impropriety to reveal such of our feelings to the light of posterity. And I admit that I have seriously pondered the matter myself, occasionally prompted to delete. But since I started this "last letter," promising to share with you "my heart, my soul, my growth, my deep and sincere joy, my sorrow," I have concluded that without some of the "physical" details, much of our "love affair" will be lost for all time – and the value of our *Letters of Love* perverted. Surely, in an age which – for the most part – has darkened the physical yearnings between man and woman into an ugly, perverted SEXUALITY, there is a time and place to affirm again, the untarnished sanctity and beauty of the union of the flesh. Upon deep reflection, I have come to believe that the sweet and pure delight of the man who loves – and the woman who joys in his love – is one of God's greatest gifts to man.

God bestows it as a blessing – and a God-given right – to those who unite their bodies, their hearts, their souls into one. This is the *oneness*, ordained by God – that man might fulfill his responsibility to "multiply and replenish the earth." In such union, each Adam is gifted – by his Creator – to find sweet and pure delight in his Eve. And each Eve, entrusting her beauty and her innocence to his tender care, yields herself into the strength and joy of her husband's love. Thus they become one body, one heart, and one soul in the sight of their Maker. Only Satan – or man – could turn the Garden of Eden into a bed of sin!

And this, my still dearly beloved husband, is what I solemnly believe. And this is what you and I joined ourselves to do on that wonderful day when we stood in God's presence, and solemnly vowed: "I do." And this is what sustained us in our thoughts of each other, during those long, long months of absence. And this, dear love, is what I learned from *you*!

My September 5th letter to you is not an "anniversary" letter, because I really think – from your letters – that you are on your way home. And I am almost daily expecting a telephone call or a telegram from New York. Thus I only write:

> You know, my darling, I don't care how many of my ribs you crack when I get that first hug – but you'd better watch your own ribs. I think you're going to be slightly surprised at the amount of loving that's damned up in me and that's no lie. I never knew a person could want loving like I do. But I don't want it from anyone but you. As I tell you goodnight this night, I find myself more in love with you than ever before in my life. I still "loves ya!" [And I mean *body*, as well as heart and soul!]

But back to you and the letters of September, which will find you still in the hospital until the end of the month. You are grateful to be there, because of the continuing cold and rain and mud. On the last day of September, you will have written me 22 letters, comprising 74 pages! And in every one of those letters you will tell me of your friends' visits to bring you the newest rumors, and every day you are sweating out your fate. You write:

> I just saw some of the old gang – they are shipping in a couple of days. . . Understand that the 592nd is in camp right now but as I can't leave [the hospital] I haven't seen any of the guys. Maybe they'll come up tomorrow. . . .Now you can see just what is going on over here. Nobody knows nothing nohow. There were a couple of low-pointers killed themselves when they were told they had to go back to Germany. That shows how the guys feel about the whole thing. Those two were nuts but the average attitude is mighty low over here!

And along with your uneasiness and vacillation about your travel orders, I find great introspection. And constant longing for me. For instance you write:

> Years ago I got the habit of playing a lone wolf hand and being independent for what I thought was happiness – but when I met and married you, that soon folded away into the past. Now the only happiness I ever had or will have, is centered on you. I know that without you, darling, there shall be no peace and contentment in my soul. You are so vitally important in my soul – so vitally important to me and my life that I am filled with pride and joy at the mere thought of you. . . Never in my lifetime do I think that anything will become as important to me as to return to your arms. To feel your love. . . makes my hope for the future a bright and lovely thing.

Because you are not getting mail, you return to reading some of the letters of the past: so, in a way, it is as though I have written you another letter. Of my letter of April 19, you write five months later:

> Of all the sweet letters I prize most the one you wrote on April 19th. It fills my heart with pride and gladness – it has been read a great deal – because it was the one you described your falling in love with me. I have felt many times, and I do honestly, that God was looking down when He gave me you. I feel also that I am entirely unworthy of such a wonderful person as you – you have my love for all eternity and I want so much to be worthy of your love in return. You need not say how much you love me for I can tell it in every line you write, and in every thought I

> have – but I have an ego that cries out for those words. Until I met you, darling, I was a self-centered ass and never knew what it was for me to love a person as I do you. I was the most important person to myself – but knowing you for the last year and a half, and being your husband the last 12 months has changed all that to the most important person to me is and always will be you and it shall be for All eternity, Your loving Neb

And on the 17th of September, you begin to get my letters, written only two weeks previously. In them I report on all the busy doings of my days and ways – 54 pages of my very busy life. I write of my Labor Day visit to Oak Creek Canyon, with Anne and her family. This is the first time I have ever been on a camping trip and I am enthused at the beauty of the area, the fun of sleeping out in sleeping bags, of wading in the creek – and even falling kerplunk into its swiftly moving waters. And then we go to Flagstaff and Williams and the whole experience pleases me. But I am longing for you – and need you. I finally get letters which indicate that you are not on your way home – it has been merely wishful thinking, but I try to remain hopeful, encouraging you and commiserating with your living conditions. And then, I suggest plans for our eventual reunion. At this time, I'm still in Prescott with Anne and attend a church program in which all the little members of the family participate and I include you in the evening:

> All of Tense's family was at the program and I barely escaped with my life. Dougie and Billie Jean love me to death with hugs and kisses – not to mention sitting on my lap. Donald is getting so he runs up, says "Aunt Helen" and gives me a kiss. He used to be afraid of me. When we went swimming yesterday, Dougie insisted on paying my way out of his own money so I told him I'd take him to a show and he's a happy kid.

I close with:

> I hope that tonight you can't sleep well, that you dream of me and that you miss me like the devil because that's exactly how I'll spend my night and what's good enough for me is good enough for you. Your loving, lonely Me

In another letter, I caution you to remember

> how hellish I can be at times so that you don't make me too good. One thing, though, we won't be under the horrible tension of our first two months together when we never knew whether there'd be any more time for us. If I never have another blessing in my life, I'll always be thankful we had no loss of life or love, just time. [I had been thinking of our song, "Til Then" as I wrote these words.] I hope I never forget as life goes on how lucky I am to have you come home – alive and well – to love for the rest of my life.

I miss writing you one evening – I've had to stay in Phoenix to see the doctor and am just too tired. But I make up for it the next day with a very long letter, in which I propose meeting you in L. A. – if you ever get there – so "we can have a little time by ourselves, before you come home to see your family. Can I, huh? Can I?" The next day I have bad news; my little brother, Jerry has been run over in an automobile accident. It's a miracle he's alive; I "got weak all over when I heard about it." And then, still thinking you are possibly, maybe, could it be on your way home, I again write: "Darling, you are going to let me come to L. A. to meet you, aren't you? After a whole year of not seeing you, I just have to see you first by myself. So please write and say it's all right."

On the 14th of September I finally receive letters of August 24th and 25th and September 1st and 7th. Now I know for sure that not only are you not on the way home but you are also in the hospital. I begin my letter, trying to be upbeat and to cheer you up:

> *September 14, 1945:* Oh yes, my darling, you can blame it on the army chow but you don't fool me a bit! Knowing you, I know you prob'ly ate just what you wanted and not what was good for you.

But I am just too devastated to hold the light note for more than a few lines. Then I write – simply beyond any control:

> I am so very disappointed . . . that I just don't care much about anything. . . I don't much care whether the next day comes or not. I know that's an awful way to be but seems like I can't help

> it. And when your coming home is the only thing that even interests, then to think it will be three to five months longer makes a big hole in my morale. Sorry, honey, I didn't mean to go off like that – must be something I ate! But Christmas seems so far off.

And you will not be with me, even then!

In response to your worry over me – and your consultation with army doctors about the pain I feel- I tell you that you will get no more bulletins about my health. "I've come to the conclusion that the penalty for being born is to feel bad. Besides, honey, I'm okay so please don't worry. I'd rather do anything than make you worry about me – even eat that raw liver [that your "consulting doctor" has suggested] – ooh, horrible thought!!!"

And then, to cheer us both up, I tell you how happy I will feel to go with you to buy your ring and put it on for you. "I'm glad you really want it because I'm so proud of my rings that I wanted you to be proud of yours too. Now you will be, huh?" [And you were. We bought the ring in L. A., together; I put it on your finger there, on our second honeymoon. You wore it for 30 years – despite the events that almost doomed our marriage - until the summer of 1975. There, on our first visit to Europe together, you had to go to a jeweler in Shannon, Ireland and have it cut off; your finger had swollen so badly on the air flight that it had to be done. We never bought another ring. In your construction work, it had more than once caused you near serious injuries when you used your big equipment – particularly the saws. I never resented the necessity; by that time I knew that much more than a ring had bound us, irrevocably, together.] I close my letter of September 17th, with a fervent plea for you to "please take care of yourself."

And thus has passed the first half of the long, hot summer for me, in Mesa. And, oh my darling, as I write about this time, how my heart pains for both of us. How did we endure, keep hope, keep faith? And above all, *how did we keep writing?*

The last half of September will end for you as you begin to get my letters of my doings in Mesa, during the first half of the month. Delighted that I have enjoyed my camping experience, you promise to take me camping, "we will see if my knowledge of the woods can't make you a soft mattress of pine needles to sleep on. I love the woods and love to spend the night around the camp fire." [I still do not understand why you never did this one thing I would have enjoyed so much – and I think our children would have enjoyed it too. When I see you again, will you explain this to me?] On the 21st you write that the papers are writing of the anger of the folks back home because the troops are not being sent home and that, perhaps because of the rumpus, the point system may be changed. On the 23rd, good news! Starting November 1st, *all* 60-69 pointers will be shipped by November 1st and *all* will be home by Christmas.

Regarding my suggested plan for our reunion, you assert: ". . . remember, darling, I want you all to myself for awhile before the in-laws start interfering and none of this "settled" husband and wife stuff either – instead it's going to be boy-meets-girl – boy-falls-in-love – marries girl – honeymoon – with a lot of laughs, fun, and, oh, 'beaucoup of love' – That is, if it's okay to you or do you feel like a 'settled wife'-ha!" On the 25th, it has turned bitterly cold and you discover that the latitude corresponds with that of Canada. [You would never have been able to withstand an Indiana winter!] There is no snow yet, but "the cold rain more than makes up for the absence of the snow." New rumor says you will be home by January 31st: "Now, honey, the question is - can I stand it four more months, or should I blow my brains out?"

Your September 26th letter is quite strange – for you. You find that you are unable to concentrate on anything:

> **26 Sep 45:** today I have felt my thought run rampant-my impressions of the day have become as the day – blue and discouraging. . . because of the rapid change of dreams and thoughts. I must say it is a hell of a thing to happen to me. . . .the cause may be because of [all the reading you have been doing.] The amount of impressions left by these books, plus the added morals of the movies, have all seemed to have been held in reserve and released today. Now this is a fine tone of a letter to my wife – it sounds more of a tone used on a friend, don't you think? So now you are not only my wife, lover, sweetheart and honey gal, but my friend also. What a combination that makes. You are indeed all of those and more. My love steadily grows.

When I have a domestic problem, you are my wife to talk it over with; when I got love to tell you of, you are my gal – and when I got books to talk about, you are my friend. Who ever heard of a guy talking books to his wife or gal – so it's gotta be a friend!! Betcha think I'm nuts!!!

[No, my love, I think you are maturing intellectually. Books and good movies (new concepts) can open up whole new realities for one, if thought is given to them. Surely you are not just beginning to see the possibility in a real marriage? It was always my thought that we would be man and wife, lovers, and *friends*. Why didn't you continue to explore those "disturbing" thoughts as life engulfed us?]

September 30th finds you still in the hospital but due to be released back to duty. Remembering that it will be exactly a year since we last saw each other you ponder the time apart:

30 Sep 45: . . . I can see that it has been much more than just a year. In it there were days that were eternities – others when I wondered if I'd ever see the light of day again. But all through the hours that passed, the only true, real thing alive was the love that is still burning so deeply within my soul. Love of life, yes, but greater than that, wherever I was, dwelt a deep, sincere love for you, my wife. And now, as then, that love is still the only true, real thing about me.

[Would you have said these words to me – if you had been able – as you lay in your bed at Hospice, waiting for 'Quill to come get you?' And will you say them to me when we meet again? That's really the only thing that matters to me now – my Eternal love for you.] But just to let me know that you are still my "lover," you end with thoughts of the flesh:

So darling, I take leave of you on this Sunday, although I would rather be there with you to play with the Twins, kiss you and sleep by your side, then you'd know I love you very much, Truly your Neb

My last letters of the month respond to you with apology for "letting things get me down;" events of the day; and then I report that, sadly, at this time there are no "white panties" available – I've been reduced to wearing pink ones:

> but I love *you* in khaki shorts as well as white ones. . . .When in your wacky way you bring up a subject like that, I know that you haven't forgotten me one little bit and that you're going to love me when you get home just as much as you did when you left. And when you say you've often felt that even though we are apart, we've been together, I know exactly what you mean. There hasn't been a night in the last year that you haven't been with me so that I could tell you goodnight and several times little things have come up and I'd wonder would you want me to do this or that and it's almost as though you were beside me. When the girls I know go out and have a gay old time dancing and stuff, I'll confess I'd like to be going too. But I know as surely as I'm living, there's no "fun" on earth can equal the "happiness" of being your wife and loving you as I do. . . .I have a greater honest-to-goodness happiness than they can ever imagine-a feeling deep inside that never leaves me and never will. I want you here to hold me tight and never, ever let me go again. And when we're together, I'll try to show you my love is true and deep and Yours forever, Helen P.S. Come on home and I'll guarantee you won't have traveled 5000 miles just for a smile!!!
>
> *September 17, 1945:* Mom's birthday is Thursday and I don't know what on earth to get her. But with the brilliant mind I have – surely I'll think of something. [And I have truly found a gift to give her. And you will know in my next letter!]
>
> *September 19, 1945:* [Hold on to your hat!] My dearest darling:. . . Darling, tonight I have something extra special to say and to be perfectly honest I'm not sure whether you'll be really glad or not. But whatever your feelings, I'm trusting you to tell me exactly how you feel. Anyhow, grab yourself a chair before I tell you that I'm planning on being baptized the 6th of October in the Temple. It was a complete surprise to everyone – but me, of course. I didn't tell anyone until this morning. I got my

recommend last night, without telling anyone and then this morning I showed it to Mom. She was so happy, she cried. [This was my brilliant idea for her birthday present.]. . . Sweetheart, naturally I believe the Gospel or I'd never accept it, but the only reason I ever started studying about it was for you. I thought it might please you. And in trying to do something for you, I found something for myself. I hope you are happy about it! Don't be afraid either, honey, that I'm rabid on the subject and would ever try to "reform" you – I love you just as you are and what you do is up to you. For myself, I'm glad it's settled in my mind. I doubt if you'll ever know how hard it's been at times – the many times that I almost gave up and went home or – now that it is over I can tell you – the few times I almost called it quits between us for the simple reason I might be a terrible detriment to you – perhaps not so much now but in later years and maybe mess up your whole eternity. I used to go to bed at night crying about it and dream all night about it. But now, I've really studied and read until I do know that it's the right thing for me. I'm glad I'm so terribly in love with you – this is just another wonderful thing that has come to me because of you.

I went to MIA tonight and had a wonderful time. It was the opening meeting of the year – a dance – and you might be surprised at the number of dances I danced. I hope that tonight you are loving me as I love you. For even more than last night, you are first in my heart.

And so September begins to speed by for me in new activities and challenges – and I will need them to endure your continuing delayed orders. On the 20th, I write you about my promotion at the office – starting next week. I've also bought a new skirt and blouse – anticipating your approval. I also am able to inform you that if you don't get home before New Years, I can hand you a $1000 on a silver platter. The 23rd is a Sunday and I'm so lonely for you. But I've had a lovely day:

September 23, 1945: Sunday School and church and even Fireside. Since everyone has found out I'm almost a member, they've been after me with a vengeance. I don't know whatever made them think of me, but I've been asked to be the drama

> director of MIA. I protested because I don't know much about MIA classes, but it didn't do any good. It's to be a five weeks course for each class beginning with the M-Men and Gleaners, then the boy scouts and junior girls and so on. It should be loads of fun-if I just have the ability to do it. Each class, at the conclusion of its course, will give a short play and that shouldn't be too hard. I've had enough training for that, I think. The only thing I'm worried about is if I'll be able to really keep them interested. Well, I'll let you know after next Tuesday night.

[You know, Neb, it never once occurred to me that with my expanding life in the church activities, you might feel as I did, when your life back in March improved as you were in France and re-united with the Dog House Gang. If you felt deserted, dear, please forgive me. Everything I did there in Mesa was done with happiness of you in my heart. And the hope that you would be proud of your little wife. And everything that I would do in future years was always in the same hope. Every triumph of yours was a gift to my heart – and I never thought that you would feel differently. Again, why couldn't I have known?]

September 26, 1945: I inform you that:

> I had wonderful success with my drama class last night. In fact, some of the kids told me that they enjoyed themselves so much that I had actually converted them to spending Tuesday nights at Mutual. The only trouble I had was that some of the teen-age [I, myself, am still 18, but they don't know that – nor do you!] M-Men thought they were going to give me a run for my money and hold a little meeting by themselves but I soon put a stop to that. I just folded my arms and sat down and told them when they were ready for a class to let me know and we'd go ahead. It didn't take two minutes before they were ready and willing to see what I had to say. And now we're all good friends. Now next Tuesday I won't be nearly as shaky as I was last night.

And on that same day, I have written you a second letter, saying that if you are not going to be home before Christmas or New Years, I'd like to go home for a little visit. It's been seven months since I've seen any of my folks. "What do you think? And I want an answer -

don't ignore this question."

The 28th is again full of my activities – [and I just now, writing this, realize that I have missed writing to you for four nights this month. Did you realize that as my letters came in?] I am busy with a new job at the Highway Department, and I am thoroughly involved in MIA.

> *September 28, 1945:* Last night was the MIA officers and teachers convention and it was pretty late before it was over. I had a wonderful time and really learned something... Have you ever directed a play and had to have it all ready inside of four weeks? Well, believe me, sweetheart, it isn't easy! In fact, by the 30th of October, I shall probably be a gray-haired wreck. But I want very much to put on a really good performance and if hard work will do it, I will, too! So darling, keep your fingers crossed for me.

My sister, who has just turned 17, has written me about her social life and in that context I write you in this same letter:

> Seems like my life is passing so quickly; just being swallowed up in waiting for my life to really begin. Sometimes I feel terribly old. When you come home again, though, I know I'll gain back ten or twelve years and then you really will be married to a "child bride." I tell you that I've gotten thinner and my face is not as round as it used to be but I've an idea it will disappear when once again your arms are tight around me and your kisses on my lips. If I could even talk to you, some of the terrible ache would go. Since I found out you wouldn't be home for awhile, it's gotten to be just like a stone were in my breast, sometimes so heavy it's almost too much to stand. . . .but I'll hold out til you get home. . . .more than you'll ever know I need you and with all my heart I love you.

My last letter of September tells you that I have been to two sessions of Conference and it was a wonderful experience: "I marvel more and more every day at the people of our church." [Notice my unnoticed usage of "our church." I have not yet been baptized but somehow inwardly I know that "I've come home." As I reflect on this, it is really somewhat similar to how we fell into the usage of "our apartment" in those days so long ago when we were courting.] As I write you this night:

> beautiful music on the radio has made me awfully sad and awfully lonesome for you but somehow I think – or at least hope – you've been lonesome for me. . . In ten days it'll be a year since we've really been together but as far as loving you, time has made no difference to me except to increase my love for you a thousand fold. And perhaps to strengthen me just a little by the waiting. As far as I'm concerned there can never be another man for me. I love you too much to ever even have room enough for anyone else. Your loving wife "Me"

9
Hope Springs Eternal

October begins with you still in the Field Hospital. You have milked it for all it is worth, but now the doctor says you are disgustingly healthy and you are going to have to leave. But before you go, the Red Cross girls have a birthday party for you on the 4th, with ice cream and cake – which you are not supposed to eat – and even accordion music. "That sorta made the day for me," you write. On the 6th you write a brief note in which you tell me you don't know what to do about your mail, when you leave the hospital. On the 7th, you are afraid you are going to be turned out in the cold the next day:

> **7 Oct 45:** I mean cold – and I only got one blanket and my bag. If I can't round up some more blankets somewhere, I'll probably be right back in here with the flu or something. Looking on the bleak side of things, you can start looking for another change of address soon. It may be that my address may change several times between now and the time I get home.

Then you write that you have a feeling that you'll soon be on a boat headed for home. And then you ask about the bank account. The letter ends with these few words: "By golly, honey, but I'm nervous tonight – my hands jump all over the place. Maybe it's because I don't know what lays ahead."

My heart simply aches for you as I read the next few letters that will come from you. How can you bear up under all this stress of the army's indecision, after so many months of combat and then the hardness of the details that followed? I will only add to the uneasiness you feel by my letter of late September, telling you I'd like to go back to Indiana for a visit, since you will not be home for Christmas. So in an eight page letter, you write that you want me to be happy but you just don't know what I should do. What if you get home? Where would I be? You have to see your family but if I'm there, that's where you'll come. Where do we plan to live? You had thought about going back to school in Arizona. What about the money? I can see your poor mind is in a whirl and I am so sorry that I've even suggested it. But you end by trying your best to resolve the problem:

> I guess I could have said all this by simply saying Yes, Go, or No, Stay but you are my wife and have your feelings and voice in this marriage as much as I. This is another one of our talks and since it does concern you more than myself, you have what I think and you are the one to decide what you'll do. Honey, please know this – whatever you do about it – it will meet with my approval and I shall hurry as fast as possible to your side. May even get there before Christmas, you know. Darling, I do love you and you must believe that all this waiting is driving me insane for I need to be near you and with you. . . P. S. Tell me can you get head or tail out of this letter?

Then, on the 9th, it's back to the area again, where happily, you find several letters from me and your family. You receive my letter telling you of my forthcoming baptism and you write:

> **9 Oct 45:** I am so happy and thankful that you have been studying and have accepted the Gospel. I have so wanted you to know about my belief but I wanted it to come to you without interference from outside sources. That is the reason I was so strong in some of my letters to the folks. Darling, I am happy you have seen fit to be baptized! I guess you know, my sweet

> that I would have never let you call it quits because of what I believe and your ideas that it "may hold you back." I love you too much, very much to let a thing like religion stand in the way of our happiness. . If for some other reason you wanted to call it "quits," I would have said okay, although you must know that if you had it would have broken my heart. Even writing about it in discussion makes me tremble, for to lose you, my darling, would be to lose my life. Please, never think about that again – will you?

And then you compliment me on the "savings account":

> My gracious, so the nest egg is up to $700. What a wonderful cookie you are [and continuing on with the mixed up letter of the night before, you have new information:] . . . since that mixed up letter!! The newest is that they are to discharge all men with two or more years service. Since I have almost three years in, I fall into that category. . . They told me down at the [re-deployment office] that they were too busy to mess with me – so maybe I'll be home before Xmas after all. But you still let me know what you decide about going home for the season!. . . And my sweet, how do you think I feel about 'making wiz ze love when I also have gone without "it" for a year now! You know, of course, that it is just one year ago tonight since I made ze love to you! One whole year has passed since I have felt your arms, your lips, and yes even the twins. But you can be sure, sweetheart it ain't going to be another year. Why by this time next year little Jr should be here or at least on the way! Or do you think that is going to be too early. And I never believed you actually thought it was "dumb" either!!!

[Oh, but I did – at first!!! But maybe that was only because I was too tired??]

From the 15th to the 23rd you are shuffled from place to place – I really can't follow it. But on the 15th, you are at least in a warm tent and have found blankets for yourself. You write the following in reply to a letter I've written about the missionaries:

> Sweetheart, I'm afraid my ability to preach a sermon has been dulled. It has been three years since I spoke before a congregation and I'm afraid it would scare me worse than dodging a shell! However I used to be able to sling a mean sermon. I ought to have been able to as I spent two years doing nothing else. I hope you don't feel that my belief in the gospel is weakened because I don't live the Word of Wisdom. I assure you that it is just as strong or stronger than it has always been. Some people might say I don't believe the doctrine because I smoke and have a beer or two, but they say that because they think the Word of Wisdom is the only point of the gospel. True enough it is a point and I am many times ashamed of my weaknesses but I am proud it doesn't affect my faith in the church. Honey, I see I am beginning to rant and rave, so I'll quit. But I'll never quit loving you.

You write me no letters from the 15th to the 23rd, and yet on the 23rd you reprimand me severely because my letters have been postmarked two or three days after I wrote them and

> "Then you ups and don't write for two days – My, My, you must be getting something besides me on your mind? Hell, I don't blame you as I can imagine it is plenty tough on you having to wait all this time plus a few months more."

The tone of your letter offends me but you do close in a more friendly way.

> "Darling I think your suggestion of staying home for a little necking is the one for me. I been out to too many places now and all I want to do for quite awhile is to grab you in my arms for "necking" and for making wiz ze love – and I won't care whether it is in the bedroom, kitchen, bathroom or the attic, just so the two of us will be alone together. 'The sooner we get together, the happier we'll be' and that's how it is with me, honey chile!!" [Not unless you change your tone and your attitude, my dear, after all the letters I have written.]

On the 25th, you are being transferred to a base in Belgium, Chanor Base Section Headquarters. And here you will be driving trucks-or working as a typist. It's a sort of campus environment and all the work is done by POWs You have good living quarters – mattresses, entertainment, access to Paris, you inform me- all in all, a prime rear echelon billet. But you are not happy. Neither am I. And now I'm going to look back to see if I deserve your rebuke.

10
The Wear of Time

Looking back on the last days of our loving correspondence, I find that I am overcome by the deepest depression since the days I first heard about the loss of the 106th. And, as then, it derives not from the actions of either of us, but from the hand of fate, and the chaos of the embarkation offices and the absolute inefficiency of those in charge of everything. Mail is not being delivered to you – nor to me. You have written me 13 times in October, about 50 pages, and I have written 16 letters and over 60 pages in the same month. But my letters are postmarked two or three days after I write them, irritating you as shown above – and I am scarcely receiving any from you – except those that were written over a month ago. And, of course, both of us are getting edgier by the hour – or maybe minute. Great decisions are imminent for both us, but how do we make them in the midst of such uncertainty? I am a planner – and a "worrywart" – as you always say – by nature. Your response is more, "don't worry; we'll work it out." So as I've tried to plan – saving money as I can, thinking about postponing our child, giving all my unexpended energies to my new callings in the church and trying to keep you involved in all these activities- I can see how you would feel that you have been displaced in my framework of life. But I can't help it that as late as October 17th, you are just completing September's letters and up to the 5th of October. And you have been changing addresses so rapidly, I can't keep up with them. So is it any wonder that misunderstandings occur. And on the 17 of October, you have even told me not to write – the mail is too stacked up to be delivered. As of November 20th you will have received few of my October letters and none of my November writings. And a great shock will await you on the 23rd, when you do.

But before that, I will have received *your* letters in which I will see all the activity that you are engaged in, and my heart grows wearier and wearier.

My letters of November, written 60 years ago, still pain me as I read them today. The longing, the attempt to be cheerful. Every word is a cry of my heart:

> I dreamed of you last night that you were home – and when I woke up I fully expected to see you home. I've never had such real dream. . . I don't even want Christmas, if you're not here."
> On October 4th - your 26th birthday: "I've been thinking of your last birthday and how much fun we had that night. I think it would be close to heaven if I could see you and tell you how much I love you. Last year was sad because you were soon leaving – this year is sad because you're still gone.

I respond to a September letter just received that day.

> If after waiting a whole year for a husband, he comes home and is afraid to kiss me – I resign! And don't be "too afraid" of me – I'm not going to be "offended" if you make love to me. [What did you think I was waiting for?!?]

I write you of my baptism, my confirmation, my call to be drama director and the classes I am teaching, and the plays I am directing – one for the Stake. And I tell you of the friends I have made for us among the young couples, who invite me to accompany them in their activities. I'm trying so hard to make a life for you to come home to. Receiving one of your sweetest letters of September, I write:

> I'm glad to know my letters help make you happy and keep up your morale. But frankly, I think the whole thing is simply that we love each other so much we just read love into every word. I think your letters are perfect – you think they're boring and discouraging. You think my letters are good – I think they're awful. So there you have it. It just adds up to "I love you" on both sides! . . . .and as you say, I think that God Himself, brought us together – and I'll always believe that. . . because I never, ever, want to lose you.

On the 13th, I do tell you that I am having to see the doctor quite frequently – that I'm having severe headaches that almost blind me.

But I do not tell you I am having serious problems otherwise. I am having to go nearly every other day for injections, supposedly to see if they can help. Nor do I tell you that with my 60 mile bus ride to the State House, five and a half days a week, followed by an eight hour work day [in essence a fifty six hour work week] together with my Ward and Stake responsibilities – particularly with a stake drama in the process as well as the presentation for Ward on the 31st – I am literally worn to the nub. Particularly since I have to walk, to and from the bus, maybe five miles a day. I have lost sixteen pounds in a very short time, but have not paid particular attention to it. I am just too busy to think of it.

By the 16th, I receive letters of the 8th – the crazy one about whether I should go home for Christmas – and the one of the 9th about your happiness at my joining the church. This first causes me unhappiness that I have created such a problem for you and my response is, of course, "Think no more about it, honey, I'll go home when you can go with me. It'll be much nicer that way, anyhow." I tell you that you have hurt me badly by referring to the money in the bank as *my* money:

> *October 19, 1945:* I have certainly never thought of it and hope I have never written of it in that way. It's "our" money. . . I truly believe, Neb, that when in our marriage it becomes "mine" and "yours" instead of "ours" we will never be happy. I know, because I've seen it.
>
> As for living East or West – naturally, since you'll have to earn the living, it's your right to decide. . . .Once or twice in your letters you've said you thought of Chicago or Detroit, and yet in this letter you favor the west, so I really don't know what you prefer. But whatever it is, I'll be happy with it, just as long as I'm with you. [And that's the way it always was with me.] So there's really no problem at all. I won't go home – I don't care where we live – and its our money – not mine. But most of all, you must know I love you heart and soul – no matter what our problems are. You're more important to me than anything or anyone in the world. If I worry you and irritate you with my problems, forgive me, honey, and just remember that I'm naturally a "worrywart."

And I will end my letter of the 19th with "my only wish, my only prayer is that at Christmas I may be with you and then never have to leave you again. To have you, to hold you again, is all that I could ask." And, as fate – or God – would have it, "what might have been"- and was, in fact, almost possible – would not, finally, come to pass. [Even now, I can't help wondering what I did in the *pre-existence* to ensure that I would face so many continuous problems in *this* life!]

On the 21st, having received my "patriarchal blessing" I write:

October 21, 1945: We'll never have to worry about us not having any children because my blessing says I shall have children who will be an honor to us. . . It also says I shall be married in the Temple. . . Are you planning on ever being married in the Temple?

[We would be sealed for time and eternity in the Mesa Temple, with our children, on September 3, 1971, 27 years after our civil marriage, August 5, 1944.]

When I receive your letter of the 15th, regarding your belief in the church, despite your breaking of the Word of Wisdom, I write you a letter – not of rebuke but, I think, my testimony. I have no way of knowing whether you received this letter before coming home or not. I will only receive three more letters from you in October-following the one of rebuke on the 23rd – and then your next letter will be dated 23 November 1945. Had you received this letter, of the 15th, you would probably have been angry because I bluntly say:

> *October 15, 1945:* I know that being in the Army makes things a little different and there are more temptations but still, honey, I hate to think of you doing things that you're ashamed of and you, yourself said you were ashamed of yourself sometimes. If I'm ashamed of something, I try to correct it – not just apologize for it.

[And that is still what I try to do, even though I often fail.] But I end with:

I didn't mean to preach a sermon because I'll never try to tell you what you should do, but you have brought it up and I couldn't help but tell you what I felt. Perhaps it's because I never before had such a beautiful plan of our next life, but I feel so strongly about it. Really, in comparison to what we may receive, the few things we should do here seem so small and trivial in return that the least we can do is make an effort. Life here seems so short and unimportant to the time in eternity and I want so much to be able to live it with you through the rest of that time.

And then I ask your forgiveness, ". . . but we talk over everything else so I guess we can talk over our religion too, huh?" And what a naive question that was!

My last letter of October is the 28th, following six days of not writing per your instructions. But now that I have a new address I write a long, newsy letter, telling you about my preparations for the play we are to present on the 31st.

October 28, 1945: I worked [on the stage, etc.] from 9:30 until 5. I did everything from oil the curtains to building a window. Hurley helped me but he spent a great deal of time just playing the piano. Anyhow, I worked my fool head off, until I was almost sick. I came home at 5 and went back at 7 for dress rehearsal which wasn't over until 10. Anyhow, am I forgiven for not writing last night?

I've gotten some wonderful letters this week and I love you to pieces for everyone of them. . . . If you're not here for Christmas I'll go out and dig my grave and crawl in. But then if I did that, I never would feel your arms around me again, would I? Not to mention those "hot, passionate "kisses, you spoke of. It seems like years since I felt "hot and passionate" but don't worry, I can learn again. I was so cold in Sunday School this morning, sitting by Floyd Haymore and his wife, so Floyd pipes up, "Well, no wonder you're cold, look how long your husband has been gone." Was my face red, but it's the truth, I sure miss you to keep me warm. Incidentally, they're expecting a baby, I think.

> Speaking of babies, you mentioned that by this time next year, Junior would be here or on the way. But if that's the case, naturally, I can't go with you! [to college.] Did you think of that or do you honestly want him that soon? Sometimes I think I do and then again I don't. It isn't like people just have to have babies, whether they're ready or not. . . But our first baby is up to you as well as me, and while we can talk that all out later, I find myself wondering what you're thinking about it or if you are or what? If you feel we should have Quill III – or maybe it'll be a girl – as soon as we can, why, for you, I'd do it. Naturally, I expect to feel a great deal better when you get home than I do now. I still have my black out spells occasionally, but the headache isn't quite as persistent.

And so I leave you in this last letter with more problems to think of. But when you get home, I will know what your decision is.

11

November: "The Way Was Long, the Wind Was Chill"

Tomorrow and tomorrow creeps in its petty pace, so says the poet – and so say my letters of the fourteenth month of our separation. The "cementing" power of our letters is beginning to fail. The hurt of your October 23rd chastisement of me – ". . . you ups and don't write me for two days – My, My, you must be getting something besides me on your mind!" cuts me to the quick. And my first letter of November cries out to you in that pain – of heart and of body.

> I know I missed writing you for two nights and I know I used to write you at midnight but I don't think you can know how badly I've been feeling since about August. I'm so tired and worn out, not to mention the terrific headaches I have and try as hard I can, it's an awfully long pull to get feeling well again. . . .So there are times when I can't hold out even an hour longer. But I

deserve the lecture I got in my letter tonight and I'll try to do better. I know that letters must be meat and drink to you right now so I'll do my best to start again every night. [Last night I couldn't write because I'd had an eye exam and the drops didn't clear – I couldn't see much of anything up close.] I tried to write but I just couldn't. I don't think I've ever missed three nights in a row. Please forgive me and if you don't think I've been working very hard, ask Mom. Anyhow darling, you should know I never have anything on my mind as important as you. And you also know that the idea of not waiting for you never enters my head – no matter how tired I get of waiting. Naturally, I get tired, and it's discouraging and hard on me, but it's only because I love you so very much. I can't wait to have your arms around me and your lips on mine. Every bit of my heart, my mind, my body cries out for you until it's almost agony and to have you beside me one hour would be heaven. It's "hard," of course, to be loved completely and wonderfully for two months and then for thirteen long ones – and more to come – be completely without you. But would you want it otherwise? Would you want it to be easy? And isn't it hard for you? If it isn't, you don't love me very much.

So darling, never again say in that off-hand manner, that you don't blame me for not writing – or that I don't because it's "tough" on me. It cuts clear to the quick when my every thought is for you. Never in a million years could I love another man as you – never could I give to another man what I gave to you – the only thing I really had to give, myself. And if I wait another year or so, my love for you will never change, except to grow stronger. If I hadn't loved you, I wouldn't be your wife and when I love, I love for keeps. . . . So be patient and try to know that there's just a little too much to do.

Every night, letter or no, I send my love to you across the miles and surely you must know it's yours. Goodnight dearest,
Helen

And so my letters of November continue: the 3rd, I take a bad fall over the garbage can while trying to hang clothes out on the clothes line in the dark. 4th: I tell you of my horrid boss – a "second childhood" old man with a bald head and black false teeth, who tries to put his hand all over me every time he's near – my shoulder, my knees, grabbing my hand.

> *November 4, 1945:* He's the kind that likes to make insinuating remarks that embarrass me. I hate him so much and I can't stand him and it's affecting my work And he knows it bothers me because one time when I jerked away from him, he asked me if I were going to tell my husband and then in his cute little way remarked that you were too far away to do any good. . . .One of these days I'm going to have one big blow out with him and then this little cookie will be out on her ear.

5th November – 15 months married – Today I send you, not a love letter, but the news that the Red Cross is going to be sending you papers to expedite getting you home. Your mother has already been to see them and they feel that you have every right to be home after such a long run around and especially because your wife is truly ill. And furthermore, they have said, many men have come home in such a manner. So you will be receiving papers and you are to follow orders and get them where they should be taken. If you do, you may *be home for Christmas* after all. Knowing this is going to be a shock to you, I try to prepare you carefully:

> *November 5, 1945:* Don't be alarmed about me. It's just a matter of form. I have been going to the doctor several times a week, but it's nothing serious. She seems to feel that she can't help me much until you're home. This isn't the reason for Mom's going to the Red Cross but it's a help, perhaps. My doctor will give us a notarized paper [and several other papers and then it's up to you.] . . . and try your grandest to convince them you should come home because it's true that I need you so very much. I know that you can really make me well again – and happy forever.
>
> *November 6, 1945:* I still haven't received letters for two weeks.
>
> I'm going to warn you again tonight not to take all these letters you'll soon be getting from the Red Cross seriously. The way they sound, you'll probably think I'm ready for the grave, but

> I'm really not. Maybe I have lost sixteen pounds, but I needed to.

And then I urge you not "to get any silly idea that you shouldn't come home through the Red Cross. It's fair and square and truthful."

Creeping into these letters of November – perhaps because of my failing strength – there is almost a doleful undercurrent of fear about your still loving me: "I only hope that when you get here you'll find me as you did when you left – even though I may look a little tired. . . I worry quite a bit that you may be disappointed in me."

> *November 7, 1945:* This is the 18th day without mail – almost as bad as last winter. As usual, with mom in Prescott, it's lonely around here, but I still have that feeling of contentment. I guess I'll always have the longing for a place of my own – to be shared only with you. More than anything I want a home for us with you coming home to me each evening. I want to make our home so happy that you never get tired of coming home – that no matter how long we're married, we'll always have this love for each other. That's truly the only thing I want.

On the 10th, I go to a wedding reception – my first ever-and again the weakness of my body and spirit is evident: Writing of the beauty of the reception:

> *November 10, 1945:* But when it came to the music, it tore my heart into little pieces – I had to come home before I cried like a baby. I don't know why I'm like that, but it doesn't take much anymore to absolutely break me up, and this longing for you here lately is nearly more than I can stand. I wished tonight that it were our wedding night and that this time we'd never have to be apart again.
>
> But when you do get home, it'll be just like being married again, only, oh so much nicer, because this time I won't be so scared and we won't be so strange – or will we? After thirteen months, I'm not sure just how I'll feel!!!

I write only nonsense on the 11th. The next letter, the 13th, follows up on the Red Cross paper work and what you are to do, but I am more frank with you about my health.

> *November 13, 1945:* I haven't said too much about how I've felt since I didn't want to worry you, but I haven't been very well since about July. The summer heat took me for a loss and then on top of that I've had so much trouble with that pain in my side for several weeks. And then I've had these headaches til at times I could hardly stand them – sometimes they seemed to blind me. I'm not having them so much now, but by this time, I'm so nervous and worn out that nothing seems to do me much good. In fact, I seem to be tied in a knot inside and it doesn't take much to start me on a grand old crying spree. . . don't think I'll get any better until you are home. I need you badly.

As I've written the above just now, I feel a kind of shame at revealing such weakness. But as I think of it in detail, it's really not impossible to see that I'm literally on the way to a nervous break down. And with cause. In the last 15 months, I've undergone several "major life crises," as a psychiatrist would say today. First, the courtship, then the engagement, then marriage, then you going overseas with a Unit that is almost completely devastated in the Battle of the Bulge – and great mourning for you for over two months before I know of your safety. Then I close up my residence, move into my family's home for two months, after which I travel across the U. S. to meet your family and to find a completely strange life style. I also find, and start, a tasking new job. And then, the Hell of my first Arizona summer. And still the months drag on without you. Is it any wonder that I'm ill? If I weren't a "tough cookie," I wouldn't have survived at all! Honey, I'm surely one of war's "walking wounded!"

I fail to write you, again, on the 14th. But my letter of the 15th tells you why and sends bad news. "Your mom has been very ill with a severe eye attack – and I stayed home from work yesterday to care for her. Her pain was so bad, Dad took her to Dr. Case. She had an ulcer and so he burned it off and gave her some medicine and said if she wasn't better in three or four days, she'd have to go to the hospital. So she's still in bed and pretty well doped."

I continue my tale of woe, with an account of my experience when I returned to work the next day.

November 14, 1945: . . I went back to work yesterday feeling pretty good. But by noon, they had run me around so much, 'I no feel so good.' One of the ladies mentioned that I didn't look so good and told me to go lie down for a few minutes. I fully intended to but I just didn't get a chance. A little later, I was waiting on a fellow, had his money in one hand and before I knew, I got a violent pain like I've never had before – the money went one way and I went the other way. [I was mortified to pieces, when I finally got over it.] But the next thing I remember I was downstairs in the lounge with my shoes off and a cold towel on my face and I didn't even know what had happened. They called the doctor and she told them to bring me down to her office – and down I went in a Highway Patrol car. Results: no more work til Monday, at least, plenty of rest, and a trip to the hospital for some X-Rays. And that's all. Lot of commotion for such a little thing, huh?

Sweetheart, do you love me enough for it not to make any difference if it should take me a while longer to get straightened out? It worries me so much that I can hardly stand it. I've tried so hard to manage but I can't seem to do much. Before we were married I was never like this – you know that – so I have a deep faith that when you're home and we can be together in a normal life, I'll be okay. I really think it's been, first, getting married itself and then immediately beginning worrying about you leaving and then having you gone. But I know that when I'm with you again, I'll be the same happy and well cookie I was when I first met you. Anyhow, how do you really feel about the situation? It's only fair to tell you, because I love you so much I can't hold anything from you. If you don't think I'm worth the bother, I wouldn't even care about trying to get well. I just love you too darned much for my own good that's all!

P.S. I don't think you "love me terribly," I think you make wiz the love better than anyone (voice of experience, huh?) Also, I didn't write what I did to worry you, I just wanted to be fair with you. And please, honey, don't mention any of this to your folks. [They worry so.]

About this time, I begin to receive a letter or two from you. On the 15th, I receive your letter of November 5th, when you're living at the

11th of November Club, where you seem to be an overseer in the kitchen. That is, you are trying to control theft in the kitchen since all of the workers are civilian. As you usually do, you have made friends with everyone – the chefs, the serving staff – and you write:

> **5 Nov 45:** oo la la – I have a private room, private bath, complete with a terrace, etc. Of course it is a small room and it has only a single bed but I would be more than glad to share it with you. I may say that the mattress is the very best - feather plus innerspring. However, I'm sure it won't squeak to keep the neighbors awake!!! If you get what I mean! [Of course I do!] I guess that you know that it can't be too much longer before I shall be able to try to live up to all this talk I have been giving you. Not especially in the physical aspect but also by showing you how really bad that I have got it for you. Darling, my heart tells me such beautiful things about you and my head just can't help but endorse each little thought and action. I couldn't anymore help loving you than the proverbial cow could help jumping the moon. There is just something about you, baby, that is good for me

In this same letter, I can see that you are concerned about some of the same things that have been disturbing me:

> Here we have been man and wife for 14 months, apart for 12 [hey, dear boy, you've goofed up on your counting! I make it 15 and 13!] and it looks as if it will be still another two. Now what I want to know is; after 14 months apart are you still going to love me? Let me tell you that I am going to still love you, if it should be 14 years! That is just how strong my love is for you. . . I miss your pretty smile and lovely face – not saying how I miss your presence and talks together and making wiz ze love!!! I just miss looking at you – and I'd certainly love to have you in my arms.

In response to this letter of yours, on the 16th I reply that I'm glad things are a little better for you:

> *November 16, 1945:* , , , there in Belgium-private room, private bath, private terrace! Goodness what a Private husband I have!!!

> Even that single bed sounds all right to me since you're so willing to share it with me. After all, what loving couple needs a double bed anyhow – so much of it isn't used! I'm not worried in the least about you living up to "all this talk" you've been giving me because I remember how you make love. That's the trouble, I remember too well, especially those last few weeks. Don't know why in particular, but I have. Anyway, I feel I won't cry "quits," as you put it – betcha I last longer than you!! Twenty Yankee nickels!! Anyhow, wait til the time comes – and this time I'll know why my back aches!

And so each of us, in the midst of the details of our separate lives, continue to try to keep the spark alive. But you are not getting my mail, you tell me on the 9th. And some of the men have not had mail regularly for months.

> **9 Nov 45:** Not getting mail really gripes me – for I do need it so much. I'd just like to know what you are doing right now. If you were with me, I'd tell you what you would be doing. You'd be getting kissed and loved like you've never been kissed and loved before. I believe I got more than enough to make you hollar quits. You may hollar quits but I shall never quit loving you.

And then your letter of the 12th indicates another transfer for you because they are going to close all the Clubs; you don't know where you will go. And you despair of your mail ever catching up to you.

> **12 Nov 45:** Darling, I still haven't received any mail but I know that letters are on the way every day! One day soon I'll get 'em all at one time. . . . Dearest, I often wonder just how much longer it is really going to be before I am with you for keeps. Sometimes it seems only a short time and then again it seems like it will be ages yet. I have never wanted anything as badly as I want to look at you in person – I want to hold you forever in my arms and kiss you tenderly-terrible and rough. I want to so badly that it is an actual pain that eats down to the depths of my very soul. Yes, my darling, there is no danger of my not missing you, not wanting you. . . you are the only girl in this

> world . . . One look at you is enough to erase all the longing I have had the past year. [Now that I'm not sure how to take, dear!] Baby, how I am looking forward to that day – be it before or after Christmas – all I know is that it will be soon – and yet so far away.

I continue to write - at least every other day. I write again of the Red Cross papers; tell you your mother is better; report on the preparations for Thanksgiving on the 22nd:

> *November 22, 1945:* This is our second Thanksgiving apart and if the first was hard, this one is worse. But this day will really be one of Thanksgiving for now I know that you will return to me as you went away and except for your presence, I couldn't ask for anything more.

I also tell you that:

> The last two days have been very trying and if anything else can happen, I wish it would and get it over with. Naturally, another week without mail is tragic. I got a letter from my grandmother yesterday and she told me that mother has been in a hospital for several days suffering from a nervous breakdown. This isn't her first one and I'm terribly worried. If Mom would go to a hospital, she's pretty bad. I do wish I could see her. My darling, I feel that it isn't going to be another month until I'm holding you close and telling you, I love you so, Helen

On the 16th, you write of Churchill's state visit to Brussels and the traffic snarl it has caused, making it difficult for you to get to work on time. You also tell me about meeting "your old buddy," [everyone you meet is an old buddy] and painting the town with him. Naturally, you went to a night club, where you tried dancing, but gave it up since there was no floor – and because the only

> gals that hang around cafes here, as in Paris, are "business" gals and they flock around a couple of soldiers. The cheapest bid was 200 francs for the night – the highest was 850. Bob and I had a fair time but we had to catch the 11 o'clock tram. .

> ..Darling, I am now going on the 4th week without the morale lift of your letters . . .Lots of boys have told me they have had no mail for 6 or 8 weeks – at least I am a little better informed than they, eh?

I will get this letter on the 30th and I reply that I'm glad you and Bob

> had a good time painting the town red. But what you said, little chum, what you said!! Quote! "The cheapest bid was 200 francs for the night, the highest was 850. Bob and I had a fair time etc,". No reason why you shouldn't have had a super time because 9 to 11 is a long time!!! It didn't use to take us that long and over here we hear tell that for those Belgian girls the duration is six minutes! What's the matter honey – are you slipping? Big joke, huh? Better be!!

And so I try to write faithfully all the long, cold month of November, but like you, I skip a day now and then. The song is not ended – only the melody lingers on. Trying to express this and accepting your apology for skipping a day occasionally, I write:

> Honey, I know how it is. I know that neither one of us write this last month as we used to but if your heart is as mine, it's not that there's less love, only that there is nothing much to say when everything is always the same. I think you're wonderful to write as often as you do. . . [And I try to explain my own failure:] I've lost completely the little ability I once had. I can't seem to express myself at all. There is music and love in my heart for you but the words don't come. Perhaps it's because I've used all my words expressing my love or perhaps it's the fact that every day my love for you has increased until it's become so great it's useless to even try to convey it with pen and paper. However, I know you know this so until I can show you, I won't worry about it.

And then I "call on each memory" of every day we have spent together – our Sundays, your stopping in the middle of the street to kiss me – and how the kisses "made me weak clear to my toes – even worse than Singapore Slings!" I end with "What's happened to Junior?" And I add that I've been to a Church dance and danced every dance from 9 to 12. And I want you home to take me to the

Gold and Green Ball at the Mezona at Christmas.

You will write three more letters in November, that cold, cold month for me here in Mesa, with only a little gas heater in the apartment to keep me warm. I am used to coal furnaces that blast heat to every room. And I am longing to see my mother and my family in the old familiar places. But your letters will tell me of your wisdom tooth which has broken off and must be surgically removed; the flu shot that has caused your arm to hurt, "Everything happens to me all the same day," you write on the 20th. And "in three days it will be just a month since I got any letters from you." And so that will mean you have probably received *none* of my faithfully written November writings. But on the 23 November 1945, you will write me this startled letter:

> **23 Nov 45:** My Darling Wife, For a month I don't hear from you and then yesterday I get all these papers through registered mail. I must say that they came as a complete shock and I certainly hope that you are in no actual danger. I can understand the nervous strain you have been under and I realize that your health hasn't been too good – now I am worried for fear you are quite ill. Darling I hope that you are somewhat better and that soon I'll be home with you

Then you explain that you have immediately started the process:

> but I have heard these cases have taken three weeks or so but I have hopes of getting it all done next week. Then it should be only a short time before I am with you. Take care of yourself, my darling, cause I am trying to hurry home to you.

And then you give me instructions to immediately quit work, and to start the process to have the Army reimburse me for all medical bills. The army is responsible and the army should pay!

> When I get home we are going to find out what's wrong with you and get it fixed up for good – but in the meantime, you take it easy and don't worry about a thing – I'll be home before too long and then we'll really celebrate my return to civilian life.

Darling, I love you so very much and it hurts me to know that you are ill – So get well, my sweet and I'll see that you stay that way. Now don't be foolish about anything and you quit working.

And then you threaten to" raise a little hell over here with some stubborn T/Sgts-officers or whoever tries to give [you] the run around. "I love you, darling."

On November 26th, you write that the papers are ready for final approval.

26 Nov 45: After that, it should be a short time before I'll be on my way. All together it will take about two weeks for everything. I don't know which will be faster in getting me home now. I was told I'd be on orders the first of December to go home on my points. However, going home on emergency should cut the trip by three weeks. In 5 to 8 days, I'll know if our Home by Christmas has the final approval. I got the papers all filled out and approved as far as they could be here in Brussels. Tomorrow they will go the Theatre Headquarters for the last step. The Red Cross man said that it was a cinch on being approved on account of being notarized. I believe in two weeks I'll be on a boat coming home to you and that I'll be home for Christmas!! Great day!

You end this letter by again telling me to quit work, quit church, quit everything and just rest. And then you do one of your very rare things: you apologize to me.

Honey, I'm sorry about writing you concerning your letters. I must have been feeling mighty blue that day and I thought I put it in such a way that you would know I was kidding you. Baby, I feel it a pleasure for you to write even one letter to a monkey such as I. And I do feel greatly honored that you love me as you do. Course I'll bet you a million Yankee nickels that my love for you is just as strong. I love you so, Your homecoming Neb - Kisses to you!!

30 November: You are now beginning to get my letters regularly

although there are some that will probably come after you get home. The letter about your mother and my fainting has worried you:

> **30 Nov 45:** Sweetheart, you must quit working and get away from the strain because I don't want you to be passing out too much until I get there to catch you – I can do that pretty well you know! It shouldn't be long before you'll be in my arms and I can take care of you as I should be doing now. Darling, I love you so – be careful with yourself – and tell mother to hurry up and get well too – Love for Always Your Neb

In this next to last love letter you will send me, you give the details of your return. The next day or so the papers are approved – and you should be on the first boat possible. After that, the fastest you can get home will be about two weeks. It takes 6 days on the fastest boat to reach New York – then it will be another 6 or 7 days' train ride home. But there might be a chance of catching a plane once you get to N. Y. However, if the next boat available is a Liberty Ship, it is a slow crosser and will take about two weeks to reach the States. As you say, you'll have to hurry if you want to make it by Christmas! And again, you want me to find out how to get the Army to fund my doctor bills.

On December 4th, your approval is yet to come in but should be by tomorrow. You are waiting for a teletype from Frankfurt, Germany. [Oh, the efficiency of the Armed Forces!] You have received my letters of the 21st & 23rd and are slightly relieved about me but:

> **4 Dec 45**: I can't help but worry about you for I know how our pet pain used to get you, Maybe you'll be rested up by the time I get there and I had better not find you working." You tell me that you hope to get home in time for Christmas dinner and to "grab a rabbit [how you loved fried rabbit and I learned to cook it just the way you liked] fatten the bunny and I'll have me some good meat when I get home – eh? Good meat in more ways than one, eh!!! Sweetheart, I want to hurry home to you so I can just hold you close, kiss you tenderly and whisper in your ear, Darling, I love you.

This will be your last love letter to me in your service abroad. And my letter of December 2nd will end our literary romance:

> *December 2, 1945:* Tonight I'm so very lonely for you that I'm afraid I've indulged in that strictly feminine cure-all, a little crying. I've been lying in front of the fire for the last hour or so reading your dear letters. That always brings you closer and I long for you til I can hardly stand it. And when I go back to your May and June letters with all our plans for a summer that is several months past and you're still so far away, it tears my heart.

And remembering how different we both are I write: "I hope that in our life together, you'll never let me hurt our marriage when I get bothered by some little thing. Seems like sometimes little things hurt me terribly and in return I hurt you. If you took me seriously, anything could happen."

And on December 14, 1945, exactly three weeks after application for Emergency Orders have been initiated, you will embark for the United States of America, exactly 13 months following your departure for the European Theater. And you will arrive in New York, on 2 January 1946. I will learn all this, long after the fact. The warrior-lover's return home is still to come.

Book Two

The Book of Life

January 1946 – September 2005

"Let me not to the marriage of true minds
Admit impediments. Love is not love
Which alters when it alteration finds....
O, no! It is an ever fix-fixed mark,
That looks on tempests and is never shaken;
Shakespeare: Sonnet 116

Part I

Living the Dream

Adam's "DREAM" -- he awoke and found it "TRUTH"

Keats 1817

1
And Then Our Life Begins

My only love and husband,

As I begin this second book which is to be part of my final "Love Letter" to you, I am acutely aware that I have undertaken an almost impossible task: to chart and understand the happenings, the joys and sorrows of our next 56 years of married life – and to strive to make sense of them. To guide me, I will no longer have our wonderful letters – written from the hearts of two separated lovers – to hold me to the straight and narrow path of truth and understanding. Furthermore, I cannot give you, through my knowledge of your heart and mind, the opportunity to speak for yourself – to address from your point of view the joys, the sorrows, the reasons for your choices and your actions, in all the circumstances of the years that we would share together. For, as time passed in the pressures that all newly-weds experience and in the difficulties of readjustment to a peace time world for both of us, often, as I sought to understand, to share with you your thoughts and feelings, you shut me out. Before, in our long and lonely months apart, with the breathing spaces afforded by distance and the slowness of the postal system, there was always time to think, to adjust, to "cool down" over seeming offense or hurtful feelings. And trusting one another, we wrote straightforwardly of our feelings and our needs. We shared intimately, without fear or rancor, all things of our lives. Anything and everything. But after your return, and in the immediacy of adjusting to our real road of life, such communication often failed. And in the times when we most desperately needed to recognize and verbalize our love and need and sympathy *for* one another and *to* one another, we withdrew into ourselves. My love, for 15 long months of distance and danger, we talked to each other from our hearts, holding nothing back. But such "entrusting of *my* heart," you did not seek, nor did you want, as time went by. Nor did you seek or want it for yourself. You came, progressively, to clothe your heart and mind, at least to me, in an unfamiliar armor of *Silence*!

And so, my dear, in writing of our life after the war, I can only depend upon my memories, sharp and accurate as they may be, reinforced not by letters from our hearts, but by photographs, public records, etc. And *you* reading my account, can only depend upon my sincere desire to be scrupulously honest in all that I remember – and upon my growth and understanding that has come with age. In the end, this is all that I can offer. I do not know the answers. I cannot solve the riddles. But you must believe, as God's own truth, that *I loved you then; I love you now; I'll love you to the end.*

And I hope that you can say the same to me, when "we'll meet again!"

Forever, Helen

2

I Shall Not Love You In December

I have no record of when I would have received your last letter dated December 4, 1945, but I'm certain it could have been no earlier than the 11th or 12th, given the mail situation. But on the 6th of December, when you wire from Bruxelles: "Papers approved. Starting home Sunday. May be there by Xmas," I am filled with hope that you will be with me on Christmas Day. But Christmas is over and you have not come. Only after anxious days do I receive a cablegram, dated 26 December 1945: "Delayed at Azores, Land about two weeks. All well."

So, as I had written you on the 19th of November, "my only prayer . . . that at Christmas I may be with you," would have been a possibility – had not God or fate decreed a wicked hurricane in the Azores Islands, which nearly wrecked your ship and caused delay for repairs, somewhere in the wintry mid-Atlantic. [It was in this terrible storm that you lost most of your possessions, as I remember – and

Junior! For you never spoke of him again.] But now, for sure, I knew you were *en route*. Again, I must live on tenterhooks until I receive your call from your reception base in New York. Those days seemed endless! Fortunately, I had had the wisdom not to quit work as you had instructed – choosing to take my accrued vacation time when you got home, while at the same time drawing my salary. So mercifully, I was able to keep busy – though so edgy I must have been an irritant to everyone. Then, finally, you call. You are at a reception base in New York, but all the troops on your ship are quarantined. *An outbreak of scabies!* All must be deloused and re-outfitted with clothing. It will mean another week or ten day delay. Then, because you are on "emergency" status, you hope to catch an Army transport plane to Fort MacArthur where you will receive your papers for leave, before you are demobilized. Then, God willing, we will be together, in Los Angeles, for our long awaited reunion and "second honeymoon."

And so we wait some more. But on the 8th or 9th of January [I really can't remember now] at the state office, on the west side of Phoenix, about 10 a.m., your phone call comes. And once again, I am "On the Merry-go-Round" – just as I had been 17 months earlier in July of 1944, preparing for our wedding. You are, you say, at Fort MacArthur, outside of L.A. awaiting clearance and orders. As soon as you have them, you'll go directly to Hollywood, where you will try to get accommodations from the Red Cross, if possible. I am to meet you in Pershing S0quare, just as soon as I can get there. You will wait until I come, in the square – and we'll "work it out" from that point. And so, for the first time in over a year, we hear each other's voices – and are filled with joy.

Darling, I would have met you in Timbuktu if you had asked, but you've no idea how frightened I was with your instructions and all the details. In the first place, I had never flown – and was scared to death of flying. Now, I not only had to fly, but I had to make flight arrangements, get back to Mesa (30 miles by bus), get my suitcase, get back downtown to get a bus to the airport – if I could get a ticket – and then find out how to get to this Pershing Square of which I had never heard. All in time to meet the love of my heart before he grew tired of waiting for me! So, as 17 months before, there was, for me, pressing uncertainty and activity, with my fellow workers rooting for me all the way. Well, I managed it all! I was able, luckily, to reserve a ticket on the last flight to L.A. that day. My faithful bus driver, with whom I rode both morning and evening to and from the center of Mesa, broke every possible speed law between Phoenix and Mesa *and then* actually drove me down from the normal stop downtown to 120 S. Lesueur *and waited for me to pack my suitcase* before *he delivered me directly to the airport, with the consent of the few passengers.* Would anybody, in this day and age, believe that? Of course, the airport was very small, and the traffic was that of a small town today, but I have never forgotten this driver's solicitude for me, his passenger, that most important day of urgency. Without him, I would not have made my flight.

And how I managed to get from the airport to that Pershing Square – to this day I don't really know where it is – and *then* to find it a huge place, with hundreds [it seemed to me] of people milling around, most of them uniformed service men, I shall never understand. I only know I searched the crowds, bewildered... Oh, how am I to find you, my love? I wait. And I wait. And you are not there. Am I in the wrong place? On the wrong day? At the wrong time? I begin to grow afraid.

Then suddenly, just as in my dream I'd told you of, I see you! And you see me! And we are running. And I am in your arms. And you are kissing me – hard and terrible, as you have promised. And I see your sweet face. And then, at last encircled tightly in your arms, I know that all is well.

The Soldier Returns

3

But I Shall Love You in January, In Hollywood, Ooh, la la!

After that – as after our wedding ceremony so many months ago – the events are a blur. I don't remember if we ate – it had been a long day for both of us by this time – but I do remember that you stopped three times, in the middle of the sidewalk, to kiss me thoroughly, as you had done so many times before in Indianapolis. And I do remember that we had to hurry to the Red Cross housing office, hoping against hope for a hotel room to be found for us, in this busy city now overrun with service men on leave. But finally, the gods were with us: after what seemed an agonizing time, an available room was located in the old Hollywood Hotel, convenient to everything. But one drawback: the time limit – strictly enforced in fairness to all service personnel – was four nights per reservation. We had hoped for more time. But it was now late evening – and both of us were very tired – so with our permit in hand, we hurried to ensure the precious place for our reunion!

The Hollywood Hotel, now past its prime, was certainly not the swank Chicago Stevens, but it was clean and the bed was good. I remember you laughingly "tested" the springs for their "squeaking" quality and remarked that it was at least a double bed, unlike the single bed you had offered to share with me in your "private" accommodations in Belgium. And I remember that I had told you a single bed was perfectly adequate for loving, since half the bed was wasted. And in such idle talk, we ease the tension. But as we unpack, we discover that there is no *en suite* bathroom: that accommodation is "down the hall." We laugh and conclude that, well, we'll manage. And then, the easy talk, the "busy" work is over and suddenly, just as on our honeymoon, you are reaching for me; you are telling me you love me and I am so beautiful. And you enfold me in your arms, as though I had never left them. And this time there will be no need of lessons. Nor is there hesitancy, on either side. But soon, without words, before we unite as one for the first time in fifteen months, I know that you have decided we should wait, at least a little time, for Junior. And I am grateful for your care of me.

Well dear, I have no letters to remind me of that night – nor of the three more nights to come – either in your words or mine. But I remember. There was no fear, no holding back by you or me. You had, indeed, saved all your strength and love, for me. And I had waited for it, wanted it with all my being. And I remember that I had not had time to pack my Paulette Goddard negligee. But it didn't matter; I had no need of it. Nor did you. And I remember clearly all that night. We loved and then we slept; and then we loved again and talked; and then we loved once more. And you assured me, again and again, that the "twins" were as lovely as ever and that they still "knew their daddy." And finally, we slept again. And all night through, my passion met your passion. And neither one of us cried "quits," all through that night and early day. And sweetheart, in those hours of loving, I knew that you had found no lack in me and that you proved for yourself, beyond a shadow of a doubt, that I did not think "it" dumb!

Much later, about two the following afternoon, exhausted by love and the eager talk that follows, we decide we ought to replenish ourselves with food, since neither of us had eaten since breakfast the day before. So, showered and refreshed in our "bathroom down the hall," we went for food. And then to shop for your wedding ring. By this time, we had both agreed that you had earned it. In fact, I have assured you that, despite your fears expressed in several letters, you are "man enough" for anything – even Junior when that time comes. We ate a mid-afternoon lunch – or early dinner – at the beautiful just-opened Clifton's Cafeteria, near us. And it was, indeed, a beautiful place in 1946. A professional photographer took our picture there and that wonderful photograph hangs in my den, showing – if one looks knowingly – your familiar [to me] morning-after smile of satisfaction and pride of ownership in me. And my smile and eyes reflect what I know is my perfect joy and happiness with you. [I do not point this out to others – only you and I will know that that photo reflects the joyous melding of our bodies, hearts, and souls.] And then, having explored the grotto and the other beauties of this new type of dining room, we go to buy your ring. And that evening, before we once again make love, I place it on your finger as a token of our commitment, faith, and love.

I do not remember vividly, just what we did those next three days. I know you wanted continual activity, despite the loving tiring of the nights. I know we went to Long Beach and you carried me up a long, steep hill to the amusement park, because my pain was troubling me. And I protested all the way – but you were so proud of your strength and loved to show it off. And we spent the day in Long Beach. And we explored the shops of Hollywood. And we went to some quiet afternoon rendezvous bars, where you enjoyed your beer or two. And we went dancing. But always I knew that night would bring us back to "Yankee nickels" and "the twins" and "making wiz ze love." And I was eager – and content.

But then, our fourth night was up and money was running low, so you decided that we should take the bus to Mesa, in the afternoon of the last day. And I do remember how very tired I was and how long and uncomfortable the trip. Remember, I was not really well. But I slept on your shoulder all the way, covered with a blanket. And you were full of care for me. And then the Second Honeymoon was over! As your family welcomed us at the bus depot, late that night, I realized we would not be alone again for many crowded days of family, friends, and stress.

4

"You Can't Go home Again"

The happiness of your father and mother as they met us at the depot was touching and tearful. I watched them welcome home the son they had not seen in two years, and knew their joy. Your dear mother, bless her heart, clung to you and sobbed. And your dad's well-camouflaged pride would only be equaled by yours, when nearly 24 years later, you would see your own son commissioned, at Quantico, as a new lieutenant in the United States Marine Corps. Quickly, the plans unfolded. It was too late – and expensive – for us to get a motel room for the night. So, it was decided that we'd stay with your parents at least the next two nights. Then Stell had planned a family reunion and dinner at her home in Phoenix, and then, we could begin to make further plans. We'd have to go to Prescott to see Anne and Tense; then, in three weeks, you were under orders to return to Fort MacArthur for your formal discharge from the Army. So shortly, all of us were in the tiny apartment that had been my home – mine and your mother's – for the last ten months. I hadn't thought to tell you, in all those months, that I slept on a made-up couch in the living room – or with your mother, if Dad was traveling. And it was on that couch that we would sleep tonight – since Dad was home and there was only the one bedroom. I wondered if you were thinking then – as I was – of our dear apartment that had welcomed us in Indianapolis after our return from our first honeymoon. I'm sure your parents were aware of your dismay – I certainly was – but what was there to do? Why had I not made better plans – despite the uncertainty which had clouded all our actions for so many months?

But what was *was*, I thought, and we'll survive!

That was my thought. But that was not your intent! And on that night in Mesa, we had our first disagreement. I simply could not "make wiz ze love" with your parents in the adjoining room. And, rebuffed and furious, you could not ease your frustration by smoking a cigarette in bed, in your mother's house. So you had to get up and go outside, and I knew your displeasure with me. And in the morning, after a restless night, for both of us, I could not make you coffee and bring it to you, and smother you in kisses, in apology. But your mother made a marvelous breakfast and you forgot – or disciplined – your discontent. Later, when I took you for my usual long walk down to the center of Mesa – just to free you from the pressure of the house – you had one of your famous no-nonsense "talks" with me, firmly declaring that you would have no more shyness from me about our making love. You hadn't held off "loving," for so many months, to be thwarted now that you were finally home. And your parents should understand that, you said, and if they didn't, too bad! And that's how it was to be; you had spoken! [And here, I might remark that I did end up sleeping, all our life together, on the right side of the bed – despite my declaration, some months earlier in a letter to you, that the left side was mine or that one of us would end up sleeping on the floor.]

But when through the years I acquiesced with you, [as I would following your "talk" that day] it was never out of fear. Always, I simply tried to honestly consider your point of view – and to agree with it, if it were possible. Or else, as in the case of which side of the bed to sleep on, I loved you and it didn't really matter. And that night, when we went to bed, I "forgot" your folks in the adjoining room, and gave myself to you as you desired. And, as always, you were careful about Junior.

I don't believe, until the writing of this letter, that I ever consciously considered your pressures, as you returned to your family "source." I should have been more aware, remembering my own difficulties in coping with your family's strange new ways when I first came to Arizona. For, as you returned to their midst, your family was, essentially, unchanged. And you were not. No longer were you the callow youth of 22, raised in a hard life of depression years, with only two years of college, and a just-completed two year church mission, before you were drafted. Now you were a nearly 27 year old battle-hardened, newly married man, of unimaginable experience and complexity. During the last three years, you had thrown off of necessity, and choice, many of the socially imposed restraints of the past. You had emerged whole – at least on the surface – from a harsh, completely male-oriented world of survival and self-interest. And never again could you be what you once had been. And I instinctively had realized this. But unfortunately, your family – especially your mother – had no such understanding. You were welcomed back into the family as a hero – but more importantly, as the only son of a deeply religious, older mother, and the "little brother" of three adoring – but critical and bossy – sisters, with families of their own – each of them with busy, pre-occupied husbands. In essence, you would be grist for their mills of discipline and reform and I would, in the years to come, be entrapped in your never ceasing conflict. Now, in retrospect, how it seems so like the family circumstances into which I had been born – a martinet of a mother, no father's presence, and an overwhelming need to escape into something for which I would not be responsible. As I had fought for my concept of freedom, so you would come to do – however disastrous your way might be or how indefensible your motives. And sometimes, now, I almost understand. And I forgive.

But to get back to the welcome home. Two nights in Mesa, then off to Stell's for a welcome and a family dinner. Here we will be asked to stay the night and Rae gives up her room, and the bed squeaks, but we make love, and you're happy with me. [And I'm hoping everyone sleeps soundly.] But the next day, Dad suggests that since he has two days of work at the Capitol and can take the bus, if Stell can't give him a ride, that you and I take his car, do what we want, and then spend the next night in Mesa in the apartment, by ourselves. Then, we can pick him and Mom up the following day and we'll drive up to Prescott where we will be welcome to stay with Anne or Tense's families.

Now those who didn't live through the years of war won't know what a wonderful gift it was to be given Dad's loan of a car – especially out here where Mesa and even Phoenix are still little more than large towns and public transportation is almost nil. In the city where I had lived all my life, public transportation was taken for granted. And in the cities where you had been – Paris and Brussels and Frankfurt – such travel was the norm. But here we had a car – thanks to Dad's thoughtfulness. And tomorrow was my birthday! And you had remembered what I had written you on our 9th month anniversary: "I sure would like to go out on a fling, like I have once or twice in my life – you know a couple of Singapore Slings and a double Tom Collins. . . I'm so tired of being good I could scream. So darling, when you get home, you can just plan on taking me out for a good howl!" And that's what you planned for my birthday. We would go downtown to the Adams Hotel and have dinner in the Sapphire Room – and dance 'til I was so tired I'd drop. And so we did. And I have a beautiful picture taken there, on my 19th birthday – but it's 22 to you – and I am wearing my little black hat with the pink feather and am smiling with happiness. And you are handsome and smug with – is it expectancy or complacency? [Either way, I know what you have on your mind.] And we did dance, and I'm wearing the pin you bought me for our anniversary. And as I've said in my letter, you do "drink lightly to see that I get back home okay, but one night is mine!" And it was. In ways I could never possibly foresee.

My Nineteenth Birthday

But we do get home safely. And the house is ours, and I now know, for sure, what that look on your face has meant. And we are alone; and we explore; and we kiss. And our passion mounts. But almost at the moment of crisis, you realize you do not have "the step" to prevent Junior. Then, well, it's too late! And I remember thinking, at the instant of consummation, "I'm probably unable to conceive anyhow." And then, as I had said when I decided to marry you, the die was cast and without words or thought, we are suddenly fulfilled, replete: exhausted – as never before – by our encompassing passion. We sleep until noon the next day. And I will never forget this night of my 19th birthday because, in my moment of waking, I *sense*, instinctually, that in our overwhelming passion, we have engendered our son! And I remember the dream I'd written you of just six months ago:

> "You were home and we were really having a wonderful time. We were in Phoenix window shopping and in one window was the most beautiful black gown and negligee, also a slip and brassiere and I remember that I wanted them so badly. But instead of buying them, we stood there and laughed because I was pregnant and couldn't wear them."

Had I thought of this dream in time, would I have made sure you stopped by the drugstore that night? Or more importantly, and happily, when I discovered I was pregnant, would I have told you, laughing in delight, as I reminded you of that dream? It doesn't matter. At this time, I hid my thoughts from you. And when you apologize for your failure to be prepared, I neither scold nor predict. Neither, however, do I encourage you to further tempt fate this morning – after eight nights and sometimes days, I need a rest. And I do not want to be the first to call it quits! But I am supremely happy with you, anyhow. Because fulfilling the promise you had made me exactly eight months ago, I know from you I have, indeed, had "the loving of my life!"

5
Interim

We make our trip to Prescott and meet with all your family and then we seek out your old friends and I get to know them and hear of your youthful adventures – and mis-adventures. You were a wild one, I learn. We go to your favorite hangouts and I see you in the western milieu that you love. Western music, western barn dancing. Men and women in levis and boots – on the dance floor! Raucous, wild to me. But you are having fun and I join in to the best of my ability. And you drink more than you should – just as you did in Chicago – and the next day, your mother is angry. But this is your furlough, your reward for all the horrible days of war and the consuming wasted days of your life, and I do not complain. As long as I am with you, I know you'll be okay. And then the furlough time is up. [I've had no rest from you at all, but since "that night," you've always been prepared, so I waste no time in worry – reassuring myself with the thought that we had tried seriously for two whole months to get me pregnant – without success.] So it's time for you to make the trip again to MacArthur for your final discharge. Then you'll return, a civilian at last – and we will begin to make plans. And we decide that you should make the trip alone, since it will be strenuous and quick, three days at the most. We'll save my fare and besides, I should return to work. But just in case, while you're gone, I make an appointment to see Dr. Vernetti. And I do not tell you. But I come to wish I had.

6
"The Best Laid Plans . . . "

My visit to Dr. Vernetti devastates me. Despite my premonitions, I cannot believe that I am almost definitely three weeks pregnant! I have no need to ask *how* it had happened or *when* it had happened. But I am furiously asking *why* it has happened. After all our discussions back and forth in our letters; after all our decisions to wait; after all my pleas for a little time to be just your wife and your lover; after all the inconvenience of your preventive measures; after all my careful planning to be financially ready for our Junior; but especially after all those months of worry that I might *never* conceive, *why has God let this happen now?* And I am so angry with *God* for the collapse of all my plans and for all my useless worry, that for the first time in our short life together, I will act, as I have said earlier, "in a way not to make you proud of me." I was so caught up in the resentment of my condition that I'm not even sure how I broke the news to you. Nor do I recall your reaction. But I have every reason to think that you were not at all appalled by learning that we were, indeed, to have a child. After all, you had been desiring Junior ever since our wedding night, and had more than once expressed in your letters the thought that we should take advantage of any opportunity offered us for pregnancy. I truly believe that your response must have been – as it had been to many other problems we had faced, even before our engagement – "Don't worry about it; we'll work it out." And your family were, of course, ecstatic. But I was, as I remember, an absolute hellion of resentment. Now, I knew, there would be no chance of going to college – either for you or for me. Now you would have to choose, decisively, a line of work you might enjoy; now we must quickly find a place to live suitable for a baby; now I would shortly have to quit my job. And on and on my worries went. When we went to find a place to live, the first question seemed to be, "Is your wife pregnant?" One place we could have got, we lost because you insisted I could not be endangered by the steep steps I would have to climb to the above-the-garage apartment. With all the service men and their wives looking for a place to live, pregnancy seemed anathema to many owners, because of the crying and the diapers and the liability. And I took this to heart as though I had a contagious disease.

I'm explaining this to you in this letter, my dearest love, because I am not sure that in all my weeks of ugliness – at least a period of six weeks or two months – you ever understood the reason for my reaction. Oh, did you think it was because I did not want your son? I'm not sure you ever asked – or that I ever explained the very selfish, and yet complex rationale I have just revealed. And if I disappointed you severely during that time, I hope that you forgave me – as I have had to forgive myself. But I was to atone for that ugliness in suffering, before our son was safely born. And my darling, I do remember that you were still loving of me, and still loved me physically during that time, offering no rebuke that I remember, trying, I think, to let my anger run its course.

But back to the sequence of events that would precede the truths above. On the 8th of February 1946, you return to Phoenix, a civilian at last. I meet you at the Depot and greet you for the first time as, "my husband, *Mr.* Nebeker." And we are both happy to be together again. Stell has offered us the use of a small bedroom in her home, while we make plans as to our future. And we have thankfully accepted. Already we've found housing in Mesa – or Phoenix – almost impossible to get, and your furlough money was nil and your mustering out pay has been exactly $141.72. I have, as I remember, about $750 in the bank – and I'm still employed. Also, I think that you had a small monthly subsidy still coming from the government – but I'm not sure. Anyhow, on your trip back to Phoenix, you're planning to discuss with me our future. You've realized that decisions will have to be made quickly; the responsibilities of your civilian existence are upon you. And then you learn the news that you are to be a father. And all things change in the realities I have just explained.

Grateful as we are for your sister's generosity of room and board for a time, both you and I know that the basic necessity for us, as newly weds – for that is what we really are – is to be alone. We need freedom to move about, to make decisions, even to fight, without family intervention. And more than ever, you sense that I will need your physical response to me as a woman. [Or is that your need, too?] And your frustration mounts, for we've been at your sister's at least six weeks, and intimacy grows more difficult. Both you and I are suffering. This is not the extended honeymoon season we had planned. Still we've had no success at finding anything. And with your refusal to rent that last apartment with the steps, I'm wallowing in my anger.

I think it is at this point you finally reach your limit of exasperation with me [which you have carefully concealed before] – the point where it becomes necessary for you "to turn me over your knee" as I'd expressed it to you in one letter. [Or, as I wrote in my famous letter of rebuke to you about your demotion because of the wine-keg episode: ". . . I do think you need to do a little thinking just for your own good. Don't be angry, darling – someday our roles will be reversed and you can call me down."] And you do "call me down." Or rather, quite uncharacteristically, you apply your hand to my rear, so to speak. Not in my gentle way with you, but in harsh words that shock me into sensibility. I can still hear the steeliness of your words, the harshness of your voice: "Quit acting like a knocked-up teen-age-er."

Oh my dear, how I needed those words. And how grateful I was for your courage in uttering them. For immediately I recognized the truth. Of course, that's really what I was – for I was barely 19. But you had *married* a *woman,* I thought. And that *woman* had wanted your child. And that *woman* had conceived in a beautiful night of passion, with her *beloved, yearned for husband.* And that *woman* should have faith in her *"Adam."* And that *woman* should look to her *Maker,* in gratitude for this blessing that had come to her, after all her fears and indecisions.

And I swear to you, my dear, that in that epiphany, I was freed from the dark anger that held me. And I rejoiced in you and in your love. I don't know whether I ever expressed these ideas to you. Or even whether it was necessary. But I do know that after the jolt of your words of reproof, I was glad in my pregnancy and I tried to show you that, in my every action in the days to come. And I hope you understood that. Or I hope, at least, you understand it now. But how I wish that I had written you a letter to thank you for your wisdom and to tell you all of this. Or how I wish that you had written me.

After your return, and as I've lost my bitterness, we learn to find some privacy by eating lunch down town, where we investigate and discuss what you would like to do as a vocation. And you decide to see if you can get an apprenticeship as a carpenter. You've enjoyed the building you had done in your war experience and you'd also taken some training while in the camps. The government will subsidize your apprenticeship – if you can get a job – and if you can get into the Union. But your search reveals that the process is a kind of Catch 22 – you can't get a job without being a union member – and you can't be a union member without having a job. So you start out to beat the system – and you finally do.

But before you start employment, I beg you for the promised trip to see my family. I know that after the baby comes, this won't be possible. And you have promised me! So in April, we decide we can go for a week or ten days. But, at the last minute, you think you have a place in the apprenticeship program and refuse to go – saying that we don't have the money and that you need to find a job and a place for us to live. I am terribly disappointed. We have enough money in the bank for us both to go – and still have a backlog to draw on. And you have promised me!! I think you believe that without you, I just won't go. [Or maybe, I think, this is an excuse – to give you time alone. Maybe you're just tired of me!] But I am fed-up with being at Stell's, and I really *need* to go. My doctor has told me I must quit work and thinks the trip and rest would do me good. And I haven't been home for over a year and my mother has been very ill. And besides, I'm not pleased that you have broken the promise you had given me last winter that, if I didn't go at Christmas time, when your arrival home was imminent, we would later go together and visit the old places of our courtship. So about the 12th of April, I defiantly make my journey to Indianapolis, for the first time in fourteen months. And it is while I am there, having a wonderful time with my relatives, old friends, even an old "boy friend" or two – [so there!] that *you* will disappoint me as deeply as I have failed you in the "pregnancy" matter.

And this time, I have your letters – and two telegrams, and a "gift card" – to prove everything. I think I'll let your letter of April 20th speak for itself. But I'll comment on it as I read it, as you did my letter of reproof so many months ago.

My Darling Wife:

By the time you get this you will probably be here with me – but I think it [the gift you have sent me] will ship to you by Friday night when you get on the plane. [I still haven't decided just when I'm coming home. I am not pleased with you!] Baby, I sure need you cause this empty feeling is rough. [Here is my proof that all is well with us, after you've "turned me over you knee," metaphorically speaking.] Besides I am more or less in the ranks of the unemployed. [You could have gone with me after all.] And I love you too much – it hurts when you're not here. [I knew it – you need me!]

Now I'll tell you of my doings other than school and such. Last Thursday we went to work to find the job shut down on account of Lillywhite going bankrupt. . . so we've got to wait for that money, consequently the bank account is down again. [I'll bet this is the crux of the matter – you're preparing me.] I got my first check from the V. A. I put it into the checking account and bought some clothes – I got two pair of trousers and a couple of shirts. [You're entitled, but I wish you had waited for me. Your taste in clothes is abominable.] Besides all my clothes are dirty waiting for you!! Wife of mine!!. ["A woman's place". . . Keep 'em barefoot and pregnant!]

Saturday night I dashed around for apartments – one nice place close to town was rented about five minutes before I got there. Then some shacks – and some of the $100 a month type. However, there were a lot more advertised than usual and I think we'll have a place soon. [We have had no privacy for three long months; I don't believe we'll ever have a place of our own.]

[And now I come to the real point of your letter – and the real reason you were too late to rent the apartment, I believe, and I am really angry about this.] Before I went apartment hunting, I ran into a gang of girls that knew you – Naturally Chauncey was along. [And now I know exactly what's coming] We ran into Bob Groves – a Prescott lad, and another kid from up there. They had their gal friends so we dashed out to the Mecca Club – and there was Vera and some more Magazine gals. I danced with Vera and an Irene. They wanted to know when you were coming back. They all looked pretty well tight – but

> maybe it was the couple I'd had. I'm getting purty fed up with this drinking stuff – anyway it cost too much dough. [And now I *really know* what has happened. You are back in the care free days of your overseas "boys." And while I know the "girls" mean nothing, I am more angry and hurt than you will ever know. And once more I have that ominous feeling that I am trapped by pregnancy. And I know that you have blown our bank account!]
>
> Darling, hurry home to your poor unworking husband and we'll have a vacation together before the job starts up again. [Neb, as you write this letter, were you feeling any guilt? Or were you so dumb you wouldn't have a glimmer of how this would make me feel after refusing to keep your promise of taking me to Indianapolis? And then you have the audacity to end with your real need of me, my body!] Besides that, I find that sleeping without you is much worse than sleeping with you, on your most sleepless nights. Darling, I love you. See you Saturday morning.

But following that letter, I do not choose to come home on Saturday. And you know that I am angry. So you send me flowers the same night you have written the letter. And the next day I receive a telegram: "About crazy missing you. Are you coming home Saturday. I need you, I love you." And again, on Easter Sunday, a telegram, "Happy Easter darling, tried to send flowers too late. Get a dress, have more fun, but I miss you sumpin awful. I love you."

So having let you stew an extra five days, I return to Phoenix. But the damage is done. You and your old friend, Chauncey Hill, have wiped out almost the whole bank account in carousing – far more than you and I would have spent had you come to Indianapolis with me. [And this will be the pattern that will begin to emerge quite early in our life. A spur-of-the-moment-night-out-with-the-boys, followed by, occasionally, sincere remorse, but always without explanation or a phone call to relieve my mind, and eventually, without evidence of guilt. But those days are as yet on the horizon.]

7
Deja Vu

Following my return, and your repentant confession, and my swallowing of bitter words, the days pick up for us. You have managed to find us a really nice room, with adjoining bath, in a comfortable home near about 3rd Avenue and Culver, if I remember correctly. And though we have no cooking facilities, we can at last be alone. I am nearly four months pregnant, but I'm showing absolutely no signs of pregnancy. And you tell me I look lovelier than ever. And I can wear my black negligee – and my red and my white – and I revel in our sexual freedom – now there is no need of caution. You are at the height of your virility and, having found another apprenticeship opening, you eagerly hurry home from work each night. And as we inevitably make love, I think sometimes my ardor almost overwhelms you. Perhaps you had forgotten my warnings in my letters, that I was by nature passionate. But you no longer have the least need of your "little book."

And darling, I think that both of us are completely happy. Perhaps more than we will ever be again. Of course, we have to eat our meals out, but that's not too expensive in those days, and with your V.A. checks and the small apprentice salary, we make out okay. Often, in the middle of the night, after we make love, you dress and go to the all night drug store to bring home sandwiches and coffee and we talk and plan for our baby. And sometimes we make love again. You seem to have no need of anyone but me, now. But sometimes I wonder how you have the strength to work; I can rest all day, if I like. [Just as I did when I had my ruptured appendix.] The memories of these days and nights are still precious to me. And they got me through some very rough spots in times to come.

I have the freedom of this time since I have been forbidden to work by the Ob/Gyn specialist that Dr. Vernetti has insisted on. She fears a possible miscarriage for me, but I have not told you that, and the specialist – whom I came to hate with a passion – is only concerned that I'm not showing any obvious signs of fertility; I haven't gained weight at all. In fact, to the very end I never needed a maternity dress. The same was true when I had our second child. So unlike most fathers-to-be, you can delight in my body as you have always done – and this is important to you all our lives. And we do now, indeed, have a lengthy second honeymoon, alone.

And then, we luck into a small garage apartment at the rear of a large home – in fact, the address was 711 E. Culver. First, we rented a rather dreary, old section of the garage, where the pipes dripped and the clothes closet was right off the bath and had mold in it. But we didn't care. We didn't even think of the lovely little apartment of our marriage. And though the bed springs creaked with every movement, we didn't care about that, either. And I rode the street car every day, downtown to the meat market on Washington St. where the butcher kept his still limited supply of meat open to me. And I chose the best available and I cooked for you morning and night – and packed your lunch each day. And we walked downtown to the Paramount theater once a week, and to the drugstore each night for a soda. And for me at least, the world was bright. You seemed happy, too, though I have no notes or letters to remind me. But I think I knew.

And then, we got the much newer and nicer apartment next door, with a really modern kitchen, and a bright new bath and a bedroom with a bed that didn't squeak! The living room wasn't much, sunken so that the rain came in. But it felt much more like the place I'd had when we'd met. And a friend from your work and his wife moved into the apartment we had left, so we had friends nearby. [I can't remember their names, but I still remember that terrible trip we took with them to Pismo Beach. Who on earth ever heard of Pismo Beach?] And I had access to an old washer – not at all like the ones we have today – and I could wash your carpenter overalls, and your shirts. You may not believe this, but I was truly happy. I tried to go to work again, but you may remember, I just didn't have the strength. And we managed. But we knew that we'd have to leave by the 1st of November, when the baby came. The owners did not want a baby crying and disturbing other renters. And so we were always looking for a house to buy and trying to save the money to do it. Then, in July, we had the opportunity to go to Heber with your boss, Russ Keltner, to help build a fancy summer cabin. I really loved that – and I have pictures of us together, me in shorts and halter and you in your working clothes – and no one can tell I am six months pregnant. And you look so handsome and strong – and happy. But again, I have no way of really knowing what you thought, or if you were satisfied. But I knew you loved me – and were so proud of me. [But it just occurred to me – maybe you'd have liked me to look pregnant? And I think I'd have liked it, too!] And do you remember the really horrible sun burn I got? I had no idea that in the mountains, under clouds, one could get burnt to a crisp. I didn't think I'd ever be able to wear a shirt on my back again.

When we come home, Melvin has found a little house under construction that we can buy – built by a jack-of-all-trades member of the church, just outside the city limits at 1724 E. Oak Street. It won't be ready until November, but that's just about right for us. And with management, we can barely swing it. [How I wished that you hadn't dissipated all that money running around with Chauncey Hill. Did you ever regret that?] And so the worry about having to move is off our minds. And now, it's August and we have only about three months to wait for Junior, who is due, the doctor says, October 20th.

8

The Blessed Event or Count-Down Time

Returning home the last of July from Heber, the heat is withering. And in my visit to my obstetrician, when I complain about the extreme tiredness I'm feeling, he tells me it's the heat – and anyway, that's how a woman feels when she's six and a half months pregnant. I still have gained not one single pound and no one believes I'm really pregnant. But he says it's a small baby, and sometimes that's natural. I tell him that I think something is wrong – I just don't feel right. He says it's my first baby and I don't know what pregnancy is like. You realize, of course, Neb, that now there are all kinds of tests that doctors make and instruments that take pictures of the baby in the womb. But there was none of that for me. The stethoscope, occasionally a pelvic exam, blood tests. That's about all that I remember. So I tried to stop being concerned. I'd fainted a couple of times the last few weeks, but that wasn't so unusual for me, so you paid no attention to it, and I tried not to. In fact, I had fainted a week before when our friends next door were there, and I remember hearing you say as I revived: "Oh, just leave her lay; she'll come out of it." The concern you had felt for me months earlier had dissipated with time. And it lay dormant to the last days of your life, I believe, even in grave times. It was a hardness in your make-up that came to hurt me deeply, emotionally. And to cause me unnecessary pain, physically. I have seriously tried for many years to understand this emotional sterility in you. But the only rationale I can find is that you truly had no feeling of love for me. Or the possibility that you had seen so much suffering in your months at war, that all emotional energy had been drained from you. Either way, there has been little consolation for the hurt that I have felt through many years. Maybe sometime in the next life, you can explain this all to me, and wipe away the many tears that I have shed over what I saw as callousness.

But to get back to the point. You weren't concerned about my fainting; I wasn't concerned about my fainting; the doctor wasn't concerned about my fainting – except to take another blood test. But I had been with Stell two weeks before and had blacked out completely in the aisle at Woolworth's. It was a lengthy blackout and medics had been called and she was worried. But I hadn't said anything to you. Now I have to honestly admit the prospect of delivering a baby appalled and frightened me. Happy about the baby I might be, but the process of childbirth, itself, was horrifying and dehumanizing. I simply did not know how I was going to get through it. But I tried as best I could not to show my fear to you. My hospital bag was prepared, and I think in my own thoughts I had come to grips with the idea that "I would just have to get on with it!"

Then, on August 5th, you and I have gone to celebrate our second wedding anniversary with dinner at the American Kitchen and a movie. We walk home from the Paramount – I'm not sure how long a walk that was, but as I prepare for bed, I discover that I'm bleeding. And for once you are concerned. It's too late to call the doctor, but early the next morning you go to phone to see what we should do; of course, we have no phone. And I'm alone all day. But the doctor has said just to stay completely in bed – getting up only to go to the bathroom, which is probably only three feet away. I've already fixed your breakfast and made you lunch, and you go off to work – you are pouring cement at the old Balsz School half way to Tempe. We have no car, of course, but your friend next door takes you off each morning. You kiss me and strictly warn me to do exactly as the doctor has said. I lie quietly reading all morning and then I have to go to the bathroom. I get up, take two steps, and blood is gushing from me. I'm covered in it; the floor is covered. And all at once, I'm too weak to stand. I remember thinking, "I don't know what to do. I've got to get help. And fast!" On my hands and knees, I am barely able to crawl to the back door of the main house. I manage to knock weakly – and finally my landlady hears me and sees that I am in my gown and covered with blood. The rest is again one of those blurred events. I think they call Stell and then I'm in St. Joseph Hospital, surrounded by nurses. And then the doctor is there. And I'm calling for you. But you aren't there. And I'm afraid. I know I am dying. And Stell is telling me that someone has gone for you. And then, all goes black.

When I regain consciousness, I am in a fresh gown, and glucose is dripping in my vein. But there is no blood for me. I have a rare AB/RH negative blood – and there is absolutely none available. They've sent out an emergency call, I learn, but the Rh factor is a new discovery and there are no registered donors available. I think I understand that my life is truly hanging in the balance. And then you are with me, and holding my hand, and I know you won't let anything happen to me. I don't want to die. I've just begun to live.

9

The Nightmare Begins

For two long days, I lie on a gurney in a hospital corridor. The maternity ward is filled to overflowing with the wives of veterans, and there simply is no room in which to put me. Neither is there blood, yet. And I am growing weaker. Finally, the Rh negative type is found and the life-giving blood begins to flow into my veins. I am never to know what kind of consultation occurs about me. Are you involved?

Do they tell you what is at stake? Do you know, as I have been told, that the baby's life – in this hospital – takes precedence over mine? And did they tell you that I had a *placenta previa* – a complete abruption of the placenta? And that survival for either baby or mother in such a situation hung on a thread? [The only thing you tell me later is that when you came home that day and found the floor soaked in blood, you thought I had committed suicide. Now why would you think that?] They didn't tell me any of this – until it was all over. And then V.E. congratulated himself in front of me, saying that "ten minutes earlier and the baby would have died and ten minutes later, you [meaning me] would have." That told me exactly why I had had to wait so long for anything to be done for me. Did he ever acknowledge that to you?

But all this will not occur until nearly a month later. In the interim, I will have been first, bedded in the doctor's office; subsequently in the "Delivery Room" section for three days and nights, where the groans and screams and procedures of the delivering mothers will cause me to weep in constant fear – and where you are permitted to visit me not at all. Furthermore, I will receive little personal care – washing, a comb for my hair, brushing my teeth – because I am neither in labor nor "post-delivery." And the nurses are feuding, because of their heavy duties. And you do not know this, because I'm allowed no visitors. At last a bed is found for me in the new mothers' wing. And here in the two-bed room, you are allowed to visit. And your presence strengthens me. But here I will watch other mothers come and go with their new babies; and here, too, every evening the supervising nursing Sister [a white-robed Nun] comes in to say goodnight, telling me she expects a Nebeker baby in the nursery the next day [as though the delay were all my obstinacy]. During all these days, I am begging you to take me home, promising to never get out of bed without someone there. But, of course, you dare not. And I *hate* you for leaving me here in this hostile world. [Years later, in 1994, when you suffer a stroke and I cannot bring you home, until you have had the best rehabilitation possible, I understand your *hatred* for *me,* as I surrender you to the necessary care of a rehabilitative nursing home.]

And I *hate Dr. V.E.* He will tell me nothing – will not discuss with me at all what is happening – and is going to happen – to me. Following a long and stressful exam in the "stirrups" about the tenth day, I do learn that the baby is in a "breech presentation," that the placenta may completely detach, and that the baby needs every possible hour in the womb, if he is to survive. I vow *never* to speak to him again, after I ask him the next day, whether I will have a C-section. His arrogant response is, as he lounges in my doorway, "Well, I'll tell you. I'm going home today and read up on it in my medical book and when I find out, then maybe I'll tell you." So, when on the 26th of September, in the late afternoon, I begin to bleed and to suffer intense back pain, I will not ask for him. But fortunately, for me, my observant older roommate quickly summons aid.

At 5:10, on that same day, a Thursday [and our son, as he matures will always be "full of woe" as Thursday's child is doomed to be!] almost a month early, our son, Aquila Chauncey Nebeker III is born, by Caesarean section. And he weighs, I'm told, a healthy 6 lbs 3 oz. Whether you got there in time for his birth, I don't think I ever knew. I awaken some hours later, in a beautiful private room, with French doors looking out on a beautiful garden of flowers. And I know that I have this special room because my baby is dead. And so I believe for ten days, despite your assurance that you have seen him. But because he is not brought to me to hold, and because I am not permitted to get out of bed to go to him, I believe it is a lie to protect me – even when you tell me it is because he has some problems with his breathing. And then, about the tenth day, I am sitting up. And you are with me. And the nurse brings in a bundle. And with your arm around me, I see, for the first time, our son. And weeping, I hold him in my arms. And I know that I am really a mother. And on the 15th day of October, after your 27th birthday on October 4, 1946, we both come home from the hospital. And another new life begins.

My love, as I am writing of these memories so many years later, I re-experience the emotions of those days. And I clearly recall my concern for you. But I have absolutely nothing to tell me of your feelings through all these days of worry. Were you afraid for me? Did you wish that you had never married me? Did you remember that just a year previously, you had been in the hospital at Camp Lucky Strike, pining for me and waiting for my letters? And who was taking care of you with me not home? But as far as I knew, you were measuring up in every way and this cheered my heart. And when at last you brought us both home, I have the sweetest picture of you holding our son, wrapped in a blanket, close in your arms. He is so tiny – and you look so proud. But you also look scared to death!

Neb and Quill

10
Home at Last

When I come home after such a long time, your mother is there to take care of the little son I have finally delivered safely, and I am grateful. I am forbidden any activity, consigned to quiet bed rest, because there is danger of further hemorrhage and the potential rupture of the low cervical incision. However, I am deeply concerned over you – wondering what you are feeling about all the problems I have caused, as well as how you will feel about me physically – hating illness as you do. I know you will be sexually tense – I see the signs. And when you come home in the evening, there is the tension between you and your mother. And there is not a minute – or space –

to be by ourselves. Mom fusses over your smoking, protests your coffee drinking. And I feel caught in the middle. Then she is nearly 70, and I feel terrible because she is sleeping on an uncomfortable couch in the living room, while we are in the bed. After you leave in the morning, she bathes "Nebbie," as we will call him, but after the third day home, every morning she says, so I can hear, "Now tomorrow your mommie will do this." So I try. And then you come home and give me hell for not obeying the doctor's orders. And I just don't know what to do. Nebbie has a "spastic stomach reflex" – typical of 8th month babies – and has to be fed every 45 minutes. But he throws up within a few minutes – in a violent spewing – and then the feeding has to be done again. And I have never once fed him in the hospital. I feel like I am in hell. And suddenly I'm overcome with uncontrollable weeping, which goes on for days. I don't know what's wrong with me and I visit my friend next door, hoping for relief. But I simply can't control the overwhelming grief and tears. No one knows about post-partum depression, in those days. Especially you – and your mother. And one day, she simply packs her bag and leaves. I guess she got disgusted with me or else felt she was to blame. I just don't know. But I grieved over her reaction until the day she died, without the courage to ever bring the matter up.

But it's better for us when Mom leaves, and we are private in our lives – and in our bed. My weeping stops; I'm gaining strength; and you can at least begin to know that I will be your "wife" again. And that patience will prevail. [I hope all young men are clued in to this now.]

11
The New Home

The middle of November comes and it is time to move into our new home. We have little to move except our few clothes, some dishes, some cooking utensils. We haven't had the money to buy much furniture, but we have bought a bed and dresser, a couch, two chairs, an *ice box* – refrigerators are too expensive and scarce to afford. And we have a small table and chairs. And I have no washing machine or laundry tub of any type. We do not realize how hard that's going to be with a new baby. And we are literally out in the country, without transportation. There is no floor covering – no tile, no carpeting – just cold cement throughout the little 650 square foot house, far smaller than my apartment had been. There's an arterial irrigation ditch across the front of our property and the builder hasn't leveled the lot at all. It's a third of an acre pile of dirt, front and back. Our lot irrigation ditch runs across the back and there is no fence between us and the neighbor behind us on the next street. Furthermore, we discover to our dismay, that there is no furnace – we had not even thought of that. We have one small gas pipe in the living room for a heater that cannot possibly heat the house. And we haven't bought the heater yet, so it's cold. On top of that, the plastered walls throughout the house haven't begun to "cure," and are already "sweating." It seems a dismal place, but for us, it was our own.

But honey, looking back on it in the pictures – and remembering our vicissitudes – how did we ever get through it? And how did we, in our own small way, make such a success of it? Thinking now of all the plans we'd made while you were gone, and of all the suffering we'd endured up to this point, I know the answer to only two things: first, I know that I'd still choose to be your wife; but second, I'm sure I would have made you stop at the drug-store the night of my 19th birthday – or else you'd have slept in a much colder bed!

Now let me remind you of our – or rather my – first day in the new house. [All of this is true!] We're up in the cold November morning at 5 a.m. I feed and change Nebbie and then get your hearty breakfast on our little gas stove. Next I pack your lunch. You have to walk down to 16th and McDowell – carrying your toolbox with saws etc. – by 6 o'clock to catch your bus out to the school near Tempe, where you're pouring cement and working on basic foundations. I give you a kiss and send you off, knowing you'll have a miserable day in this weather. Now I've got to sterilize the bottles and prepare the baby's milk for the day, before I give him his bath. That done, I wash and sterilize by hand the diapers and other baby things, praying Nebbie will sleep for awhile. He doesn't. It's feeding and throw-up time again. Then I set up the portable drying rack – I have no clothesline yet – outside of the back door and I get everything strung out to dry. I no sooner get them hung out in the wintry sun, than a wind comes up and knocks the rack down in the dirt. As I begin to wash again, the water pipes break and I don't know how to shut the water off and the house starts to flood, before I can figure out what to do. Nebbie is now screaming his head off and I've got to try to feed him again, but the whole house is flooded, so I've got to get the water out somehow, but I have no push broom. And so it goes. I have no phone. I know no neighbors. I have no idea how I get through the day, but when you, poor thing, get home, I am bawling, and Nebbie is howling and I'm still trying to get the water all swept out of the house. And you, horrible man, are hungry from your ten hour day and expect your dinner to be on the table. I truly don't know how that day ended. But as I write these vivid memories, I am chuckling – no! I'm laughing. And I know why God made sex so enticing and addictive that it could catch us off our guard. Had he not, how would the human race survive? [Incidentally, our only granddaughter, now 30, called yesterday to tell me she is expecting our first great-grand baby. What do you think of that? Or perhaps you already know? Debbie has always told me she knew your father, who died, you remember, just ten months before her birth.]

Things will, however, get better. Perhaps most providential is finding that we have wonderful neighbors living just behind us. Fritz is German, still speaking with a heavy accent, and Gertrude, his wife, is a registered nurse, from a strict Lutheran background, and her specialty is in maternity and baby care. She saves my life. And Fritz becomes your good friend. Remember their five children, four boys and a girl? And our little "Nebbie" soon becomes the Vierck "pet." Gertrude helps me learn how to feed our little son, serves as baby sitter when we need her, and the children become Nebbie's big brothers and sister. Once Fritz even lends us his little two-seater roadster with a rumble seat for a night out at the movies. Do you remember that? And you, dear heart, work like a slave to grade our lawn and plant the seed and keep it mown. You are never still. Just as you had been on the front lines in Europe, you are building a shed, or making a fence, or adding a convenience inside. And as our son grows, making a swing and a slide set, a sand box. And as he learns to walk and talk, we adore our little Neb. He is a beautiful tow-head – just as I'd predicted on our first anniversary – and he follows you around like a little puppy, as he grows older. But that's still in the future. Before that, Fate has more in store for us.

In the winter of 1947, there is the beginning of another depression. Conversion from the war-time economy has been slow. There are too many veterans dumped into the employment field, without industry keeping up its growth. Without jobs, men can't buy cars, men can't buy clothing, men can't buy houses. And so there is at last no job for you. Although still in the apprentice program, you are not being paid. And in January, we decide that I will have to return to work or we will lose our little home. They want me back at the Highway Department, and so I go back to work in the Drivers License Division, at the same salary I have made before. I'm much closer now than I was in Mesa, but I still must walk the mile to the bus morning and evening, and I still must work a five and a half day week. And I must leave my little son in the care of Gertrude – who is glad for the money I will pay her. But I have come to enjoy him and being home so much that going back to work is a real sacrifice for me, though I accept the necessity.

But just before I start, your dad calls and says that he has received his new car – because as a mining inspector, he is high on the priority list for one of the scarce new automobiles. If we will come up to Prescott and get it, we can have his old 1936 Chrysler, with its 100,000 plus mileage. We are absolutely delighted and so you buy bus tickets for us to Prescott; we leave Nebbie with the Vierck's; and we head north. You, however, have unknowingly purchased tickets on a bus going only to Wickenburg. And, to make a long story short, you expect me to hitch-hike, after midnight, the rest of the way. I am appalled. I have never hitch-hiked in my life! And never will I hitch-hike after midnight! And that's that. Do you remember how angry you were with me, because we had to stay in a motel that night? [But I remember you weren't too angry not to take advantage of it!] Looking back on it, I can see how easy a thing it would have seemed to you – I have only recently read your details of hitching all over Europe. But weren't you able to see how impossible that would have been for me? So many times, in your letters, you had told me how you disliked the type of women who joined the Services – the type you wouldn't want your wife to be. But nevertheless, you don't seem to have much understanding for the "type" your wife is – for the differences between us. Some things I could do for you. Some things I couldn't. But you seldom give me credit for the sacrifices I willingly make.

Anyhow, once we got the car, you gained a freedom you had not had. Now you were better able to look for work – and you could take jobs at a further distance. But also you now had a different kind of freedom – one where you could join the boys after payday, and have "a beer or two." This would bring the serpent into the Garden, eventually. But as you used the car to look for work, you seldom seemed to think of taking me to work – or even picking me up from the office, except on payday, when we ate out. Time after time, I came home exhausted, further tired by walking from the bus along the unpaved road, only to find you home and reading your paper, and the car parked in the driveway. And after I had picked up our little boy from Vierck's and wanted to spend a few minutes just resting on the bed with my high heels off and playing with him, you grew upset with me, because you were hungry and wanted your dinner. I truly had so little rest.

Unfortunately for both of us, my body, less than four months from serious child birth, survived the strain imposed for only four short months before it broke again, the first of May. Again the ovarian growths were on the rampage and I would once more need surgery. This time I was left with barely a quarter of an ovary. And you may remember the serious kidney infection that kept me hospitalized for nearly two more weeks. That, too, was a fluke, because Dr. Merrill, my wonderful surgeon, foreseeing no problem, had left town for three days. When he returned, I was in high fever and he was furious with everyone on the staff. They had not called him; they had done nothing to alleviate the pain; and I was burning up. He immediately started treatment. But I suffered kidney and bladder infections for many years. I returned from this hospital experience, determined that never would there be more surgery. And especially, I determined there would not be another pregnancy. But during my hospital stay, Gertrude Vierck wrote me daily letters, letting Nebbie tell me about his day. I still have those letters and I read them often, vicariously participating in his actions of the day.

Following recovery, I again go back to work. I'm very good at the work I do, but I hate every minute of it – except when I wait on customers. But you have work now, at least temporarily. And you've worked so hard on our small house, that the lawn and flower beds are the pride of the neighborhood. And always trailing you is your little shadow, Nebbie. He adores his da-da. And he loves his two-gun holsters, and he loves to run through the hose as you water the lawn. And we love to take him to Encanto Park to see the ducks and the geese. *And we are a happy family!* Except on the occasional nights, when I have supper waiting on the table, you do not come home – at 6 or 10 or midnight. At work, you've found Tucker – another Del or Kirk - and you "boys" "dash off" to have a "beer or two," just as you used to do in the camps overseas. "Tucker" becomes an unwelcome name in our home – at least to me, though I try not to be rude to him. But then, after your spree, you'll apologize and sweet-talk me and I'll try to make the best of it. And it doesn't happen again, until a month goes by, or two weeks. And then. . . .

One Sunday, I remember, after you've been "off with the boys," I'm so upset, I will not even talk to you. You've spent money we didn't have, the night before, and I'm worrying. Unknown to me, you go down to the dry-goods store – was it McClendons? – and spend your last three dollars on a make-up gift. A bright, gaudy Mexican designed table-cloth! And you know, Neb, my heart just broke over what I sensed as your true remorse. The fact is that with one little beer, you were caught – like a chocoholic or a caffeine addict. It wasn't as though we had arguments that set you off, or problems that we couldn't handle. I could, perhaps, have understood that. It simply was that once you had one drink, you were gone. And I worried about you to the point of tears. And increasingly I feared that you would end up like my dad. But you know, I treasured that ugly cloth until it finally wore out. And there were so many gifts like that, to ease the sting.

So I look at my pictures of these passing days of late 1946 and '47 and into '48, and see our modest home beautified, our bright, beautiful little boy with his happy smile, and his own little lawn mower following you as you do your work. And I read him his stories and sing him to sleep. And most nights I go to bed in your arms. And I know we're a blessed, happy family. [But we do not have contact with the Church, which is quite far from us, downtown. And we are not contacted.] And I am now well. But I am still working.

12
Moving On

Although you have had work sufficient for our needs since mid-47, the construction trade in the Phoenix area was always erratic. And the fact of the matter is that while you were becoming an excellent carpenter and would qualify shortly as a journeyman, you simply were not happy working under the direction of others – particularly when they knew less than you. You had lost one job in August, because you spent too much time at the water thermos. Another time you were fired for disagreeing with a foreman. Another, you simply walked off the job, fed up with everything. You were just like you were in the front-lines, energetic but averse to the slightest unnecessary discipline. Your need for freedom was a growing force within you. [I understand you so much better now, Neb, because of our grandson, Derek. He is the spitting image of you – although not as handsome – and he simply will not tolerate boredom to any degree. I truly think he has a brilliant mind, and he's had several worthwhile jobs since he graduated from college. But he is an *independent* of the first order. And working for himself, he told me just last week that at the age of 27, he has just reached the half-million mark in his financial portfolio.] So when in the summer of 1948, your dad asked you if you'd like to come up to Prescott and on your own, and by your plan, remodel one of his three homes, I urged you to take on the responsibility. It was to turn out for us as a pleasant experience – and for your parents, it gave them a chance to be with their little grandson and to give them a legitimate excuse for helping you on your way.

I loved the summer. I watched you plan the remodeling, do the buying, execute the work. And above all, be with me. For I had declared *my* independence and quit work. I felt I'd carried my share for long enough and now it was my right just to be a mother and a wife, after nearly four years of marriage. I really don't remember too much about the particulars of those two or three months that we were up there. I think we had a room in one of the houses; and I remember having fun with Anne and her family. And mom and dad spoiled Nebbie rotten. But I do remember we went dancing – and I think we took a trip up to Las Vegas with Howard and Jimmy, while Anne kept our son. And I won $35 with my first quarter ever in a slot machine. And you were upset with me for not giving it to you to play – or playing it myself. But I was saving it to buy you a sport coat on your upcoming birthday. And we stayed at the new Flamingo. Remember, Las Vegas was brand new, prices were cheap, and we could afford anything. And we had fun, almost like on our honeymoon in Chicago. Sundays, with the family, we went to church and Sunday School, together, as we had seldom done since Nebbie was born. And I so enjoyed being back in the framework of the church.

Most of all I remember being with you. And especially our afternoon breaks we took across the street at the little cafe-truck driver stop, where we got pie and coffee, and talked together about the things you were doing. And do you remember how extremely angry your mother got at that, because she hated the stopping of those trucks on her street, and thought the drivers were all criminals? But I also remember that these were the last days we would have to know your dad. And I used to walk down to the courthouse, when he was through for the day, and walk back home with him. I loved him dearly. [Our son turned out to be so much like him in his middle age.] And I have a marvelous picture of Dad as he kneels to hug his name-sake grandson. It would be our last picture of him. And he looks so proud of Nebbie.

13

"Be Happy for This Moment: This Moment Is Your Life"

In the early autumn of 1948, we returned to our home, and you found work on the completion of the new East Phoenix Stake building at 17th St. and Brill. And because of the requirements, you observed – at least while on the job – the non-smoking, non-drinking non-coffee restrictions, and for the first time since your return from war, we were fellowshipped by the Elders Quorum. And soon you were involved in not only work on the building, but in the priesthood quorum – and we went to Sacrament Services together – although, like a lot of the young fathers, you seemed to spend more time walking in the hallway with your son, than in the meetings, themselves. But that was okay – at least we were there.

I was called almost immediately to be the teacher of the nine year old Sunday School class. These boys were known as young rascals. At that time in the church, all classes sat with their teachers, not their parents and I took those noisy, restless deacons and within four meetings had them complimented by their Bishop, as the most exemplary Jr. Sunday School class, because of their reverence. I loved those boys. And still remember the names of many of them. But in April of '49, I was called to be the teacher of the Gleaner Class. I remember how very unprepared I felt for that appointment, but determined to do the very best that I could, knowing that the Spirit would help me every step of the way.

In this same period, you had been tapped for the soft ball team, because of your pitching arm. And we made many friends, as the wives and I attended every practice, every game. We brought our children to the big ball field there on the grounds of that lovely new edifice that was slowly readying for dedication. And at your memorial service in November of 2001, there were some of those brothers and sisters in attendance. They remembered you and they remembered the Summer of 1949 when you led the Phoenix First Ward to major victories. One newspaper article I am reading now states: "Phoenix First Ward, leading the Latter Day Saints Church Softball League with 25 victories and one loss,". . . .and A. C. Nebeker was the winning pitcher in all of those games. [And I am looking now at the sweet picture of you, taken as you prepared for a game. You have the happiest smile and your beautiful teeth remind me of this trait in our children, perfect, white teeth. Oh that I should have been that fortunate.] Unfortunately, after pitching the team to the regional finals, the team manager, because you threw a few wild balls the first inning, took you out, replacing you with another pitcher, who lost the game to George Stapley 8-6. Neither you – nor the team – could forgive the manager. All felt you were entitled to pitch the game, win, lose, or draw, after your wonderful season. But Earl had the say-so. It took me a long time to forgive him – for I think that quick decision affected our lives severely. But more of that later.

It was during these times – the Gleaners and the ball games – that we were to meet Beth and Darwin Wilkins, who became my dearest friends. You didn't get to know them as I did, but still today, I count them first among all my married friends. And later, they will play a most important part in my life. And it was during these same times, that I, as Gleaner leader, was able to hold what was called the "Binding of the Gleaner Sheaf," with 18 young women having met the requirements. That same year, I and six other young women would become "Golden Gleaners" – under my direction.

It was also sometime during this time period, my husband, because of my deepening love and respect for you, that I knew beyond a shadow of a doubt, that I wanted, again, to bear your child. This was no rash decision on my part, for I knew, already, it would entail another Caesarean section, with all the seriousness such surgery still implied. I remember the night that I told you of my desire and I sensed your hesitancy. But I never knew the reason for it. Was it fear for me? Was it worry over additional responsibility? You didn't discuss it with me. But I knew you were thinking it over, seriously. And I waited.

It was also during these happy days of growing love for you, that your father, in May of '49, unexpectedly died of a heart attack, while in the Prescott hospital, waiting transfer to a hospital in Phoenix for prostate surgery. I think you never forgave yourself for not going to Prescott to see him. But the old Chrysler was acting up, and you thought he'd be in a Phoenix hospital within a day or two. So you decided to defer the trip and see him at the hospital here. This sudden death, I think, and the widowhood of your mother at the age of 72, ultimately marked a drastic turning point in your life, that would only surface some months after the funeral. At Dad's burial, you gave a wonderful dedication of the grave. [Your son would not be alive to dedicate your resting place.] And for the second time – the first at the blessing of our son – I saw you exercise your priesthood. And I was stirred. But for a time, you and I continued with our activities – playing ball, working in the church.

And finally the dedication of our now-completed and paid for Stake House was to take place. The party preceding the dedication took place on October 15, 1949. There was entertainment and dancing. And you and I won the dance contest that evening. People always said of us – even our daughter – that when we danced, we were as one. And on that night, we were as one in every way. For on that festive night, against all physical odds for my conception, in perfect love and harmony and passion, our daughter was conceived. As with our son, I knew, intuitively, that the seed had been sown. And I knew with great joy that a second time I had been given God's grace.

Never in my life did I carry greater peace and happiness within my heart as within the next eight and a half months. Everyone said I shone with joy [as they had said when we were married] – though again I showed no overt sign of pregnancy. I was determined that I would cause no pain or trouble to you and that you could look forward to our child's birth without fear of any kind. The surgeon who had performed my last surgery – and had become my permanent doctor – had agreed to deliver the baby (we had no sonograms to foretell sex, then) even though he had just given up obstetrical work. But, for me, he agreed to make my child his last delivery. And you were pleased because you knew I had great trust in Dr. Merrill. As time drew near, he gave me the choice of either having the surgery July 1st or of having a Fourth of July birth. I chose the 1st, a Saturday morning at 8:00 A. M. Do you remember taking me to the hospital the evening before and how the nurse refused to register us until she had called Dr. Merrill? We'd come in after visiting hours were over and she was going to refuse us admittance. And then I told her I was there to have a baby. And she said to me, "When, in nine months?" And even when I told her next morning, she put in a call for confirmation. The specialist, Dr. Warrenburg, coming in that evening said that if he didn't know better, he'd think they were removing a small tumor the next day. But, again, I delivered a six pound baby – this time a beautiful baby girl. Just as we had planned six years ago in so many letters, we now had our "Junior" and our Deborah Paige – and before your 31st birthday, as you had always desired. I was now 23. And this time we knew there would be no more children.

That afternoon and evening there was a truly dreadful thunderstorm. Crashing thunder and lightning, pouring rain. You came very early to the hospital, but left quite soon, as I was in dreadful pain and under heavy sedation. That night you wrecked the brand new Hudson that we'd bought from your mother at your father's death, a purchase we really couldn't afford to make. But Mom needed the money and wanted you to have it, so we had purchased it a few months earlier. I wasn't told about the accident; there was some fear for my health the next three days after the Caesarean and you held the news from me. But on the fifth day, you brought Nebbie down to see his new baby sister. He wasn't allowed in the maternity ward, but I held the baby up to the window, and you had him down below so he could be the first to see his little sister, whom he would idolize – at least until she walked, and ruined his tinker-toy creations. And then when I was warm and happy, you told me of the accident. You had "of course" gone out to celebrate the birth of your new daughter with your "buddies." Unfortunately, the car was a disaster, so we would be car-less for the next six weeks. And you had to take me home from the hospital on the 20th day, in a truck, borrowed from the construction company you had just begun to work for.

I still remember the terrible jolting to my incision. But most of all, I remember the jolting to my confidence in you. And the greater pain that was yet to come.

14
Days of Bliss

Remembering the difficult days of nearly four years ago, when we had brought our Nebbie home from the hospital, you and I had made careful preparations this time to see that no catastrophes would occur. Of course I hadn't counted on your "night out with the boys" and the wrecking of my transportation home from the hospital, but I survived the shaking motion of the truck, while I tried to hold my precious new daughter safely in my arms. I would guess that since the accident had occurred two weeks before, I had prepared myself for the uncomfortable trip and the unceremonious delivery of my precious cargo to her new home. Otherwise, all was excitement and happiness in our home, as Nebbie greeted his little sister, and the neighbors exclaimed over her. And you and I were at peace with the world. Learning from past experience, we had engaged a highly recommended maternity nurse, who would be with me the first two weeks, leaving me time to recuperate and for my incision to heal. You would have a company truck to get to and from work. And I now had a brand new washer, and a clothes line in a beautifully sodded lawn. And you, dear husband, had installed, in a hall closet, a new central heating system for the winter to come. The baby's bassinet was softly and pinkly feminine; you had made a bedside table for me so I could easily care for this beautiful new daughter of ours. I knew, beyond a shadow of a doubt, you loved me – and our child.

And she was, indeed, the dearest, most placid and loveable child imaginable. Delivered two weeks early, she slept twenty hours a day, having to be wakened for her bath and feeding. I would become so concerned about her quietness that several times an hour I would go into the room to be sure she was breathing. We called her "our treasure." I adored her; her brother adored her; and you were a loving daddy. I was entirely happy. And I knew that I was happy and I knew how and why I was happy. I had you; I had Nebbie; I had Debbie; I had our home. God had blessed us. Who could ask for greater bliss?

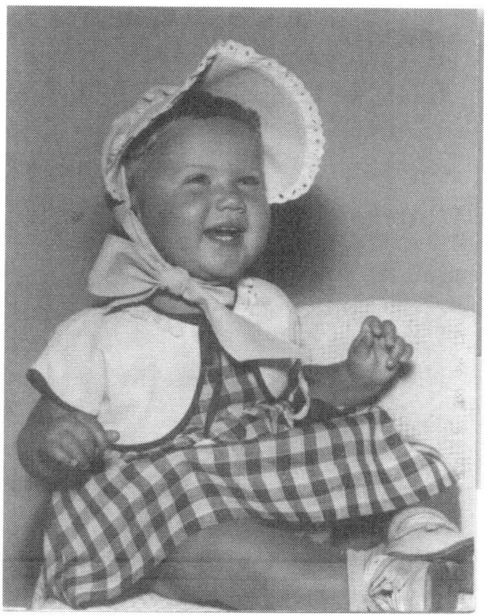

Deborah Paige Nebeker

But my dear, what was your state of mind? Did I ever think to ask you? Or did you ever think to discuss it with me? You had a good, steady job with a growing tract home builder and you worked long days and seemed happy in your work as a finish carpenter. You took pride in your abilities and turned everything on the job into a competition. How many more doors could you hang today than yesterday? How much better were your joints than yesterday? Always you were looking for whatever could enliven your days. I sensed that, I think, and I felt your growing restiveness. But what did I do about it? I was always there for you physically – even when you came home in the middle of the day. And I tried to see that we had entertainment – I had made new friends for us just down the street. The Finches had a son and daughter exactly the same age as our children, and I sought social opportunities with them. But you were no longer involved in church activities – in part, because of your hurt over the ball game, I think. I didn't nag you about it. But your mother did. And I did try to have her to dinner or to stay overnight with us, in the days to come, so that she could be with the family. Each time, I did, however, she ended up in a nagging bout. About coffee and smoking and not going to church. And each time that happened, I knew that before the week was out, you would be off with the boys "for a beer or two." And then the outings grew more frequent and my hurt more constant. And I remembered the letters that you had written so long ago, declaring you would never hurt me. "Even the times I made you angry come back to make me feel sad! That I could do such things to hurt you!!! My! My!!. . . I love you so." And as "hurts" increase, I wonder if you do love me so! And the flowers in the garden begin to turn brown.

Then, by inspiration, I know what to do – you need some excitement and freedom from stress and work, so I engage Mrs. Tyner – the wonderful nurse – and you take a week off and we make a trip to Los Angeles and then to San Diego, in our newly repaired and painted car. And we have fun and love together, much as the two lovers we had been in Chicago just six years ago. We eat our last meal at the Brown Derby in Los Angeles – a salad was all we could afford by then – and we return home, and we are broke! But you do not seem worried; in fact, you seem calm again. So peace prevails. And Nebbie is now six and ready for school, and our baby girl is nearly two and a half.

15
Meditations

As I am writing these words, looking at pictures of our little family and reviewing the happiness they reveal, I keep trying to piece together the signals that should be obvious and pointing to the changing times that are to come to us. It would be easy to skip over some less-than-happy memories and leave only the triumphs alive in this final love letter of mine. But that seems the coward's way. Surely,

Neb, Quill, Debbie and Helen

as I write to you, for at least one last time I should be free to exchange with you the thoughts of my spirit, to indicate my questionings, my searchings of the soul. I want to understand what is happening to us in these years. I want to understand you and what drives you. And I need to understand myself. I know that I am happy in my home, in my family, in my church work. And I know my love for you is still basically the essence of my being. But I also know that your drinking bouts are more frequent and of longer duration. When I try to talk with you about it, you are angry – accusing me, as you have accused your mother: "You're trying to get me under your thumb." This is your continuous response to any attempt at discussion. With each episode, of what is becoming to me personal betrayal, I realize that I am increasingly unable to bear the now constant emotional upheaval that is slowly eroding away my trust in you. And I realize that as trust is being lost, my physical response to you is becoming more guarded, less responsive in frequency and in ardor. Without conscious intent, this withdrawal has been a "response" to your actions, not a "cause" of them. But you turn it into a "cause" as you begin to accuse me of not being sexually responsive. How does a woman make her husband understand – when his mind is set against wanting to understand – that the sexual act of love is a matter of the heart and mind, as well as of the body? Sexual "love" is the act of giving, of surrendering, for a woman. And when that "integrity" or wholeness of heart, mind, body is gone, such surrender can become debasing, for some women. [You would have understood – or at least discussed this with me in a "little talk," when we were writing love letters years ago. Just as I understood when you taught me about love and children in your "little talks," during our courtship.]

But as I'm writing these thoughts of mine to you, I'm thinking of what you are thinking during these times of which I write. And perhaps I'm beginning to understand. Were you thinking that life was rapidly passing you by? You were always terribly age conscious and 40 is coming on. Were you thinking of your adult life as essentially a cage? Two years of college – not exactly a holiday? Two years of a restrictive mission? Three long years in the service? All of these years without essential freedom of any kind? Seven years of your life lost? And since those seven years, another seven of marriage and fatherhood and responsibility? Like Jacob, did you feel you had served fourteen years of unremitting toil? In your own way, were you seeking now the freedom that I had sought at the age of 15 – only to surrender it to you in marriage?

Or were you driven by guilt? Guilt over your father's death without your visit to see him? Guilt over the concern that you should have for your mother in her widowhood, but couldn't because of her nagging? Guilt over your failure to live up to your responsibilities in your religion? Guilt over memories of the war, and the friends you had lost in battles, and perhaps the things you had had to see – and perhaps to do? Guilt over hurting me? I just don't know – and I never will in this life. But as I seek to understand, I can lose some of my feelings of sadness – and perhaps my own sense of guilt – knowing that each of us has to find his solitary way to greater wholeness – or else die spiritually and psychologically. A psychiatrist might explain this growth to wholeness as the internal, psychological drive to "individuation." But for me, I express that inner drive as the guidance of the Holy Spirit. And that is exactly what drove me to begin my college and university experience at the age of 25, when my son began his first grade in the public schools. But first things first.

16
New Beginnings

In the summer of 1952, in the upheaval of emotions I have just shared, and moved by forces that probably neither of us understood at the time, you and I, dear love, began to move toward greater freedoms – and different freedoms – in both our lives. You, having ended your employment with the company building tract homes (they had finished their units), had, with my complete support and confidence in you, taken the State Contractor's Licensing test and gone into business for yourself as Nebeker Construction Company – specializing in remodeling and residential contracts. You had no financial underbase at all, but you had made some interesting contacts in your last two years and I was willing to take the chance that "we'd work it out," as you had said so often in our early months together. This was absolutely taking a leap into faith, on my part. But I knew your longing to be free from the restrictions of others; I knew you were a talented workman; and I knew you had real creative talent and could draw plans almost as well as a beginning architect. Furthermore, I felt your own business might be an answer to the drinking problem – if you were excited and involved in this new beginning, you might not need the release afforded with your "buddies." As you began to get small contracts and make fair money, I offered to help by keeping your books, being a business partner in a sense. But you scotched this involvement – you wanted "no interference" in your business proceedings. So, rebuffed by you, I became extremely restless and worried about what I was going to do when Nebbie was in school all day. And what would sweet Debbie do when her "Bubba" was no longer her special, all day playmate?

My 25th Birthday - January 16, 1952

Thus it was, in the late summer of 1952, in the midst of these changing circumstances of our lives, moved by a force I did not understand then but which I now know beyond question to have been the Holy Spirit – I suddenly decided to enroll at Phoenix College as a freshman. At the age of twenty-five, mother of two children, ten years out of high school, frightened to death by my daring – I made a leap into faith for myself. I don't remember what your actual response was. Did I ask your permission? I don't know. Did we talk it over? I don't know. You must have given at least tacit agreement because there were fees to be paid – and I had no money of my own, not having worked since my pregnancy with Debbie. You must have agreed to my use of the car – you now had your own construction truck with your name on it. And I would have to have money to pay for a sitter for our little girl. But that I had already arranged with Beth Wilkins, for she had two little girls – one a year younger than Debbie and one a year older. And she was delighted to keep Debbie four hours a day, for the $10.00 a week I felt I could pay her. That was a good addition to her limited family budget and for Debbie it would mean two little playmates to make up for the loss of her brother's company. But obviously, that money would have to come from you. And, in your usual way, you probably acquiesced in my decision – as you had done, for instance, in the matter of my working at the service men's club while you were overseas, hoping I would ultimately change my mind. But again, I just don't know how you really felt. I do know that you would have cut me no slack, so to speak, in any family responsibility. The home affairs would be completely mine – as they had been since our marriage. Shopping, cooking, housework, care of the children would continue to be my major emphasis as far as you were concerned.

As I look back on my entry experience in the world of education, I am almost overcome by the courage it took. In 1952, there were no supportive women's groups or academic counselors. Older women were at home, "where they belonged," as were their wives – so thought many of my instructors. And how alien I felt amidst the stares of the eighteen and nineteen year olds, who promptly dubbed me the Matron, disliking me as a grade-point raiser and an intruder into their teen-age world. Did I ever feel free to talk to you about this? Or did you ever really concern yourself with my feelings? Did you know that some of the young women in the church were forbidden my friendship by their husbands, because no "nice" woman would ever "desert" her family, as I was doing? Therefore, I must be after only one thing: men! Did you think that, too? Did you realize how difficult it was for me to be the "superwoman" that my cooking, cleaning, shopping, nurturing role demanded? Did you realize that I prepared for classes in the early morning hours while you and the family slept? And did you ever see that I always arranged my classes – through all my succeeding years at the University – so that my children were never without my presence before or after school? And did you know that I was always the parent who made cookies for the children's school parties? And did you ever realize that you actually, at times, threw every possible obstacle in my path to keep me from succeeding? And whatever the "family plans" you made, I was always there for you and the children?

Do you remember that when I played my first role in a drama production at the college, you could not bring yourself to attend? And when I received my associate of arts degree – I was the first student ever asked to present the valediction and had won scholarships to the university – I guessed you forced yourself to come, overtly proud of me. But shortly after the ceremonies, I remember that you left me to drown your sorrows in the company of sympathetic buddies at the local bar. And I went home alone.

Long after the fact, I do remember that we laughed together over some of the trauma of the past. Some things, however, we never could admit to the light of laughter. Some things you adamantly denied to the last days of your life. But there were many times, my dear, when I silently laughed [as I had done in the days of our courting, when you discovered my "Rogues' Gallery] as, in obvious self-approval, you told new acquaintances of the part you had played in my successes, having "married me young, brought me up to please yourself, and put me through school." You never did see the irony in this. Such was your growth. Proving, perhaps, that time does, at last, heal all wounds.

Not to leave this part of our story unended, let me just say that you endured my journey to the very end, seeing me through all the milestones that were to come: graduation with my undergraduate degrees and my final degrees; my appointments through all the ranks of academia – from Instructor of English to Assistant Professor,

Associate Professor, and my final appointment as Professor of English – and Associate Chairman of the English Department. But this is the process of many years of study, of teaching, of publication, and of sorrow. But I have written of these years extensively in a publication of the Modern Language Association – which you probably never read. However, you endured most of the triumphs and the agonies of these days with me, so let that suffice.

17
Meanwhile, What of You?

As I embarked upon my strange, new path, you were working diligently to make your business a success, and I was so proud of you. I saw you, step by step, win a reputation of skill and honesty. You never advertised. Every contact you made was word of mouth by a satisfied client. And then you made the acquaintance of a very prominent architect, through whom you were given not only contracts for significant projects but also access to a wealthy and sophisticated clientele. And shortly, you were in the company of a few Hollywood personalities and their social swirl. Unfortunately for you – and for me – that milieu went to your head and you were soon caught up in their cocktail parties and the headiness of their personal lives. Now the late nights became later nights and more and more drinking occurred. I worried endlessly about your driving under the influence and perhaps being involved in an accident – and all this was through a process of at least three years. Although I learned later that you had been invited to include me in the activities, of course you never did. You knew I would have objected. Furthermore, I would have cramped your style. I discovered also, from one of the "crowd" – when he met me and expressed surprise at my being such a"beautiful woman," – that you had told everyone I was a "drab little school-teacher type" who wouldn't be at all interested in the social life.

Was that how you really came to see me, my husband? Had my education changed me that much? Or had it only changed your concept of me? Did you never realize in all those months of writing and in all our years together since, that I was a person of mind as well as body, of special spirit and soul? I remember, at a party with friends in the church, when the game of the night was to tell something about one's mate, your response had been, "When I married Helen, she was a sexy little blond with a great body – and then she became a "brain." [But in the same game, you had to tell what color your mate had worn to bed the last night and you remembered that my gown had been blue!] *A brain?* Was that why you became cold and distant from me? Maybe I did turn out to have a "brain," but I was still me. And I still loved you, and our family, and our life that we could have together. I had neither intent nor desire to be a career woman. But my fate was clearly ordained by higher powers to be what was to be. I know that now, as surely as I knew – and know – that our union was destined to be. For better or for worse. The path was pre-determined; the walking of that path would be a matter of choices. For both of us.

18

"The Reckless Choice"

During these years I have just written of, you choose to walk your path in ways already predicated by your past. As you had written to me almost exactly ten years before, when you were in the hospital in France:

> Years ago I got the habit of playing a lone-wolf hand and being independent for what I thought was happiness – but when I met and married you, that soon faded away into the past. Now the only happiness I ever had or will have, is centered on you. I know that without you, darling, there shall be no peace and contentment in my soul.

As I have re-read these words of yours, I am struck by how often we pronounce, out of our own mouths, the very nature of our condemnation to come. Thus, as you choose to return to your days of "playing a lone-wolf hand," of selfish independence and freedom from me, you are laying out your own punishment. As you pursue your pleasure, in parties and drink and family irresponsibility, there is, indeed "no peace and contentment" in your soul. You are angry at everything. You have no time for your family. And I am on the verge of a nervous collapse. One early morning, you return from your activities so drunk that you crash your truck into the side of our house. Demolishing the service room completely. Only then do you seem to come to your senses. And completely stricken and contrite, you spend the next two months of all your spare time from the jobs you are then doing by rebuilding the whole back of our house, adding on a large new playroom and bedroom for the children, a new office section for yourself, and a larger service room in place of the one you have destroyed. As you return to the center of your family – to me, as it were – you become happier, your health is better, and for a time, I am reassured and we draw closer to each other. But also by this time, my spirit has been deeply wounded and I am seeking some insight into resolution of my problems from a noted family psychiatrist. One has helped you in the early days of your return home, and I am hopeful of some relief for my own concerns. I don't think I ever told you that about this time, my first cousin, Betty, has died in a mental institution in Indianapolis, having suffered a nervous breakdown. She dies during a shock treatment. And Betty and I had been close. And she was only a year older than I. And Dr. McGrath has told me in no uncertain terms that I am on the verge of a similar breakdown. Unless your pressure upon me ceases. And so the path you have chosen – and will choose – will have ramifications for me. And for your children. By this time I am in my last year of my bachelor degree at the university. And the pressure there is growing.

But three months of repentance are all you can bear – and once again you are in the pursuit of what you think is happiness And my despair continues to deepen. Then, with the beginning of the next academic year, I have been offered a paying position as the first "teaching assistant" the English Department has ever hired. With that position will come greater responsibilities – and also I will be continuing with my graduate studies. My choices become crucial.

19
"The Moving Finger Writes and Having Writ Moves On"

Thus it was that in the trauma of these on-going events, an opportunity arose for me that I could not possibly have envisioned. And no one, not even you, ever knew the whole truth about the decision I was to make. In February '55, my psychiatrist tells me that my collapse is imminent – he cannot predict anything but that, unless the circumstances of my life change drastically. . . . Without such change – meaning you must evaluate your actions and take up some of the concerns of the family – he predicts a mental breakdown severe enough to entail a psychiatric commitment, where I could be isolated from you for treatment. I sensed, Neb, that he was right. But what could I do? I had tried every way I knew to tell you what was happening to me. Your only response was your now constant, "You're just trying to get me under your thumb," routine. And I *was* falling completely apart.

Then, miraculously, it seemed to me, a way opened up, a truly impossible thought on the surface. Off-handedly, I told you about a three month European study program, offered by the university, for graduate study. Expensive – but conceivable. In all honesty, I thought you would immediately dismiss the program as costly and impossible for a married woman with young children. In fact, I think I hoped you would. You didn't! Your immediate acquiescence – your enthusiastic endorsement of a three month absence from me – told me one thing for certain. You were anticipating, with my absence, your complete freedom. Now what was I to do? Staying home in the same old circumstances meant for me a serious illness. On the other hand, taking another leap into faith, and making the many plans that would be necessary before I would go in June, might bring you to your senses – might make you realize that you and the family not only "needed" me but also "loved" me enough not to want to see me go. I really hoped that such a re-evaluation on your part would occur. It did not. Again, the die had been cast. And there was no turning back. For better or for worse.

To make a long, involved story short, let me simply remind you of how I made the plans for our children's care with a reliable woman for the next three months; of how you, without recrimination, paid the rather handsome fees for such a long travel period. And of how you let me set off, with an overtly happy heart – but with the deepest soul-sorrow I had felt since *you* had left *me* those eleven years ago in Indianapolis. What would be the result? And how would we meet again? If you had simply said, "Honey, I don't want you to leave me. I love you so." I would have flown into your arms, without thought or regret. But as I write, I am looking at your picture – as serious and unsmiling – you tell me goodbye. And I am wondering what your feelings really were. And the picture you took of me, as I board the train, shows me with, I think, a quizzical look on my face – as though, even then, I'm wondering "How could you let me go?"

I leave to study in Europe.

20
Another Life-Changing Trip for Me

I will keep on this three-month study tour of Europe, a complete journal of my experiences with people, my travels throughout most of the European countries and capitals, and some of the personal changes within my mind and spirit. But I have kept hidden in those writings the deepest feelings of my heart. I wrote you letters, of course, but they were not the letters of longing and passion I had felt when you left me. Nor will they be letters in which I repine for home and family. During the week I spent in Indianapolis, before I took flight on KLM for our first destination in Europe, my heart was so heavy with loss and longing for all that really mattered to me – you and my children and my home – that I cried myself to sleep every night. Each day I longed for a phone call or a telegram saying, "Please come home. We can't do without you." And I would have been with you on the next flight. But like so many years ago, when we first met, "you did not call" and, as then, "I wasn't surprised. Either you didn't feel I was necessary or you had other fish on the string" – as you did that night so long ago in Indianapolis. So realist that I am – at least on the surface – I simply squared my shoulders, stuck out my chin and "got on with it," as I have done through most of my life. But I was determined to make the most of this adventure of my life.

The three months were to change me in ways I could never have anticipated. I now was personally familiar with all the places from which the history and the literature I would teach for so many years derived. I learned foreign customs, and visited with those who had suffered in the war in which you'd served. I met interesting and different people. I was introduced to a man attached to the American Embassy in Rome – and he took me to an Embassy party. I could have gone much further in a relationship with him – and other men I met. But I didn't. I attended three beautiful operas at the Baths of Caracalla in Rome, with a companion who thought me beautiful and fun – not "a drab little school-teacher type." At twenty-eight-and without you – I learned that I was still desirable. I crossed no forbidden lines – my sense of honor precluded that – but I learned to know again – free from your restraint and obligation and neglect – that there was still life. And fun. And freedom, if I decided to take it.

It's interesting to me that while, of course, you wrote me, I saved none of those letters. I wrote you, too, but not as often as you seemed to expect. But I wrote my children and I longed for them every day. And I knew from Mickie, who wrote me every week, that they were well taken care of. And that you were spending time with them – as you had not been doing for many months. [In fact, that July, you took them to the opening week of Disneyland.] But I was under no delusion about you; I could read from your letters what I had predicted before I planned the trip: you were enjoying freedom from any sense of restriction. It has always been interesting to me that it is only when you feel threatened by others in a relationship with me – in other words, only when your green-eyed monster gets aroused – that you zero in on your feelings toward me. How sad – for you, and me. I, on the other hand, feel the greatest love and physical passion in a situation of absolute trust and confidence. How very different we are. But as I have written the above about my friendships with various men, I'm wondering if your "catting around" is your need to prove to yourself that you are physically attractive to others, and important. And since you have always been able to take my love for granted, that just didn't count?

Because you shared with me long ago your visit to Paris, I think I will include here – from my journal – my visit to the same spots:

> No visit to Paris would be complete without a tour of the night life and that I had. Leen took six of us to places not usually visited by tourists and there we saw real French night life. I can't say I was embarrassed, although I had never seen such completely naked shows – it was Paris, and part of what I had come to see. [Like you, Cpl. Nebeker!] We went to Pigalle, with the prostitutes prowling the streets – they even propositioned, in our presence, the three fellows who were with us. We visited the "Latin Quarter" where we saw real "Apache" dancers – in fact, I had a dance with the male member of the team. After I

> finished the dance – he was an excellent dancer – I knew something about the smells of Paris! I don't think he'd bathed in a year. We couldn't leave without a visit to the Moulin Rouge, where we had a bottle of champagne and saw an excellent show. This is a tourist place and lacked the spice of other places we visited. In the small, wee hours of the morning, we turned homeward for a few hours of needed sleep. We had seen Paree at night; the tour was complete.

So now, my love, after 55 years, you can enjoy my trip to Paris – as I had "enjoyed" yours so many years ago! Interestingly, I discover that instead of writing now, you are phoning me in Rome and in Paris. Both times you want to know why I am unavailable at such late hours of the night – or morning. But surely everyone knows that Intercontinental calls are extremely difficult – as well as expensive to complete? But you always persevered, until you got me. I wonder why? [I hope you don't read any venom in this?]

On Friday, August 26, we take the boat train from London to Liverpool – a four hour trip – where we embark on the Australian liner *Empress of Australia,* to arrive in Montreal, Canada on September 3rd, after a brief docking in Quebec. You are to meet me there for the drive home. Before departing, I penned this little farewell for my fellow travelers:

Tour Blues

In a moment of weakness when our minds went astray
We went on a tour to lands far away.
In a bus we entitled "Shake, Rattle, and Roll
We toured all of England – the tour guide's main goal.

We traveled the Highlands; we traveled the Low
Our muscles were aching, our minds full of woe.
We saw cathedrals, old castles, in down-pouring rain,
Til the mention of "ruins" nearly drove us insane.

But at last Britain we finished and o'er the North Sea
We took a short trip to the famed Zuider Zee.
We toured Belgium, Germany, Switzerland, too
Then Italy, France, before we were through.

Then after a century – or at least so it seems
We traveled by ship to the land of our dreams.
To the land where the food is the best to be had,
And the beds are so soft they make your bones glad.

Where we don't need a passport to cross over the border
And drinking water with meals is not out of order.
Where the plumbing is good and bathtubs are free.
Where to get in a bathroom, you don't need a key

Where the "lifts" really lift – don't get stuck between floors.
And you don't have to jump or get caught in the doors.
And this we have learned – that though far we may roam
When it gets down to facts, THERE'S JUST NO PLACE LIKE HOME!

21
"So, It's Home Again, Home Again, America for Me"

After having flown to Ireland at the beginning of our tour, the journey home by ship was tedious, boring, and rough – perhaps even dangerous. The skies were overcast and ominous the whole eight days, and almost everyone in our group was deathly sea-sick. Fortunately, I seemed to be a born sailor – even the roughness of the English Channel crossing had left me untouched, while others hung over the railing almost the whole crossing. The ship had absolutely no recreational facilities and there seemed to be no staterooms, as such, only tiny two-bunk closets in which there was scarcely room for one person – let alone two – to dress. Remember this was 1955, and tourist travel was almost unheard of. I imagine that we were on a ship which had been used for troop transport after the war.

By the time of our arrival in Quebec in early evening, on Friday, September 2nd, everyone was eager to be on deck as the few Quebecan travelers debarked. I, of course, expected to meet you the next day in Montreal – though truly I would much have preferred to come home by train, rather than make the long auto trip. But you had insisted on meeting me, so I was packed, ready for the morning's debarkation. And thus I was free to stand at the rail and watch the departing passengers. Suddenly, as I looked down, I remarked to my friend, "that man down there looks exactly like my husband." And then, as "that man" waved and yelled, I realized that he was you! For whatever reason, you had indeed come to welcome me in Quebec! And so I rushed to get my luggage up and off the ship and then, you were kissing me and hugging me tightly and I knew, once more, that I was home.

We stayed that night in Quebec, where you welcomed me with a husband's proper welcome for his long gone wife. But the next day, I didn't get to see anything of Quebec. You had – unknown to me – purchased a new 1957 Chevrolet, picking it up from the factory in Flint, Michigan, before coming to get me. Now you were eager to start the long journey home, making only a brief stop in Pittsburgh, Pa., where I could see my sister and her husband for the first time since my marriage. Before that, however, we stopped at Niagara Falls, where we spent several hours, as you may remember. These visits concluded, you began your mad drive across the countryside. This is one thing that had always bothered me about you. Taking a trip always meant driving straight through – ten hours at a stretch, if necessary – but always so stressful for me. I think we spent three nights in motels, making the distance in four days, all told. In those days you were stopped three times by State Police, receiving your only ticket when we got to Apache Junction, I think. But I had had seven weary days at sea, sleeping in a narrow, uncomfortable bunk, one night of visiting with my sister, and now this frantic dash. I was exhausted – and irritable. And you had not yet told me what I could expect when I got home. Had I known, I might have stayed in Quebec! However, all the discomfort was negligible, in some sense, because I wanted to get home to my babies.

As we drove homeward, we talked of many things – my experiences, your business, the children and their activities, how you came to purchase a brand new car without discussing it with me, the trip to Disneyland. But finally, the real confession came out. You had almost missed meeting me when I docked, because on the day you were to leave Phoenix to pick up the car before going on to Quebec, you had been jailed for drunk driving. *And* in order to be able to leave in time to get me, you had had to pay a bribe of $800 plus the fine itself. Darling, as I write this, I am truly laughing – as I'm sure I did not laugh then. But that is because I can almost feel your anguish – and your sinking heart – at having to make this confession to me. I imagine that if you had felt you could hide it from me, you would have. But you were more afraid to have someone else tell me than to tell me yourself. Needless to say, the rest of the trip took place in an icy silence. Except for your breaking the cold with the news that you had just signed a contract to build a palatial home in Paradise Hills, which would make you – or break you.

22
Home, Sweet Home

After this long time, I cannot, of course, remember just what day or at what time we finally arrived home. I only remember my complete dismay and anger, when I discovered that your mother, upon learning of your trip to meet me, had installed herself in our home, having fired my housekeeper, Mrs. Jones, without consulting you. [Your mother was then eighty.] The children were in a state of upheaval. Mom was always too controlling and Quill, for that is what "Nebbie" had declared himself to be by this time, was in a state of rebellion. And the house was an absolute mess. Without my knowledge, you had started making and installing beautiful handmade cabinets in our kitchen. That, in itself, would have been a wonderful surprise. But everything in the former cupboards was now piled in stacks on the kitchen table and floor – including all the food supplies in the house. Everything was in chaos and I was so tired that I just sat down and bawled.

Naturally, your mother took offense, thinking, she said, that she had done us a favor. And I know I emerged as the villain of this comic opera. My husband, what were you thinking of? How could you not at least have tried to prepare me for what I would find at my long awaited – by me – homecoming? Oh, well, this too passes. And I've been baptized by fire, again!

23
And Life Rolls On

Shortly after arriving home, my new school year begins. And this year of 1955-56 will be an especially sweet one for me, because my dear little Debbie and I will be going back and forth to the university together every day. She is enrolled in the Payne Training School kindergarten program, which is a delight for her, and how she loved her teacher, Mrs. Pescha. Quill is now in the 4th grade and doing fairly well, and you, my dear, are busy building two beautiful houses. All is going well, except for an occasional "lapse" or two on your part. And I am psychologically much stronger, after my three months freedom from stress. But in September of 1957, at the age of 30, I will have a new occurrence of the old "pet pain." After two months of extreme agony, and just before the new semester of my teaching as an instructor is to begin, I must undergo an emergency operation for ovarian cancer which, having spread to the uterus, becomes a hysterectomy. This is unfortunately, Neb, the period in which you have just begun building our new home, with all the stress of that added to your concern for me. I have determined with all the force of my will to recover quickly and to not cause you any undue trauma. But the fact is that I could not protect you fully, as I had done with my surgery when you were overseas. I could not hide my pain from you. And I could not keep your sister, Stell, from over-dramatizing the effects of that operation on one so young. She had been through the same operation in the first days of our marriage and because of her failure to have children, it had deeply affected her. I, however, had two children – and enough experience with other surgeries to know that the effects were only temporary. And I was always, as you said, "a tough cookie." You had been especially solicitous during the hospitalization – no wrecked cars, etc. – and I had come home after two weeks, was on my feet, and preparing to go back to teaching within another two weeks.

One evening during that time, Stell had offered to keep the children overnight and I had prepared an especially nice dinner just for the two of us. You were not home at your usual time, but I wasn't worried. You had given me no reason to expect an "out with the boys" episode for some time now. And I was always hopeful that you would outgrow this need. But seven o'clock came, then eight, then ten, then midnight. And you weren't home. Suddenly, the back door burst open and you were standing there, reeling, not in apology as you had been that night in the first days of our marriage, but in furious anger. And amidst the torrent of other words I heard, "You're not even a woman anymore!" Already devastated by the hours of waiting for you, and for the first time in my life, I reacted in uncontrollable, infuriated anger. I picked up a china bowl of mashed potatoes from the table and instinctively, hurled it at you. Incredibly, it hit your arm just below your left elbow, shattered into pieces, and the blood simply poured from you! I don't know who was the most shocked. I don't remember much of what happened next except, stricken, I tried to stem the heavy flow of blood, with little success – at least for several minutes. And then? Nothing is really clear. I'm sure you were appalled – and angered. Perhaps you even left to drink some more. But I do know that my hurt at your words was so deep, that all these years later, I can still feel the pain. Certainly, in those six words, you had more than compensated for any dismay that I had caused you the morning after our wedding night, when I had thoughtlessly – and in ignorance – told you that I thought "sex was kind of dumb." And today, in writing this, I'm wondering if you even remembered these cruel words to me – spoken in a time of my extreme vulnerability. I never spoke of them to you. And you never apologized. But you bore the scar of my deep hurt and anger on your arm to your dying day.

I clearly remember, however, that even in my anguish of spirit, I realized that through me – and through no fault of my own – you felt your manhood to be threatened. And again, my pain was for you. But what could I have done? Or how could I have helped you to discover how wrong you were, except through time and patience? For the time being – at least in your own mind – you had your excuse for acting as you would. And the path you choose leads almost to disaster. For all of us.

24
The Seeds of Time

Dating from the sad events of my 30th year just related, it is difficult for me to substantiate factually the major events of the next three years. We move into our new home at 2102 E. San Juan, Phoenix, Arizona in February of 1958. At this time I am concluding my Master of Arts degree, having received my Bachelor of Arts with the outstanding achievement of the highest grade point average, 4.0, for all colleges. I have also won several awards at tournaments for my speech competitions. And I have become an Instructor of English, at the university – working full time and receiving a less-than-adequate salary. You are busy building three houses on our own lots and we are spending a great deal of time working on our landscaping and completing the decorating of the house proper. Quill is now 12 and Debbie, 8, and both are doing well in school. I have recovered completely from my hysterectomy, and in several small vacations that we have taken since, I have more than proven to you quite satisfactorily that I am still a *woman.*

It's interesting to me, that in the course of our lives, when things get their very worst between us, you almost always take me off on a short vacation and things come together for us – at least on the surface. In Mexico or San Diego or Tucson, we can throw off the restraints and responsibilities of every day living and come together as lovers and companions. We can dance, and you can buy me presents. And you can forget that I am a "brain" and have a drink or two in my company, with no accompanying guilt. In the same way, during the holidays of Christmas and New Year, when the company of the "boys" always beckons, you assuage your guilt with beautiful presents – usually of clothes in which you can be proud of me. During these years, we join the Arizona Builders Association and have a place to dine and to dance and to co-mingle with fellow builders. In this way I hope to negate your need to throw off restraints in your ever-ongoing search for that elusive "freedom" which you seek. We also have joined a group of church bowlers once a week and you enjoy that competition. So as time has passed, we have moved on. Together.

And then, the Nebeker clan – your mother's children and their progeny – has a wonderful reunion. And it is a truly wonderful gathering. But it is in this activity that your mother again begins to apply the pressure for your reformation. Of course her motives are of the purest intent. She wants you to reform your life so that you can have me and our children sealed eternally and of course, that is what I have been desiring for nearly fifteen years. The desire of my heart has been to have *you*, a dedicated priesthood holder, at the head of my family. *But you simply cannot have another person's testimony for him! You* have to make up your own mind – and I know you will not do that through any pressure applied. So once again you are in rebellion – through many weeks of unendurable misery, for me and the children. Finally, after one horrible night, I ask you to leave our home. And, under protest, you move into an apartment. Again, I think, the die is cast!

But now not only are you free, but, in the weeks to come, I think you realize that I am also free. And this you do not like. Or else you come to realize that you do love me – and our family. And in early February or March of 1961, you plead to come home. I am extremely skeptical, but I remember you convinced me that you really did want to become the man you knew you should be – but that you would need my help. And you gave me a solemn vow, that if I withdrew my divorce proceeding, you would not let me down. And you must remember, dear, that I had known the "inner man" of you through all those wonderful days and letters of our first two years. And I had hope. And love! I dropped my suit. And you came home. And life begins anew.

25
Against All Odds

The early months of the year of renewal, as we might call it, began for me in hope and in trepidation. I had had your promises in the past so many times, with failure, that the first months of your return back to our home found me holding my breath each time the evening drew to its close and it was time for your return. But steadily, surely, you kept your promise not to be late, to call me if there were a delay, and not to create episodes of stress relating to your drinking. As I remember, we had a family trip to Disneyland. We also visited Mother and her new husband who now lived in Ventura. Christmas of '61, we made our annual trip to snow country to choose our tree, hacking it all to pieces when we got it home – as usual – so that you could restructure it to the perfection you demanded in your creation. And early in the Spring of 1962, we took a trip to Yosemite, leaving Debbie with my mother. Slowly, but happily, my faith in your promise to reform grew. I had never asked for any further commitment of reform than that you stop your drinking, for that alone precipitated the emotional crises which I knew I could no longer bear. The smoking I could endure. At this time, I was nearing the end of my doctoral studies and you had just negotiated your first contract for a large commercial building in Tempe. The children were happy and increasingly proud of their father. I was working in the Sunday School. Life had seldom seen me more contented.

But what of you, my dear? I have so little to go on as to your feelings, your hopes, your fears. Oh, for a precious letter, a card, in this our 17th or 18th year of marriage, and our 5th or 6th year in our lovely new home. You always had called me a "worry wart" but I am wondering now, if you were not really the one who ran scared, worried more than I. I have always been contented with the little satisfactions of life. Even now, I can scarcely remember when I actually panicked over anything – except you – and my love for you and our children. Somehow, in my view of life, whatever befell, one "just got on with it." So I was never to know what – after 16 months of sobriety – so frightened or angered or enticed you that you devastated the complete trust I had finally found in you and destroyed the very foundation of our home. Was it the new office project? Was it the fact that you were nearing 43? Or was it me? Had I in some way failed you again?

In the final analysis, it didn't matter, The hard fact was that on your daughter's 12th birthday, with me waiting in stricken misery, that at 3 a.m. you pull up in the driveway, storm into the house in a drunken rage and inform me that you will do what you damn please, when you damn please, and with whomever you damn please. And then you start to leave again. But I know that you can't be permitted on the streets in your condition and I threaten to call the police if you try to leave. It is truly a terrible scene. The upshot is that you spend the rest of the night sleeping in your car. But I – for only the second time in my life – will, in an act of fearful rage and grief at the destruction of my trust and faith in you, *hammer to pieces* my treasured, wedding rings, the sacred symbol of my love and commitment to you, my beloved husband.

When the morning comes, you shower and shave without a word. And then out it comes again. You want your independence. You will not leave the home again. I can either acquiesce and go along with you or??? And then you leave. But with the morning, our children are crying, confused, and our son tells me, in no uncertain terms, that he no longer has respect for me, letting you, his father, treat me as you do. These words make my decision inevitable. I cannot let my children witness such a scene again. It is now up to me.

My first decision is to call the Bishop to see if he will come to our home to counsel with me and you. I make an appointment and you agree to be at the house when he comes. And you are there. But there is a veil of darkness around you. And when the Bishop tries to talk seriously with you, you inform him that all the troubles are because of me. If I would just, "adapt my thinking," forget the church, be with you as a wife, and let you do what you want when you want, there would be no trouble at all. Our poor Bishop is speechless. What does one say in the face of evil? And that is what it was. And I knew it. And I knew I had no choice. Before the end of the week, I have found an apartment and the children and I have moved. Fortunately, this is summer and I have until September to get my house in order before I begin teaching again. Your building project is to start the middle of August and I am afraid a notice of divorcement might be of harm to you, but I must do what I must do. Before I file for divorce, however, I take a few days to go to my mother's to think carefully about our situation. Debbie is at camp – she will write me the sweetest letters from there on August 1st and 4th, in which she tells me she has already made a friend who will be at her new school in the Fall. [My dearest daughter, even then, never failed to love and assure me in whatever way she could, as she would you, when help was needed.] Quill is off to the World's Fair in Seattle, with a friend and his family. So I need worry about neither of them. What you are doing in our home I do not know.

In the peace and cool of Ventura, where there is nothing to do but think and pray, I make my decision and I send you the following letter, which you somehow kept:

> . . . This trip has been good for me and I have been able to think over our situation objectively and unemotionally, I believe, and I know beyond a shadow of a doubt that I must leave you. I have tried to think of all the good things I could to counteract the pain of these last six weeks and I realize that we have really shared very little except the problems of the business, living in the home together, and the physical presence of the children. We have not actually even shared them. We haven't laughed together or truly enjoyed each other for a long time. Intellectually and emotionally we have no meeting ground and spiritually we are miles apart. In spite of all this – a hollowness between us that eats into my soul – we could have made it if you had only been mature enough not to subject us to another of these terrible emotional crises, for me at least. Or even if once started, you had called it to a halt when I pleaded with you to stop before it was too late. Now it is too late and I know I can never bring myself to go through another of these episodes which have periodically been the basis for the destruction of our marriage. If you cannot control these outbursts, which, I know, are a result of pressures (many of which I believe are unnecessary) then you are too immature for me to love. If you do them deliberately to hurt me, then you are a sadist. If you do

them subconsciously to hurt yourself, then you need help because you are sick. Whatever the reason, I can endure no more and would rather get out now while I still have sympathy & compassion for you.

As I said before, I am badly hurt. I feel you have driven me from my home and been most unfair to me for my efforts of 18 years. But I can understand how your mind works in excusing yourself for this so I can forgive you – but to forget is a different story.

It's hard to face the fact that at my age I must face the world on my own with not really enough to make ends meet and still give my children the life they are both entitled to. But I will do it! I want you to maintain a loving relationship to your children and I will do all I can to foster that relationship. However, I want you to realize that I am going to live my own life and do not want you to bring emotional pressure to bear on me. You gave me up in favor of your "independence" so our responsibility to each other is over. This is hard to realize but it is a fact that must be accepted. The divorce will be filed Monday and this play is over.

What happens then, I don't know. But it can't be much worse than the past. I do know that if there is any future for us together, it must be on an entirely different basis. I do not love the man you are; I might love the man you could be if you truly wanted to. Once before you said you needed me to help you be that man, but I couldn't help you for more than sixteen months. So now, whatever you become, it will be on your own. You'll owe me nothing. You can truly be the self-made man you want to be. And then perhaps you'll know whether you really love me or whether you just need me. If you love me, you could then accept me without resentment of my strength and independence – qualities you once admired. . . .

. . . Hope your Tempe job is okayed and the house has a prospect. Take care of yourself.

It is only as I have copied the letter above that I have realized I was just completing my PhD. studies. Was this what was bothering you? How could I have even suspected that – when every success of yours, I counted as a success of mine? Oh my dear, what happened to us?

26
"Oh, That Way Madness Lies"

I file the papers for dissolution of our marriage of 18 years. The item is published and "everyone" seems to know immediately. And sides, inevitably, are taken. No one at church knows what to say to me – so they say nothing, avoiding me out of embarrassment. Only one dear friend has the sensitivity to speak to me and to offer her help, if possible. You send me three dozen roses on our anniversary date – something you have never done before. You come by the apartment to see if I need help. Succeeding Sundays, you appear in church, sitting several rows behind me – but obvious to all. I can feel their looks and hear their whispers. And I know their sympathy is for you, "poor Neb." Our son has decided that he should move back in with you – you need him more than I do, he says in his defense. But I know it is really because you are bribing him, taking him and his close friends out to dinner every night. I have so little money and you have refused to grant me any and I will not demand of you what you will not freely give. Debbie, bless her valiant little heart, has started bravely in at her new school. I do not know what she is thinking, but she never complains. Though I know her heart is aching over this dreadful fact of her parents break-up.

I have started teaching, but it is taking every ounce of my strength – my discipline. In retrospect, I cannot recall at all the classes of those first days. One afternoon, I find myself sitting alone, in our living room – at home. And I do not recall how I have gotten there. I must have driven; the car is outside. In the apartment, the phone rings; you are calling again. And the phone rings the next day and you want to see me. And on it goes. But I know there is no real hope – that you want, always, only what you cannot have. And I resist. And I know that I am falling apart. You come past the apartment; you want to talk; you tell me, "All of this is your fault and the children are suffering. And I love you. Just come back and we'll work it out." And you want to make love. And I know that all I have to do is say yes and we'll start all over again. But I simply cannot. And you finally leave.

One day, in the midst of these endless pressures, I find myself downtown, sobbing in the streets as I seek my psychiatrist's new office. It's in an out-of-the-way private cul de sac center and I cannot find it. And when I do, I find that I am at the back door – not the entrance – pounding for admittance, weeping, seeking help before it is too late for me. Finally, a nurse hears me and I am taken in and the doctor administers a sedative, and makes me sleep, then sends me home, to await a future appointment. [And you, Neb, never know this, but as I am writing, now, my tears are flowing and I do not know if I can continue.]

The next day, I am in such despair that I call my Relief Society president – a dear friend – to come and visit with me – I cannot be alone, I think. She spends the day, and I cry out my heart to her. She shares my pain. She leaves at early evening. I am spent from weeping, worn out. There is no more that I can do. But suddenly, in the midst of hopelessness, I am absolutely calm. I see the answer to it all, all the pain of you and the dear children. *I am, as you have said, the crux of all the problems.* [As my mother had so often told me in my youth.] If I could only do what you had asked, all would be well. With you – and without the "intrusion of the church" and all that it implied in my life – we might still be a family. The choice is mine. But there can be no turning back for me, this time. And such a choice I know, will be, irrevocably, the end of "me" – will be the death of my spirit, the end of "Helen." And for the second time in my life – the first being my choice between you and Jack Roberts when you had given me my cherished and now destroyed rings – it seemed that I was faced with the dilemma of impossible choice. I know I cannot negate my spiritual Self, what I am in the essence of my soul; therefore, I cannot live with you. Neither can I, since you will not leave me in peace, "live without you." How often had I written you those very words – I cannot live without you – during the dark days of the European conflict. And ironically, how often had you pledged your love to me "through all eternity." I had made the choice between you and Jack so many years before – and through all the years could not atone for harm I had so carelessly done him. Could I atone for any choice that I now made? And in the end, I clearly saw that only *God* could solve my dilemma.

Quite deliberately, dear love, I wrote you a final letter of goodbye, swallowed the pills, lay down on my bed – completely at peace. And left the choice to God!

27
The Infinite Wisdom of God

I cannot recall fully the events of the next twenty-eight hours. I dimly remember that I was in a white room, with busy people in white hovering over me. I think I remember seeing you – and wondering why the Bishop was there? But it is much, much later, the next late evening, before I awake sufficiently to understand that I am in our home, in our bed, and you are sitting beside me, your face pale and strained. When my comprehension clears, you tell me all that has occurred. And your love and concern – and even anger – is there for me to feel. This is what I recall your telling me. I can only hope I have not distorted the events in any way.

The previous evening, earlier, you say, for some unknown reason you had become strangely concerned about me and had tried to phone – hoping that I might possibly go to dinner with you. When I failed to answer, your intention had been just to forget it and go eat alone. But unusual for you, you say, you had felt prompted, repeatedly, to go by my apartment – just to see if I needed anything. And so you did. But then, I wouldn't answer the doorbell, after repeated ringing and calling out – and you could see that my car was in its parking space. And suddenly, with shocking impact you confessed, you knew that I was in danger, that you must get to me. You go to the back door, manage to force the lock. You call out to me, but failing to get an answer, you go into the bedroom, find me on the bed. I am asleep; you cannot waken me. And then you see the note, and realize what I have done. I must be gotten to the hospital immediately, you think. You carry me to your truck parked just outside my back door, and within minutes, I am in the emergency room under the doctors' care. And there they tell you that there had not been much time to spare. But now, you are telling me, I am home with you where I belong. And I am in your care. And you assure me, with a solemn vow, that never will I have to fear again that Serpent in our Garden. And I know, beyond a shadow of a doubt, that you are speaking truth. And never do I know that fear again.

And so it was. God in his mercy and wisdom had had me in His care all that dark night. And now the choice of "life" or "death" – both physical and spiritual – has been clearly evidenced for you. The *choice* is *yours*. *God* has made *that* decision! But only *you* can chose the pathway you will follow. And you choose life – not death. And together, through the years, we try to walk that path.

My dearest love, as I conclude these deeply personal revelations that mark the crucial turning point in what will be another thirty-nine years of our earthly life together, I want to give you my solemn word that never, in any way, were my choices meant to "get you under my thumb," to "teach you a lesson," to exert any control over your life as far as your freedom was concerned. And certainly I had no intention of threatening you with responsibility for my death. I truly believe that as inevitable as was my falling in love with you – and your falling in love with me; as divine an intervention as was your return home from battle; as uncontrollable and traumatic as was our son's conception and advent into the world; as blessed as our daughter's happy birth to us, so was the inescapable necessity for you (1) to feel the absolute desolation of my spirit; (2) to foresee – in terms that you were emotionally and intellectually able to understand – the consequences of the choices you *had* made and still would *have* to make. For myself, I do not seek to avoid any condemnation – such as lack of faith or serious guilt – that could and might be made in my choosing what is most often called suicide – or a way out. I can only say that in my mind, I chose the course I did as a sincere casting of my burden upon the Lord, with the knowledge that every choice has its inevitable consequence. If my choice made it possible for us to go forward together and as a family unit, with all its joys and sorrows, and failures and triumphs then I am content to pay the necessary price, whatever that might be. I am so grateful to you that you kept your solemn promise made on that night so long ago. That choice has made it possible for me to endure the worst that fate could ask of me, in years to come. I write these words in the love of my heart, as I begin a new Book in our life together. Yours, forever, if God wills. Helen

Part II

The Testing Begins Again

1
If We Can Just Keep Hope and Faith and Love

> *March 8, 1945*: My darling . . . .I do love you with every part of my being and I pray with all my heart your feeling will always be the same for me. Keep wishing on that Star, because I wish too, and between our God and our star, things are bound to break for us. For now and ever, your loving wife Helen

So I wrote you, the love of my life, nearly eighteen years previous to the events I have just so painfully recalled. And as we were to begin, again, our "new life" together, I could have reiterated those same words in absolute truth, and hope, and faith, had I thought to write you once more a love letter from my heart. In perfect trust, I let you have the divorce decree set aside by your lawyer – and returned to you open-heartedly. I think you did the same for me. And our physical love was renewed without a doubt. But whether your contentment, your love for me, was less than mine, I may never know. Perhaps you felt less "free" than you had been for many years, but nevertheless, you kept your commitment to me. And as I read the records of the passing years, as I ponder the faces in the pictures that preserve our life's history, I am content with what I see. And I think that you were happier – or at least more satisfied – than perhaps you ever realized. Happiness is, after all, a matter of such small things – holding hands as we sit together in church, going for a walk together in the coolness after a cleansing rain, a simple comment of appreciation and love from the one who matters most, feeling our children's arms around us as we tuck them in their beds at night. Of such small things are the memories – and the happiness – of our lives composed.

I want us both to remember – me here and you beyond the veil – that despite our difficult problems in the early years together – we were always good parents. Our son and daughter were the joys, and the pains, of our whole life. And, my dear, you were a wonderful father! Hard sometimes, in discipline, and in requiring responsibility of them both – but always there, whatever their need or problem. I have so many memories of you and your dedication to our children: your labor in building their playhouse, in the swing-teeter-totter-sand box unit you built for them, your daughter's hand-made dresser you designed and built and finished so beautifully for her sixth birthday. And you and I, together, never missed our son's Little League games through all the hot summers, you never ceasing your efforts to help him build up his self-confidence. And I will never forget the day in the 8th grade, when he came home from a class on sexuality [without our being forewarned] completely confused and perturbed, and your giving him a man-to-man clarification and assurance about the physical and spiritual aspects of love and responsibility. Of course, I didn't hear that talk, but you gave me the gist of it and I knew his heart was at ease. And I had such admiration for you. Then I remember when Debbie was in the 5th or 6th grade, and we put on, for all her classmates, a Halloween carnival, in our back yard. And you made every booth, every game, yourself. And I provided all the refreshments for some forty ten year-olds. What a labor of self-giving love. Of such events were our lives composed.

And every birthday, there was a party for each of them. And Debbie had her pets – hamsters, and gerbils, and cats (even though I was deathly afraid of them). But never a dog, until when her brother went off to the University of Wisconsin, she sneaked in a fluffy, little puppy, and won me over into keeping him. (Even though I was deathly afraid of dogs, too, having been bitten by a rabid dog when I was about six and having horrible memories of the 21 rabies shots I had had to take every day – given right in the middle of my stomach with a *huge* needle!) But thus it was that we acquired *Chauncey*, our beloved pet and consolation of nearly sixteen years. I want to leave in this letter to you, Debbie's recollection of "her daddy," her deep love for you, which she spoke so beautifully at your memorial service in 2001:

> The most prevalent feelings that I recall from my earliest childhood are that my Dad loved me and would always keep me safe from harm. These feelings have stayed with me throughout my life, no matter the place, no matter the circumstance. What

> a blessing for a child to feel such love, such safety. I was not a particularly pretty child. But I knew that in spite of my crossed eyes and my stringy hair, I was beautiful to Daddy and that I could do anything and that Dad would be there with outstretched hand to help should I falter in any endeavor. I was a child that grew up in love and safety. Indeed I was "Daddy's Little Girl."

Oh my dear, when I read such words from our beloved daughter, I love you so much and know of a certainty that I made no mistake in marrying you – and that my personal sufferings and mistakes had not been in vain. And then our daughter writes further of her childhood days:

> I have very fond memories of my childhood. Memories of a little vanity table that Dad built so that I could be as pretty as I could be, of Christmases of bikes assembled and doll houses built in wee hours of the morning. . . Dad took us to Disneyland the first year that it opened and practically every year thereafter. We grew up in Disneyland and Dad loved the place – the gadgets, the innovation. There he was just like a kid and partook in its ever-giving magic – an experience later enjoyed by his four grandchildren as he delighted in taking them to Disneyland and Knott's Berry Farm in their youth. These memories are not of things – but of "happenings." Dad taught us to enjoy the simple things – choo choo trains made from brown boxes and palaces made in sand. We were cowboys and cowgirls, superman and wonder woman in boxes transformed into forts and rockets. We took trips to Prescott and Sedona, enjoying the history of his roots, neighborhood rodeos as horses were broken, the best spare ribs ever, and nature's wonderment. Dad loved the outdoors and he passed this love on to his children. I was a child that grew up with mirth and fun.

Dear love, these words are testimony of the Spirit I saw within you in the days of my own youth, when love was newly sprung and still to be tested in life's hard crucible. I did not err in judgment or faith in you then, nor through the years. And then Debbie writes of her memories of her high school years:

> I got to know Daddy best during my high school and college years. [And these would be the years following your solemn vow to me and the start of our new life.] Starting in my freshman year in high school, Dad became the surrogate father of a rather large group of my friends and Quill's. Every Friday, Dad would pile all my friends into the car and take us to the Camelback football games. On Saturdays, it was off to the lake for a bit of skiing. My friends adored him and there wasn't anything that he wouldn't do for me or my friends. My fondest memories are of the long-standing daddy-daughter date we had every Saturday that ASU played a home game. From 1964 until one year after his stroke in 1994, we attended ASU football games together – that's over 30 years!. . .No matter where I was or who I was dating, these nights belonged to Daddy. And I wouldn't trade one of them for anything in the world. . . Daddy never let me go on a date, but that the young man didn't come in and meet "the parents" – much to my date's dismay. He never let me leave the house without a dollar and a dime in my pocket – a dollar for a taxi cab ride and a dime to telephone him should I ever need help. He would always be there for me no matter what. I was a teenager with a Dad who cared.

And these last words I quote from Debbie's tribute to her Dad are a summary of a part of the "path you chose to follow" in your mature years. And I take pride in you, as does she.

> I remember much during these years. Dad, being quite athletic himself, enjoyed watching his son grow in stature and athletic prowess in baseball, wrestling and track. As an Eagle Scout leader, Dad was diligent in teaching young men scouting skills which he himself had learned as a young Eagle Scout. Dad believed in these skills and he rejoiced as "his boys" achieved proficiency. Perhaps the most vivid memory I have is the visible pride my Dad showed when Quill graduated from the Marine Corps as an officer. My Dad literally picked up his 190 pound son off of the ground and gave him the biggest hug I had ever seen him give. Together, they were bursting with pride. This was one of the crowning moments in Dad's life as he saw his only son mature into manhood.

[And, my husband, as I write this, I know that all the pain and trauma of this our only son's birth so long ago was worth every fear, every sacrifice, every tear of mine, as I brought him into life. Through *me* you had this happiness in life. And I hope that I do not presume too much if I give myself a little credit for helping you to do all the things that you did to give Debbie such pride in you and such happiness in her memories. I was there beside you all the way!]

2

"Love Opens All Locks; It Heals All Wounds"

And you were there beside me in times that brought me happiness. I'm not quite sure of how to develop this part of our life. In decades of experiences? In special events of pleasure? Or just a hodge-podge of conversations – as we did in those sweet letters of loving and sharing and longing so long ago? Perhaps I'll just begin with what we did in the first months of our renewed union. In 1963, we put in our swimming pool. And this brought happiness to our children – Quill, especially, because he had his graduation party here with all his friends of the church, before he left for his first year at the University of Wisconsin. And here we entertained the Elders Quorum, with luaus and dinners, and the MIA had its first new Stake party here – and the punch bowl had a crack in it and broke as I poured my special concoction of frappe into it. But it didn't matter; we just had ice water and the Stake officers minded not at all. And in all these parties, you sweetly set up tables and chairs and helped in every way you could.

And this summer, my sister and her husband and little daughter, Jane, visited us on their way to life in California. And this was the year that we had two house guests from the United Nations' diplomatic corps of Nigeria and the Ivory Coast. Abi Abiola had been educated at Oxford, and black as the night, he spoke faultless British English. He was a Muslim and could eat only certain foods. Mr. Manuan – I forget his first name – was French and was educated at the Sorbonne, speaking only French. And being by religion an "animist," he could eat scarcely anything, as I remember, since all life was sacred. I really don't remember how I fed them. But we had a wonderful two weeks in their company – and I took these two black men to Church – at their request – and one member of the congregation, seeing them, said "I'll be g-damned "and turned around and walked out. And another member said, "Trust Helen Nebeker to try to integrate the church." Do you remember that? But I wasn't offended at all – I had forewarned the Bishop and it was okay with him. I remember how thrilled I was, because of this friendship, when *all* qualified males could receive the Priesthood and a mission was subsequently established in Nigeria. From their background of subordination of women, neither man could understand that *I* was the *professor.* They both thought you were and that I was your wife, chauffeuring them around. And remember how Mr. Manuan went off to the plane, to return to New York, wearing his new Stetson hat and carrying a set of your plans of our house proudly in his hands, intending to build a house just like ours, when he returned to his home? I remember in their own continent of Africa, these men were bitter enemies – and of course, couldn't speak each other's language. But in our home they ended up respecting one another and becoming quite good friends. Due to revolutions in their countries shortly thereafter, we didn't know what happened to them. They never wrote.

And the next year we hosted six Japanese college students for two weeks – two young men and four girls. They had studied English for several years and could read but not speak English at all fluently. And, as a treat, thinking them poor university students, you gave them a hundred dollars to go to the western town – Rawhide – and later learned that one of the group's father was a multi-millionaire. A maker of armaments, who could buy us up in a minute. But our children and their friends learned so much from this experience with people of other nations. And this was the year I was invited to give my first "paper" at a national convention at the University of Washington. And it was highly successful. And I think you were proud of me.

In 1964, you took me to San Francisco, and at the opera house, we saw a London production of *My Fair Lady*, starring Julie Andrews. We had to sit far up in the balcony, because it was a sold-out performance. But I didn't care. It was wonderful. Though my back was so bad from the slope of the seat that I had a difficult time just walking, for the rest of the week. How could I ever thank you for this wonderful experience? But look how I've rattled on – just as I did in all those nearly 400 letters that I wrote so long ago. And are you bored? Or do you still wait for my ramblings of love? Or can one even think of such things in the place where you now are?

Thinking back, do you recall that in the Fall of 1964, our seventeen year old son went off to the University of Wisconsin – the choice which he had finally made – and the only one of his choice that we could possibly afford? I remember how the grief of the leaving of my first-born simply overwhelmed me. I had been entirely unprepared for this emotional upheaval. And I cried and cried, every day, when I got home from work. Part of my grief, I think, was that you didn't seem at all to miss our son – to sense that the first of our family was gone. And life would never be the same. It was only one day, when I was sobbing on our bed, and you sat down beside me, took me in your arms and said, "Honey, I miss him too," that the pain was assuaged and I could go on, comforted by the faith that we would always have each other.

The years of '65 through '67 were especially hard for us, financially, and if it hadn't been for my salary – poor though it was, I don't know how we would have managed. Though your mother had died in September of '64 – shortly after we had begun our new life – relieving us of the financial burden we had borne for her after a stroke two years earlier required a nursing home – the expenses of an out-of-state university stretched us mighty slim. But we had promised our children that they could choose their own university, *if at all possible.* We knew they would learn much from their choices and their experiences of being away from home. And subsequently, they both did. Both of them learned that the heavy expense was not worth the education they were getting. The famous professors they were promised actually taught only advanced students; the moral climate was beyond their toleration; and finally, I could assure them places in the classes of the very best of the professors at ASU. So subsequently, they came home and both Quill and Debbie received degrees from the university where, because I was faculty, I could subsidize their expenses. But Quill did receive one advantage from the UW and that was his acceptance into the Naval Reserve Training program. And when he transferred to ASU, he kept his enrollment current and received a small stipend each month, while he remained in college.

But as I remember these changes in our home structure, I remember the closeness that increasingly drew us together. And I also remember that at your mother's death, you seemed, somehow, more free. I know you loved her dearly, but I think your sense of "failure" lessened when her presence no longer made you feel guilt. It was during this time that I bought season tickets for the symphony; you weren't exactly happy at my choice – thinking this was "snobbery" on my part. But how you came to enjoy symphonic music. In fact, you enjoyed it more than I – an hour was enough for me. But I think because your hearing was deteriorating, that you heard sounds you had not heard before. [It is a fact, that being on the big guns during those months of training and war had seriously affected your hearing. And at the time of your death, I think you heard scarcely anything at all.] Then, having accustomed you to the "social life," I indulged in season tickets to the opera [which I loved beyond all else], to the Little Theater – and we often bought extra tickets, taking friends, by turn, as guests. Most of all, I loved the musical theater – opera, and productions like *Fiddler On the Roof, Camelot*, 1776. [And much later, in our travels to Europe, you would indulge me by taking me to every play or production you could. We saw *Les Miserables* in its first London production. And then we saw it again in Edinburgh. And we saw a wonderful production of *Driving Miss Daisy* and too many others to list.]

But in these years, we still took our short trips, to the coast or to Mexico, and once, to Seattle. And I had my teaching and I was now being published by solid professional journals. But building was down in Arizona, especially as foreign investors were buying up the available building sites, and small contractors could not compete. But you were active with the Scouts and I was teaching Sunday School and all seemed well. But your Nebeker Cough of the war years had returned with a vengeance. And I began to worry about you. And wished you could stop smoking.

So time passes and in 1966, Quill has completed two years at the university and has announced, on his own, that he has decided to go on a mission! Can you remember how astounded you were? Given your own missionary years, and your dislike of the restrictive life, you felt it was the last thing that he should do – for if ever a son was like his father in his rebellious, freedom seeking needs – Quill was yours. Despite your advice, Quill perseveres and receives a call to the Finnish

Mission, of 30 months – 2 ½ years – and enters the mission home in Salt Lake for exactly *one week* before he is sent immediately to Finland. He arrives on June 21st, 1966, three months before his 20th birthday. He has had two years of Russian language, but no training in the Finnish [which is probably the most difficult of all European languages!] Debbie is now a sophomore in high school, with all her demanding – and happy – experiences before her. And you now have another house contract. All seems to be going okay. There are football games for you and your daughter and her friends. And you have an outlet for your high spirits. But you don't like the fact that you are nearing fifty. I am forty-one, and it doesn't bother me at all. But maybe it bothers you? And then, I become slowly, but increasingly ill.

The illness that will overwhelm me in the time that Quill is gone reminds me of how ill I had become in the months before you returned from Europe. But this time it was much worse. Day by day, I weakened, becoming increasingly unable to eat, losing weight, and finally hospitalized repeatedly because my blood pressure would drop so alarmingly that I sometimes could not even stand, let alone walk. I was diagnosed with Addison's disease, and they did painful biopsies – not Addison's. Then something else, then something else. In my last hospitalization, the doctor came in one morning, sat down by my bed and abruptly said, "Helen, you're dying – and we don't know why." And they didn't know why. But they were calling in one more specialist. This time I was diagnosed with having a rare collagen disease, and sent home with prescriptions for, among others, prednisone. And slowly, I began to recover. [Prednisone was, indeed a magic drug for me. How I wish the doctors had started Debbie on that before she became so ill with an auto-immune disease, just as mine had been.] Fortunately for us financially, I was on a semester's Sabbatical leave at that time. And I had time to get my health and strength back. You were so wonderful to me during those awful days – and I know how hard it must have been for you. But I think that only in the days of our courting were you ever as loving of me as you were then. And I never forgot your love and dedication. Without that I think I could not have survived. [But I needn't have feared your sainthood – you would return to your less compassionate self quite easily, following my recovery.]

Of course during the times of this illness, our little daughter suffered. And had it not been for our wonderful home teacher and his wife, I don't know how any of us would have made it. Janie Rhoton, alone, made it possible for me to get Debbie off to Grinnell College, in August of 1968, because I was almost too weak to even pack her clothes. And Janie brought you her wonderful deep chocolate cakes, and Dow gave us his great spiritual support. In the meantime, Quill is fighting his battles in the mission field, worrying about his mother – for although we have tried to keep our problems at home from him, some dear soul in the church has written to inform him that his mother is dying. Along with that, the costs of his mission have increased almost doubly. He now has so grown since he left home, that he has to have new clothes; his food expense is double, and he has great trouble with the language. His first mission president has encouraged his teaching English at the local college, his involvement in track events with the Finnish college students – as a form of "media publicity" for the church (which was virtually unknown in Finland at that time) – but the new president has nixed all such activity as improper for the missionary work. Nearing the end of his missionary months, Quill is suffering intense spiritual anxiety, questioning his reason for being there at all. Not in terms of his testimony of the truthfulness of the Gospel, but of his own place in it at this time. Illness, money, and spiritual agony! Surely God has sent his own version of the plague of locusts upon the Nebeker household. So much for the popular idea that with a family member on a mission, all will be well! Perhaps that may be so, at least for some. But my experience suggests that it might be far better to prepare a family to expect that it may have to *just endure* and *hold on to its faith* in the face of all the darts of the devil that can be thrown at them.

Neb, I have just reread many of the twenty-seven months of Quill's letters from Finland and I am so much more aware of your struggle – the sense of guilt and unworthiness you were still struggling with, even as your son was struggling in the mission field. And it was in the 27th month of his tour of duty – having complained to his president of feeling quite ill for several weeks and being rebuked as goofing off – that Quill's appendix ruptured. One Saturday morning – warned of something amiss by the Holy Spirit, I believe – you suggest, for the first time in 27 months that perhaps I would like to put in a call to our son. That is forbidden in the mission field in the year of 1968. But we start trying to get through a call. Do you remember it took us nearly all day? And when, near evening, we are finally connected,

Quill has just emerged from the recovery room – having received 12 pints of blood transfusions during the process! Looking at this fact now, how strange that our son should be undergoing almost the same ruptured appendix process that I myself had endured, nearly a quarter of a century earlier. It is still my opinion that Quill's premature death, at the age of 52, was caused by the blood transfusions he received there in Finland. An autopsy could never clearly delineate the cause of death for the record – only that all of his internal organs were damaged severely, especially his liver. And Quill neither drank nor smoked to the day of his death. Nor was he sexually amoral. His death, 25 years after that appendectomy in Finland would be in accordance with what we now know about the contamination of blood products and hepatitis infections.

Be that as it may, when our son returned home *three months early* – after *27 months of service* – [with permission from his president – I have the letter] he returned home in a kind of semi-disgrace. Today, the church's system would have provided for an honorable return home on the basis of his health. Quill was not accorded such sympathy – even after 27 months of arduous service. This was to be one of the greatest tests of my faith as you know, my husband. And all of us – but Quill especially – would be traumatized deeply because of that early return. But you never voiced a word against the church; even though I know you suffered, too – if only because of my great grief.

And as though this weren't enough, In the midst of our trials, our 18 year old daughter has fallen in love! And has left for Grinnell College – a very prestigious Liberal Arts and Science college near far away Ames, Iowa.

3

"I Did But Touch the Honey of Romance"

To get back to our daughter's falling in love – the details of which you may not remember or wish to remember: on December 31, 1967, Debbie, now taking classes at ASU before leaving for Grinnell in

August, had reluctantly agreed to go with a girl friend to a New Year's Eve dance at the Institute. That decision was to be a fateful one because, almost like her mother before her [me, you know], that night she fell head over heels in love with a young man who just happened to drop in at the dance, being home from Berkeley, where he was finishing his Master's degree in electrical engineering. [Doesn't that recall the events of our meeting to you? Was their love fated, just as was ours?] Although I saw immediately that he was much too old for her – almost six years – I knew the first time I met him, with one of my uncanny instincts, that Chuck was to be my future son-in-law. I remember that first time, when he came to pick her up for their date, that I reminded him that Debbie was only 17 and that there were family rules about curfew; he must have her home no later than midnight. I remember his instant indignation – he was twenty three and not used to being told when he must bring a date home. The sparks almost fly between us, but he knows the rules now and he reluctantly concurs. Chuck is a recent convert to the church, and I am hoping that means he can be trusted with my treasured daughter. [Perhaps I am remembering you on our first real date?] But I am not yet prepared for any blossoming romance. She has a whole life ahead. Marriage is far off.

To make a long story short, you know that Debbie goes off to Grinnell. Graduating from Berkeley, Chuck takes a job at Honeywell, in Minneapolis, where he can be near enough to visit her in Iowa. Subsequently, having saved money from his job, he sends himself on a two year mission to Argentina – waiting for Debbie to graduate and taking a chance on being classified as 1 A in the draft. When he returns – and Debbie has graduated from ASU with high honors, and with her Bachelor of Science degree – they are married in the Mesa, Arizona Temple, on January 28, 1972. All of our family are in attendance, except Quill, who is in Japan with the Marine Corps, waiting possible deployment to Vietnam. But now we have to back-track in order to fill in the glaring gaps that you may or may not remember. Actually, I think our daughter's wedding day may have been one of the unhappiest days of your life. In fact, that evening – after the Temple sealing of that morning – as we are getting ready for the reception at the church, you simply disappear. You are already dressed in your tuxedo [and you are so handsome and I am looking at your picture right now and remembering how I loved you that day] so

I know you are ready. But where are you? And suddenly, I am terribly afraid. I sense what you are thinking – and fear what you might do as a result. You never told me, my dear, but to this day I believe that you were remembering our wedding day and were grieving in your heart, wondering if this man, to whom you have given your beautiful and beloved daughter, will bring her the grief, the heartache, that you have brought her mother, me. When I see you again, this is one of the questions you must answer for me. And if you were thinking of us, and our wedding, was it with the joy that we both once felt? Or had you come to regret your decision to marry me, so long ago? But you didn't go out to get drunk and drown your tears, as once you would have done. Again, you have kept your promise given me ten years ago. And suddenly, you are with me. We are on our way to the reception. And again, all is well.

Helen, Debbie and Neb

The reception is beautiful. The newlyweds go off to the hotel until tomorrow when they will come to our house to open their gifts. And then they will leave for their new residence in San Diego. That night, we, too, will sleep in each other's arms. But the next afternoon, when the weary couple depart, two weeping parents open the sweet gift of love that their daughter has quietly left in parting, and they realize, after twenty-eight years of marriage, that unless they are truly "one" they cannot survive the sorrow of their empty nest.

Playing "King of the Roost"

4
Segue

But in the meantime, as they say in books, Quill, having returned home from his mission, has graduated from ASU, and qualified for pilot training at the Navy Air Academy in Pensacola, Fla. Unfortunately, he will not qualify for pilot's wings, because his chronic sinus condition is too severe to pass the physical required for that certification. He does, however, choose the Marine Corps as his emphasis, rather than Navy, is commissioned a Lieutenant – in the summer of 1970 – and is attached to a Marine air wing. You and I and Debbie attend his graduation at Quantico, and the buttons nearly burst from your jacket in pride. I, his doting mother, am truly impressed with the never-vanquished determination of this son of mine – who was often the scourge of my soul, but whom I loved beyond measure. Quill was always to say in the future that if it hadn't been for his stint in the mission field – with all its trauma – he would not have been able to make it through the Officers Training Course he endured at Quantico. He never did say which was the worst. [Incidentally, Neb, your precious granddaughter would also complete almost the same brutal training at Quantico, one of only four women, thirty years later. What would you have thought of that? What a progeny you and I bred, my love! At the very least, they kept "hanging in there!"]

To make Quill's story complete to this time, he, too, fell in love at first sight (I think it was the white boots she wore) and married, somewhat disastrously in the long run. But he provided us with our first and second grandsons – whom we also loved, though their mother would, in time, alienate them from us. Quill, too, had a Temple marriage and all our grandchildren were "born in the covenant." And this comment must take me back, again, to the time of Quill's mission. For it was at this time that I accompanied him for his endowments, receiving mine at the same time. I still remember his comment when he saw me there in that special place: "Mother, you look just like a queen." But I remember sobbing my heart out – even as I rejoiced with him – for you, the love of my life, had chosen not to go with me. I was not your eternal mate, nor were our children sealed to us for eternity. And you did not know until years later that in the Temple, I did not bear your name. In those holy records, I was Helen Elizabeth Helfrich – a name I had not borne for 40 years or more. And my hollow, lonely pain was almost unendurable. Though you did not seem aware.

But that is not the end of the tale. For some six years later, when Quill was ready to be married in the Los Angeles Temple in 1971, planning on a September date – I informed you firmly that I would not be attending our son's marriage, alone, without his father. And although you struggled to make me change my mind, I was adamant. I knew I could not endure that pain again. So finally, after 27 years of marriage, after much soul-searching and struggle, you gave up your smoking, prepared yourself fully, received your recommend, and on September 3, 1971, you and I were sealed as man and wife in the Mesa Temple and our son and daughter were sealed to us, as a family unit, that day. Was I wrong to bring that pressure upon you? In doing so, did I deprive you of your precious agency? I still do not know. But I do know, my dear, that you suffered the torture of the damned to give up your smoking habit of so many years. And you persevered. Having made the commitment, you did not back-slide. But your reformation was ultimately too late for your physical health. Slowly, but surely, your lungs were succumbing to the dreadful emphysema – the seeds of which had been sown on the battle front so many years before. And once more we learn that every choice must have its consequence. And yours was to be excruciating pain, long before your death. And I would suffer your pain – and ultimately, the loss of you. But in your final hours, did you think of me with love? with hate? or with regret for that first night we met so long ago? And are you waiting for me now – beyond the veil? These are the questions of my heart – as I wait for you.

Part III

These Were the "Days of Our Lives"

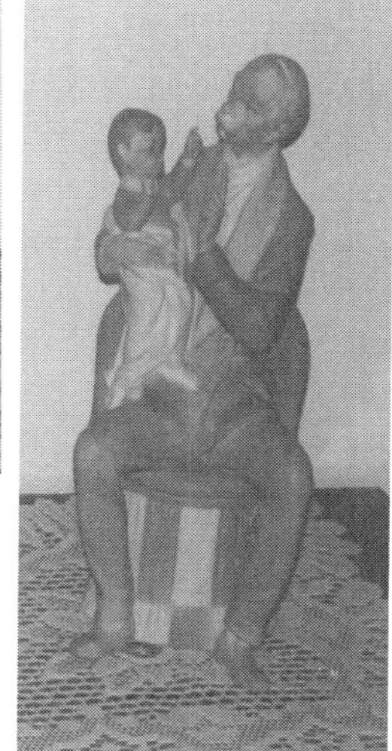

1
"What Is Our Life? A Play of Passion. . . "
Spenser

The years of the 1970's were probably the happiest times of my life, since the days of our courting and our short married life together, before you departed for the battle front. But like those days, there was in this time much sorrow and pain and even loss. How can I best recall – or perhaps re-create – not the *events* but the *passions* – the intensity, the emotional involvement in the happy, the chaotic, the sometimes stormy events that would crowd our lives in those few years? Suddenly, I know, for there before me on a shelf in my bookcase, I am looking at three treasured art objects which I have had for years. First is a Lladro porcelain creation of a Victorian suitor in his dapper suit, high buttoned shoes, top hat, and his proper English umbrella, seated on a high-backed wrought-iron bench with his beautiful, fashionable, prim lady love. With a smile on his moustached face, he is extending to her averted gaze a delicate rose. Of temptation? Next to that expensive work of art is a kind of "Mexican piece," – a serape clad peasant, sombrero in hand, his work-worn wife standing at his side, her head on his shoulder, his head bent to hers, their arms wrapped securely around each other, while their eyes are closed as in sleep. I happen to know that this piece has a monetary value of less than $10.00. The third piece on the shelf is another expensive porcelain piece of an older Victorian gentleman, clad in a smoking jacket, seated in an arm-chair holding, presumably, a grandson on his lap, as the young and the aged shake their forefingers at each other. [As the generations always seem to do.]

These three pieces are symbolically precious to me. They seem to encapsulate the emotions of our life together. The first piece requires no explanation. It is a reminder of the days long gone, of wooing and of love. The third piece is also self-explanatory – the changing reality, the multiplying and replenishing which is to *come* because *we before* have sown the seeds of love and multiplying, as was commanded in the *"beginning."* Thus life goes on! But the middle treasure – and the one which I would rescue first in case of an emergency – is to me a final representation of us, of you and me as husband and wife, clinging together as one – paradoxically in the *beginning* of the *closing* years of our life!

In its entirety, it is as though this little grouping is saying to me: "In youth you found each other in 'love and war'; then, you were tested in the conflicts of 'freedom' versus 'responsibility'; now you will develop each other in the contradictions of strength and softness, of yielding and prevailing, of joy and pain." It will be in these final years that the true joining of body and mind and spirit – blessed by the Holy Light of Christ – *may* make us one in the sight of God. Does this make any sense to you?

I don't think I ever told you what that little gift of the Mexican couple – which you brought home to me in the aftermath of our daughter's leaving to make her own new life – meant to me. It told me that you had begun to understand, at least emotionally, what I have been trying to express [though you might never put it into words]. You had seen the little couple in a drugstore, on your way home from work. And with completely uncharacteristic sentiment, you had had it wrapped and, without words, gave it to me with a kiss and a hug that evening. And told me it had cost you seven dollars and ninety five cents!

* * * * *

And thus it was that these years of this '70s decade began in love and loss and pain so inter-mixed we could not separate one from the other. Our children left us in their "joy" of love and our "loss" of beloved children. We lost their presence, their need of us, their companionship. We gained in closeness to one another, in little ways as in your gift, our sensibility to one another's need. My joy grew greater each day in your increased activity in the church.

When our first grandchild was born on a Sunday [I, too, was a Sunday child], June 24, 1973 – your namesake, as his father had been before him, and you had been for your father, and his father before him – we took a trip together to Dallas for his blessing and what a wonderful thing it was to hold the little spirit in our arms. And then Debbie & Chuck provided us with our only little granddaughter, Sabrina, born almost on Thanksgiving day, Tuesday, November 25, 1975. [I never did decide whether grandchildren in their early stages were as wonderful to granddaddy as they were to grandmother. But I know you came to love that little girl and her brother, Derek, born 19 May 1978, in La Jolla, CA., just after the birth of Kevin, Friday, September 17, 1976, to Quill and Linda, who had moved to Fullerton, California.]

Shortly after the birth of Kevin and Derek, both Debbie and Quill returned to Phoenix where they bought homes and for more that ten years those four little cousins were all to live near each other and enjoy a close relationship. And those years were filled – at our house – with birthday parties and cook-outs and sleep-overs. And sometimes this grandmother was so worn out she could hardly function, but she loved every minute of it – and so did you, you wonderful granddad you! And I think we still had our boat for some of these years, but I'm not quite sure. And sometimes I was greatly saddened because Quill's wife, Linda, didn't like me, no matter how hard I tried to let her know

I cared for her and would help her in anyway I could. And when Quill put in a pool, the boys did not come to visit as they had. But they still came for birthdays and Christmas, until they finally moved, because of Quill's work, to Salt Lake, where they were until their father's death. In such joys of life are the sorrows also woven. And the heart and spirit must expand to encompass them all.

But these years were also hard ones for me in the professional world. Since I have written of these problems extensively in a published work* which became quite famous in its own way and is available commercially, I will not relate them here, except to say that I fought hard battles and eventually won justice, in addition to shaking up the academic world! But the emotional toll on both of us, my dear, was not a light one. And you gave me your emotional support in many ways.

I have not yet recalled for you the things we did for ourselves – just for us. In 1975, somewhat reluctantly for you, I think, we took our first trip abroad together – a three week tour of Ireland. We were lucky to make good friends with a couple, from the mid-west, and explored all the by-ways and pubs of Ireland – but we drank only cola drinks and had a wonderful time. Most fun of all, I think, was our evening at Bunratty Castle, in Limerick, and I have a lovely picture of you with the medieval waitress and her arm is around you and you're laughing, while I'm being kissed by a Jack of Knaves. It was "touristy" all the way. But is was totally enjoyable. Then, we went to Trinity College and saw the Book of Kells, and to the Abbey Theater, and you kissed the Blarney Stone, hanging by your heels and having your picture taken – incidentally, you never did get the picture for which you paid. And remember the wonderful time we had at the Irish dance festival that was held in the ballroom of our hotel. And on the jaunt to Inverness, that awful ski hotel lodge we had to stay in, while the tour guide basked in comfort in the beautiful hotel, itself? And in the summer of 1978, the new stake house was finished and we have a lovely picture of the two of us, together, in front of it. And happiness is evident in the smiles of both us and your arm is around me, possessively and protectively.

*Nebeker, Helen E. "Out of the Dark." *The Road Retaken: Women Reenter the Academy.* New York: The Modern Language Association of America, 1985, pp. 38-45

Dinner in Bunratty Castle

Neb and Helen in front of the new stake house.

There are two letters of these years that I want to share with you in this final letter of mine to you, my only husband. The first is from Linda, Quill's wife, and because of their divorce sometime in the future, it has special meaning for me. It tells me that you and I were not failures in trying to help them in their relationship – or in rearing our son. On October 2, 1977, just before your 58th birthday and just after Quill's 31st, on a Sunday afternoon, Linda writes:

> Dear Mom,
> As Quill and I sat this Sunday evening reading the scriptures. . . there was a keen spiritual feeling in the air. . . . I pondered the many blessings the Lord has given me. . . . I pondered the power of the Priesthood in this home and the love that we strive to have for one another and then I thought of you Mom, Quill's Mother - the trials and tribulations you have gone through to raise two fine children. You and Dad raised two children in the Gospel and Temple marriages who - as I see in Quill, are striving to become better each day. This letter is just to thank you for all you have done in doing such a wonderful job. You also have made me feel like your own daughter and I truly appreciate this and love you for this and much more. . . . I ask your forgiveness for prejudging you and I am so sorry - you are one of the dearest ladies I know . . .the words come freely from my heart. Thank you so much for just being you. I truly love you and Dad for your love and kindness and the effort you put forth in raising my husband. I truly pray I might have God's help to raise my sons as well. Love, Linda

Oh, Neb, how I wish we could have helped Quill and Linda to hang on and work for better times. How sad our failures – unless they strengthen us and others.

This second letter you wrote yourself, on August 5, 1974, our 30th wedding anniversary. It is scribbled on a now much-folded piece of paper, because I carried it in a secret compartment of my billfold for twenty-seven years – from the day I received it until your death on November 1, 2001. It was my talisman of love – and of endurance for the days that were to come. Thank you, my love, for that next to the last letter I would receive from you.

> For 30 years I have loved you - but not as much as I do now - For your "anniversity" present [there] will be a ring of your choice. I want to get one for you but you have to be with me. I love you ,"Me"

This is truly a treasure of my heart. And I hope the words of love are still in your heart.

It is in the last year of the decade – 1979 – that we bought a lot in Scottsdale and you began a "spec" house that would eventually turn out to be the beautiful home of our dear daughter and her family. It is still their residence and grows more beautiful as time passes, thanks to the skills and persistence that Chuck has shown in refurbishing and updating it these last two years. You would be amazed at his care and dedication in all his work. And Debbie loves her "dream home," built by her daddy – but up-dated by her husband. And now I will "shut up the story of our days" in all the personal and political strife of these turbulent '70s. They were days of love and war and fun and sorrow. They were the days of growth. They were the days of our lives.

2

"It was the best of times, it was the worst of times."

1980's

I hardly know where to begin in this part of our story, my dear, whether with a summation, a prediction, a prevailing motif, or just surrendering of myself to the meanderings of my mind. As I look through my journal entries of the days and months of those years, I am struck by two prevailing motifs: expansion and casting off of restraints in your life – and deeper, darker introspection – and loneliness – in mine. The new decade begins with us selling the "spec" house you were building to Debbie and Chuck, after which you have taken a position, in August, as a consulting Project Manager with the nationwide Ramada Inns Hotel Chain. This position entails both the overseeing of the remodeling of the Ramada Inn in Scottsdale, and also extensive traveling – often at a moment's notice – throughout all of the U. S. to control quality of construction and the cost factors for the extensive re-modeling projects Ramada is currently undertaking. You never read my journal – and it's a good thing you didn't for in it I express my deepest inner probings – but of this new venture of yours, I have written: "He [you] loves the travel and the hub-bub and I'm glad that at 61 he has the opportunity to do something different because I know his life was getting 'stale, flat and unprofitable.' I think it may be too hard on him but I'd rather have him drop dead of a heart attack than waste away in boredom."

And how you did love the hub-bub, the dashing off to Canada, or to New York, or to Pennsylvania, or wherever – all without the trouble of making reservations as we think of it today. You flew with a special kind of pass that precluded trouble and delay. On Thanksgiving of '80, you flew to Atlanta, Ga. And were five days in returning. This is an interesting excerpt from my journal about that trip:

> Neb called about 5:00. He said it was freezing. He wouldn't take a coat with him, in spite of my urging so he was very cold. Especially since he couldn't rent a car as he usually does because his driver's license had expired. I have been nagging him for nearly two months to renew it – prophesying just such an eventuality. But Neb never takes anyone's advice. He always learns the hard way. And I know it was the hard way for him to be without a car! I'm afraid I laughed and said, 'I told you so.' Thank goodness I didn't go to Atlanta with him. [You had urged me to – and been upset when I wouldn't go.]

And so it would be with you to the end of your days. Stubborn! Stubborn! Stubborn!

You return on December 2, from Atlanta, only to leave the next day for Billings. And so it goes, day after day and week after week. And then, month after month. And my spirits hit a low not seen since those ominous days of 1962. At Christmas we are all ill – Debbie and her family are down with the flu; then she started to hemorrhage and is taken to the hospital. I am so ill that I can't get out of bed to help her – the flu has settled in my vulnerable back and I can move only in extreme pain. Quill and his wife are having severe problems and they do not even bring the boys over for Christmas. In summation I write on 29 December 1980:

> As though this were not enough, I feel that Neb [you] was more ungiving than he has been in many years. He spent no time with

> me in preparing for the holiday, never went shopping with me, took me to lunch or anything. As I write this, it sounds very petulant and little, but I have so little to look forward to in terms of sharing with anyone – that this loss of Christmas activity together looms large in my eyes. . . .Were Neb to read this he would be angry for he tells himself and me that he must work 15 hours or more a day in this new job and if I will be patient, things will be more normal soon. I however believe that his obsession – unnecessary – is an excuse for not having to let anything else enter his life. I am afraid of what the outcome may be for us. [And I was afraid – for you have now resigned from your church responsibilities and are seldom home for Sundays. And you need that spiritual renewal.]

Can you see, love, in reading these words that I wrote in a time of great uneasiness, how time has changed both you and me? If I can write these words in my journal, why can I not write them to you in a personal letter that you can read, mull over, grow angry at, and then write back to me? Why have *you* sent me no love notes in all these days in which I write so despondently:

> These thoughts are difficult to write but they are true. I feel desperately alone, achingly hollow, so that I am on the verge of tears unless I force myself to be hard, uncommunicative.

And as you can see, my motif in this time is darkness of the spirit and soul. But I conclude the year's comments with a realization of my own failure: "I realize that the whole truth of the matter is that I have too little "oil for my lamp" and it cannot be bought in the marketplace nor the light borrowed from another. . . . May this trauma within me end soon."

But, as the philosopher says, " this, too, shall pass away." And so it does. And as the New Year of 1981 comes in, I write:

> I felt the gloom and the despair of the last few weeks lifting from my heart. . . I seem to have fresh courage taken and I am ashamed of the dark, selfish thoughts of the last writing. In fact I almost ripped the first pages out of the journal, thinking I would start afresh, today. I am torn between expressing my thoughts honestly and uncensored or writing only the good, uplifting thoughts and events of life. One would like to leave

> behind only one's better self. But the fact is that unless one is able to see and understand the darkness of the forest, the light of the sun/Son is never quite as dazzling.

And I conclude my entry with:

> My husband, who is dear to me despite our difficulties and differences, has made the morning sweet for me, although he has since gone to work, even though it's Sunday. I know he, too, has his despair of the spirit and I must try to help him more so he can find his own spiritual direction.

And so the 1980s proceed for us "joy in the morning," and "despair in the night." You share with me a working trip to San Francisco, and I have a wonderful time. I have received my full Professorship and am Associate Chairman of the Department, with more responsibility and greater salary. But in the dark time of the nation, President Ronald Reagan has been wounded by a gunman and has a bullet removed from his lung. Three other men have also been seriously wounded. Remembrance of the murders of J. F. Kennedy and his brother, Robert, and the murder of Martin Luther King – along with more recent attempts on President Ford's life, and on President Carter's, and the terrible murders of all the little black children in Atlanta – surface in the national psyche. Surely the forces of darkness seem to encompass our world. The nation as a whole breathes prayers of gratitude for the recovery of Reagan, whose courage and humor has brightened the gloom and gained him the respect of even his detractors.

In the midst of these tragedies of the "night," my book, Jean Rhys: Woman in Passage* has been published and receives good reviews. I am pleased with it. But also in the midst of the light, John Sarager has died, after his long struggle with cancer. And in the trauma of his death, I have descended into my own night of Gethsemane. I think John's death and the realization of how his tremendous spirit had triumphed over his devastating illness had made me conscious of how I was wasting my life, had awakened in me all my inadequacies. More personally and devastating to me, you and I were drifting further apart with each day. Once more in my life, I sense, my soul was reaching toward death, because it could not reach for growth. And I was caught

*Nebeker, Helen. *Jean Rhys: Woman in Passage.* Montreal: Eden Pres Women's Publication, 1981.

in a desperation so deep, I could scarcely even struggle. Then, God, I know, moved me to see our Stake President, whom we knew well, and with him and his prayers and compassion and strength, I was able to work out the pain that was consuming me. I write of these dark days:

> I think I have come to an acceptance of certain things in my life. I have let go of griefs; have really learned, I think, that we can only do the best that we can in the light and knowledge and circumstances in which we find ourselves. Ultimately, we must trust God; we must hope; we must not give up.

Scarcely was this crisis and resolution over than Christmas was here and you had returned from D.C. On the 23rd, you were nervous, tense, but made a special effort to be pleasant on Christmas Eve at Debbie's with the children. However, we had no tree, no presents, and for the first time in 37 years of marriage you had gotten me no gift, not even a card. My primitive, symbolic nature saw presentiment in this. On December 26th, I had to go to New York to present a paper at the very prestigious Modern Language Assn. Annual meeting. You were to have gone with me. But at the last moment, you chose not to go. Football, your friend, Kelsey, the dog-races – possibly a few beers, I think – were more important to you. And when I came home, you were off again, to D. C. In January I became quite ill and was sent to the hospital for a biopsy with a possible diagnosis of kidney cancer. It turned out to be only poly-cystic kidneys and a small stone. Beside the unnecessary expense, I felt cheated – I had really hoped for a cancer diagnosis. I didn't really mind the thought of dying. "No more papers to grade, no more having to go to work, a few months of suffering and I can start my new life!" Again, how God must laugh at us. And you, my husband, were not here with me, to give me comfort.

But in February, despite my heavy responsibilities at the university, you insisted on my coming to Washington for the grand opening of the now completed Renaissance Hotel. I'm sure your real intent was not my presence but rather the opportunity to show me how important you were. And I was impressed with the scope of your accomplishment. And we did see a wonderful play together. I met many people and you seemed quite proud to introduce me as your wife. But I recognized once more how easily you were falling into a pattern of life that I had thought was over twenty years ago. And I have deep misgiving. [It is during this time – and I must insert it here because I have only re-discovered it – that I receive your very last letter to me. You are leaving on another trip very early in the morning and evidently not wishing to waken me you have left the note on your pillow beside me:

> Now the time has come to go, I don't want to go. Even for only a couple of weeks before I see you, I have a feeling of loss already. You see, my love, I do love you greatly and I know I have caused you pain and worry since I got this job. . . Remember, I love you,
> "Me"

Such as this are the sweet memories that somehow keep us going through all the years of our life. How glad I am I kept them all.

You finally do get home from Washington and things do settle down. Then, in late 1982 you are terminated after 27 months; the country is now in the grip of a growing depression. Your termination is a great financial loss to us – but I am not sorry. But then Quill is terminated – he has been at Ramada for several years. And ultimately, he will have to sell his home and he, with his family, will move to Salt Lake City. But for the time, his looming divorce has been cancelled. And we are happier at being together. You have gotten a new job as Project Manager for a 200 unit apartment building, which you hate. You are essentially well at age 64 – and you look ten years younger and are still so handsome – except for a malignant skin cancer, which is surgically removed. How do I see myself during all these days of the '80s? When I am being photographed for the picture on my book, at the age of 53, I write in a journal entry:

> I really don't mind at all being that old – I accept it – but the funny thing is that I still feel pretty much like I did at 30. I joy in life; my body is strong and agile; I weigh 110 pounds, and stand 5'4, wearing a size 4 dress, so I'm reasonably attractive. Yet I suppose younger people look at me and think of me as being more than middle-aged. Sic transit gloria!

[That description would still be essentially the same, today, except that

I weigh 102 pounds and wear a size 2 dress. And I'm still reasonably attractive, for one approaching 79. I hope you would find me so.]

And about the same time, when I have won my fight at the university about promotion, I write of myself words that for me are still true:

> I wish I didn't have to fight so often just to obtain justice. That, however, seems to be a fact of my life; nothing comes easy to me, nothing, that is, except learning and teaching. Those are, I suppose, my personal passion and gifts. But those gifts themselves complicate my life, and set me apart from others. I am, so I am often told, intimidating to others. I find this sad because I care so much for people and want to share and be a friend. But I have only three or four close friends who know that I am not awesome at all, but basically sensitive and vulnerable. I guess my facade says otherwise to most people, however. And rejection is a reality for me; one which causes me deep pain from my earliest memories.

[Perhaps one never forgets, my husband, the feelings of their early life. How I wish I had shared more memories of your growing up. Though I did come to recognize many things about your early life – and I hope I understood you better for my knowledge.]

During these tumultuous years, we will see our grandchildren baptized; our home burglarized twice. Debbie has earned her Masters degree in Industrial Engineering and has been working for SRP and then for Intel. You have finally, after 15 years, bought yourself a new truck – and given the El Camino to Chuck. He will spend thousands of dollars rebuilding it, through the next twenty years. And you have taken the big step and declared yourself *retired*! On our 40th wedding anniversary, Deborah will have the most beautiful anniversary dinner for us and I have marvelous pictures of us, together, with your arms around me and a happy smile on your face. She sends us for a vacation at the marvelous L'Auberge Inn in Sedona, where we eat and sleep and still make love! This is the year I decide to have our kitchen remodeled and you are angry with me. After 26 years, you see no reason for change of anything around our house. But I prevail, because *after all* I too am earning substantial money and am entitled!

Perhaps the first five years of this time can be summarized in the words that I use in the conclusion of a specific year:

> Illness, job loss, betrayal by a friend, but the year still seems good! I have my family all with me. Sweetness between husband and wife prevailed over bitterness and disappointment. We have our health, our home, our bills are paid, our hearts are strong. [And how especially sweet are the many memories we shared with our grandchildren. I will never forget, as I look at all the pictures we took, the fun we had together.]

Our 40th Anniversary

And in conclusion, I comment: "Isn't it miraculous how cycle follows cycle – high follows low, joy follows sadness – *if* we just hang-on, endure to the end as the Scriptures admonish." [As an afterthought, I might say here that during these years, the Block Program for the church was first instituted. I hated it at the beginning and I am only tolerating it now. So in this, if nothing else, I am truly "enduring."]

This first half of the 80s decade ends for me with the sweetest, anonymous letter I ever received from a participant in my Sunday School class. I simply must end with parts of it to show my efforts, to show that all in my church life was not "just enduring":

> Dear Sister Nebeker, ... Every time I hear a lesson from you, it tears my heart. The Holy Ghost tells me that what you are

> saying is true, and that I should take heed to the message and listen. I wanted you to know that you inspire me to do what is right, more than books or bishops. As many times I've heard the messages you speak, they never fail with me. You have a way that makes them stick. I think about things you spoke of in class, weeks, months later. . . May life bless you . . . Love, a friend (a sister)

Now who could ever ask for a greater reward for effort and prayer than to have touched a sister like that? My heart is filled with joy! But I remember, as I always do that this is a gift from the Lord. I write, under the letter just quoted:

> The Lord has blessed me richly in giving me a true talent for teaching and I never forget nor deny that it is His gift. In my heart I think the greatest call is to be a nurse – to give physical comfort to the sick. But then, the Lord may have known this would not be my real strength and has called me in other ways. Perhaps to feed the weary mind and spirit.

3

Retirement: Another Snake in the Garden!

"What is food for one is others bitter poison."

At the age of 65, you, my love, decided to retire! You had worked hard all your life; given up your contracting business to work for Ramada, finished up the apartment job you had taken after that; and finally threw in the towel. I should have been glad for you but I was not. I was jealous! I read now what I wrote at the time and I am surprised at my malice:

> At 65, like it or not, he seems to have retired! He seems to enjoy it well enough, but I certainly do not! I guess it just never occurred to me that long before I would be free to quit work, he would be a man of leisure. It rankles in my soul as I leave in the morning and he still is sitting at the breakfast table. I do not like

> my littleness of spirit, but I have not yet learned to overcome it! Perhaps though, if one takes into consideration that I have made the same 35 mile trip to the university almost daily for nearly 30 years, I may be forgiven a little of my resentment. Actually, I want desperately to quit work and do other things. But so far have not had the courage to do so. And it truly does take courage to give up the real measure of security I have achieved for myself – for one who has come from a childhood of poverty, [my salary] is an amazing accomplishment. I guess what I'm really looking for is one of "life's accidents" to happen to me. This is the easiest way to engender change because one does what has to be done in the circumstances! But I don't think the Lord will make it that easy for me. He never has! He makes me choose, initiate for myself. And I don't like that!

And I will continue to chafe at your freedom – and *interference* in my internal home affairs. You rearrange every kitchen drawer (and I am already immaculate in my household organization.) In a drawer in the den, I have kept over the years, in the constantly changing ward boundaries, a roster of past years so that I have reference to those from whom we are now separated. You *organize* the drawer, throwing away every valuable, to me, record of the past. Evening after evening, you are sitting in your chair, comfortably reading, when I come home from a hard day of work and the exhausting drive home. And of course you are waiting for me to fix dinner. As you have almost always done. But we are still paying for a yard-man – although you do take care of the pool yourself. What else you do through the day I do not know.

But I do know you never so much as put a potato in to bake to save time with dinner. One evening I came home in an envious and foul mood and I gave you my well-known (to our family) signal that all was not well with me, banging the cupboard doors as I prepared the meal. You have the temerity to yell out to me, "What in H. . . is going on out there?" Already in a snit, I come into the family room and say, "Well, how would you feel if you came home from work every day and found me sitting there waiting for you to fix my dinner?" Your unwise reply – that was to determine your fate – was, "Well, hell, we'd eat out!" That, my dear, was your undoing. For though it broke every precept of my sense of duty, from that time on, whenever I was tired and did not want to cook, without apology, *we did eat out*! Haven't I always said that out of our own mouths we pronounce our doom? Well, that taught you to think before you spoke!

But, all in all, this was also a special time for me – and I hope for you. We had been called together, in our newly organized ward, to teach the Gospel Doctrine class. And for the first time in all our years together, you attend Sunday School with me – and hear me teach. And although you never said, I truly think you were astounded, because sometimes, after a class, you just squeezed my hand – and I knew. And you never once missed a class for any excuse. You were such a help to me because the class was so large – and you took attendance and knew every student's name and made sure that I knew the names and the faces. It was such a privilege to serve with you, and I often told you so. And during that time you were asked to serve as Second Counselor in the High Priests Group, while at that same time, we were invited to participate in a Family Home Evening Group, and made such good friends. And as a group, we attended the Temple together every month. Blessing upon blessing just poured out upon us. My heart was glad in ways that it had never known. Thus, those days of retirement took on a glow of their own. And my resentment waned. And my confidence in the future grew.

And it is now 1986 - the decade draws apace.

4

The Courage of Making a Choice

In October of 1986, I finally decide to make my bid for early retirement as of July 1, 1988. I have been a Professor and Associate Chairman of the department for nearly ten years. Before making such a life-altering decision, I have agonized, projected consequences, prayed constantly, and have finally found the courage to cast caution to the wind and do what my mind and heart and spirit truly desire to do. Of course, if I'm completely honest, I will have to admit that the death of the huge tree which has been outside my office window for my whole tenure at ASU is the final determinative fact. For to my symbolic, *primitif* soul, it is as though the Lord Himself has said, "It is enough, Helen." And so I hammer out a great retirement deal in exchange for all my tenure rights, which still have years remaining. [I have since been told that many of my younger colleagues were subsequently enabled by me to make retirement decisions that they had never been aware of – and that the University still uses my proposal as a basic format for bargaining.] I maneuvered, to my great profit, two years on a fiscal contract. And as of October 1987, I have been on leave for seven months and it is marvelous! I've loved every minute of it and I have never been happier in my life. In the Spring, before my leave, I have given a big faculty party at our house, at which Nick announces my retirement to the absolutely astounded – and smitten, I truly believe – English Department faculty. Never for a moment have they suspected such an action. The surprise is complete; the party is beautifully done; and I have honored George Herman – another long-time faculty member – in his retirement. There are 60 department faculty in attendance. And the cost is more than compensated by my colleagues' enjoyment. [I'm not sure you would agree with me on that, Neb.]

On the 15th of October, you and I leave on a five week tour of Europe. It has been 12 years since our trip to Ireland, and two years since we had gone to Seattle and Victoria, British Columbia. We arrive in London the morning after the whole of Europe had been devastated by a hurricane of the century. Having in no way been warned in advance of landing, we find the airport at Gatwick almost abandoned, British Rail completely shut down, no transportation of any kind seemingly available. And the arriving passengers in complete pandemonium. We eventually manage to flag down a London cab and after nearly a whole day, we arrive in London, at our hotel, confused, exhausted, and $100 poorer for cab fare. Of course nothing has been made ready for us because the electricity and water had been shut down; in fact the hurricane had left destruction equal to that of the bombing raids in the '40s. Whole buildings are demolished. Apartment buildings are left sheared in half. It was indeed a baptism of fire for a weary traveler. Had there been any departing flights, I think I would have left the next day without a backward look.

But as things worked out, we were able to leave on our appointed tour the next day and although things went from bad to worse the first two or three days – cold, rainy weather, bad accommodations – you and I had a great trip together. I wonder now – though I didn't think of it then – if you had been reminded of the dreadful winter you had spent in '44 & '45 in the areas to which we would go before our journey was complete. My love, you may never know how much those days with you meant to me. I do know, for a fact, that in every city we visited where you had been "faithful" to me during the war, you indicated your faithfulness to me" then" by making love to me "now." I know, because you told me so and showed me so! So in Heidelberg, and Paris and Frankfurt – and in our stay in Vienna, where we celebrated a belated 43rd wedding anniversary – we knew, once more, a rekindling of our love. And there, in Vienna, to the music of an extraordinary orchestra, we waltzed together in the great ballroom of the Schoenbroeun Palace. But I really think you enjoyed more your group dance with the enthusiastic and inebriated Viennese – who engaged in a "romping" somewhat similar to our American square dances.

Unfortunately for you – and to my great worry – you developed a horrible cold and bronchitis in the rainy mists of Germany and the Alps. I was afraid I might have to take you home – but by the time we got to Italy, you were much better. We visited Reid and Lela Ellsworth in Rome, where their mission president had granted them leave to be with us for a day or two. And then we spent some time in Venice, where you bought me my beautiful Venetian glass. And in Nice, you had already splurged on my Lladro "Hunter and his Lady." Never in my life had you so spoiled me.

But the best of all were our last four days in London at the Tara Hotel, from where we learned to get around well on bus and underground. And we walked the city streets and went to the theater and ate lunch in the pubs. We decided right then, that before we were too old, we would return to London, on our own. And then the days are over. When we return home in mid-November, our dear daughter and children met us at the airport and had a lovely welcome waiting at our home. And it was so good to feel the love of Debbie and of Sabrina, and of Derek and of Chuck. Truly, there is no place like home.

That Christmas we were all together and had dinner at our home, with Debbie and her family. Quill came to Phoenix, alone, for a weekend business trip and was also with us. And I had invited dear long-time friends, Mickie and Gene Finch, to dine with us. And so another year ends with feasting, football games and the usual sense of "finish" that comes with the end of another year. It was good to be alive.

And the next years speed by in busy-ness for me. I do the same things I have done for years. But I am extremely happy about not having to work. Never once in all the years that have passed, have I regretted my retirement. I am seldom bored. I teach Sunday School and Relief Society. I give a baby shower or a wedding shower or a dinner party. Our family home evening group changes occasionally as one couple moves and we add another. Reid and Lela come home from their mission and it is good to have them back. We go to a movie together or to a play or a symphony, and we enjoy it. I'm studying Hebrew, but in the midst of the course I come down with the dreadful flu that I have gotten periodically since that first winter of our marriage. In one entry of a journal I note, on a Saturday's boredom: "I'm always alone [on Saturdays - and Sundays] because of ball games. How destructive sports on TV are to relationships. But one must learn to accept what cannot - or will not be changed."

But I help Debbie with her house, or I wall-paper, or I read, or I study. And I grieve over the death of two dear teachers I have known, Professor Louis Myers and Wayne Edland. Both of them contributed to my growth and professionalism. And I speak at their services. And so each year goes by in the little activities that make up all our lives. I summarize the wisdom of one year with these questions: "Why are we all made so self-centered? Why does it take so long to realize that *love* is a matter of giving rather than taking?" And I conclude with the wisdom I have gained : "We spend so much of life expecting someone to *make us* happy, when happiness can only come from inside."

But I have not been as well as I might be. And I am worried about you, my dear.

5
"The Ever-Whirling Wheel of Change"

And so the satisfying days of my life in retirement slip by. I measure them in the little, meaningless actions of happiness. I keep a sporadic journal – usually dependent upon my sense of guilt for not doing as the Prophet has told us about such writing. And in my entries, I see the desultory quality of our life from day to day, week to week, year to year. I am still involved in teaching – Sunday School always, but now I am going twice weekly to read to two fifth grade classes in a less-than-wealthy elementary school. Who would have thought that little ten-year olds would actually love and look forward to an old lady, such as I am now, coming to read to them books like *Tom Sawyer*, *Where the Red Fern Grows*, Poetry, for heavens sake! But they love me; their teachers say I am the highlight of their week; I am the mom or grandmother they do not have. So I continue, despite the travel time and the inconvenience of the schedule. I give book reviews periodically at Phoenix College, where the attendees seem to enjoy my sometimes controversial views regarding the current popular choices of the "professional" reviewers. I also have taken up the study of Hebrew, which is extremely difficult, involving travel time as well as study. And we are studying French, together, at Phoenix College. I am a Visiting Teacher; I'm involved, with you, in our "family group," hosting them periodically. I get edgy in my "leisure," so I start pulling up the floor in our little pool house – which ultimately, will turn into lovely guest quarters. Once I start the project – to your dismay, of course – you are there to join me – or to take over from me – in every process. You are also a Home Teacher and the High Priest work keeps you busy. Then you are called as assistant financial clerk for the Ward. My colleagues – and friends who have never worked – ask me whether I am bored? How I spend my time? What do you do since your retirement? As for me, I answer, "Well, I do the same thing that you have done all the years you haven't worked." And I wonder how we ever had time to work. In one entry of 1988, I have written:

> Didn't do much today except paint in the pool house [Cabana, we call it] and go grocery shopping. Saw a young man standing on the corner asking for work for food. Didn't have work – too late in the day and it's going to rain but took him a sack of groceries and $5.00 which was all I had. No one should be denied money/work in a wealthy country like this.

Another entry, another time, reads:

> Hebrew lesson tonight! Hard! Cleaned house, studied Hebrew, took up old carpet, worked in yard, cooked a roast, ordered a curio cabinet for living room. I'm much too extravagant. Got to stop spending money!

And in one terse comment on my life and self, I write, "I didn't do anything of value to anyone. Is just enjoying life really a waste?"

And during all this time, I find in my re-reading – and to my surprise – that I have often been really ill. I cannot seem to shake a kind of flu-like illness – much like that I had had in Indianapolis so many years ago. [And for the first time in all my years of teaching the Gospel Doctrine class, I am so ill at the last minute that I have to send you to teach in my place. And everyone said you did a wonderful job. Why was everyone so surprised?] But at our house we seldom indulge in "pity parties" that can't be kept in control – or beyond our acknowledgment, at least – by a challenging "project" of one kind or another. And when I can't go on, Deborah brings me her special, healing chicken soup. For my body and soul.

But despite all, keeping the promise that we had made to ourselves, we go to England and France again in 1988, for a restorative month of freedom, and learning, and fun. And love. And this time, we are on our own. And you are such a marvelous guide and organizer. Only in these trips do I ever remember that I feel absolutely free, without the need to plan or to exercise discipline in any way. You are the leader, the planner, the reader of schedules, the maker of reservations. And I think you have really learned to love travel. And how we both love our journeyings on the first class trains that take us all over England and Wales and Scotland. Seldom do we even have to make reservations; first class at that time meant almost empty cars. [The only complaint I have to make is that you stubbornly refuse to let me help you in any way with the luggage. No one could travel lighter than we do, but you could at least let me carry my own little travel case.]

And in France, we also manage very well on our own. Though I get caught in the gate at the train station and am scared to death because I can't remember how to yell for help in French. And more than once, the "odor of humanity" on a metro bus forces us to get off before we reach our destination. One day, you make me walk the "Rues of Paris" for such a distance that in complete exhaustion, I sit down on the curb and refuse to go one step further. To your disgust, despite your prodding, you have to pay the taxicab fare to our hotel. But mostly on foot, we see all the sights, explore the Latin quarter, enjoy the food, as we had not been able to do with a tour group. Yet, I remember that here in Paris, you spend much of your time searching for *les toilettes.* And your cough grows worse. And again, I am worried about you. You are now approaching 70. But you have never been ill – beyond a severe cough and cold – in all our 44 years of marriage. And you have never seen a doctor – except when you've been injured on the job. I do not know what is to come.

> Friday, 4 May 1989: Neb became very ill today. Thinks he has the flu - refuses to see a doctor.
>
> Saturday, 5 May: Neb much sicker. Called Chuck to administer to him. He seems to be breathing better but still quite labored.
>
> Sunday, 6 May: Came home from church to find Neb seemingly better but by 5:00 I knew I had to do something – even against his will. Called Jim Anderson [he was our Stake President and not even your doctor, but he knew that if I would call him on a Sunday under those circumstances, things must be really bad. Thank God he came!] and he came and took him immediately to the hospital. Very close to pneumonia. Lucky I called Jim and he came immediately.

My journal entries from here on are lost – I cannot find this book anywhere. But perhaps I had no time to write for you were truly sick unto death. You were in intensive care for days; you developed complete shut-down of your kidneys and almost had to undergo dialysis. To the day of your death, practically, you denied all that I have written above. You simply had no memory of it. Jim told me later that loss of memory was very possible in the case of kidney shut-down, but from that point on, you were to accuse me of making the story up – and to tell our friends that I was to blame for subsequent illnesses because I was overly cautious. You recovered rather slowly, but in October – five months later, we again went abroad. This time only to the British Isles. I insisted that I didn't want to travel on the continent – but I was really trying to protect you from what I was then able to see as the greater stress for you of being in non-English speaking areas. You were simply not as strong as you had always been. And I had misgivings about travel itself. But we had an enjoyable trip – as usual. In fact, we made some very special friends whom we would enjoy on further travels. We would travel again until 1994 when, again, all things would change. [But you accused me so often of not being "adventurous" in my traveling, that one day, in absolute exasperation when you were chiding me in front of friends, I finally blew up and told you the truth to your face – and to their embarrassment, I think. But you never again made such an accusation. Sometimes, Neb, you were an intolerable jack-ass!]

The last days of the first year (1989) of your what-was-to-be continuous illness end with short journal entries. On the December 24th, I have narrated the Christmas cantata for the Ward. It has turned out well. Christmas Day we have a family dinner, with Reid and Lela as guests. I write: "I worked too hard – am exhausted. Flu is all around. Glad we had shots. Kids (Debbie and her family) were thrilled with their gift." [Remember, we gave them a month's vacation in Hawaii in July?] And so my entries go: Football, shopping, teaching, reading, Scripture study. And, as always, I am not pleased with myself. I write: "So far I have done nothing of merit in the new decade. Oh, how shall I begin?" And in another entry, I simply say, "Oh, why would *anyone* ever want to read this journal?"

But there are two entries I do feel important enough to record. This is contained in an overview of events:

> At October Stake Conference, I had the marvelous blessing of being chosen by Brother Neal A. Maxwell, of the Quorum of the Twelve, to bear my testimony in the Sunday morning session. It was a terrifying – and totally unexpected experience to hear my name called out before so many people, with absolutely no warning. I could scarcely make it to the podium because I was way back in the cultural hall. And to be called for a testimony when one's preparation has not been to that focus is especially difficult. I was praying for the Spirit all the way down the long aisle. I know my prayer was heard and my testimony was to the heart of all I know to be true. Afterward, Brother Maxwell held my hand and said, "I have been wanting to meet you for a long time!" How full my heart was that he should even know my name. But the Stake President told me later that Brother Maxwell had indeed – not he, the Stake President – selected me. That conference was a red letter day for me. (This was the October Conference 1983.)

Interestingly, Debbie was to tell me that she also had been selected at her Conference to do the same thing. I hope neither of us was found "wanting in the spirit of testimony."

One other experience I want to report from my journal because it is important to me to show two things. First, why I am often "disliked" – or perhaps why I am often "disturbing" is a better way to put it – to my fellow Saints. Secondly, I want to testify to the impetus of the Holy Spirit within me at various times, when despite my personal desire, I am literally pushed to my feet to speak. I cannot account for it in any other way – for I truly *do not like to speak out in large groups and especially where the Priesthood is concerned.* But I must quote from 21 January 1990 general Sunday School meeting – where the new Church budget directives from Salt Lake were discussed:

> Sunday School meeting today was about the new budget directives. I was thoroughly appalled at the whole tenor of the presentation and discussion. The whole point was how to, in a sense, subvert the system and to support the quite elaborate programs the Ward now has in place, particularly for the Scouting program – skiing trips, house boating, trips to Hawaii, etc. [We were a wealthy ward and one man after another was on his feet offering to fund this activity and that activity, outside of the budget process. Do you remember that, Neb?] Suddenly, I had to speak to the issue of what I thought the changes from the Presidency really implied – equity within expenditures throughout the Church, rich or poor and a retrenching from the really extravagant rewards – or bribes – which were being offered young priesthood holders for achieving awards of various kinds as well as for "activity." I really didn't want to speak out but my hand was up without my volition. I was truly embarrassed (and so were you, my dear) and scared that I had been out of place. [Afterward, not one person spoke to me as we left the meeting and I knew what they were thinking!] But President Davis thanked me afterward for speaking out. Said I went right to the heart and said what he wanted to but didn't feel he could because he is in the Stake Presidency.

My point in relating this is simply to say that when the Spirit truly inspires me, *I have no choice but to obey!*

On the 29th of January, 1990, the month ends on a really upbeat note for me, and I record it here for special remembrance:

> Our FHE group met at the Temple and went through a most inspirational meeting. Neb and I were asked to be witnesses and that is so special. The session was quite small but we all had a nice warm glow. It's a real joy to hold your husband's hand as you leave the Celestial Room together. [My dear, this memory joys my heart and brings tears to my eyes. It's been so long ago! And we would never be witnesses again.]

On March 8th, I record: "Vern called this morning to say thanks for last night [we had taken them to the theater] and to tell us he and Bonnie have been called to an English speaking Mission Presidency. They are naturally thrilled. They will be wonderful. I envy them."

And despite all this, I write at the end of the month: "My life is such a nothingness. And yet, I'm not bored or restless. It's just that I feel I should be more actively engaged."

And yet I do not write again until June 28th when I exclaim disgustedly, "122 degrees today. An all time record. How far can it go?" And darling, do you remember so long ago when I had written, after my first summer in Mesa, that I would never spend another summer in Arizona again? How time does make liars of us all.

Then on July 26th, Debbie and her family are off to Hawaii for their Christmas gift of a month. I write: "I hope they have fun together and return refreshed in mind, body, spirit, Boy, do I need such refreshment! I have the three dogs for the next month! O, woe!"

And then, with the last entry I will ever write in any journal, fate will once more lift her heavy hand, preparing to lower, again, the boom on the Nebeker family.

> 27th July 1990: Neb had doctor's appointment today, preliminary to his cataract surgery. Seems like all my life is right now is waiting for things to happen. I really am not feeling at all well. I hope it is just the heat!" [How predictive could I be?]

Meanwhile, in comings and goings of every day events, and before your scheduled surgery, Quill and Linda have been divorced and a bitter custody battle is being waged. Linda does not really want the children, especially Quill, but she is determined Quill shall not have them. It is unfortunate that Linda was very like my mother; she feared having children and she was not at all maternal after their advent. She was simply an essentially unloving mother. She fussed and she stewed but she knew absolutely nothing about what motherhood should mean. [In my view, that is.] She had been married at least once before marrying Quill – in the Temple. Had that marriage rescinded. Married Quill – and had that second marriage rescinded. And to my knowledge has been married at least twice since that. According to her experience, *all men* must be beasts. Maybe so. But you and I certainly suffered, along with Quill.

Now to get back to the point. You, for the past two years have been driving practically blind – refusing to face the fact that your eyesight is diminishing – until we have an accident in our nice car. At which point, you finally see Doctor Meador who determines that you have advanced cataracts and the surgery is scheduled for Tuesday, July 31. We arrive at the hospital about 5 a.m. and just before you are taken to the pre-op room, you faint. After a great hub-bub ensues, new blood tests are taken – something is not quite right but the doctor decides we can either go ahead with the procedure – or return at a later date. You decide to go ahead. All goes well and I am with you in the recovery room, when the room seems – to me – to be swarming with little gnats or mosquitos of some type. I disregard it and take you home, with instructions and an appointment for two days later. At home, you seem to be okay and then you develop a fever and are in great pain. Where, you do not tell me. But I awaken in the night to find you sitting in a tub of hot water seeking to ease the pain in your prostate, apparently. We return that morning to see the ophthalmologist who, immediately, calls a proctologist and has you in his office within the hour. Your eyes are doing well. But I mention to Dr. Meador the swarm of gnats I had been seeing since the recovery room and I am in his chair immediately and go through an exam so painful, I faint in the chair. I have a retina which may be detaching and I am instructed that after I take you to the proctologist, I am to return home and be extremely careful of any activity until I return in another three days for another exam. So, I take you immediately to the proctologist where your pain is relieved shortly and I am instructed to take you home, until you return to see him and for further tests in two days. After which, in all probability, you will have to have prostate surgery. And so you will.

I do not have to have surgery – the retina has not yet detached but I am to be very careful. No strenuous activity of any kind. Perhaps the detachment will not occur. You are to have prostate surgery in early August, after your blood is built up, if possible. But now, you are miraculously able to see clearly and you cannot believe it when for the first time in years you can see plainly an airplane flying far above the horizon.

You have your prostate surgery in late August but your blood level is still quite low. However, the hospital discharges you – without the doctor's permission – and sends you home still bleeding heavily. The second night home, you are in such pain I have to call 911; they transport you by ambulance to the hospital, where you remain until early morning and are then sent home with the bleeding stanched. I call the doctor the next morning as the hospital requires. But the doctor's nurse refuses to make you an appointment. The following night the bleeding continues, but the hospital refuses to admit you because you haven't seen the doctor [and that means they won't get any money for your admittance!]. I simply do not know what I am to do. The bleeding is serious and you are in terrible pain. Finally in desperation I call Jim and he tells me, discreetly, to take you to the hospital where your surgeon is chief of staff and *he will have to see you and have you admitted*, if necessary. By this time, you are too weak to know what is going on and I am so exhausted I hardly know what I am doing. But after some twelve hours you are finally in the hands of your original surgeon and he is all apologies and you are admitted for further surgery and kept until the surgery seems to be completely healed. I wonder now, how we survived all of this. But we do, and we return once again, in October, to our haunts abroad.

This year, however, you have finally agreed to my pleas to let us upgrade to first-class even though, as you have always insisted, "the back of the plane gets there as soon as the front." That little decision – which we could well afford – will make all the difference in our comfort and health. And even you will agree, after the fact, that the cost was well worth it – at least for people of our age.

This is the year that we will have the wonderful experience of meeting Yuriy Nikitin, a minor official in a Russian Trade Delegation from Russia. Do you remember how we were dining in London at the

Forum Hotel, and this silent, glum little man was sitting next to us? And I felt so sorry for him, I leaned over and asked him if he were a "Rusky." Of course, he didn't respond at first, but I remember finally, that he and I could actually converse, although neither one of us could speak a word of the other's language. We talked about his family and how we lived. Remember his astonishment at learning I was a Professor – and that we had a whole, three bedroom house to ourselves? I have often thought about that meeting and wondered whether that was an experience of "conversing by the spirit." I was able to do that a time or two in Germany with people I met – but this was an experience beyond comprehension. He invited us to his room the next day and you took him all the different U.S. coins you had, to take back to his son who collected foreign money as a hobby. I have a lovely photo that you took of Yuriy and me. And we sent him and his family some "luxuries" – coffee, sugar, etc., after we returned home and we received a card written by his son from Moscow to wish us Happy Holidays. That was the year governments fell in Russia – and we never heard from them again. Perhaps they were "purged."

Helen with Yuriy Nikitin

When we return, we are both restored in enthusiasm for life and seemingly in health. The next year will see you in fairly good health, except for two serious skin cancers, one of which will entail extensive grafting from the chest area to your face. But you heal without disfiguring scars. You have, however, grown more hard of hearing and your disposition has grown sterner, more fault-finding, and less endurable for me. But we still have friends in our evening group, you are still acting as ward clerk and I am still teaching. You, however, are angry with me because I have made some upgrading of our home. You want nothing changed in this home you have created some 46 years ago. Thus, all is not happy in the Nebeker household!

Until, that is, our dearest daughter, ever thinking of your pleasure, gives you a computer for your birthday. My dear, that was to be the postponing of your days! It had been years since I had seen you so enthused with something new. And you mastered the d. . . d thing! I could not believe, only admire, your tenacity. The fly in the ointment was, though, that now you were able – through the computer – to keep track of every single penny that was spent in our household! You became a despot. Not that I was extravagant. But your need to control everything – which had always been an aspect of your character – was now unleashed to almost demonic fury. When I went to Salt Lake with Debbie and bought a bird house at Gardner's Farm – your maternal grandfather's polygamous home in West Jordan – you knew about it and its cost even before I got home. It was like having the FBI on my trail at every step I took. And while I'm laughing as I write about it, I was not laughing then. Never in our life had we argued about whose money was whose, [and actually *you* were the one who let money slip through your fingers] and I did not like the power of that "invention of the devil" in our home. As a consequence, I refused to let you tutor me in its "joys." I knew that to let you "instruct" me would be to "destruct" our marriage. I think, if you can be aware where you now are, that you must be laughing at the many hours – and the many frustrations I have endured – as I have toiled these last three months over this little "last letter of love." And I will admit that I use e-mail occasionally, especially to keep in touch with Sabrina, but I still read books and I still pay my own bills by hand written checks *and I will never submit to the dehumanizing power of the computer!* I admit, though, that I'm glad I don't have much longer to live!

It is difficult for me to follow the events of the next two years. I did not keep my journal, but I have kept my calendar notations through the succeeding years and I know that about this time you were called to be the Regional Representative to oversee all the Church reconstruction in the various wards. It was a time consuming task – and you did a truly responsible work in that very demanding situation. And you saved the church much money in your careful oversight. You served under the Stake President until your stroke. The years are a blur of hospital emergency rooms for you, always with an admission and a stay of from five to ten days. [And always you refuse help until the wee, small hours of the morning.] Your lungs are finally giving completely away. In 1993 we will have made our last European trip – again first class, but we both knew this would be the last effort you could make. I had tried to dissuade you from even trying but I think you went just for me – and perhaps for yourself, as well. You collapse on the flight both going and returning home. We spend a very quiet – for us – last visit to the places we have shared together and prepare to rest. It is about this time that Quill re-marries – another disastrous choice.

Prior to the trip, you have had one emergency after another and I, too, have had another surgery – and I remember it well. I had to go to the hospital on the afternoon of the pre-New Year's Day downtown parade in Phoenix, December 1992, and you were quite put out with me because you would have to miss games on TV as well as travel across town to the hospital in the difficult traffic conditions. You made me feel so guilty – as though I had planned the whole operation to interfere with your holiday. And then, later in the day, you had to miss games to come and get me. For the tenth time in my life, I would be undergoing general anesthesia and each time I knew that I was possibly going into the dark of night. Recovery was never an easy process for me, and I was always aware that I might not recover. It hurt me deeply that you did not in some way understand this. But you didn't even bother to stay with me.

Evidently, my illness of the past two years had been triggered by kidney/bladder inflammation. And so I had surgery – to discover that there was a bladder cancer and the surgeon felt lucky to have found it in time. I was warned that there was a 90% chance of recurrence and 21 months later, in September of '94, I would again undergo surgery. This time, however, you would not be able to take me to the hospital.

You would have to sit at the table, still semi-paralyzed from your recent stroke, as a priesthood brother functioned in your place. I think I saw in your face at that time sorrow for the previous hospitalization, when you had been so unloving. Though being you, you said nothing.

In June of 1994, my calendar tells me that you had another prostate surgery and that again, you bled severely upon returning home, had to return for emergency treatment and then were sent home from St. Joseph Hospital on the 15th. Two weeks later, on July 4th, 1994, on an unusually hot day even for Phoenix, you were not feeling well. But despite my protests, you insisted on working on our spa – in the sun and in the heat. I took you out some water and begged you to quit and come in the house. As usual, your stubbornness won out and you continued to work. To make a long story short, the next morning, having slept in another room, I thought it unusual that you weren't up. But wanting you to rest if you could, I pulled the door softly closed, so as not to awaken you. A short time later, you received a call from the ward clerk, so I went to call you. And found you slumped over the side of the bed, trying to move. You had suffered a stroke sometime that morning. And our life would never be the same.

6
The Night Descends

When I discovered you lying athwart the bed, unable to move, I was so shocked that my wits completely deserted me. But I finally realized I must call 911, again. They were there within three minutes and you were soon at the hospital. I don't know how much of this you could remember; you couldn't move, speak, and the medic said your blood pressure had slumped to a life-threatening level. The first thing I had to do when I arrived quickly after the ambulance was to give permission for a blood-transfusion. After that, you were in the hands of the specialists and all I could do was wait. But I knew that the situation was critical. And I'm sorry to say that I can remember the absolute anger I felt, as I waited that long day in the hospital and returned home that evening, alone. I was so angry with you that if I had had a sledge hammer, I would have pounded my bathroom vanity into pieces! *This was your fault. Your damned stubbornness, your inability to use common sense after so much trauma only two weeks before had resulted in real tragedy. Would you never learn?*

I am ashamed, even now, of having to write these words. But at that time I hated you with all my heart! Still, my heart was overwhelmed with pity for your suffering, for your humiliation at your dependency upon others. I knew this would be the sharpest wound of all for your proud spirit.

Within five days you will be transferred, without my knowledge, to Good Samaritan Hospital's Rehabilitation Center. I will finally find you there – and in my fear and frustration, I am bawling like a baby. This irritates you and the nursing staff: why such emotion? And it is there, in that horrid place, that my heart will almost break for you. [I cannot write this without weeping.] I see you struggle to bend your proud spirit in order to survive. You do everything you can to be co-operative with the nurses, the treatments, with the physical therapy. I come everyday to be with you and I watch you struggle as the young girl-women who are the therapists put you through the exercises. But your lungs are gone now and these female "children" do not have the strength of experience to force you – they, too, are filled with pity. So when the hospital committee meets, they decide you are not making progress and in conference with me, they say they will send you home – and you will be in a wheel chair the rest of your life. I know you too well; *I will not let this happen to you*!

So I search out the best Rehabilitation Hospital I can find and I engage their private services and have you transferred from the hospital directly there. And you are so angry with me. As I had been with you before Quill was born and you would not take me home. But when you see the place I have chosen – Phoenix Mountain Nursing & Rehabilitation, in Scottsdale – you are reconciled, and within minutes of your entering the foyer, you have been shown how to tie your own shoes. You have a private room and we bring your TV, and a better mattress. I will also manage, after conference with the staff, that you will have only male therapists – you are too much a hater-of-dependency-upon-women to learn from the gentler sex. You will need hard-nosed male oversight. I come to see you every day – a twenty mile drive – and we will have dinner together. You will spend our 50th wedding anniversary in this center – and almost for the first time since 1962, that 18th anniversary of pain, you will worry about remembering it in some way. So in the middle of the hottest August day, amidst a terrible sand storm, I must come out to hear the amateur orchestra that entertains the patients play "The Anniversary Waltz." And to eat cake and ice-cream supplied by the staff. My dear, you never cease to amaze me.

But for the most part, you are almost oblivious to the fact that my life has been altered as much as yours. When I see you suffering and I cry, you simply *do not understand why*! To you, you are the one whose life has been changed. And you will in no way let me enter in to console or feel or talk. The psychiatrist at Good Sam has told me that after his examinations of you, he knows that I must accept the fact that *emotionally, you will never change - you simply cannot.* He will not – or perhaps professionally cannot – tell me why. But I will have seven long years to discover this is truth.

You return home after two months of therapy, able to walk, although with difficulty – which you hide from nearly everyone, refusing even my help. And after weeks of concentrated effort, you learn to write legibly with your left hand. And you spend hours at home with a speech therapist and your talk improves day by day. You never give up. I marvel at you. I want to tell you so. But you never let me beyond your defensive wall. And I wonder, as I write this, if you have changed beyond the veil? And could you now put your arms around me and let me cry? And cry with me? As you will not do until the day of your death. Did you know that I grieved deeply through the coming years and that one day, severely rebuffed by you, to assuage my overwhelming sorrow, I wrote this poem? Did I even try to share it with you? Or did I build my own wall? And has it become a part of me?

The Waste

He could not speak the words
Within the granite of his heart
Like seeds that struggled to break earth
And feel the light replace the dark
Wherein they lay.

He did not know the way
To say the wintry dark that snowed his heart,
Which only she
Could bring to Spring
And leave it green.

His soul could stretch to feel the heal of her,
Yet leave her warm, rich "give"
Untapped, like tree that waits in spring
The tapper's touch
Which does not come.

The nourishment was there to share
If only he could break the ice
Of wordless freeze
So she might know
The heart of him who lived in dark
Aloof, alone;
Half-riven stone.

To my husband

And this is "real poetry," my love. And can you understand it? And weep for loss?

7
As Darker Grows the Night

When you came home, in late September, you were *not* in a wheel chair. You could walk slowly and carefully – but without a walker (you were too proud to use one) – but you had a terrible open sore on your ear, which the visiting doctor at the rehabilitation home refused to treat in any way, saying it was just a little open sore. When I took you to a specialist, it turned out to be a malignant tumor and for three months, I had to take you each day to the dermatologist for x-ray treatments. The tumor never healed – and until you died, you underwent excision after excision of cancers all over your face and body. In the end, they were untreatable and at your death, the malignancies were there. In addition, you were in and out of the hospital, year after year: lung failure, prostate relapses. Finally, after nearly bleeding to death before I could get you hospitalized, you had a colonoscopy for the removal of bleeding tumors at which time you went into shock on the table – and the doctor was at his wits end as to what he should do – your death was imminent. But I told him to do what he could, and you survived. This was the story of our lives. Our son, the unbeatable quipster, joked that he had asked for leave so often that his boss's standard reply, when we summoned him to come home again, was "What's the matter? Your father dying again?" And the fact is that you were! Except you refused to go. Grimly, you hung on – at least five years beyond what any doctor would predict. And you continued to try to do some of the work for the church – I took you over to the regional office, every week, to sign the checks and confer about various projects. And you learned to use the computer with only your left hand. And I was torn between admiration and grief.

Now here I want to remind you of how wonderful our children were during all the time of your illnesses. In fact, I gave Quill an opportunity to throw one of his "dramatic hissies" when I had you transferred to the Rehabilitation Center. He stormed; he accused me of trying "to warehouse his father." He threatened to come down to Phoenix and carry you back to his home where *he* would take care of you! [In his basement apartment, of course, with 30 steep steps to climb.] I could always count on Quill's dramatic flair to give me a real laugh. You never knew about this, of course. And in the end, he agreed that I had made the right choice for you. For the first time in his life, I think, in your illnesses, Quill learned to show how much he cared for you – and me. He put himself out to visit, to call, to show his love – despite your holding him off from exuberant demonstrations of affection. [Even with your own son, you could not let down the defenses.] And always, despite his own troubles, Quill was ever upbeat. The last words you ever heard from him, as he was leaving for Salt Lake, were these – having come back in to make his last joke: "Well, Dad, looks like I'm going to have to die first – and come back and get you!"

And then he was gone. Never to return again. I will always wonder if he had had a premonition. And I will also remember, as he left me at the airport, his last words to me: "I love you, Mom."

And our ever-loving, ever-supporting, ever-suffering daughter, Deborah, was my sustaining rod of steel and, forever, your "little girl." [I remember that this was what you once called me, in early days of love.] How glad I was that I had had the courage to give her to you as my greatest gift. Although I don't know whether you ever thought of this in all the years we were to share together. You already know, in this letter, of the words of love she spoke for you, at your services. I hope you were able to hear them for yourself. Somewhere above.

And she was just as loving and thoughtful of me. In May of '96, she took me on a short trip to Seattle, where she had to go on business. Debbie had, against your wishes, taken a position as a Vice-President with a company in Chicago, after your stroke. It was a wonderful opportunity for her – but you never quite forgave her. You just could not approve of her leaving her family – even though the children were now adults – Derek a senior in high school and Sabrina at the university. Perhaps that is how you had felt when I started on a path of education, so many years before. But in the long run, I think most husbands are often at the root of the choices their wives make! And times do change. I so enjoyed the trip and it was the first vacation

I had had in more than two years. And I think I had not even been to a movie since your stroke. And you were filled with resentment because I required Chuck and others to check on you each day – and I, too, called each evening. And I think you waited for that call.

At birthdays and dinners and our usual family Christmases, all the family gathered round you, and Sabrina and Derek visited often. But with time, your weakness grew and the oxygen was necessary twenty-four hours a day. We did, however, against your wishes, get you a mobile scooter. You were indignant, at first, and then learned to use it as a vehicle of freedom. Sometimes you would travel four or five miles away – to shopping areas, to friends. Friends would say, "Surely that wasn't Neb that we saw at" – and they would name some distant place. And "surely" it was you. And despite my worries, you refused to carry the mobile phone I got you so you could call and let me know where you were. Did you *ever once* think of easing my burden in all those years? And yet, I loved you despite everything. Until, in the end, it became almost too hard. And so time passed and we did the best we could.

Our last photo together.

8

"Of grief I died, but no one knew my death"

T. Roethke

In early October of 1998, just about six weeks after Quill's last visit in which he threatened to "go first" and then "come after you," Debbie and I had planned to take a short trip to San Francisco, since she had business there. Quill was coming to stay with you – having planned, unbeknownst to you, to try to take you to the coast on a trip by car. He had undergone some shoulder surgery after leaving us on his visit and had been a little under the weather, thinking he might have flu, but he called the week before he was to come to tell us he was better and would be here. Saturday, Quill's birthday, Chuck came over to the house very early in the morning – you were in the den watching the news. He seemed very strange, telling me I'd better sit down – he had some news to tell me. Immediately, I thought of the children: "Has something happened to one of them? One of the dogs? Not Debbie?" And so my mind tried to comprehend Chuck's sadness. And then, as I sat, at my son-in-law's insistence, Chuck gently told me the unbelievable! Our son was dead!

My mind and heart were iced rejection. My son, my baby boy? It couldn't be! This child of mine who had come bursting into life in blood and trauma and near death for both of us, weeks ahead of time? That chaotic soul who lived his life in that same precipitous way, always in the heights of joy or depths of woe? This stalwart man, upon whom I now leaned and hoped for comfort when you died – our son had left this life as he had come, almost without warning. He had simply taken a shower, lain down on his den couch, closed his eyes, and gone to sleep, with a smile upon his face. [His neighbor found him, alerted by Duanne – when Quill had not responded to her frequent calls from Texas, where she had gone on business.]

I heard Chuck's words. I could not scream nor cry. I must be calm for you. And Debbie had not yet been told. She would be inconsolable – and she was far from us, somewhere in California. How could God ask such further grief from us? From whence my strength? I steeled myself. *And, without tears, I went to break your heart.*

Oh my dear, as I write this – weeping now – I must confess I do not remember much. I don't know whether I reached out to comfort you or not. I think not. I think you, too, were steeled to bear the next blow – already having suffered so much. But in the long run there was nothing we could do. Debbie had to be reached. Duanne had to be called. No plans could be made because we knew that there would have to be an autopsy – Duanne had told Chuck that. And so on Saturday 26th, our son's 52nd birthday, the day went by in shaded hues of night, while we waited for the light of Sunday. That morning I taught my Gospel Doctrine class, a lesson I had for some unknown reason continued from the previous week's discussion. But now I knew the *why*. At last I *felt* the Book of Job. And I was later told the Spirit had been in the class that morning.

The autopsy was finally over and Duanne held secular services in Salt Lake the following week for all Quill's business colleagues. And Debbie and her family and I were there. But you could not go. Our dear friend, Vern Watkins, came and sat with you that day. [And Vern later said you talked about the ball games.] But I knew your pain and my aching thoughts were with you every moment. The following day or so, Quill's body was brought to Phoenix to be entombed in our family plot. The coffin was opened beforehand and, alone, without my arm or the support of anyone, you climbed the steps of the mortuary and went to see for the last time the body of your only son. My heart breaks again at that memory of you, alone. But it also breaks for me – because you did not reach for me or cry with me. But you wept with your grandsons.

We had a memorial service for our son the following week and I think everybody in the East Phoenix Stake was there. And there were many from the University. And many neighbors. You sat, surrounded by our family in the pew – while Debbie and I sat on the stand. We remembered and spoke of our Quill with love – without a tear, without a falter. And the same priesthood speakers who had spoken at his missionary farewell so many years before gave the Invocation and the Benediction and President Vern Watkins gave the message. And afterward, the dear, sweet sisters of Relief Society provided enough food for everyone in attendance to be invited. But my husband, did you feel my love sustaining you and merging with your grief? I don't believe you ever spoke of Quill again. I think you could not bear the pain. But I spoke of him constantly; he remained alive in my heart. Though I believed I was forever inured to grief. How wrong I was.

9
Joy Cometh In the Morning

Almost exactly eight months after Quill's internment, a joyous event took place in the garden of our family home. Our dear only granddaughter, Sabrina Paige Falls was married to Ryan N. Hemphill, of South Africa, June 5th, 1999. You were able to be there and to have your picture taken with her and it was the happiest event of her life, she says. She had about a hundred guests, and a band and dance floor, and a lovely reception dinner. And she was a beautiful bride. Ryan's friend, a minister, performed the ceremony and the weather had not yet turned unbearably warm. Following the wedding, Sabrina and Ryan took a wedding trip to his home in South Africa, going on a safari. Sabrina says that was the hardest thing she ever did. [My honeymoon was one of the hardest things I ever did, too. But subways can't compare with lions. I would bet no one could compare with you!]

This is the last happiness you and I would share together. You would continue to decline and your unhappiness with me seemed to grow each day. I could not please you. You knew you were dying. Though you were fighting with all your strength, you knew the darkness was coming on. And I think you hated me because I was alive. The final year and a half you were under hospice treatment, at home, but you really wouldn't let them help us. The only relief was that I didn't have to get you to the doctor by wheel chair anymore – I knew the nursing staff reported to the doctor and he was on top of medication. At least I knew that you were getting the best care possible. And then, at the end, I collapsed. And the nursing staff recommended a week's respite care for you in the hospital. I could not handle the dressings on your cancerous wounds, one of which had now burst open; you would not let me even see the wound. So I let them take you – for a week of respite care, only.

I did not comprehend then that you would die there. You had

cheated death so many times before. But in seven days, you, the love of my life, were gone, in one last night of struggle against a series of strokes. And I was not there beside you. [And there would really be no life for me thereafter.] A little after our 57th wedding anniversary, on November 1, 2001, you died at the Baptist Hospice Care Center, with your beloved daughter at your side. I had gone home for a rest and I was called too late to get there in time to say goodbye. I missed our last farewell by five minutes. And the sad final memory I have of you was your anger with me – the night before when I was trying to feed you some tapioca that I had brought you – because I could not understand what you were trying to say. I think, however, that Debbie – who had flown in from Connecticut that evening – was meant to have those special last hours with you. For she had missed being with Quill when he died and had never gotten over that regret. And she has such sweet remembrances of her time with you. How she promised you that she would care for me and then released you with "Daddy, it's time to go to Quill." And she says that without a gasp, your spirit was gone. And she felt the rush of joy. And with her remembrance ends our love story, on this earth. But not this love *letter*. I still have thoughts to share with you.

10
Sequel

But now I will quickly bring you up to date on what your wife has done since you left her to take that final trip alone. I lived in our house for one year, after which I knew I could not sustain the work load any longer. So following the inspiration given me, I relocated to a gated community in Mesa – where I first began my Arizona life and not far from where I lived with your mother while you were gone. I love my unit – most of our possessions have fit in well here and my home is very beautiful – and I have made some very special friends. Here, we have a club house, pools, library, exercise room, TV room, computer stations, pool tables and card room, anything one could wish for. I think you would like it here, too, although it might be small for both of us. Jerry Hearn lives quite nearby and comes to see me often. And I am only four miles from the Temple. Friends from Phoenix come to see me and I meet them for lunch every once in awhile. You have provided well for me in the beautiful home you built us and in its sale. You would not believe the sale price. I have a comfortable guaranteed retirement and a nice portfolio to leave our family when I go. *Also, splurged on a new Lexus which I love – and which you would probably read me the riot act about.*

And so, my love, in material things, I am fortunate. But I am very lonely for you. And for our son. And Deborah is still far away and so busy I seldom see her. And she is not well. But we both manage and get on with life. This life review has been my only task since I began it exactly three months ago. And I have figured up the hours I've spent in writing – and in the nearly 800 letters we originally wrote to each other and which I have put together to preserve and become more accessible – and it comes out to a grand total of about 1500 hours or 37 forty-hour weeks. In the process, I have lost 12 pounds and have shed that many pounds of tears.

And now I'm asking myself, what has been the purpose of it all? Would you be pleased – or are you pleased – with what I have done? And I will have no way of knowing unless – or until – I am with you again. But for now, as my final burden, I must ponder the sum and substance of my work. Then, in the very last effort of this mortal life, I will conclude my last love letter to the man I pledged to love, honor and obey, in sickness and in health, not 'til death do us part' but through all eternity. "Till Then, I'll Draw On Each Memory."

Helen

August 23, 2005

My Eternal Love,

And so I have finally reached the end of this labor of love which has consumed me in memory, in happiness, in deepest melancholy and sorrow of the soul, and finally, at last, in a kind of overwhelming joy and acceptance of the process of *our* life – which is perhaps more representative of life in general, than one might think. As I have progressed through, first the sustaining letters of our youth – our life apart – and then the years when we were actually together and measuring out our little span of days, I have become acutely aware of the very essence of life itself. Life, like the war in which you fought so bravely and with such fervent intent to survive, is likewise a battleground. It is a field of constant struggle; it is a rocky road, pockmarked with hope, with joy, with loss, with pain, and sometimes with overwhelming despair. And some fall soon in the strife. But for the lucky survivors, perhaps this treacherous road is marked by the triumph of battle and at the end – for those who fight most valiantly – by God's own Medal of Honor, the great gift of Love.

How brave we must have been in the pre-existence, when in hope and faith – but probably also in fear and trembling – we opted for this "war of life." And surely those warriors who even hold the course at all are worthy of remembrance – and of respect. And dear, *we held the course* – according to our understanding, and our strength. Perhaps you now know whether you have won the Medal of Honor or whether perhaps you are still under consideration. But I must wait for death to know my fate at all.

But even as I write, in a sense I know that what I have last written is not true at all. I have *possessed the Medal of Love for years: I have loved*, for I loved you almost from the time we met. And *I have known love,* for you loved me from almost our first meeting. And in our many *letters of love* were the sustenance of life, the "honey hope" of youth, and the physical passion of the body. These were the "salad days" of life and we ate of the tree of life and knowledge, eagerly. And we *loved.* And *in love* we were faithful to one another. And when you had won a real battle of war in the Ardennes Bulge, a survivor, if nothing else, you found me waiting patiently for you, *in love*, with the dreams of the still truly young.

Then you came home and the battlefield of life stretched ahead. And you found you had – as the song said – to "put your dreams away for another day." And *with love*, I tried to sing a duet with you. Though often not in your key nor to your satisfaction. But we *loved* and multiplied and replenished the earth, so the battle could continue for other young lovers. And in that *love* we found the delight of our children [and often, the delight of each other] and always the sorrow and the pain, and eventually, the implicit *loss* that seems to be an eternal companion of *love*. And we learned through the years that "the heart has its seasons, for and against"and we tried to hold steady in the buffetings of strong winds and cold blasts, the artillery of life that threatened to destroy us and *our love*. And always we tried to recoup the losses and to strengthen the defenses. And almost always, to persist in the face of the enemy, with the weapons we could find.

In conclusion, my dearest *love*, I must admit that our 57 years of guarding together the battle front appointed us has often been, for both of us, almost too difficult to bear. But as I have contemplated our successes and our failures through these last weeks, I have recognized again a simple truth – a truth that confounds the mathematical maxim that "the whole of a thing can never be greater than the sum of its parts." The whole of life's battle – the tally of wins and losses – the whole of our life and our marriage is much more than the sum of its parts – much more than joy and sorrow, much more than young love, parenthood, empty nest, grandchildren, old-age, sickness, pain, even hate, and finally, death. That struggle – or battlefield – that we call Life or Marriage – is the long, hard growing process of acceptance of one another for what we are, of devotion, of forgiveness, of endurance in the face of all that the enemy can throw against us. It is, in the final analysis, the illuminating triumph of the Spirit over the body. And in this triumph of the Spirit lies the *ultimate gift of God*, to those who even try to hold out faithful to the end.

Thus, the whole of the journey of life – and of Marriage – is crowned by the *undying love* of man and wife, in the *light* of the *undying love of God*. And this *undying love* is our gift – or medal – from God, *love to* and *for* each other. Oh my love, do you understand what I am saying? That in *that* hope of our Saviour's redeeming love and mercy and grace, I have hope for you and me, for our eternal love!

But in the end, my husband, if His *love* cannot – because of our own natures – encompass us, then I still say to you: you were the choice of my heart; you were the father of my children; through you I came to knowledge and to endurance and to eternal hope. *You* have given me the medal of life! Because of you, I have loved. Because of you, I have been loved. Because *I* love *you*, I hope to know love again – in your arms of welcome – when "I'll Be Seeing You," Beyond the Veil.

Forever yours, with my undying love,

Helen

"Ah, when will this long weary day have end
And lend me leave to come unto my love?"

Edmund Spenser